PELICAN BOOKS
Arthur's Britain

Leslie Alcock, FSA, FRHistS, is Professor of Archaeology at the
University of Glasgow. He was educated at Manchester Grammar School
and Brasenose College, Oxford. Since 1947 he has carried out
archaeological excavations in North Africa, Pakistan and widely in Britain.
For many years he has lectured, both in the British Isles and in North
America, at both academic and popular levels, on the archaeology of the
period covered by this book. He has also made significant contributions
to our knowledge of the period by his writing and by a series of excavations
in western and northern Britain, including the five-year campaign at
Cadbury-Camelot.

Leslie Alcock delivered the O'Donnell Lecture in the University of Wales
in 1966, and in Edinburgh University in 1978; more recently he has given
the Jarrow Lecture 1988, and the Rhind Lectures 1988–9. He was
awarded the G. T. Clark Prize in 1964 for work in the Roman and Early
Christian field. He has been President of the Cambrian Archaeological
Association and of the Society of Antiquaries of Scotland. His publications
include *Dinas Powys: An Iron Age, Dark Age and Early Medieval
Settlement in Glamorgan* (1963), *Culture and Environment: Essays in
Honour of Sir Cyril Fox* (edited with I. Ll. Foster, 1963), '*By South
Cadbury is that Camelot . . .': Excavations at Cadbury Castle 1966–70*
(1972) and *Economy, Society and Warfare Among the Britons and Saxons*
(1987), as well as numerous articles in learned journals.

Leslie Alcock

Arthur's Britain

History and Archaeology
AD 367–634

PENGUIN BOOKS

PENGUIN BOOKS

Published by the Penguin Group
Penguin Books Ltd, 27 Wrights Lane, London W8 5TZ, England
Penguin Books USA Inc., 375 Hudson Street, New York, New York 10014, USA
Penguin Books Australia Ltd, Ringwood, Victoria, Australia
Penguin Books Canada Ltd, 10 Alcorn Avenue, Toronto, Ontario, Canada M4V 3B2
Penguin Books (NZ) Ltd, 182–190 Wairau Road, Auckland 10, New Zealand

Penguin Books Ltd, Registered Offices: Harmondsworth, Middlesex, England

First published by Allen Lane The Penguin Press 1971
Published in Pelican Books 1973
Reprinted with a Revised Preface and a Supplementary Bibliography 1989
Reprinted in Penguin Books 1990
10 9 8 7 6 5 4 3 2

Printed in England by Clays Ltd, St Ives plc

Contents

List of Plates

Sources of Plates

Copyright Aerofilms Ltd: pls. 1*a*, 1*b*, 2, 3, 4*b*, 10, 11, 13. Photo J. K. St Joseph, Cambridge University Collection, copyright reserved: pls. 4*a*, 7, 8*a*, 8*b*, 9, 12*a*. Photo L. Alcock, copyright Camelot Research Committee: pls. 5, 6*a*, 6*b*. Crown copyright, reproduced by permission of the Department of the Environment: pls. 12*b*, 25*b*, 26*b*. Copyright National Museum of Ireland: pls. 14*a*, 14*b*, 16*a*, 16*b*. Photo Anthony Kubiak, copyright Herbert Art Gallery and Museum, Coventry: pl. 15*a*. Copyright British Museum, object in Lincoln City and County Museum: pl. 15*b*. Photo W. T. Jones, objects in British Museum: pls. 17, 18. By permission of the National Museum of Wales, objects from the British Museum: pls. 19*a*, 19*b*, 19*c*, 20, 21, 22. Copyright Department of Archaeology, University College, Cardiff: pls. 19*d*, 25*a*, 26*a*, 27, 28, 29, 30. Copyright British Museum: pls. 23, 24. Photo L. Alcock: pl. 31. Photo National Museum of Antiquities of Scotland: pl. 32*a*. Photo M. J. O'Kelly: pl. 32*b*.

List of Text Figures

    The figures have mostly been redrawn – and sometimes simplified – from existing plans, drawings, and photographs by David Lloyd Owen (DLO), Gloria Stephenson (GS) and the Author (A). The final form of the illustration is, however, the responsibility of the publishers.

List of Maps

Preface

This book is about the Arthur of history, and about the Britain in which he lived. It will demonstrate that there is acceptable historical evidence that Arthur was a genuine historical figure, not a mere figment of myth or romance. He achieved fame as a great soldier, who fought battles in various parts of Britain in the late fifth and early sixth centuries. We cannot know his dates with complete certainty ; he may have died in 539, or more probably in 511. This chronological ambiguity should not perturb us. At least two dating schemes are possible for the great Babylonian ruler Hammurabi, yet no competent scholar doubts his historicity.

The Britain in which Arthur lived and fought was undergoing great changes. In brief, an island which had shaken off Roman rule fell victim to raiders and settlers from overseas, the Scots and the Anglo-Saxons. Arthur played a major part in resisting the Anglo-Saxon invaders. In order to understand his role properly we must examine how the Roman diocese of Britannia came under pressure from external foes, how it became independent and for a while resisted barbarian onslaughts, and how in the long run it lost both its unity and also much of its territory. This gives the chronological limits of the book: AD 367 saw the first major barbarian attack on Britain, AD 634 saw the failure of the last great British counter-attack. Arthur himself, whatever his precise dates, stands at the mid-point between these events.

Our historical information about this period is always limited, and frequently vague and inconsistent as well. We can, however, fill out the picture with the aid of the ever-increasing material evidence provided by archaeology. A fairly full account of the culture of the Britons is attempted here, and this is supplemented with sketches of their enemies — the Picts, the Scots, and the Anglo-Saxons.

I like to think that this book could only have been written within the academic framework of the University of Wales: hence its dedication. Apart from my general debt to colleagues at all levels — undergraduate,

graduate, and staff – certain more specific thanks must be recorded. The University contributed largely to my excavations at Cadbury-Camelot, which first focused my attention on Arthurian problems. By honouring me with the O'Donnell Lectureship for the session 1965–6 the University invited me to consider the relationships between Roman Britons and pagan Saxons, which form one of the leading themes of the book. On linguistic matters and the evidence to be derived from Welsh texts, I have benefited from the advice, always readily given, of Professor Melville Richards (Bangor), Professor Thomas Jones (Aberystwyth), and Professor A. O. H. Jarman, Dr Glyn Ashton, Miss Morfydd Owen, and Mr Ceri Lewis (Cardiff). Much of my text has been improved by the comments and criticisms of Professor H. R. Loyn (Chapters 1, 2, 4, 5, 9–12), Professor W. H. Davies (Chapters 1 and 2), Professor R. O'Gorman (Chapters 1–3), and Dr M. G. Jarrett (Chapter 4). Mr Richard Wainwright read the entire typescript, and helped me on innumerable occasions to clarify my thoughts.

Outside the University, the British Academy made large grants to the Cadbury-Camelot excavations and to the wider research which they necessitated. One of these grants paid for the discovery and exploration of the Arthurian-period hall, another for the contemporary gate-tower, and a third enabled me to visit Arthurian sites in Dumnonia and elsewhere. The assistance and stimulus of Sir Mortimer Wheeler have been both prop and goad to me. Finally, Dr Ralegh Radford, doyen of Arthurian studies, has been generous with encouragement and advice over many years.

It may be useful to indicate the spirit in which I have approached my subject. As a historian, I was trained to regard record-history as incomparably superior to chronicle-history. In applying this principle to the documents for fifth- and sixth-century history, I have been further guided by the techniques of source-criticism which are now well developed among Celtic scholars. As an archaeologist, I have been brought up to regard the recognition of valid associations between objects and structures at the moment of their recovery from the soil as central to all archaeological thinking. Obvious though it may seem, this idea is worth stressing simply because it is currently out of favour.

Finally, no reader can be more aware than I am myself of the degree of compression which has been necessary in writing this book. At least one chapter merits a book to itself, and many paragraphs could easily be *expanded to the length of a section. Inevitably, compression has entailed some distortion of the arguments and hypotheses, perhaps even of the evidence itself. Another way of putting this is to say that the present book is a preliminary sketch for a vast canvas. In justification, I would claim that a sketch may reveal the main lines of its subject as faithfully as a more elaborate work, and perhaps more clearly.*

University College, Cardiff: January 1971   Leslie Alcock

Revised preface, 1987

Arthur's Britain *was written during the two final years of my excavations at Cadbury Castle, or Camelot. Those excavations coincided with a great upsurge of interest in the archaeology of 'Arthurian-period' Britain, and indeed they helped greatly to stimulate that interest. Consequently, the last twenty years have seen an explosive increase in archaeological research and discovery, and a corresponding increase in speculation and interpretations about the period.*

At about the same time, a fresh generation of students of the written word – historians, linguists, literary scholars – began a new attack on the supposed verbal evidence for the Arthur of history, and for the events which framed his activities. Whereas the new archaeological evidence has added both richness and complexity to the account that I gave in Arthur's Britain, *the new verbal critiques go far beyond the rather timid scepticism which I had expressed occasionally. Consequently, they have largely undermined the case which I had advanced for the historic Arthur: indeed, some scholars would claim that they have destroyed that case completely.*

As a result, Arthur's Britain *is no longer a reliable guide to the present state of knowledge, hypothesis and opinion. I am most grateful, therefore, to Penguin Books for allowing me to remedy some of these defects by adding a new critical, and even polemical, bibliography to the original references. In this, I have tried to take account of major relevant contributions in both the archaeological and the verbal fields. The innocent reader should be warned, however, that the new bibliography is by no means comprehensive: to achieve that would require upwards of a thousand entries to cover the archaeology of Celtic Britain and Ireland alone.*

University of Glasgow: June 1987   Leslie Alcock

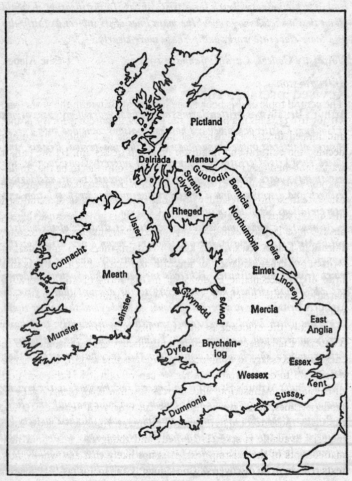

Map 1. The British Isles in the 5th–7th centuries AD.

One

The Nature of the Evidence

Introduction

The central topic of this book is the history of Britain in the years from
AD 367 to 634. This is a period of the greatest importance for the island,
and indeed for the English-speaking peoples as a whole, because it
decided the cultural and linguistic make-up of Britain. By the end, it
was established that the dominant political group was to be the Anglo-
Saxons, and the dominant language English. Regrettably, although we
can state these broad results with confidence, we have only a confused
idea of the steps by which they came about. This is not because there is
an absolute lack of evidence; compared with much of the second,
third and fourth centuries of Roman Britain, there is a good deal of
written or verbal evidence for the fifth and sixth. The trouble is that
little of the acceptable evidence is in the form of straightforward
narrative, while much of the apparent narrative history is unreliable.

Certainly the evidence is not at all like that to which students of
Victorian England or the Tudors and Stuarts are accustomed. It is
therefore necessary to examine its nature at some length, and in some
detail, and to demonstrate how far we can rely on it.[1] If the technical
discussion of manuscripts and sources is unfamiliar to historians of
modern times, it is not unlike that customary in biblical studies,
especially those devoted to the New Testament. In both fields the basic
material available is severely limited; and though we may find new
manuscripts of the existing texts it is not likely that any wholly new
texts remain to be discovered. Consequently the major task of research
consists in looking at the existing texts in new ways. Here the student
of Arthurian Britain has much to learn from the biblical techniques of
source criticism and form criticism. Already a new appreciation of
some of our fifth- and sixth-century texts is developing, and it seems

likely that over the next decade many of our current interpretations will be revolutionized.

Whereas the verbal evidence forms a more or less static body, our other chief body of information, the archaeological, is in a state of constant and increasing growth. This is sufficiently well known in the case of new discoveries, for these are frequently reported by press, radio or television. Many of them are, of course, the result of deliberately planned excavations; and since the number of active field workers engaged in post-Roman studies is itself increasing, the yield of finds from excavations is growing likewise. But many discoveries, even important ones, are in fact chance finds, the accidental by-product of quarrying, deep-ploughing, road-making and building works. Since all these activities are expanding, and since the workers engaged in them are more archaeologically aware than they would have been a generation ago, the number of chance finds which come to be recognized and reported is also rising.

All this is obvious enough; but there are two other factors which the layman, or even the historian who is not himself an archaeologist, may not appreciate. The first is the rediscovery, by active research, of material which for decades or even generations has lain buried in our museums; this adds constantly to the currently usable evidence. The second is the re-examination of old finds, and the dogmas based on them, in the light of each new discovery.

The work of the archaeologist is sometimes thought of in terms of a jigsaw, in which each new discovery is fitted into its own correct position in the picture of the past – a picture which has objective validity because it depicts what actually happened. But a practising archaeologist might think of history not as a jigsaw, but rather as a shifting pattern like that of a kaleidoscope. The pattern, of course, is produced conceptually, not optically. Each major new discovery is like a shake of the kaleidoscope, disrupting the existing patterns, and forcing scholars to create new ones.

So much, then, for the character of the evidence. In the remainder of this chapter I shall evaluate the leading types of verbal evidence in general, and in Chapter 2 I shall examine in detail three of the key texts for the period. A discussion of the material or archaeological evidence is deferred until Chapter 6.

Manuscripts[2]

It is useful to stress at the outset that none of our verbal evidence is in the form of printed books. With the exception of certain texts which are cut on stone monuments (below, pp. 238 f.) it consists of books or other documents, written by hand on the specially prepared animal skins known as parchment or vellum. One of the advantages for the historian of vellum as against the papyrus which had been used earlier is that whereas papyrus does not survive in the climate of western Europe, vellum lasts so well that many books written on it are as legible today as when they were first penned.

Despite this, however, no fifth- or sixth-century manuscripts directly relevant to our study have survived. Instead we have to make do with later manuscripts that had been laboriously copied from the original documents of our period at a time when they were still in existence. Indeed, what we normally find is that we are dealing with copies of copies . . . of copies. Thus we may have a twelfth-century copy of a tenth-century compilation which includes annals written down in the fifth century; or a thirteenth-century copy of a poem composed orally in the sixth but not written down before the ninth century. Over this lengthy period of transmission, in the process of repeated copying, various accidents may happen to the original text. It is no part of my purpose here to give a comprehensive account of these accidents, but some typical instances must be indicated.

Firstly there are simple scribal errors. One has only to write a letter to be aware of these oneself; the omission of minor words, or the dropping of letters, especially at the end of words, which in an inflected language like Latin can be crucial for the meaning. These scribal errors are immediately compounded when the writer is engaged not in original composition but in copying someone else's work. The early scribe had first to read and understand his original, which itself probably contained errors; he then voiced the text quickly, while writing his own copy. A contemporary account of a medieval *scriptorium* or writing room describes the sound which came from it as like the humming of bees. Understanding the original is of course crucial to the process of accurate copying. Unfortunately some of the key documents for the history of western Britain were copied after the Norman Conquest by scribes who knew no Welsh, so that Welsh personal and place-names have suffered considerable mutilation.

It is not only letters or single words that are likely to be lost or become corrupted; whole lines or groups of lines can be lost. This is particularly likely to happen when two lines of the original end with the same word: the scribe completes the earlier line, then picks up from the end of the later one, omitting all that is in between. This phenomenon can be seen even today in printed works which are prepared in haste, such as the daily newspapers. Omissions of this kind are most serious where the original consisted of annals or other historical data arranged in columns.

Apart from purely accidental errors such as these, major corruptions can occur through the good intentions of a scribe who tries to improve on his original. At the simplest this takes the form of modernizing spelling, dropping case endings, and generally bringing up to date a text which sounded archaic to the scribe. The temptation to do this must have been strong as Primitive Welsh and Old English developed into Middle Welsh and Middle English. Such modernization is disappointing to the linguist, who hopes to find early forms of spelling and grammar preserved, but it is not a significant obstruction to the historian, provided that the scribe has read the ancient name or word correctly and modernized it appropriately. If he has not, we may be left with a spurious place or person.

The most serious danger for the historian is the scribe who knows, or thinks he knows, more than his original, and who cannot resist the temptation to insert his knowledge. This is especially important in the case of Arthurian history. It is universally agreed that tales about Arthur were expanded and elaborated from the ninth, if not from the late sixth, century. A scribe of say the tenth century might have in mind a fairly evolved complex of stories about Arthur, most of them fictitious. If the original document that he was copying contained an authentic, but very cryptic reference to Arthur, the scribe would be tempted to fill it out. Of course, the material which he interpolated might itself be derived from a good source, or it might be wholly fabulous and fictitious. We shall see that the difficulties of distinguishing between authentic and interpolated material form one of the major cruxes of Arthurian scholarship (pp. 48 f.).

One final general topic deserves consideration before we look at the actual documents, namely, the question of the age of manuscripts. Much attention is always and rightly paid to the actual date of the manuscripts from which we work. Except where there is direct evidence – for instance, in the form of a codicil telling us who wrote it – this date is decided essentially on palaeographic grounds, that is, by the study of the handwriting. The layman might well imagine that faced with a number of copies of the same text, of varying date, the historian must always prefer the earliest, but this is not necessarily so. A manuscript of the thirteenth century may be a fairly accurate copy of a ninth-century copy, now lost, of a sixth-century original. It might well be preferable to an eleventh-century copy, heavily modernized, of that same original.

What matters, in fact, is not the date of the manuscript but the source which lies behind it. This is true even when we are dealing with variant manuscripts of the same ancient original. But it is even more true when we are dealing with different, even discrepant versions of the same historical situation. The dates of the manuscripts become virtually irrelevant here, and the first task of the historian is to discover the nature of the sources which lie behind them. From this he may establish the antiquity of the sources, and from that in turn he may evaluate their probable historical validity. We shall see later how these principles apply to the verbal evidence for Arthur himself (pp. 45 f.).

Easter Annals[3]

Obviously our best historical sources are those which were written down at the same time as, or at least in the same year as, the events which they describe. In the Christian areas of western Europe, in the period of our interest, there was one form of historical writing which essentially meets our requirements – entries in Easter Tables. These frequently record the accession or death of a king or ecclesiastic, or an important battle.

The Easter Table is a piece of ecclesiastical apparatus made necessary by the fact that Easter is a movable feast, related in a complicated way to the phases of the moon. In our period and for some centuries both before and after it, the complications were increased by

disputes within the church about the precise way in which these calculations should be made. To assist individual churches to celebrate the
Christian year correctly, various scholars prepared Tables showing the
date on which Easter should fall over a number of years.

In 457 a certain Victorius of Aquitaine produced such a Table giving
the date of Easter for every year from the Passion or Crucifixion down
to his own day. He then continued to calculate dates into the future,
and discovered that in the five hundred and thirty-third year after the
Passion, Easter would fall on the same day of the same month and at
the same phase of the moon as in the year of the Passion itself. Victorius had thus discovered, accidentally or at least empirically, the
so-called Great Cycle of 532 years.

The layout of a modern Easter Table is seen in Figure 1, while
Figure 2 is a transcription of a Table for the period AD 969–987. The
left-hand column gives the date year by year. In early Tables the year
would be cited in terms of some secular, non-Christian epoch, such
as the year of an emperor's reign, but in 525 Dionysius Exiguus introduced an epoch starting from the assumed date of the Incarnation, or
birth of Christ. Thereafter the use of the era of the Incarnation spread
throughout the Church until it became normal for Easter Tables and
ultimately, of course, for all chronological reckoning. The other
columns of the Table deal with technical matters involved in Easter
calculations – Epact, Golden Number, and so on – and column seven
or eight gives the actual date of Easter Day, *Dies Paschae*, in each year.

Nothing we have seen so far is of direct interest to us, but when we
turn to the right-hand side of the Table in Figure 2, the case alters.
Very frequently the columns of ancient Easter Tables did not fill the
page, but left a wide right-hand margin. It became the practice to use
this margin to record events of the kind already mentioned against the
year in which they actually happened. Such a record is conveniently
known as an Easter Annal, and from it a framework of dynastic,
ecclesiastical and military history can be constructed.

It should be said at once that Easter Annals may include one class
of entry which palpably was not written down at the time it occurred.
In addition to the deaths of saints, we may find their births recorded.
It is obvious that when St Brigid or St Dunstan were born, no one
could have anticipated their future sainthood. These entries must in

Year of Our Lord	Golden Number	The Epact	Sunday Letter	Sundays After Epiphany	Septua-gesima Sunday	The First Day of Lent	Easter Day	Rogation Sunday	Ascension Day	Whit-Sunday	Sundays After Trinity	Advent Sunday
1920	II	10	DC	Three	Feb. 1	Feb. 18	Apr. 4	May 9	May 13	May 23	25	Nov. 28
1921	III	21	B	Two	Jan. 23	9	Mar. 27	1	5	15	26	27
1922	IV	2	A	Five	Feb. 12	Mar. 1	Apr. 16	21	25	June 4	24	Dec. 3
1923	V	13	G	Three	Jan. 28	Feb. 14	1	6	10	May 20	26	2
1924	VI	24	FE	Five	Feb. 17	Mar. 5	20	25	29	June 8	23	Nov. 30
1925	VII	5	D	Five	Feb. 8	Feb. 25	12	17	21	May 31	24	29
1926	VIII	16	C	Four	Jan. 31	Feb. 17	4	9	13	23	25	28
1927	IX	27	B	Three	Feb. 13	Mar. 2	17	22	26	June 5	23	27
1928	X	8	AG	Five	Feb. 5	Feb. 22	8	13	17	May 27	25	Dec. 2
1929	XI	19	F	Four	Jan. 27	Feb. 13	Mar. 31	5	9	19	26	1
1930	XII	0	E	Two	Feb. 16	Mar. 5	Apr. 20	25	29	June 8	23	Nov. 30
1931	XIII	11	D	Five	Feb. 1	Feb. 18	5	10	14	May 24	25	29
1932	XIV	22	CB	Three	Jan. 24	Feb. 10	Mar. 27	1	5	15	26	27
1933	XV	3	A	Two	Feb. 12	Mar. 1	Apr. 16	21	25	June 4	24	Dec. 3
1934	XVI	14	G	Five	Jan. 28	Feb. 14	1	6	10	May 20	26	2
1935	XVII	25	F	Three	Feb. 17	Mar. 6	21	26	30	May 31	23	1
1936	XVIII	6	ED	Five	Feb. 9	Feb. 26	12	17	21	May 31	24	Nov. 29
1937	XIX	17	C	Four	Jan. 24	Feb. 10	Mar. 28	2	6	16	26	28
1938	I	29	B	Two	Feb. 13	Mar. 2	Apr. 17	22	26	June 5	23	27
1939	II	10	A	Five	Feb. 5	Feb. 22	9	14	18	May 28	25	Dec. 3
1940	III	21	GF	Four	Jan. 21	Feb. 7	Mar. 24	Apr. 28	May 2	12	27	1
1941	IV	2	E	Two	Feb. 9	Feb. 26	Apr. 13	May 18	22	June 1	24	Nov. 30
1942	V	13	D	Four	Feb. 1	Feb. 18	5	10	14	May 24	25	29
1943	VI	24	C	Three	Feb. 21	Mar. 10	25	30	June 3	June 13	22	28
1944	VII	5	BA	Six	Feb. 6	Feb. 23	9	14	May 18	May 28	25	Dec. 3
1945	VIII	16	G	Four	Jan. 28	Feb. 14	1	6	10	20	26	2

1. A modern Easter Table, from the Book of Common Prayer of the Anglican church.

De Computo Ecclesiastico

Anni domini	Indictiones	Epactae	Concurrentes	Ciccli lunares	Dies XIIII lunae	Dies paschae	Luna ipsius [diei]	
DCCCCLXIX	XII	Nulla	IIII	XVII	Non. aprelis	III id. aprelis	XX	
DCCCCLXX	XIII	XI	V	XVIII	VIII id. aprelis	VI kal. aprelis	XVI	
DCCCCLXXI	XIIII	XXII	VI	XIX	Idus aprelis	XVI kal. mai	XVII	
B DCCCCLXXII	XV	II	I	I	IIII non. aprelis	VII id. aprelis	XIX	
DCCCCLXXIII	I	XIIII	II	II	XI kal. aprelis	X kal. aprelis	XV	
DCCCCLXXIIII	II	XXV	III	III	IIII id. aprelis	II id. aprelis	XV	
DCCCCLXXV	III	VI	IIII	IIII	III kal. aprelis	II non. aprelis	XIX	
B DCCCCLXXVI	IIII	XVII	VI	V	XIIII kal. mai	IX kal. mai	XIX	Obitus eadgari regis.
DCCCCLXXVII	V	XXVIII	VII	VI	VII id. aprelis	VI id. aprelis	XV	
DCCCCLXXVIII	VI	VIIII	I	VII	VI kal. aprelis	II kal. aprelis	XVIII	
DCCCCLXXIX	VII	XX	II	VIII	XVII kal. mai	XII kal. mai	XIX	Hic interemtus est rex eadweardus
B DCCCCLXXX	VIII	I	IIII	VIIII	II non. aprelis	III id. aprelis	XXI	
DCCCCLXXXI	IX	XII	V	X	IX kal. aprelis	VI kal. aprelis	XVII	
DCCCCLXXXII	X	XXIII	VI	XI	II id. aprelis	XVI kal. mai	XVIII	
DCCCCLXXXIII	XI	IIII	VII	XII	Kal. aprelis	VI id. aprelis	XVII	
B DCCCCLXXXIIII	XII	XV	II	XIII	XII kal. aprelis	X kal. aprelis	XVI	
DCCCCLXXXV	XIII	XXVI	III	XIIII	V id. aprelis	II id. aprelis	XVII	Depositio adelwoldi episcopi.
DCCCCLXXXVI	XIIII	VII	IIII	XV	IIII kal. aprelis	II non. aprelis	XX	
DCCCCLXXXVII	XV	XVIII	V	XVI	XV kal. mai	VIII kal. mai	XXI	

2. A transcription of a late tenth-century Easter Table, possibly used at Glastonbury, with marginal entries for the deaths of king Edgar and bishop Ethelwold of Winchester, and the murder of king Edward the Martyr.[4]

fact be interpolations, added most probably at the same time as the death was entered. We cannot know how reliably these birth-dates were calculated. Nevertheless it must be stressed that the inclusion of a little material interpolated in this way casts no doubt on the general authenticity and integrity of Easter Annals.

It might be expected that once the years covered by any particular Table had passed, the Table would have no further use, and would be discarded, so that the historical information contained in it would be lost. This is not necessarily so, and that for a number of reasons. In some cases, it appears, a short-term Table was incorporated, along with its information, into a Great Cycle which took as its notional starting point a date considerably earlier than that at which it was actually compiled. Again, an Easter Table may start with an explanation of the chronological theories on which it is based, followed by a brief chronicle exemplifying its chronological method. At its briefest, this introductory matter might take the form of a *computus* or set of *calculi*, summarizing chronological information about events before the opening date of the Table. This information was probably derived, in part at least, from the Table for the immediately preceding cycle. Most important of all, the Easter Annals could be detached altogether from the Easter calculations to form a set of annals pure and simple; or their historical information might be used to form the chronological framework for a continuous narrative such as a saint's life or a secular history or chronicle. Material derived in this way from Easter Annals has been detected, for instance, among the early entries of the *Anglo-Saxon Chronicle*, and in Bede's *Ecclesiastical History of the English Nation*.

Narrative history

Very little narrative history was composed in western Europe in the Arthurian age. The monk Gildas, whose dates overlap those of Arthur, purported to write a history of Britain up to the time of his own birth. Bede and the compiler of the *Historia Brittonum* treated this as a major and reliable source, but we shall have to examine its claims more critically (pp. 22 f.). Among saints' lives, that of Germanus of Auxerre was written not long after his death, so it is likely to be reliable in outline and in many of its incidents. It gives us information about religious, political and military events in Britain on the occasion of Germanus' visit in 429 (below, p. 100). There are also suggestive snippets in the writings of early Byzantine historians, but their reliability is lessened by their distance from events in Britain. The *Lives* of other saints who were active in our period were mostly composed so long after the event, and are so full of stock hagiographical incident, that they may largely be discarded.[5]

Inscriptions

The Christian practice of setting up funerary inscriptions to important persons, whether lay or ecclesiastical, provides us with a group of texts which at least have the virtue of being contemporary as a compensation for their brevity. Their value for social and political history, as well as the archaeological problems which they pose, are discussed in Chapter 8 (pp. 238–48).

Genealogies

Genealogies can provide important clues about dynastic history and a useful framework for political history, if their recording and transmission have been accurate. On this point two contrary views have been expressed. The first is that in a barbaric, heroic society like that of the Britons or the Anglo-Saxons, the lineal descent of kings and nobles was so important a factor in holding society together that it was necessarily remembered with accuracy. The mechanism by which it was remembered was the recitation of genealogies on important public occasions, such as visits from king to king or funerals of great nobles, when the common memory would correct or prevent errors in the oral tradition. The other view is that in an heroic society, in which changes of ruler might be frequent and violent, bards could always be found to fabricate acceptable lines of descent for *de facto* rulers.

What is quite certain is that once genealogies came to be written down – and obviously it is only the written ones that we can use – inconsistencies between the versions preserved in different manuscripts become obvious. This necessarily leaves us little confidence in the preceding oral transmission. Moreover, there is reason to think that at certain periods – the age of Offa in England, that of Hywel Dda in Wales – genealogies were very much in fashion. They were therefore compiled or completed for various leading dynasties of the day, and in some cases a dynasty was given a long and respectable ancestry by 'borrowing' names from another family altogether. Critical study makes it clear that genealogies are far from being simple and trustworthy documents.[6]

Despite this, they are often used by historians to provide not merely a relative framework but a chronological scheme for early history. This is done by taking a known and securely dated person late in the genealogy and working back by dead-reckoning allowing thirty years to a generation. This may seem an unreasonably high figure for the military class in an heroic society. In fact, the fairly well documented case of the dynasty of Dyfed suggests that twenty-five years might be more reasonable. But it must always be remembered that any such reckoning is calibrated to a framework which is feeble in the extreme.

Homilies and other religious tracts

The types of verbal evidence we have examined so far – Easter Annals, narrative history, and even funerary inscriptions and genealogies – were all originally composed as some form of historical statement. But we now turn to documents where the original purpose was not historical at all, but where none the less some information relevant to our purpose can sometimes be inferred.

One important class is that of homilies and other religious tracts. The *Confession* of St Patrick, for instance, is a contemporary document, written originally for polemical or at least apologetic purposes, but it incidentally contains much information not merely about the church in Britain and Ireland but about secular affairs as well. So too does Patrick's *Letter to Coroticus*, in which he asks a supposedly Christian prince of south-west Scotland to return some of Patrick's own converts who had been carried off into slavery.[7]

The most extensive work of this kind is the 'little admonitory work', as he called it, of the monk Gildas. The major part of this is an exposition and denunciation of the failings of church and state in western Britain in Gildas's own day, around the middle of the sixth century. Much of it is fire and brimstone, froth and verbiage; but it contains, incidentally, many interesting snippets of historical information about both the political and ecclesiastical organization of the period, and we shall therefore look at it in detail in Chapter 2.

Laws

We may be sure that both the Britons and their enemies possessed systems of customary law: in the case of the Britons, the old Celtic tribal customs somewhat modified by Roman influences; in the case of the Anglo-Saxons, Germanic tribal law with no such modification. The Anglo-Saxon laws of Kent, the most sophisticated of the English kingdoms, were first written down in the days of King Æthelberht, late in the sixth century or early in the seventh. According to Bede, this was done at the prompting of the church in the person of St Augustine: written law was a new idea to meet the situation created by the introduction of the church into the body of pagan barbaric society. Recently, however, it has been claimed that all those laws of Æthelberht which deal with secular matters – in fact eighty-nine out of ninety clauses – had already been committed to writing, presumably in runes, before Augustine's arrival in 597.[8] Whether this was so or not, they were certainly framed for a non-Christian and therefore a pre-Christian society; and they provide essential evidence about its character.

Welsh tribal law, on the other hand, was not set down in writing until the reign of Hywel Dda in the tenth century. Moreover, none of the manuscripts that we possess is earlier than the thirteenth century, and it is quite certain that the laws as originally written down had been modernized during the post-Howellian centuries when Welsh society was undergoing considerable changes, first under English and then under Norman influences. But, in contrast to the modernizing elements, there are also some very primitive-seeming clauses in the Welsh laws. Altogether they form a highly stratified document, but regrettably little has been done to distinguish the various levels. None the less some aspects of what we might call Common British Law – the law or customs of the Britons before they lost the northern and eastern parts of the island to the Scots and English – have been disinterred from the Laws of Hywel, and we shall be able to use them when we come to examine the character of early Welsh society (below, p. 322 f.).[9]

Poetry[10]

It needs no saying that early poetry – whether in Primitive Welsh, the language of the Britons, or in Old English – is part of the cultural history of Britain. Equally we can expect it to throw light on social history. But what is under discussion here is something more than either of these, namely, the possibility that early poetry may also provide a source for political and military history.

There is good evidence that poetry was composed and recited to celebrate the deeds of the aristocracy among both the Germanic and the Celtic barbarians. Posidonius, a Greek historian and geographer of the late second century BC, who appears to have had a first-hand acquaintance with the Celts of Gaul, wrote about the bards, or 'poets who deliver eulogies in song'. He informs us that 'the Celts have in their company in war as well as in peace companions . . . who pronounce their praises before the whole assembly and before each chieftain in turn'. Tacitus's account of the Germans of the first century AD is not based on first-hand knowledge, but it is none the less circumstantial. He refers to their 'ancient songs, which are their only form of remembrance and history'. One element in these songs seems to have been the recitation of genealogies going back to the divine ancestor Tiw, just as the early Anglo-Saxon dynasties traced themselves back to the god Woden.

Verses of this kind continued to be composed in the period of our interest. The British monk Gildas, in his diatribe against the sixth-century ruler Maelgwn of Gwynedd, adds this to his other criticisms: 'When the attention of thy ears has been caught, it is not the praises of God . . . that are heard, but thine own praises . . .' There is no doubt that Gildas is here referring to the eulogies of court bards.

The *Historia Brittonum*, a work essentially of the early ninth century, gives us the names of five British poets of the later sixth century. Although we know nothing further about three of them, we still have copies of poems which may reliably be attributed to the other two, Aneirin and Taliesin.

Aneirin was a northern Briton who wrote a long poem, *Y Gododdin*, about a counter-attack launched from the region of Edinburgh against the nascent Anglian kingdom of Deira. The poem is a primary source for our knowledge of weapons and tactics in the period (below, pp. 327 f.), and it also provides information about the contemporary social structure. Most of Taliesin's poems also have a northern setting; but Welsh tradition makes the young Taliesin the hero of a conflict with Maelgwn of Gwynedd, and one of his poems is in praise of Cynan Garwyn of Powys, so we cannot attribute him exclusively to the north.

The poem of Cynan Garwyn is particularly relevant for us here, because it belongs to the primitive genre aptly designed as 'battle-listing' poems. Four lines will adequately reveal the character of such verse:[11]

> A war attack on the Wye – innumerable spears –
> Men of Gwent were killed with bloody blade;
> Battle in Anglesey – great and fair – renowned the praise:
> An expedition beyond Menai – the rest was easy . . .

A eulogy of this kind, however much it may exaggerate the military prowess of the ruler to whom it was addressed, does at least provide contemporary notice of his military and political ambitions.

Unfortunately, the use of Primitive and Old Welsh verse as a historical source is not so simple as this might suggest. For a start, not all the poems which praise the martial valour of British heroes were composed to be recited in their presence; some of them are actually elegies to long-dead heroes. Typical here is the elegy to Gereint ab Erbin.[12] Some stanzas might well have been declaimed at Gereint's own court:

> At Llongborth I saw slaughter,
> men in turmoil and blood on the head
> before Gereint, his father's great son.

But the poem was in fact composed after Gereint's death:

> At Llongborth Gereint was killed,
> and brave men from Devon's lowland.

Moreover, although the basic political situation reflected by the poem is that of the sixth or seventh century, the date of composition is placed in the ninth or tenth. Consequently it lacks the historical value of a contemporary piece. When we find Arthur taking part in the battle of Llongborth, we do not know whether or not to take this as a historical fact. It is altogether more likely that it reflects an early stage in the development of the Arthurian romances, in which his name is coming to be connected with traditions about other heroes.

The problem is compounded because we possess no early manuscripts of the relevant Welsh poetry, which was recited for centuries before ever it was written down. The elegy to Gereint, for instance, comes from a manuscript of the late twelfth or early thirteenth century. The text of *Y Gododdin* that we actually possess was written about the middle of the thirteenth century. One version of it, to judge from its spelling and language, was copied from a manuscript probably as old as the ninth or tenth century. But this is still a long time after the late sixth when Aneirin first recited the poem. Because of the development of the Welsh language over the intervening centuries, some words or phrases of the original poem would have become archaic, obscure or perhaps even unintelligible. They would therefore have been modernized by the scribe who first wrote *Y Gododdin* down, and further modernized by the later copyists.

Modernizations apart, there is also the possibility that later material was grafted on to the original poem – and this is far more disturbing for the historian. As it happens, *Y Gododdin* has a couplet of first importance for Arthurian studies. The poet says of the hero Gwawrddur:

> He glutted black ravens on the wall of the fort
> although he was not Arthur.

Here we see Arthur regarded as a commendable example of martial valour. What we cannot prove is that this reference was in *Y Gododdin* when Aneirin first recited it. If it was, then Arthur was already celebrated as a hero by 600. But it is always possible that the phrase 'although he was not Arthur' was inserted when the poem came to be written down in the ninth or tenth century. There is good evidence, for instance in the 'Marvels of Britain' section of the *Historia Brittonum* (below, p. 41) to prove that by that date wholly fabulous tales were being attached to Arthur's name. We cannot therefore say whether the reference to Arthur was interpolated in *Y Gododdin* under the influence of such tales.

When we turn from the British or Welsh evidence to the Anglo-Saxon, we find that the Old English poems which have come down to us are not so immediately relevant to the historical personages of fifth and sixth century Britain. It is sometimes suggested that the Hengest who is referred to in *Beowulf* and *The Finnsburh Fragment*, the second-in-command of the Danes in the fight at Finnsburh, is the same as that Hengest to whom Vortigern gave land in Kent. The suggestion is incapable of proof, but even if it were true, it tells us nothing directly about politico-military events in fifth-century England.

Nevertheless, we cannot doubt that just as the *scops* in *Beowulf* recite poems in praise of the exploits of the nobility, so likewise at the courts of English kings, the great deeds of both ancestors and contemporaries were celebrated; and for the early English, as for the Germans of Tacitus, these poems passed as a major source of historical knowledge. The poem of Widsith[13] proves that this included a knowledge of continental ancestors and kinsmen:

This is the testimony of Widsith, traveller through
Kindreds and countries; in courts he stood often ...
Attila ruled the Huns, Eormanric the Goths
Theodric ruled the Franks, Thyle the Rondings ...
Offa ruled Angel ...
With single sword he struck the boundary against the Myrgings where it
    marches now,
fixed it at Fifeldor. Thenceforward it has stood between Angles and Swaefe
where Offa set it.

It has been suggested that this verse, celebrating the fixing of a frontier by Offa of Angeln in the fifth century, was recited at the Anglian court of Mercia in the eighth century. It then inspired a later Offa to the equally heroic task of fixing the boundary against the Welsh on the line of Offa's Dyke. However that may be, verse of this kind provided one of the historical sources available to chroniclers when, in the eighth and ninth centuries, they attempted to write histories of both the English and the Britons.

Chronology

None of the various sources which we have examined is of great use for historical purposes unless the events which it describes can be accurately dated. If we are to write narrative history, this means that events must be dated to the nearest year. But for a variety of technical chronological reasons this is rarely, if ever, possible in our period.

Readers accustomed to the sort of history in which events can be placed with confidence on a certain day of a certain month of a certain year AD may find this difficult to credit. But it is worth reminding them that even today we make use of a number of different reckonings for the start of the year. We may think of it as starting on 1 January, New Year's Day. But it would be more reasonable to think of the year of our Lord as commencing on Christ's Nativity, 25 December. The Christian year itself, however, begins with the first Sunday in Advent, four Sundays before Christmas Day. Our financial year, on the other hand, does not begin until 6 April, whereas the academic year begins in October.

Similar confusion obtained in early times; indeed, from our point of view it was compounded.[14] We would write of the academic session 1969/70, meaning that which began in October 1969 and ended in September 1970. But the early historian thought of the year of our Lord itself as starting on 25 March, the assumed date of the Annunciation; or on 25 December, the Nativity; or on some essentially pagan date which had Imperial Roman prestige behind it, such as the year of the indiction, the 1st or 24th of September; or even, in accordance with Roman civil practice, on 1 January.

A concrete example may help to make this clear. An early chronicler might refer to an event happening in October in the year of our Lord 700. Unless we know which particular reckoning the chronicler is using, we cannot tell whether the event is to be dated to October 699 or 700 AD in our own reckoning. So we must always expect a possible error of one year in early dates, even in the case of those gleaned from Easter Tables.

So far we have been considering a narrowly circumscribed cause of error. But the possibilities are extended when our sources, or the ultimate sources on which they depend, were not themselves using *anno domini* dating. The very idea of dating from the Incarnation was only conceived late in the period of our interest – in AD 525 by the monk Dionysius Exiguus. Before that, various systems were used in the Roman Empire to designate a particular year. It might be reckoned in terms of an era, calculated for instance from the supposed date of the Creation, or from the assumed date of the founding of Rome, or from the accession of an emperor. An alternative system, that of consular dating, identified each year by the names of the two consuls currently in office in Rome.

After the invention of the Dionysiac system, it spread slowly to the western fringes of Europe, and probably did not reach Britain and Ireland before the seventh century. From this it follows that if we find a date from some earlier century expressed in *anno domini* terms, this date must originally have been reckoned in accordance with some other era. It then had to be recalculated as a Year of Grace. It is therefore not an original date, but a computation, and in the computing there was a large possibility of miscalculation. The most readily detectable error occurs when the original was reckoned not in accordance with a pagan era, but by the alternative Christian era, that of the Passion of our Lord. It has already been mentioned that Victorius of Aquitaine had compiled a Great Cycle Easter Table which began with the Passion. This was dated conventionally to the consulship of the two Gemini, AD 28 by our reckoning. Victorian Easter Tables were widely diffused and served as a framework for Easter annals. When events from a Victorian Table came to be copied into a Dionysiac Table, the difference in era was not always noticed, and the annals would then be entered twenty-eight years too early. A large error like this is fairly readily discoverable; but smaller miscalculations in computing from one era to another may be quite undetectable unless we have other chronological evidence.

So far we have been concerned with dating in a Christian, literate and more or less civilized society. It is reasonable to expect that in a pagan, pre-literate, barbaric society the problems of chronology will be far greater. Despite this we find that in narrating events during the century and a half before the first Christian mission to the English, the *Anglo-Saxon Chronicle* uses *anno domini* dating to record the invasions of Kent, Sussex and Wessex, as well as for important battles and the accessions and deaths of rulers. It does not ease the problem here to say that the compiler of the *Anglo-Saxon Chronicle* took some of his dates from Bede, for this creates the twofold problem, how did Bede compute *his* dates for pagan Saxon history, and how did the chronicler compute dates for the events not mentioned by Bede.

It is generally considered that the data for these pre-Christian computations were provided by king lists or regnal lists. That is to say, the various tribes or nations of the Anglo-Saxons maintained lists of their successive kings together with the lengths of their reigns. Given such lists, it would be possible to work back, by subtraction, from a known king of the Christian period to establish the dates of accession of all his predecessors. Within each reign significant events, such as important battles, might have been remembered as occurring in the *n*th year of the reign of King X.

These lists are not merely a hypothesis to account for the fifth- and sixth-century dates in the *Anglo-Saxon Chronicle*. Bede mentions 'those who compute the times of kings', and we actually possess lists for Wessex and Northumbria in the Preface to the 'A' manuscript of the *Chronicle* and in the Moore manuscript of Bede's *Ecclesiastical History* respectively.[15] What is in question is their reliability. It is agreed that regnal lists cannot be accurate to the nearest year, simply because lengths of reign are unlikely to be expressible in whole years, and regnal years are unlikely to correspond with Years of Grace. But is there any guarantee that the reign-lengths were accurately recorded? In the centuries before literacy was introduced in the wake of Christian missions, historical information can only have been retained by fallible human memories and transmitted by word of mouth. What has been said already about the inaccurate transmission of genealogies (above, p. 10) applies with even more force here, since it was necessary to remember not only a list of names, but a series of figures as well.

In a small way, the accuracy of the transmission of information about reign-lengths can be tested. The Northumbrian regnal list agrees with statements made by Bede as far back as the reign of Edwin – that is, over the period from 737 back to 633. It also agrees with Bede's date for the founding of the Northumbrian dynasty by Ida in 547. The kings listed between Ida and Edwin cannot be cross-checked against Bede because he himself does not mention them. But the agreement between the regnal list and Bede's statements is scarcely surprising when we consider that the scribe who wrote the king list had just finished copying the *Ecclesiastical History*, and then annexed the list to the final folio. This can scarcely be accounted an independent cross-check.

The case of Wessex is more instructive. The preface to the 'A' manuscript of the *Anglo-Saxon Chronicle* includes a regnal list, while the main body of the *Chronicle* gives the accessions and deaths of the rulers of Wessex against the appropriate Year of Grace. If we assume that the dates of Cynegils, the first Wessex ruler to be baptized, are likely to be fixed from a contemporary Easter Table, we can work back by subtraction from his accession in 610/611, and so compute the dates of his five precursors. At no point do the dates calculated in this way correspond with the *Chronicle* dates. In three cases there may be a systematic error of exactly ten years, which could be explained as the result of a simple scribal error. But the most startling discrepancy is that of Ceawlin, who, according to the *Chronicle*, succeeded his father Cynric in 560, was possibly supplanted by Ceol in 591, and was finally driven out in 592. To him the regnal list allows merely seventeen years.

We can observe this discrepancy between the early king list recorded in the *Chronicle* and the chronology of events which supposedly was based on such a list. But this presents us with a further dilemma – should we believe the regnal list, and recalculate the dates of reigns in accordance with it? Or should we believe that another, more accurate list lies behind the *Chronicle* dates? This dilemma cannot be resolved by any of the normal techniques of historical research, and we must therefore accept the position that no reliable chronology is possible in Wessex before the reign of Cynegils.

We may sum up our discussion of the chronological problems presented by our written sources on these lines. Once Dionysiac Easter Tables had become established in the west, we can believe that dates are accurate within a year. Before the adoption of the Dionysiac Tables, however, we may expect that events which had been entered contemporaneously in Easter Tables using some other era may be subject to dislocations of as much as twenty-eight years. In the case of the pagan kingdoms, we can have no confidence whatsoever in the chronology of events.

Two
Three Key Texts

So far we have examined the general character of our verbal evidence. Now we must scrutinize three major texts which together provide the bulk of the evidence for Arthurian Britain, and which exemplify many of the problems involved in its study. These texts are: the *De excidio et conquestu Britanniae* of the monk Gildas; the anonymous *British Historical Miscellany* contained in the British Museum manuscript Harley 3859; and the relevant annals of the *Anglo-Saxon Chronicle*.

De excidio Britanniae[1]

If ever there was a prolix, tedious and exasperating work it is Gildas's *De excidio et conquestu Britanniae*: 'Concerning the Ruin and Conquest of Britain'. A large part of it consists of biblical quotations which are chiefly of technical interest to students of bible translations. Its historical section, as we shall see, is largely untrustworthy. The whole is written in a Latin which though technically correct is so involved in style and so obscure in vocabulary as to be always difficult, and at some points impossible, to understand. Why, then, is this a key text?

The essential answer lies in the use that Bede made of the *De excidio*, and the wide circulation which was thereby given to its historical statements. When Bede came to write his *Ecclesiastical History of the English People* he was faced, as we are today, with a dearth of material for the crucial period of English settlement between the end of Roman rule and the mission of St Augustine to Kent in 597. He had access to brief notices of the visits of Germanus of Auxerre to a Britain in which the Saxons were already a military force. He heard traditions about the settlement of Kent, which had been handed down by word of mouth for two and a half centuries. But there was little else available except for the historical sections of the *De excidio*. This had been written within a century of the chief events which it described; indeed, the most important incident of all, the British victory of Mount Badon, occurred in the year of Gildas's birth.

Bede, therefore, made large use of the *De excidio*, cutting out some of the rhetoric and turning the Latin into something more readable. Occasionally, in his attempt to make Gildas comprehensible, Bede silently gives his own meaning to a phrase that was ambiguous in the original, and we shall find it necessary to challenge Bede's interpretation on at least two occasions (below, pp. 103 f. and 107–9). But the most important point is that Bede's version of the story told by Gildas has remained the fundamental account of the Anglo-Saxon settlement of England from the early eighth century, when Bede wrote, almost to the present day. Only in the present generation has this account been seriously challenged. In so far, then, as the Anglo-Saxon invasions created the Arthurian situation, a knowledge of the *De excidio* is fundamental to our purpose.

We possess the *De excidio Britanniae* in manuscripts no earlier than the eleventh century; but Bede's use of it enables us to know to some extent what the original document was like, and his reference to the Britons' 'own historian Gildas' makes its authorship certain. About Gildas himself we know little, save what is revealed by his own writings, because the two *Lives of St Gildas* are so late in date as to be of little historical value. He was almost certainly a Briton, and a westerner at that, though it is doubtful whether we should place him in Wales or in Strathclyde. He was most probably a monk. He was regularly known as Gildas Sapiens, and it seems that the term 'Wise' means specifically that he had mastered the learning of the civilized Roman world, written in Latin, as opposed to the oral vernacular learning of the Celtic peoples. He died, according to the Welsh Easter Annals, in 572.

The date of the *De excidio* itself has usually been placed about 530, and certainly no later than 540, give or take five years. The key to the dating is provided by Gildas's diatribe, in Chapters 33 and 34, against *Maglocunus insularis draco* – Maelgwn of Gwynedd. The implication of Gildas's attack is clearly that, although Maelgwn was well advanced in his reprobate career, he was still very much alive. But according to the Welsh Easter Annals, a document which we shall examine shortly (pp. 39–40), Maelgwn of Gwynedd died in 549 as a result of plague: *mortalitas magna in qua pausat mailcun rex genedotae*; the Great Plague in which Maelgwn of Gwynedd died.

If we accept the date of the Annals for Maelgwn's death, and accept further that Maelgwn was relatively old when the *De excidio* was written, then a date close to but certainly before 549 is inevitable for the work.

But can we accept this date for the death of Maelgwn? Since it is recorded in an Easter Annal, it had probably been entered contemporaneously in an Easter Table (above, p. 6). But this could not have been a Dionysiac Table (above, p. 18), and there is therefore a possibility of some chronological dislocation when the annal was transferred from the original Table to the Great Cycle Table in which we find it (p. 40; pp. 54–5). Against this, it has been argued that the *mortalitas magna* of the annal is most probably the severe outbreak of plague which we know from various Byzantine and western writers. Starting in the east in 541/2, it had spread to southern Gaul about 544, and is likely to have reached Britain within the next few years. Consequently a date between 545 and 550 would seem reasonable for the *mortalitas magna* in Britain, and for Maelgwn's death.

The main objection to this dating is a passage in the *British Historical Miscellany*, Chapter 62, which implies that Maelgwn was a contemporary of Ida of Northumbria, and also of the renowned early Welsh poets, including Taliesin and Aneirin. This passage may be the source of the tradition that there was a conflict between Maelgwn and Taliesin, or alternatively the tradition may have independent roots. Whichever is the case, we must admit the possibility that Maelgwn and Taliesin overlapped. This, however, would make it highly improbable that Maelgwn was dead by 549, because Taliesin's poems can definitely be dated to the second half of the sixth century. If Maelgwn and Ida were contemporary, this would point in the same direction. Bede gives Ida's date of accession as 547; and even granted all that has been said above (pp. 19–20) about the difficulties of using regnal lists for chronological purposes, there can be no serious doubt that Ida flourished in the third quarter of the sixth century.

If these arguments were sound, we would have to think of a date after, rather than before 550 for the writing of the *De excidio*. This could have important repercussions for the dates of Arthur (below, pp. 53–5). Meanwhile, it can be said that this later date for the *De excidio* does no violence to such scanty internal evidence as it contains.

What, then, is the *De excidio et conquestu Britanniae*? Gildas describes it as a letter – *epistola* – and a little admonition – *admonitiuncula* – but its 110 chapters, covering sixty pages in the standard text, belie this description. The work may be divided into four sections. Section A, Chapters 1 and 2, is an introduction, in which Gildas states his theme: the sins of contemporary rulers and churchmen, and the woes which had been visited on the ancestors of the present generation because of their sins. Section B, Chapters 3 to 26, is apparently a description and history of Britain from the period of Roman rule down to Gildas's own day. But it is a history intended to illustrate the central theme; a homiletic and admonitory history rather than one intended to set out the course of events with factual accuracy. Section C, Chapters 27 to 63, is a denunciation of kings and secular authority, which begins with a diatribe against five contemporary rulers of western Britain, and then proceeds to denunciatory or cautionary quotations from scripture. Finally, Section D, Chapters 64 to 110, is an attack on ecclesiastical authority, beginning 'Priests Britain has, but foolish ones', and ending 'May God Almighty preserve his very few good pastors from all evil . . . Amen.'

Attempts have been made, by leading scholars in this field, to demonstrate that we have here not one, but two, works. In effect it has been claimed that the authentic writing of Gildas, sometimes referred to as the '*Epistola* proper', comprises Sections A, C and D only. On to this original text a wholly spurious history, the '*De excidio* proper', or Section B, was grafted a generation or more after Gildas's own day. The *De excidio* was available to Bede, who used it in his *Historia ecclesiastica* as we have seen, but it is inferred that the *Epistola* was not available, or at least was not used by him. If this is so, then these two documents, the *De excidio* and the *Epistola*, were still separate in the early eighth century.

Despite the authority with which this hypothesis of the twofold character of the work has been expounded, there are grave objections to it. In the first place no convincing motive has ever been advanced for the creation of a spurious *De excidio* and for its fostering on Gildas. Secondly, if the spurious *De excidio* was grafted onto a pre-existing *Epistola*, the graft was very cunningly achieved. A close study of the developing argument of the work shows that Chapter 2 provides a synopsis or programme for Section B, while the final sentences of Section B pick up the main denunciatory theme in anticipation of Section C. In terms of argument, then, we have a unitary work. The same is true in terms of theme and style. And a recent very detailed study of the vocabulary, syntax and style of Gildas has shown negatively that Section B lacks the tricks of style of the particular school at whose door the forgery has been laid, and positively that there is no significant difference between Section B and the rest of the work.

Finally, we may consider the evidence of Bede. Throughout the earlier chapters of Book 1 of the *Historia Ecclesiastica*, Bede used Section B of Gildas very closely as far as its final chapter. He then added: 'among other unutterable deeds of crime, which their own historian Gildas relates in mournful words, they added this, that they never preached the Gospel to the English'. There can be little doubt that the 'unutterable deeds' and 'mournful words' are Bede's passing reference to Sections C and D of Gildas, which for him had no historical interest. If this is so, the argument that the *De excidio* and the *Epistola* were two separate documents in Bede's day cannot be maintained.

It may therefore be accepted that the *De excidio* – or *Historia* as it is sometimes called – no less than the *Epistola*, is a work of Gildas Sapiens, written about the middle of the sixth century. What is its historical value? The answer must be that this is on three levels. The lowest, the most untrustworthy level, is that in which Gildas deals with the history of Roman Britain, Chapters 5 to 18. The essential point here is that he ascribes the building of the turf wall of Antonine, and the stone wall of Hadrian – both works of the second century – to the years after the usurpation of Magnus Maximus in 383. Now it is no defence of Gildas to say that archaeologists still dispute about the precise dates of the two walls, and therefore we cannot expect Gildas to know any better. The very fact that he falsely attributes two major works of military engineering to the late fourth and early fifth centuries demonstrates that his knowledge of that period is scanty. Again, it has been argued that genuinely historical Roman activities underlie Gildas's story, whatever muddle he has made of them. But we can attempt to disentangle the muddle only because we possess other and acceptable historical sources for the late fourth and earliest fifth centuries. When these sources give out, as they do in the crucial middle generation of the fifth century, we have no means of sorting out the straightforward truth from the writings of a man already proved to be a muddler.

The second level concerns the period immediately before Gildas's birth. He has given a lurid account of the devastation wrought on Britain by the northern and western barbarians. He has told of the ultimate failure of the Romans, in the person of Aëtius, the commander in Gaul, to respond to a British appeal for help. Thereafter, under the threat of renewed invasions from the north, the Britons decided, under the leadership of an unnamed *superbus tyrannus*, 'outstanding ruler', to call in the Saxons to their assistance. This is in Chapter 23; by Chapter 24 the Saxon mercenaries have revolted and are ravaging the whole island. Their devastation continues almost unchecked until, at the end of Chapter 25, under the leadership of the romanized general Ambrosius Aurelianus, a victory was gained by the Britons. 'From that time forth, sometimes the Britons were victorious, sometimes the enemy, up to the year of the siege of Mount Badon, which was almost the most recent but not the least slaughter of the gallows-crew.' This was also the year of Gildas's birth, and in the forty-four years of his life the island had enjoyed freedom from external attack though not from internecine strife.

It is reasonable to believe that, within Gildas's own region of Britain, his lifetime had seen an abatement of Anglo-Saxon military activity against the Britons. Granted that his motive is exhortatory and homiletic rather than historical, his credit as a preacher would surely have been destroyed if he had referred to a long period of peace when the experience of his audience was one of continual warfare. We can also infer, on the very same grounds of Gildas's credibility as a preacher, that Mount Badon had been a signal victory for the Britons over their enemies. But how far back is this argument valid? We can believe in the existence of Ambrosius Aurelianus, who appears also in other acceptable sources, and doubtless he did initiate a series of successful campaigns. But by the time we get back to the *superbus tyrannus* the particular argument that we are deploying here is of no avail, because there would have been no popular memory to act as a check on Gildas's account. We shall see that the attempt to put dates to Gildas's story at this point reduced even the Venerable Bede to inconsistency (below, p. 108). And the idea that the Saxons were first called in to assist in the defence of Britain about the middle of the fifth century is quite irreconcilable with the archaeological evidence (below, p. 92).

A fair verdict on Gildas's story of events between the unsuccessful appeal to Aëtius and the victories of Ambrosius Aurelianus might be that it reflects an indistinct memory of one incident in the complex relations between Britons and English. Likewise, his picture of fire and slaughter on the one hand, flight and destruction on the other, shows one aspect of those relations. But the internal inconsistencies of Gildas's account would be enough in themselves to prove that he does not tell a complete or even a coherent tale. As we shall see, the evidence of archaeology is making it increasingly impossible to believe that the settlement of eastern Britain by the English stemmed from a single invitation to Saxon mercenaries around the middle of the fifth century. Gildas's *De excidio* was the foundation on which Bede, and centuries of historians after him, based their assumptions concerning the English settlement. We can now see that the foundation was insecure.

Despite this criticism of his account of the mid-fifth century, we have seen reason to credit Gildas's statement about the siege of Mount Badon, and this account deserves further consideration. It is frequently suggested that the British victory of Badon in itself halted the Saxon advance for almost half a century – presumably because the fighting manpower of the invaders had been wiped out for a generation. But Gildas does not really allow us to infer this. He describes Badon not as the last slaughter of the enemy, but as 'almost the last' – *novissimae ferme stragis*; and also as 'not the least' – *non minimae*. If it was not the last, if it was not of itself a single decisive event, why does Gildas, always so sparing of names and details, single it out for mention? It is tempting to think he did so because, forty-four years later, Badon had already acquired the glamour which it was to display in British tradition and in Arthurian romance.

This leads us to the question, who commanded the British forces at Badon? In Chapters 25 and 26, Gildas has described Ambrosius as a 'moderate man', *vir modestus* – perhaps in contrast to the *superbus tyrannus* – whose parents 'doubtless endowed with the purple' had been killed in the previous strife. Under his leadership the Britons had gathered strength and had forced the enemy to do battle:

... by God's aid, victory came to them. From that time forth sometimes the Britons, and sometimes the enemy, were victorious (that the Lord might try, in customary fashion, whether the modern Israel would choose him or not), up to the year of the siege of Mount Badon.

This is one of the two early statements that we have about Badon, and it leaves the name of the general in doubt. It is possible to think that what Gildas means is that Ambrosius won the first victory against the Saxons, and thereby initiated a series of campaigns of fluctuating fortune up to the decisive battle of Badon, all under his own leadership. Alternatively he may mean that Ambrosius' campaigns led to the first victory; and that thereafter there was a long series of battles not necessarily all under Ambrosius' leadership. This would leave the question of the commander at Badon open.

It may seem strange that Gildas should not name the victor of Badon, and this line of argument would incline us to infer that Ambrosius is the subject of all this military activity. But two further points arise. First, Gildas is altogether sparing of names of persons and places. In the whole of Section B, apart from biblical passages and classical writers whom he wishes to quote, he names only two Roman emperors, Tiberius and Diocletian; three British martyrs, Alban, Julian and Aaron; the usurper Magnus Maximus; Aëtius the commander-in-chief in Gaul; and Ambrosius. Even in the critical incident of the invitation to the Saxons he names neither the *superbus tyrannus* nor the Saxon leaders. We may therefore be gratefully surprised that he should name Ambrosius and Badon at all. Secondly, bearing in mind that his purpose is homily and not history, we need not expect names, and the name of the general might fit oddly with that of the battle in what is, in the main, a sermon. It has been said, 'what English bishop, castigating the vices of his compatriots about 1860, would be so clumsy as to allude to "the battle of Waterloo, *which was won by the Duke of Wellington*"?"[2] (Original author's italics.)

The one certainty to emerge from this discussion is that we cannot necessarily infer that Ambrosius was the leader at Badon as he was at the first God-given victory. The ambiguity of Gildas leaves open the possibility that the traditional attribution of Badon to Arthur was sound. We shall see below (p. 53) evidence suggesting that the attribution may even go back to the time of the battle itself.

It remains for us to examine the third level of historical credibility in the *De excidio*. This is represented by Sections C and D – Gildas's attacks on the failings of contemporary church and state. Here he is an immediate and contemporary witness to affairs, and this in itself compensates for the distortions due to his viewpoint and his purpose in writing. Sections C and D of the *De excidio* are quite simply homily, if not invective. Their two themes are: 'Kings Britain has, but usurpers; judges has she, but ungodly' and 'Priests Britain has, but foolish ones.' Violently prejudiced though Gildas was, he tells us a great deal about both the political arrangements and the ecclesiastical organization of western Britain in the sixth century. He tells it, of course, as much by his assumptions and his silences as by his rhetoric. But without his witness, our ignorance would be almost total.

The British Historical Miscellany[3]

We turn now to a document which, in contrast to the *De excidio*, was compiled with a historical purpose in mind. It is a compendium of source material for British history, which was collected together by an unknown historian about the middle of the tenth century. The document is sometimes referred to as 'Nennius' *History of the Britons* with appendices'; or as 'British Museum Harleian MS 3859', but the first of these descriptions is inadequate and the second is positively misleading. In view of the material it contains I propose to call this document the *British Historical Miscellany*. What form does the actual manuscript take, and what historical material does it comprise? The answers to these questions are somewhat technical; but some understanding of their details is essential if we are to establish whether or not Arthur is an acceptable historical figure.

The manuscripts catalogued by the British Museum as Harley 3859 form a curious collection of documents to find together within the same binding. They include orations from the golden age of Latin literature; a late Roman work on military affairs; part (only) of a sermon of St Augustine of Hippo; an obscure Scythian geography; and the British material. This medley was acquired by the Harleian Library in 1729, and nothing relevant is known of its earlier history.

Our concern is solely with folios 174–98, which originally existed as a separate codex or book. They were written in a beautifully regular and legible hand about 1100 or a little later, but they were actually copied, at one or more removes, from a compilation which had been put together originally in the second half of the tenth century.

Despite the care taken in writing it, the codex as we have it is unfinished in two respects. First, the scribe had intended to pick out the individual paragraphs by starting each one with an enlarged initial letter, occupying two or more lines of text, and coloured red. But this was done only for the first quarter of the codex. Thereafter, paragraphs were marked by insetting the first two lines, to leave room for the enlarged initial, but the initials themselves were never written, let alone coloured. This, however curious it may seem to us, is not uncommon in the case of such manuscripts. It is the result of the decorative work – coloured initials, illumination and so on – being done by someone other than the scribe who had copied the text. It may be that the original intention was to furnish the codex with an illuminated title page, but in this respect again it appears to be unfinished. The copyist was able to write

FINIT AMEN

at the end, but there is no title page, no author, no list of chapter headings, in fact none of the apparatus which customarily stands at the head of a book.

This again is not an unknown phenomenon with early manuscripts – indeed later copyists frequently fathered texts which had come to them without author or title on to famous writers of the past. In a way, therefore, we may be grateful that our codex is anonymous and has no title, because this means that we can make inferences about it unhampered by any spurious attribution.

First of all, for convenience sake, we must provide it with a title. Folios 174–98 of B.M. MS Harley 3859 contain a great deal that is found in other manuscripts, notably a *Historia Brittonum* or *History of the Britons* which elsewhere is attributed either to Gildas or to Nennius; but they also contain much that is found only in this manuscript and another one derived directly from it. This unique material provides a significant part of their historical value. The work as a whole – and by this I mean the original which lies behind our copy – was a compilation from various sources of raw material for writing a history of Britain down to the writer's own day. The term *British Historical Miscellany* exactly describes it.

Internal evidence shows that the *Miscellany* was put together in the second half of the tenth century. It contains a set of Easter Annals of which the framework continues to 980 in order to complete a Great Cycle. But this is not necessarily the actual date of the compilation of the *Miscellany*. The last event recorded, in year 510 of the Annals, was the death of the south Welsh prince Rhodri ap Hywel Dda, which probably occurred in AD 957. The Annals are followed by a series of Welsh genealogies, of which the latest is that of Rhodri's youngest brother, Owain ap Hywel Dda. All this is consistent with a date of compilation in the second half of the tenth century, but it would be unreasonable to press the evidence further than that.

The compilation of the *Miscellany* may reasonably be attributed to the *scriptorium* of St David's. To judge from the interest which the later annals take in St David's affairs, they were entered in a Great Cycle Easter Table at that monastery; and it was there, most probably, that the compiler extracted the Annals themselves from the Easter Table. Again, the Welsh genealogies are very detailed for the kingdom of Deheubarth, that is roughly Pembrokeshire, Cardiganshire, and Carmarthenshire, whereas they are relatively incomplete for the south-eastern kingdoms of Gwent and Morgannwg. If we think that the original of the *Miscellany* was compiled at St David's in the period 960–70, and that our actual manuscript was copied there in the early twelfth century, this would fit the available facts. Misspellings of Welsh personal names suggest that the copy was written by a scribe ignorant of the Welsh language, and this is most likely to have occurred

after St David's had come under Norman influence on the appoint-
ment of Bishop Bernard in 1115.

The Welsh annals and genealogies which help us to locate the place
and date of compilation of the *Miscellany* are themselves interpolated
into a medley of historical materials, most of which are known from a
number of manuscripts quite independent of Harley 3859. It is this
earlier medley, a work of the first half of the ninth century, which is
usually known as the *Historia Brittonum*. Some of the copies of this
are anonymous, but two groups of manuscripts attribute it respectively
to Gildas and to a certain Nennius. The attribution to Gildas is impossible, because the *Historia Brittonum* includes events of the seventh
century, long after Gildas's death. Nennius is generally agreed to have
had a hand in writing the *Historia*, but it is still disputed whether he
merely added fresh material to a pre-existing *Historia*, as the compiler
of the *Miscellany* did over a century later, or whether he was himself
the original author or compiler of the *Historia*.[4]

Fortunately we are not concerned here with that particular controversy. We can readily observe that the Nennian *Historia* is a hotch-
potch of historical material garnered in from various sources – indeed
the preface to one twelfth-century manuscript has Nennius say: 'I
have heaped together all that I found, from the Annals of the Romans,
the writings of the holy fathers, the annals of the Irish and the Saxons,
and the traditions of our own old men.' If we might continue the
metaphor, we can go on to say that the Nennian heap is like a cairn of
stones, uneven and ill-fitting, not worked into a smooth whole by the
craftsman's tools; as an example of the historian's art it is atrocious.
But it has the virtue of its defects. We can see the individual stones of
the cairn, and in some cases we can trace the parent rock from which
they came, and establish its age and soundness.

In describing the *British Historical Miscellany* in detail it is convenient to use both the section numbering which Mommsen introduced for his edition of the *Historia Brittonum* and also the folio
numbering of Harley 3859. Unfortunately the sections into which
Mommsen divides the text do not necessarily correspond with the
paragraph divisions marked by red initials in Harley 3859. Since no
facsimile of this important document has ever been published, the
student must refer to the original manuscript if he wishes to know

where the scribe thought breaks were necessary. We shall see the relevance of this for Arthurian studies later (below, p. 82).

The work begins, then, with a calculation of the Six Ages of the World – from the beginning of the world to the flood, from the flood to Abraham, and so on down to the sixth age, from John the Baptist to the Judgement (Sections 1–6, folio 174B). This in itself is a very conventional way of beginning a historical work, and it is followed (in Sections 7–18, folios 174B–177A) by an equally conventional description of the island of Britain, and of its peopling by the Scots, the Picts and the Britons. Part of this is taken from Gildas's *De excidio*, part from St Jerome and other Latin sources, while other elements represent antiquarian speculation on the lines 'the island of Britain is called after a certain Brutus, a Roman consul'. It is sometimes thought that fragments of genuine folk-memory are embedded in this; for instance, in the reference to Irish settlement in the Gower and Kidwelly districts of south Wales (Section 14, folio 176A). But it is very doubtful whether any of this is of independent historical value.

The same may be said of the account which follows of the Roman conquest and occupation of Britain (Sections 19–30, folios 177A–179B). As a historical account, this is utterly muddled. We can say this because we have better and fuller sources than the writer of the *Historia Brittonum*. He seems to rely largely on Gildas, Orosius, Jerome and Prosper. On the whole he is very faithful to his sources, except where he misunderstands them, or builds more on their statements than is justified; but he obviously has no value as a source in his own right.

The first independent section of the *Historia Brittonum* begins 'after the slaying of Maximus the Usurper, the rule of the Romans in Britain being finished'. This introduces the figure of Vortigern, and we follow his activities, both in Kent and in Wales, and his relations with the Saxons, with St Germanus of Auxerre, and with Ambrosius (Sections 31–49, folios 179B–185B). At times Germanus himself becomes the dominant figure, and so a group of anecdotes about his activities in north Wales is interpolated. But it is Vortigern who forms the main subject of this part of the *Historia Brittonum*, and the account of his doings is of very mixed value. At the one extreme, the story of his attempt to build a citadel in the mountains of Snowdonia falls into a recognizable category of fabulous tale: every time that the timber and stones for constructing the citadel are brought together, they disappear overnight. This then leads on to other fabulous and magical doings: a search for the fatherless boy with whose blood the citadel might be sprinkled, the discovery of Ambrosius, and his exposure of the incompetence of Vortigern's own magicians; the disclosure of a red badger or dragon representing the Britons and a white badger or dragon representing the English; and the prophecies of Ambrosius, anticipating those of Merlin. Clearly none of this carries conviction as it stands.

At the other extreme, however, we have statements which are historically plausible, but which cannot be cross-checked because the *Historia Brittonum* is the primary source for them. Such is the statement, quite independent of Gildas or Bede, that during Vortigern's reign three ships came from Germany 'driven in exile' – an event which in the context of Germanic society is only too likely. Even the fables about Vortigern's citadel and the conflict of Ambrosius and the magicians may contain truths about Vortigern's sphere of influence in north Wales, and about a real conflict, partly political and partly religious, between Ambrosius and Vortigern himself.

Unfortunately, the essential work of source analysis has not yet been carried out on Vortigern's biography as it is given in the *Historia Brittonum*. Until it has we can only infer the trustworthiness of its individual statements on the basis of their general historical plausibility.

From the activities of Vortigern and St Germanus we turn abruptly to the conversion of the Irish by Palladius and Patrick (Sections 50–55, folios 185B–187A). The statements about Palladius have been taken principally from Prosper, or from some writer dependent on Prosper, such as Bede in his *Historia ecclesiastica*. So far as we can judge they are correct. The account of Patrick's mission, on the other hand, is in quite the worst tradition of medieval hagiography, and deserves no further consideration.

From this worthless material we come with scarcely a pause to one of the most important parts of the *Historia Brittonum*: the elements distinguished by modern commentators in such terms as 'Arthuriana' (Section 56, folios 187A–B), 'Anglian Genealogies' (Sections 57–62, folios 187B–188B) and 'Northern British History' (part of Section 57,

Sections 62–5; to folio 189B). All this material is significant for our studies, the Arthurian element especially so, but it comes from very diverse sources, and it is necessary to attempt to distinguish them in order to judge their historical value.

In Section 55 the author has apologized for abbreviating his account of Patrick. In Section 56 he continues [Fig. 5]:

> In that time the Saxons strengthened in multitude and grew in Britain. On the death of Hengist, however, Octha his son passed from the northern part of Britain to the region of the Cantii and from him arise the Kings of the Cantii.
>
> Then Arthur fought against them in those days [There follows an account of Arthur's twelve battles (below, p. 55) down to Mount Badon] ... and in all battles he was victor. And they, while they were laid low in all battles sought help from Germany and they increased many times without intermission and they brought over kings from Germany to rule over them in Britain up to the time when Ida reigned who was the son of Eobba. He was the first king in Beornica that is in Berneich.
>
> Woden begat Beldeg ...

So we come to the dynasty of Ida and some of its doings (Section 57); the genealogy of the kings of Kent (Section 58); the genealogy of East Anglia (Section 59); genealogies of the Mercian dynasty (Section 60); the genealogy of the dynasty of Deira (i.e. southern Northumbria) and some of its doings (Section 61), returning to Ida at the end of that section. It is apparent that the genealogies are interpolated into a pre-existing account of Ida himself, which is now found split between the end of Section 56 and the end of Section 61.

The genealogies themselves came obviously from an Anglo-Saxon source – in fact it can be shown that they had originally been drawn up in Mercia in the late eighth century. Their reliability is subject to all the caveats that we have already entered about genealogies (pp. 10, 19), with the added difficulty that here the transmission has passed from English into Welsh hands, and the spelling of the names has frequently become confused or corrupted. In the same way as the genealogies are interpolated into the history of Ida, we find historical snippets interpolated into the genealogies themselves, so that we have an elaborate interlacement, as it were, of genealogy with political, military and even ecclesiastical history.

These historical interpolations, together with the account of Ida, and all that follows in Sections 62–5, comprise the 'Northern British History'.[5] It is very revealing to list all the persons named in this history. Even when we exclude those who occur only in the Anglian genealogies the list is still preponderantly English, not British. Moreover, among the English kingdoms the dynasties of Northumbria, and specifically that of Bernicia, are far the most frequently mentioned. When other dynasties or nations are mentioned – Mercians; Picts; Britons of Strathclyde, Elmet, and Gwynedd – it is frequently because they have been involved in battle with the Northumbrian kings, whether as victors or vanquished. In short, the substance of these sections of the *Historia Brittonum* is a history of the kingdom founded by Ida. It is a primary source for the sixth and seventh centuries in the north-east, because much of the information it contains is quite independent of Bede. Some of the events recorded are later than the conversion of King Edwin in 627, later even than the consolidation of the conversion under King Oswald after 635. This material could well have come from contemporary records in an Easter Table. But the pre-conversion material comes from oral tradition, perhaps in the form of items attached to individual names in a regnal list. The regnal list would give some chronological articulation to these events; but bearing in mind what we have seen already about the inconsistencies of such lists, we must not expect any great possibility of accurate dating.

Although we can be confident that a Northumbrian history of Ida's dynasty forms the basis of the 'Northern British History', the document we possess is not necessarily close to its Northumbrian original. It has certainly passed through a British or Welsh phase of transmission. This can be shown by the Welsh spelling of Old English personal names – Eoguin or Eadgum for Edwin, Osguid for Oswy, Aedlric for Æthelric, and so on. Then some Angles are given British nicknames – Oswald *Lamnguin*, White-blade, or Eadfered *Flesaurs*, Æthelfrith the Twister. Moreover, certain well-known battles are called by British rather than English names – that known to the Northumbrians as the battle of *Nechtanes Mere* is here given the British name of *Gueith Lin Garan*, the Strife at Crane Lake. There can be no doubt that the Northumbrian material had passed through British hands before it became attached to the *Historia Brittonum*.

It was presumably at the same time that the specifically British items became attached to the Northumbrian framework. These are a very mixed bunch, which repay close analysis. The expulsion of Certic, King of Elmet, is incidental to the account of Edwin of Northumbria. Dutigirn (correctly Outigirn) is a British leader otherwise unknown to us, who 'fought bravely against the nation of the Angles'. Four kings known to have ruled in south-west Scotland are named as fighting against the Northumbrian Hussa. One of them, Urien of Rheged, is further celebrated because he besieged the Northumbrian Theodric for three days and nights on Lindisfarne, and because he was later slain by his fellow Briton Morcant. These events may have come from Easter Annals, or may have been remembered in Welsh poetry, for all four kings were celebrated in verse. We may recall here that another of the British entries, one which this time has no Northumbrian connection, is that which mentions Taliesin, Aneirin, and three other bards, 'renowned in British poetry'.

Finally, five rulers of Gwynedd are noticed. Cadwallon was involved in the slaying of Edwin and his sons, and was in turn slain by Oswald, so here is another Northumbrian connection. Cadafael was likewise involved in war with Northumbria. But no such connection can be postulated for Maelgwn or his ancestor Cunedda. It is sometimes argued that the interest of the 'Northern British History' is entirely northern, and that Maelgwn is mentioned solely because he was descended from Cunedda who migrated to Wales from Manau Guotodin, north of the Forth. The argument is strained to say the least, for it plainly inverts the sense of our text. This is first that Maelgwn was a great king, and secondly that he ruled in an area which interested the compiler of the 'Northern British History', namely Gwynedd; Cunedda comes in merely as an ancestor of Maelgwn, and because he and his sons drove the Irish out of Wales. The belief that the compiler was specially interested in Gwynedd receives powerful support from the mention of the fifth Venedotian* ruler, Cadwaladr, which is inserted quite unnecessarily into the account of Oswy of Northumbria.

To the scribe who compiled the 'Northern British History' the rulers of Gwynedd held an outstanding place among the Britons. Thus Cadwaladr is described quite simply as 'reigning among the Britons'.

---

* The usual adjectival form, meaning 'of Gwynedd'.

Of Maelgwn it is said: 'Maelgwn, the great king, was ruling among the Britons; i.e. in the region of Gwynedd.' This suggests that the Venedotian dynasty was pre-eminent among British rulers. We shall see later that Cadwaladr's grandfather Cadfan claimed to be 'the most renowned of all kings' [Pl. 27*b*]; (below, pp. 136 f.). All this interest in Gwynedd suggests that the 'Northern British History' was itself the product of a Venedotian *scriptorium*, perhaps at Bangor. To judge from the archaic spelling of Cunedda's name – Cunedag – the *scriptorium*, wherever it was, had an Easter Table or similar document going back at least into the seventh century. It seems likely that items from such an Easter Table, together with others culled from Welsh poetic tradition, were grafted on to an original Northumbrian history when it was being copied at Bangor. These grafts produced the hybrid Anglian-British document which we call the 'Northern British History'.

We can now turn back to examine the relation of the Arthuriana in *Historia Brittonum* (Section 56) to the 'Northern British History'. It seems possible from the way in which the account of Arthur and his battles is fitted between the last mention of Hengist and the first mention of Ida, that it is yet another of the British elements which were attached to the framework of Northumbrian history. If this is so, then it comes from a British source, which might be either northern or Venedotian. We cannot reasonably argue here from source criticism to the geographical setting of Arthur's activities. The significance of this will become clear when we concentrate attention on Arthur himself (below, pp. 81–5).

There is little doubt about the source of the Arthuriana: it was a battle-listing poem. In brief, the nucleus of Section 56 of the *Historia Brittonum* is a Latin summary of a Welsh poem about Arthur. Such a poem might have been recited anywhere in the British–Welsh-speaking area from Strathclyde to Dumnonia; only after the Anglo-Saxon expansion would its transmission have been confined to Wales proper. Moreover, the original might have gone back to Arthur's own day, or it might have been an elegy composed long after his death, and after any sound historical traditions about him had perished. This again must be discussed more fully in Chapter 3.

From the sections with a predominantly English-Northumbrian interest, which are an integral part of the *Historia Brittonum*, the

Harley 3859 manuscript turns to material which is peculiar to the *British Historical Miscellany*. This begins with a series of chronological computations, followed by a set of Annals. Since the computations (folios 189B–190A) deal largely with Vortigern and the coming of the English to Britain, they have frequently been regarded as a summary or recapitulation of the 'Life of Vortigern' which formed Sections 31–49 of the *Historia Brittonum*. But this is most unlikely. They are absent from most of the manuscripts of the *Historia Brittonum*, and occur only in Harley 3859 and another manuscript derived from it. Since it is only these two manuscripts which contain the annals, and since we have seen (p. 9; pp. 104–5) that such computations may form a preface to Easter Table annals, it is reasonable to assign them a similar role here. It is probable that the computations originally stood at the head of an Easter Table which began in 447 but which was actually compiled in 455. In that case they stand closer to Vortigern's own day than any other document that we possess, except possibly for brief entries in two Gallic Chronicles (below, pp. 105–6).

The annals themselves (folios 190A–193A) are a curious document[6] [Figs. 3 and 4]. Since they cover a span of 533 years there is no doubt that in their final form they come from a Great Cycle Easter Table of 532 years, plus the first year of the new cycle. But in themselves they bear no *anno domini* dates. Instead, each year is marked merely by *an'* for *annus*. The decades and centuries are however marked, so that the tenth year is *an'. x*, the fortieth *an' xl*, the two hundredth *an' cc*, and so on. In other words, when a scribe with historical interests decided to extract the historical entries from an Easter Table, he regrettably omitted altogether the *anno domini* dates which must have stood at the left-hand column of the Table, and merely reckoned the years serially. So the first thing we have to do before we can extract any dated history from the annals is to calibrate them. Fortunately year 9 deals with an event which we can date because of its general Christian significance: 'Easter is changed on the Lord's Day by Pope Leo, bishop of Rome.' This is known to have happened in AD 455. If the ninth year is AD 455, the first year is AD 447. Whenever this calibration can be tested against dates known from other sources it appears to work within a year or two either way, which is the highest degree of chronological accuracy that may be expected in this period.

We have seen that the particular interests of the later entries of the annals suggest that they were compiled at St David's. But while this is true of the Great Cycle in its final form, it is very unlikely, if not indeed impossible, that the original Easter Table was computed as a Great Cycle at St David's in the fifth century. What is probable is that when a Great Cycle Table was put together at St David's – probably at the beginning of the ninth century – it was made retrospective, and both information about Easter, and also historical matter, were added from such obsolete tables as were available in the *scriptorium*. To judge from the specifically Venedotian bias of some of the seventh-century entries, one of those tables had been used in a *scriptorium* in Gwynedd. If we ask the date of compilation of the earliest of the tables which came to be incorporated in the Great Cycle, the answer is 455, simply because the change of Easter by Leo would have necessitated either the alteration of existing tables or the compilation of new ones. So though the final form of these annals was not attained until the late tenth century, the earliest material in them was almost certainly entered contemporaneously in the late fifth; and so century by century throughout the annals. They contain two crucial references to Arthur which will be discussed in detail in Chapter 3.

After the annals, the *British Historical Miscellany* continues with a series of Welsh genealogies (folios 193A–195A), which need not detain us here. At the end of these is a list of the sons of Cunedda, who had migrated from eastern Scotland to north Wales in the late fourth or fifth century. Their territory is defined as being from the river Dee to the river Teifi, and they are said to have held many regions in western Britain. The historical value of this passage is questionable, and some scholars have seen it as a piece of ancestor speculation – an attempt, for instance, to explain the regional name Ceredigion in terms of an ancestral hero Ceredig. However that may be, the passage is clearly included not because of its northern British interest, expressed in a reference to the homeland around Clackmannanshire, but because of its importance for Welsh history.

We have now reached the end of the material peculiar to the *British Historical Miscellany*, and what follows in Harley 3859 is common to most of the manuscripts of the *Historia Brittonum* – in other words, it belongs to that work. Section 66a (folios 195A–195B) has what purports

THREE KEY TEXTS | 41

to be a list of the twenty-eight cities of Britain. Some of these are in fact Roman forts and towns, but many of the places named cannot at present be identified, and the sound historical evidence of the list has still to be separated from the dross. Finally, in Sections 67 to 76 (folios 195B–198A), we come to the 'Marvels of Britain and Ireland'. These are overwhelmingly of a fabulous, non-factual nature. They include two Arthurian marvels: Carn Cabal above Builth Wells, where a stone bears the footprint of Arthur's hound; and the grave of Arthur's son Anir, which proves to be a different length each time it is measured. It is on the whole pointless to attempt rationalization of these marvels. For our purpose, the most important conclusion is that Arthur's name was being attached to fabulous tales at least as early as the ninth century, when the *Historia Brittonum* was composed.

What emerges from this discussion is that the *British Historical Miscellany*, manuscript Harley 3859, is a treasure chest of early British history. In itself it contains several caskets – a *History of the Britons* assigned to Nennius, a 'Northern British History', and a set of Easter Annals, to name only the principal ones. The caskets themselves enclose historical treasures, both British and English, of mixed interest. Some are authentic jewels of the fifth, sixth and seventh centuries. Others are no more than confections of later date. And even the authentic early jewels are now embedded in later settings, or are overlaid by spurious embellishments. The work of distinguishing earlier from later, genuine from bogus, is itself only in its early stages. Some of the criteria used in the process of analysis have been set out in this section. The items which appear to be early and genuine will be displayed in Chapter 3. It will be maintained that among the authentic jewels there are three to which the name of Arthur is attached.

The Anglo-Saxon Chronicle[7]

The primary importance of the *Anglo-Saxon Chronicle* for our purpose is that it narrates an account of the fifth and sixth centuries which is largely independent of our other sources. In particular, it gives what purports to be a circumstantial history, furnished with dates and battles, of the English settlement of Kent; a more sketchy report of the conquest of Sussex; and a very detailed history of the establishment and expansion of the dynasty of Wessex. If we could trust this record, it would give us an invaluable account of the English invasions and settlement. But before we establish its trustworthiness, we must attempt to analyse its sources.

The evidence of the manuscripts demonstrates that an original version of the *Chronicle* was compiled before 891, certainly in the reign of Alfred the Great, and possibly even at his instigation. This is a very long way from the period around 500 in which our interest is centred. But certain errors still detectable in the manuscript of 891 make it clear that this was at least two stages removed from an earlier compilation. It seems highly probable that, from the start of the mission of Birinus to Wessex in 634 and the baptism of the West Saxon king Cynegils in 635, the Easter Tables of the Dorchester-on-Thames *scriptorium* provided a framework for the setting down of contemporary annals. It is possible, but less certain, that around the middle of the seventh century a chronicler began to write a history of Wessex. For the period before the conversion he must have relied on oral traditions, which we must examine more fully in a moment.

Later, these primitive West Saxon annals were combined with other material to create the *Chronicle* itself. In so far as the other elements consist of a summary of universal history, or extracts from Bede's *Ecclesiastical History*, they do not interest us here. The important entries are those which are completely independent of the account which Bede based on Gildas. They include oral traditions collected from the other English kingdoms. This, then, is the basis for the *Chronicle* story of the English conquest of Kent, Sussex and Wessex.

One element in this oral tradition was doubtless poetry, including battle poems which recited the heroic deeds of the dynasties of Hengist of Kent, Ælle of Sussex and Cerdic of Wessex. This would have provided the later chroniclers with the names of both battles and warriors. In part, of course, we infer this poetic source – the 'ancient songs' of the ancestral Germans – from our general knowledge of Germanic society and Old English verse (above, pp. 13–16). But it has also been suggested that we have a specific pointer to a poetic source in the annal for 473: 'Hengist and Æsc fought against the Britons and captured countless spoils and the Britons fled from the English *as from fire*.' Here the italicized phrase certainly has a poetic ring.

If we accept that oral traditions preserved in Old English poetry provided information about the invasions and battles of the settlement period, we must now face the question of how these events were calibrated to a time-scale. The *Chronicle* as we know it follows the example of Bede and uses throughout an *anno domini* system of dating. How were these dates computed? In some cases, no doubt, annals were entered retrospectively in Easter Tables which stretched back before each individual English kingdom was converted. Much stress has been laid on the fact that, even before the conversion of Kent in 597, a significant proportion of the annals follow a four-year cycle. It has been suggested that this is because events were entered, long after they had actually occurred, in an Easter Table in which the leap years had been specially indicated. There are entries for the years 540, 544, 547, 552, 556, 560, 565, 568, but none for the intervening years. All of these, except for 547 and 565, are of course leap years, and it was certainly common practice to mark off the leap years in an Easter Table, so the hypothesis seems sensible. It immediately exposes the artificiality of much of the pre-Christian chronology of the *Chronicle*.

Of course, some control over dating in the period before contemporary Easter Annals began could have been provided by king lists and regnal years. We have seen how it might be possible to take a regnal list and work backwards from a king whose reign was fixed in *anno domini* terms because his accession was entered in a Dionysiac Table (above, pp. 19–20). But at the same time we saw the unreliability of calculations made in this way – and this was particularly evident in the case of the Wessex dynasty itself. In view of this, the statement that 'the assignment . . . of events prior to the adoption of Christianity . . . to particular years can have been little more than guesswork' seems moderate in the extreme.

It may be suggested, then, that the chronology of the *Anglo-Saxon Chronicle* for the period 449 to 550 or even later is artificial and untrustworthy. If we accept this criticism, then it disposes at once of one supposed historical problem – the difficulty of reconciling Gildas's forty-four years of peace after the battle of Badon (whenever that was fought) with the continuing battle entries of the *Chronicle*. The difficulty is not quite as stark as it is sometimes presented, because what Gildas actually says is that the siege of Mount Badon was *almost* the last, not actually the last, battle. But we would only be faced with a real problem here if the *Chronicle* dates for the late fifth and early sixth century had any claim to exactness.

One other major point of historical interpretation arises from the character of the sources behind these early entries in the *Anglo-Saxon Chronicle*. In the heroic – or barbaric – society of the Anglo-Saxons, warfare was a major theme of poetry. Among the early English, no less than among the early Welsh with their 'battle-listing' poems, battles and bloodshed were the chief subjects of *scop* and bard, reciting before their own chiefs in the feasting hall. It follows that any historical account which uses the poetry as a major source must inevitably concentrate on the same topics. This is why the few events that we hear about include:

457 Hengest and Æsc . . . slew four thousand men, and the Britons . . . fled in great terror . . .
465 Hengest and Æsc . . . slew twelve Welsh nobles . . .
491 Ælle and Cissa besieged Anderida and slew all the inhabitants . . .
508 Cerdic and Cynric slew a Welsh king called Natanleod and five thousand men with him . . .

and so on. This 'fire and slaughter' image of the English settlement probably reflects the character of Old English heroic poetry. It is not necessarily the whole image that we should see today; and it will be argued later that it is at the least a highly distorted one.

Three

The Arthurian Documents

Armed with an appreciation of the nature of the evidence and its limitations, and with a knowledge of the most relevant documents, we are now ready to attack the questions: was Arthur a historical person? when did he live? what did he do?[1]

The evidence of Easter Annals

Our starting point must be the Easter Annals in the *British Historical Miscellany*, because these, from their very nature, have the greatest likelihood of being contemporary with the events that they describe. On folios 190A and B of the manuscript Harley 3859 there are two Arthurian entries. The first is in year 72 of the cycle, which may be reckoned as AD 518. Expanding the contractions of the original Latin it reads:

> *Bellum badonis in quo arthur portavit crucem domini nostri jesu christi tribus diebus & tribus noctibus in humeros suos & brittones victores fuerunt.*

'Battle of Badon in which Arthur carried the cross of Our Lord Jesus Christ on his shoulders for three days and three nights and the Britons were victors.'

The second entry, coming at the end of folio 190A and running overleaf, is for year 93, AD 539, and it reads:

> *Gueith camlann in qua arthur & medraut corruerunt, et mortalitas in brittannia et in hibernia fuit.*

'The strife of Camlann in which Arthur and Modred perished. And there was plague in Britain and Ireland.'

In the past, scholars have tended to treat these British Easter Annals,

ti sunt: usq; ad decu & udenanu. anni
sunt sexaginta noue.

an   .iij. axe.   an
an   an   an
an   an   an
an   an   an
aii   an   an
an,   an   an, lxx.
an,   an   an
an   an   an Bellu badonis inq
an. Pasca co   an   arthur portauit cruce
mutatur. sup di. an   dni nri ihu xpi. trib,
em dnica cum an. xl.   dieb; & trib; noctib;
pupa leone epi an   in humeros suos &
rome.   an   briccones uictores fuer.
an. x. Brigita an   an,
sca nascitur.   an   an,
an   an   an,
aii   an   an
an Sci Patricii an   an Sci coluucille nasc.
ad dnm migra an   Quies sce brigide:
tue.   an. l.   an
an   an   an. lxxx.
an   an   an
aii   an   an
aii   an   an
an   an   an
an. axe.   an Epis ebur pau an,
aii   cit mixpo an an
an   no. cœl. etate an
an   sup.   an
an quies benigni an   an
epi   an   an. xc.
an   an. lx.   an,
an,   an,   an
aii   aii   an Gueith camlann inq
aii   an   arthur & medraut
.an   an   corruef: & mortalicas

3. The end of the computations and beginning of the Easter Annals in
Harley 3859, folio 190A. The annals are arranged in three parallel columns.
The Easter entry which serves to calibrate them is the first item in the left-
hand column. The Badon entry is at the head of the right-hand column, and
the start of the Camlann entry at its foot. By courtesy of the Trustees of the
British Museum.

4. Harley, 3859, folio 190B. The end of the Camlann entry is at the top left. The battle of Chester, *Gueith cair legion,* is at the fourth year of the right-hand column. By courtesy of the Trustees of the British Museum.

the so-called *Annales Cambriae*, as a whole; and because the last event recorded in them was the death of Rodri ap Hywel Dda in the late 950s, the Annals have been regarded as a compilation of the later tenth century. If we accept this view we are bound to think that they are so far removed from Arthur's day that they have very little value as evidence. Despite this, even the most cautious of scholars has been inclined to accept the reference to the deaths of Arthur and Modred at Camlann as authentic, whether or not the date is accurate. The principal reason for thinking that the Camlann entry refers to an authentic event, acted out by historical persons, is that all the other people – popes, saints, kings and princes – mentioned in the British Easter Annals are genuine, not mythical, fabulous or otherwise fictitious. Of course we cannot evade the possibility that Arthur and Modred are the only two fictitious characters among a hundred or more genuine ones; and some scholars would perhaps claim that simply because they are Arthur and Modred they must be fictitious. But this could scarcely be accepted as a balanced historical judgement.

Although cautious scholarship has been prepared to accept the whole of the Camlann entry on these grounds, no similar credence has been extended to the Badon entry. Of course the historicity of the British victory at Badon is undeniable because we have a near-contemporary account of it from Gildas. What is questioned, however, is whether Arthur's name can rightly be attached to the battle, especially when he is reputed to have carried the cross of Christ into battle – an unlikely, if not actually miraculous, feat. Accordingly, it has been thought that the reference to Arthur was interpolated, as a result of the development of legends about the fabulous Arthur, into a statement which originally said no more than 'Battle of Badon in which the Britons were victors'. At a later stage (p. 50 f.), we will examine these arguments about Badon in more detail.

Meanwhile, however, it may be suggested that the case outlined in the last two paragraphs shows a failure to understand the true character of the British Easter Annals. These were not a compilation put together between 955 and 960. It would be more reasonable to think in terms of a living organism adding a segment or growth-ring year by year, or at least annal by annal, until about 957, when the process of accretion happened to stop. The older growth-rings or annals are as old as themselves, not as young as the latest one. This is not to say that there was a single run of annals continuing throughout a Great Cycle from 447 to 980. We have already discussed this idea (above, pp. 39–40), and have seen that the Great Cycle had incorporated annals derived from short-term cycles which had been compiled at various earlier periods in different *scriptoria*.

We can say too that the fifth- and sixth-century items in the British Easter Annals could have been contemporary entries in an Easter Table. There can be no doubt that the British church was using such tables, and the annal for year 9, AD 455 is certainly a contemporary entry: 'Easter was changed by Pope Leo'. Moreover the *computi* which stand at the head of the British Easter Annals are concerned with events in the first half of the fifth century (below, p. 104), and would therefore be wholly appropriate to an Easter Table starting, as this claimed to do, in 447. These are pointers, then, to the authenticity of the early annals.

We know, furthermore, that the other persons mentioned in the first hundred years of the annals – Saints Patrick, Brigid and Columba, or King Maelgwn of Gwynedd – were genuine persons. Their deaths were probably entered contemporaneously in Easter Tables, their years of birth might well have been entered at the same time. This, of course, is not to say that we can calculate correct *anno domini* dates from the Annals, for we have already seen that chronological dislocations could have taken place when the Annals from one set of Tables were incorporated in a longer run of calculations (above, p. 18). Despite this chronological problem, no reasonable arguments can be advanced for regarding the British Easter Annals as anything other than a trustworthy historical document. This general judgement that the Annals are a reliable source should also authenticate Arthur, Modred and the battles of Badon and Camlann.

There is, however, an immediate objection to be recorded in the case of the Camlann entry, namely that, instead of using the Latin word *bellum* for the battle, it uses the Welsh word *gueith*. It would seem reasonable to expect a Latin-trained scribe, making a contemporary entry in an ecclesiastical document, to use the language of the church rather than the vernacular. The fact that he did not might hint that instead of being a contemporary entry, the information about Camlann was derived second-hand from a vernacular source, probably a Welsh poem, possibly an elegy on Arthur. In this case, it would be an interpolation in the Annals, which would certainly appear to weaken the claim advanced here that the Camlann entry is authentic because it was contemporary.

But the assumption of a poetic source is unnecessary. Camlann is far from being the only battle entered as *gueith* rather than *bellum*. The battle of Chester is *Gueith cair legion* while the battle in which Cadwallon of Gwynedd and Penda of Mercia slew Edwin of Northumbria is *gueith meicen*. There is no doubt that these battles actually occurred, and no reason to suppose that the annals which record them are anything other than a contemporary record of events. It is natural enough that a battle in which the Britons were one of the protagonists would be known to them by a British word – *gueith* or *cat*. It is also likely that for a scribe in a British monastery in the early sixth century, British rather than Latin would have been the natural language. The expression *gueith Camlann* does nothing, therefore, to weaken the authenticity of the entry.

We must now examine a far more serious attack on the Badon entry. We have seen that an attempt has been made to excise the whole reference to Arthur from this, and to reduce it to a bare record of a British victory. There appear to be three main lines of argument here. First, it is claimed that the battle of Badon was fought in southern England, whereas Arthur's activities, if they were historical at all, were wholly confined to northern Britain. The arguments for the 'northern Arthur' are complicated, and must be deferred until other evidence has been deployed (below, pp. 81–5). We shall then find that the hypothesis which restricts the field of activity of the historical Arthur to northern Britain cannot be supported by a reasoned appeal to the evidence.

Second, it is claimed that the Badon entry, as it stands, is out of character with the other early entries in the Annals, but, if it is shorn of the relative clause about Arthur and reduced to the stark form 'Battle of Badon, and the Britons were victors', it becomes stylistically compatible with the other early entries. It may be that there are stylistic nuances in these very terse entries which are discernible by a literary scholar but not by a historian-turned-archaeologist. It is admittedly true that the Badon entry is longer and more complicated than most of the early entries, but so too is the entry for 633, which reads:

Guidgar venit et non redit. Kalendis ianuariis gueith meicen et ibi interfectus est etguin cum duobus filiis suis. Cat guollaun autem victor fuit.

'Guidgar comes and does not return. On 1 January, the battle of Meicen, and there Edwin (king of Northumbria) was killed with his two sons. Cadwallon (king of Gwynedd) however was victorious.' While it is probable that the annalist has conflated two battles, no one doubts that there was a battle of Meicen, or that Edwin and his sons were killed in battle by Cadwallon. Yet stylistically this entry is as far removed from the normal run of annals like 'Ceretic died' (AD 619) or 'Eclipse of the sun' (AD 626), as the Badon entry itself.

The third argument is that the statement 'Arthur carried the cross of Our Lord Jesus Christ on his shoulders for three days and three nights' is self-evidently untrue because the act is physically impossible. The claim is made that we are dealing not with fact but with miracle and that the whole clause about Arthur is a piece of hagiography, an interpolation into the simple Badon entry at a time when fabulous tales were beginning to gather around Arthur's name. These arguments are, on the face of it, sound and sensible; but when analysed in detail, they collapse.

Firstly, a battle lasting three days and three nights is perhaps unlikely, but it is certainly not impossible, when we remember that the uninformative *bellum Badonis* of the annals was called 'the siege of Badon hill', *obsessio Badonici montis* in Gildas. We might imagine either the Britons or the English (and we cannot know which it was) occupying a prepared position on a hill-top, and resisting repeated attempts to dislodge them. The furthest that reasonable criticism can go is to suggest that 'three days and three nights' is a conventional, possibly poetic, turn of phrase for a long-fought battle.

Secondly, the statement that Arthur carried the cross of Christ on his shoulders can be explained in more than one way. We shall find this same idea of Arthur carrying a religious emblem 'on his shoulders' – *in humeros suos* – in another potentially early source, the battle-list in the *Historia Brittonum* (below, p. 71). In both cases it is possible that the explanation lies in confusion between two Welsh words, which led the scribes of the Easter Annals and the *Historia Brittonum* to mistranslate them into Latin. The Old Welsh word for 'shoulder' is *scuid* but there is a very similar Old Welsh word *scuit*, which means 'shield'. It is possible that the British report of Badon contained the statement that Arthur carried the cross of Christ on his shield – that is to say, an image of the cross, painted, engraved or riveted on his shield. But the scribe who entered the battle in an Easter Table misheard or misunderstood this as 'shoulder', not 'shield'. The error could equally well have occurred if the original contemporary Easter Table had an entry actually in Welsh, which had then been mistranslated when the annal had been incorporated in the Great Cycle Table in which we find it, or at some similar stage in the transmission. In other words, a consideration of normal methods of literary transmission makes it reasonable to remove the stigma of the miraculous from this entry.

An even more elementary possibility should also be considered. This assumes no translation from Old Welsh into Latin, and no errors in the process of transmission, but takes the statement at its face value, and then interprets it in contemporary terms. What Arthur is likely to have carried in battle is a relic of the supposed True Cross. The relic would have been quite small – a chip of wood, or even a strip of linen which had been in contact with the cross. It would have been readily portable, in an amulet hung round the neck or slung across the shoulder. This would be a perfectly natural interpretation of the terse phrase in the Annals. But whether we follow this explanation, or that given in the last paragraph, this at least is clear: behind the annal which we actually possess, there could lie a simple factual statement involving nothing of the physically impossible or the miraculous in Arthur's activities at Badon. It follows that it is unnecessary to see the reference to Arthur as a piece of hagiography which must therefore be an interpolation.

One final point remains. When other scholars impugn the integrity of a document actually before us, and claim that part of it is an interpolation and therefore untrustworthy, we are entitled to ask the circumstances and the motives of the interpolation. What has been suggested in the present case is that the reference to Arthur at Badon,

with its strong Christian element, was introduced some time between the
final entry in the Annals about 955 and the making of the copy which
we actually possess, about 1100–1125. Have we other evidence during
this period for the attribution of a specifically Christian role to Arthur?
The answer must be that we have not, and that this first appears in
Geoffrey of Monmouth's *History of The Kings of Britain*. Before that
work, the attitude of the British church, as it is reflected in Saints'
Lives, was openly hostile to Arthur. *The Life of Cadog*, written about
1090, portrays him as lustful and perverse, while the *Life of Padarn*, of
about 1120, shows him as an avaricious tyrant.[2] It is difficult to imagine
that any scribe brought up in this tradition would interpolate a reference
to Arthur as a Christian hero in an annal which recorded no more
than a British victory at Badon.

To sum up: no convincing case can be made for regarding the
reference to Arthur at Badon as an interpolation. We may reasonably
accept that the whole statement in the Annals is authentic and early,
as its occurrence in an Easter Annal would lead us to expect. We
might be encouraged in this view by the fact that Arthur is again
credited with the victory of Badon in another potentially early source,
the *Historia Brittonum* – unless, of course, we believe that the supposed
interpolation in the Annals took place under the influence of the *Historia*. Certainty is impossible here; but reason is in favour of the
integrity of the Annals.

We are left, however, with the problem of the dates for Camlann
and Badon which we may compute from the Annals. Calibrating on
the basis that year 9 is certainly AD 455 (above, p. 39), we arrive at
dates of 539 and 518 respectively for the two battles. We have no
independent control over the date of Camlann, but Gildas does appear
to provide a rough cross-check on the date of Badon. In an obscure and
possibly corrupt passage, he tells us that the year of Badon was also
the year of his own birth. The rest of his statement is interpreted by
some scholars to mean that he is writing in the forty-fourth year after
the battle. If we knew exactly when Gildas wrote the *De excidio* we
would be able to date Badon independently of the Annals.

But we have already seen (above, p. 23) that two views are possible
on the date of the *De excidio*. The customary one is that we must place
it before 549, because that was the year of Maelgwn of Gwynedd's

death according to the Annals, and Maelgwn was certainly alive when the *De excidio* was written. If we accept this, then we must also face the fact that the dates for Maelgwn's death and for Badon as given in the Annals are mutually irreconcilable. If the *De excidio* was written before 549 – say about 545 – and Badon was fought 43 years earlier still, then we are pushed to a date around 500 for the battle.

We have also seen, however, that the annal's date for Maelgwn's death is itself difficult to reconcile with the apparent evidence that Maelgwn was a contemporary of the poet Taliesin and of King Ida of Northumbria. Such equations could bring Maelgwn's death into the second half of the sixth century. It would then be possible to think that Badon was fought in 518, and that Gildas wrote in $518 + 43 = 561$. But before this hypothesis is pressed, some explanation must be proposed for the misdating of Maelgwn's death. It is admitted that chronological dislocations can occur when events are transferred from one Easter Table to another. This could apply, as we shall see, to the date for Badon; but in the case of Maelgwn other considerations are possible. The full entry in the Annals reads 'Great Plague, in which died Maelgwn king of Gwynedd'. We have seen reason to believe that the 'great plague' is correctly dated about 547–9. Welsh tradition certainly attributed Maelgwn's death to a 'Yellow Plague' in the form either of a yellow beast or a column of vapour. But of course the plague of the late 540s was not the only one in the sixth century. We should recall here that the year of Camlann was also distinguished by 'Plague in Britain and Ireland'. It is possible, to say no more, that a scribe finding an entry for 549 which said merely 'Great Plague', and knowing that Maelgwn died of plague, but not knowing when, added to the original annal 'in which Maelgwn died'.

That such confusions could easily arise among early chroniclers and in early historical sources can be demonstrated by the case of one of Maelgwn's successors, Cadwaladr. The annal for AD 684 reads: 'There was a great plague in Britain in which Cadwaladr, son of Cadwallon, died.' The 'Northern British History' also tells of Cadwaladr's death by plague (*British Historical Miscellany*, folio 189A). It adds that the plague occurred during the reign of Oswy of Northumbria, whose death is given in the Welsh Annals at AD 671. Calculations based on regnal lists confirm this date for Oswy's death. From Bede's *Ecclesias-*

tical History it seems that, within the period of Oswy's reign, the most noteworthy plague occurred in AD 664, and some historians have therefore attributed Cadwaladr's death to that year rather than to the 684 of the Annals. Since the latter date is probably derived from a contemporary entry in an Easter Table, it has great weight, but no complete certainty is possible. The most we can conclude is that a known plague of 664 and an otherwise unrecorded plague of 684 have become confused, and we can no longer be sure which one killed Cadwaladr.

Similar confusion may have led to the misdating of Maelgwn's death in the Annals, but again we cannot be sure. Our only certainty is this: unless we interpret Gildas's forty-fourth year in another sense alto-gether – as Bede in fact did – then the dates given by the Welsh Annals for the battle of Badon and the death of Maelgwn are irreconcilable. This, of course, is no reason for doubting the historicity of either event. But it may encourage us to make another attempt to manipulate the available evidence. It is not impossible that in the process of copying from one Easter Table to another the dates of both Badon and Camlann have suffered a twenty-eight-year dislocation. If this were so, then they should correctly be AD 490 and 511 respectively. Adding 43 to 490 we would arrive at 533 for the writing of the *De excidio*, which is itself a perfectly acceptable date. Moreover, a consideration of the events leading up to Badon (below, p. 111) will suggest that 490 is a more probable date than 518 for the battle. This would put Arthur's principal military activity in the decade either side of AD 500.

The evidence of the Historia Brittonum

We have already seen that the *Historia Brittonum* contains an account of Arthur fighting twelve battles. It is now time to study this account in detail. The version in the *British Historical Miscellany* (folio 187A) was intended to begin with a red initial:

> [T] *unc arthur pugnabat contra illos in illis diebus cum regibus brittonum sed ipse dux erat bellorum. Primum bellum fuit in ostium fluminis quod dicitur glein . . .*

'Then Arthur fought against them in those days with the kings of the Britons but he himself was leader (Duke) of Battles. The first battle

n illo tempore saxones inualescebant in
multitudine & crescebant inbrittannia·
Morcuo aut hengisto octha fili' ei' transi
uit de sinistrali parte brittannie ad reg
nu cantoru· & de ipso orti s reges cantor·
  unc arthur pugnabat contra illos·
millis dieb; cu regib; brittonu· s; ipse dux erat
bellorum· Primu bellu fuit in osti fluminis
nis quod dicit glein· secdm & terciu & quar
tu & quintu· sup aliud flumen· quod
dicit dubglas·÷· in regione linnuis·
Sextu bellum sup flumen· quod uocat
e bassas· Septimu   fuit bellu
in silua celidonis· id÷ cat coit celidon·
Octauum fuit bellu in castello guinni
on· Inquo arthur portauit imagine
sce marie ppetue uirginis sup humeros suos·
ros suos· & pagani uersi s in fuga in
illo die· & cedes magna fuit sup illos·
p uirtutem dni nri ihu xpi & p uirtute
sce marie uirginis genitricis ei· Nonu
bellu gestu÷ in urbe legionis· Decimu
gesic bellu in litore   fluminis· quod
uocat tribruit· Undecimu factu
bellu in monte qui dicit agned· Duo
decimu fuit bellu in monte badonis
inquo corruer in uno die n genti sexa
ginta uiri de uno impetu arthur·

5. The Arthurian section of Harley 3859, folio 187A. The part illustrated
begins with the activities of the Saxons; the opening lines are translated on
p. 35. A red capital I is missing from the beginning of line 1, and a red
capital T from the beginning of line 6. By courtesy of the Trustees of the
British Museum.

was at the mouth of the river which is called *Glein*. The second and third and fourth and fifth upon another river which is called *Dubglas* and is in the district *Linnuis*. The sixth battle upon the river which is called *Bassas*. The seventh battle was in the Caledonian wood, that is, *Cat Coit Celidon*. The eighth battle was in Fort *Guinnion* in which Arthur carried the image of St Mary, ever virgin, on his shoulders and the pagans were turned to flight on that day and a great slaughter was upon them through the virtue of our Lord Jesus Christ and through the virtue of St Mary the Virgin, his mother. The ninth battle was waged in the City of the Legion. The tenth battle he waged on the shore of the river which is called *Tribruit*. The eleventh battle took place on the mountain which is called *Agned*. The twelfth battle was on mount Badon, in which nine hundred and sixty men fell in one day from one charge by Arthur, and no one overthrew them except himself alone. And in all the battles he stood forth as victor.'

This seems at first sight a very circumstantial account of Arthur's military activities; but before we take it at its face value we must first ask what its source might be. We have already seen that the nucleus of this section of the *Historia Brittonum* is a Latin summary of a Welsh battle-listing poem about Arthur (above, p. 38). Its general form would be enough to tell us this in the first place, but there are further clues as well. The fact that the location of the seventh battle is given both in Latin – *in silva celidonis* – and in Welsh – *cat coit celidon* – is itself a very strong indication of a Welsh source. Again, the arguments rehearsed above about the mistaking of *scuit*, 'shield', for *scuid*, 'shoulder', apply here in the case of the eighth battle, where Arthur is said to have carried the image of Mary on his shoulders – *super humeros suos*. (In passing, we may notice that Geoffrey of Monmouth has the best of both worlds: Arthur placed 'across his shoulders a shield ... on which was painted a likeness of the Blessed Mary'.) Yet further details may be cited in this way, and there is consequently a wide measure of agreement that a Primitive or Old Welsh poem forms the main source for the Latin list of Arthur's battles.

There is less agreement, however, on the date of such a poem. We have to remember here that the Arthurian period was one of linguistic change.[3] During the fifth and sixth centuries the British language was changing into Primitive Welsh and other Celtic languages. British, like

Latin, had been an inflected language, in which the grammatical case of a noun was indicated by changes in the final syllable, but in Welsh these case-endings were omitted. It is argued that in Arthur's day the language was still British, so a contemporary poem would have been full of words with case-endings. Two generations later, it is suggested, the language would be Primitive Welsh, with one of two results: either the poem would retain its case-endings, and not be understood; or it would have lost its case-endings and therefore, as final syllables were dropped from words, the original metre and scansion would disintegrate. As a result it could no longer be recited and remembered as a poem.

Such arguments overlook our common experience that archaic diction and grammatical forms can persist in poetry without hindering our understanding. Picking at random a poem by John Donne, I find:

> Thou hast, and shalt see dead, before thou dyest.*

No one could claim that this is now incomprehensible because modern English has lost 'thou', 'hast', 'shalt', and 'dyest'. In any case the loss of case-endings cannot, in the nature of the evidence, be dated with the precision that is sometimes claimed. The only strictly contemporary texts that we possess are the inscribed stones, which cannot be closely dated (below, pp. 73 ff.). The British-Welsh personal names on the stones do retain case-endings, but this is because they are given in a Latinized form, to conform with the Latin of the inscription as a whole. This means that the date at which the final syllables were actually in process of disappearing is wholly concealed from us.

The process can be thought of most vividly in personal terms. If Arthur fought at Badon, then he was an older contemporary of Gildas. Gildas likewise was an older contemporary of Taliesin. It seems therefore a little forced to claim that Taliesin could not have understood a poem which had been recited at Arthur's court.

If, despite this, we accept the argument based on linguistic processes, we would have to believe that the poem listing Arthur's battles was an elegy on a dead hero, written some time between the late sixth century when the Welsh language had developed, and the early ninth when

---

* *Elegie on Mris. Boulstred,* line 23.

the elegy was summarized in *Historia Brittonum*. It might be added that distortions in the place-names would suggest that its composition was considerably before the ninth century, because some of the names were evidently unfamiliar to the writer who summarized the poem in Latin. But even if we might think that the poem was composed as early as the seventh century it would still be too far removed from Arthur's own day to constitute a sound historical source.

If, on the other hand, we find the linguistic arguments unconvincing, then we may ask whether there is anything positive pointing to an Arthurian date for the original battle-poem. Here the absence of any reference to Arthur's final fatal battle of Camlann may be significant. Given the general melancholy tone of early Welsh poetry, and its emphasis on the death of heroes, it is almost unthinkable that Camlann should not be mentioned, if it had already been fought at the time when the poem was composed. If this argument is sound, there is a possibility that the poem was a panegyric sung to Arthur's face, rather than an elegy over his long-dead body. In brief, it is worth considering that our Latin list of battles is based on an authentic Welsh source of Arthur's own day; and it is from this point of view that we may now consider in detail what historical information it has to give us.

It opens with one of the infuriatingly cryptic statements which are all too common in our sources: 'Then Arthur fought against them in those days.' We ask 'against whom?' and 'in what days?' One might imagine that this refers to whatever immediately precedes the Arthurian section in the *Historia Brittonum*. We have seen (above, p. 35) that the paragraph before had been a brief note about the Saxons increasing in strength, about the death of Hengist, and about the founding of the dynasty of Kent by Hengist's son Octha. It is natural to believe therefore that the people whom Arthur fought against were either the Saxons in general, or specifically the kings of Kent. In fact there are no other grounds for accepting the second suggestion, and indeed it would be difficult to reconcile warfare in south-eastern England with such information as we have about Arthur.

It might even be argued that there is no definite reference to the Saxons in general. We have seen that the phrase '*Tunc Arthur pugnabat*' begins a new section of the *British Historical Miscellany* with its own coloured initial. The implication is that the information about Arthur is separate from that relating to Hengist and the Kentish kings. A separate source is inevitably implied if the list of Arthur's battles is based on a Welsh poem, for it is inconceivable that it would have contained information about Kent. It is not altogether impossible that the poem was quite vague about Arthur's enemies, and that the phrase '*contra illos*', 'against them', had no specific reference at all. Certainly no chronological precision is intended by the phrases '*tunc*', 'then', and '*in illis diebus*', 'in those days'.

We are next told that Arthur was fighting '*cum regibus Brittonum sed ipse dux erat bellorum*', 'along with the kings of the Britons, but he himself was Duke [or 'leader'] of battles'. These phrases have been much discussed, because they provide our most important clue to the actual status of the man whom later ages saw as a king or even emperor. Taken as a whole they are usually read as implying that Arthur was not himself a king, but rather a soldier acting on behalf of a number of British kings. But this is not actually said, and in the nature of the evidence we cannot know whether Arthur was a king or not.

Meanwhile, we must look closely at the words '*dux bellorum*', for which two alternative translations have been put forward: 'Duke', a specific rank or title, or 'leader'. The late Roman military system had two titles for high-ranking officers, *Dux* and *Comes*, which we may translate as 'Duke' and 'Count'. In Britain, for instance, in the fourth century, there was a *Dux Britanniarum* who commanded the garrison forces of Hadrian's Wall and its supporting forts, and a *Comes Britanniarum* who commanded a mobile field army. Some scholars consider that when Arthur is called *Dux* it is this Roman military title that is in mind. This might suggest that he was in charge of frontier troops and garrisoned forts, defending the several British kingdoms against the English invaders. But this is the least likely of all the various hypotheses which we might formulate about Arthur's historical role, for it is based on an unduly restricted interpretation of the term *dux*. Even in the late Roman empire, a *dux* might command field units as well as garrison troops, and might have administrative duties of a civilian nature as well. In sixth-century Gaul, a *dux* was appointed by the king to administer a tribe or region, especially in an area of military importance, and he also undertook military duties in the field. If *dux bellorum* really was a Roman-style or Roman-derived title, it could well have implications on these lines.

But when we recall that our ultimate source is not a Latin document in which *dux* might have retained some precise meaning, but a Welsh poem, it becomes doubtful whether this interpretation is valid at all. Our doubts on this point are reinforced when we look at other Welsh evidence. In the elegy on Gereint of Devon, Arthur is called '*ameraudur llywiaudir llawur*', 'emperor, battle-ruler'. And in the Llywarch Hen poems, we have '*tywyssawc llu*' and '*tywyssawc cat*', 'leader of the host or army' or, in the second case, since *cat* may mean either 'army' or 'battle', 'leader of battle'. There is a strong possibility, then, that *dux bellorum* translates such a Welsh expression; with the further possibility that since this is a poetic expression rather than a formal rank or title, all we are being told is that Arthur fought in the company of the British kings, but he was pre-eminent in battle.

We come now to the battles themselves, and to the prime question of where they took place. It is clear that if we can locate them and if there is a sound historical tradition or source underlying the account in *Historia Brittonum*, then we have some basis for writing the politico-military history of the Arthurian period. At the same time, what we learn about the battles may affect our estimate of the soundness of the evidence, for if we find something intrinsically improbable in them, we are bound to suspect the evidence itself.

Unfortunately the location of the battle-sites is far from easy.[4] Even with all the assistance of modern place-name and language studies, a majority of the sites remain unidentifiable, while all but one could be set in two or even more places. The battle about which we can have most confidence is the seventh: '*in silva Celidonis, id est Cat Coit Celidon*', 'the battle of the Wood of Celidon', or of the 'Caledonian forest'. There is full agreement that this was in Scotland, but if we attempt greater precision, dispute begins. So far as classical historians and geographers like Tacitus and Ptolemy were concerned, Caledonia or the tribe of the Caledonii lay north of the Forth-Clyde line, in the Highlands. But in Welsh tradition Coit Celidon (in modern Welsh, Coed Celyddon) lay not far north of Carlisle, most probably in the Southern Uplands. This is therefore by a narrow margin the more likely location for Arthur's battle. But it is evidently a very vague

Map 2. Possible locations for Arthur's battles.

location, and from the point of view of the historical significance of the battle the vagueness is compounded because in this area Arthur might have clashed with an army of Britons from Strathclyde, of Picts from the Highlands, of Scots from north of the Clyde, or just possibly a far-flung spearhead of Angles from Northumbria.

We come now to the relatively simple alternatives. The first battle was fought at the estuary, mouth or confluence – all three are possible interpretations – of the river 'quod dicitur Glein'. On philological grounds this cannot be identified with river- or place-names containing the element 'glen' meaning a valley. But on the same grounds, there can be no objection to the rivers known as Glen in Northumberland and in Lincolnshire, for these derive, as does the Glein of our text, from a British word meaning 'pure' or 'clear'. But this seems a fairly obvious epithet to use of a river. We are bound to wonder how many rivers 'called Glein' there might have been in the sixth century AD, of which all except two subsequently changed names under the impact of English speech.

The ninth battle was 'in urbe Legionis', literally translatable as 'in the city of the legions'. One family of manuscripts adds 'which in the British tongue is called Cair Lion', and this might dispose us at once to place the battle at Caerleon, the Roman legionary fortress on the river Usk in Monmouthshire. But in early Welsh historical writings this name is used of Chester-upon-Dee as well as of Caerleon-on-Usk. In the Welsh Annals, for instance, the battle of Chester in 616 appears as 'Gueith cair legion'. There is no convincing basis, in the evidence before us, for deciding between Chester and Caerleon. None the less, one of the standard ploys of Arthurian polemics is to say that the reference here must be to Chester; that Arthur cannot have fought at Chester; therefore what has happened is that because of its fame, the Chester battle of 616 has become attached to Arthur's name; therefore the battle-list itself is discredited as a historical source. We shall see later, however (below, p. 86) that even if the ninth battle was fought at Chester this is no reason for denying it to Arthur.

The eleventh battle was fought on a hill or mountain which some manuscripts call Agned; others Breguoin (or variants of this, suggesting that all this group of manuscripts may be corrupt); and yet others give both names. Agned, identified by Geoffrey of Monmouth with

Edinburgh, cannot in fact be located. Nor is it easy to locate Breguoin, Bregomion or the rest. Certain philological assumptions which cannot be fully tested have led to the suggestion that Breguoin is the same place as that mentioned in a poem about the battles of Urien Rheged: '*kat gellawr Brewyn*', 'the battle of the cells of Brewyn'. Brewyn or Breguoin may then be derived from British-Latin *Bremenium*, the Roman fort of High Rochester below Cheviot, and the 'cells of Brewyn' might be understood as the ruined walling of that fort. This would certainly be an appropriate place for Urien Rheged to have fought a battle, and it is not impossible that Arthur also fought here against a northward-probing army from Bernicia, or against the Britons of Strathclyde. It is also possible that in the poetry a traditional battle was attributed now to one hero, now to another.

An alternative suggestion has been to emend Breguoin to read Breguein. This assumes a fairly simple error by a scribe – writing *o* for *e* – and the emendation is acceptable to cautious philologists. If it is allowed, then Breguein can be derived by regular linguistic processes from the British-Latin place-name *Bravonium*. This place occurs in the Roman roadbook known as the Antonine Itinerary, and it can be identified confidently with Leintwardine in Herefordshire. An Arthurian battle thereabouts seems no more unlikely than one *in urbe legionis*, whether Caerleon or Chester. But it will be clear that we cannot be entirely confident about either the Leintwardine or the High Rochester identification for Arthur's eleventh battle.

This attempt to locate the eleventh battle forms a suitable introduction to a discussion of the second, third, fourth and fifth battles, which occurred 'on a river which is called Dubglas and is in the Linnuis district': '*super flumen quod dicitur dubglas et est in regione linnuis*'. For a start, we should notice that two possible explanations have been proposed as to why no less than four battles are attributed to a single river. The first is that our source – whether Nennius or the supposed Welsh poet – knew that Arthur fought twelve battles, or considered that twelve was an appropriate, artistically correct number of battles, but unfortunately knew the names of only nine of them. So to make up the poetic number he multiplied one battle four times. This may seem a rather curious procedure. We know that the development of Arthurian romance came about in part by the attraction of other men's deeds to the heroic name of Arthur – this is presumably how Arthur came to have a place in the poem already quoted about the death-battle of Geraint of Devon (above, p. 14). And we know that fabulous tales were already being told about Arthur by the time that Nennius compiled his *Historia Brittonum* – witness the place of Arthur in the 'Marvels of Britain' (above, p. 41). If twelve battles were poetically appropriate, and only nine names were known, it would not have been difficult to borrow another three from other warrior-heroes such as Urien of Rheged.

The alternative explanation takes the document at its face value, and accepts that four battles were actually fought, not necessarily at the same spot, but at least along the same river-line. This would then appear to have been a line of some strategic importance – though not necessarily as a frontier (below, p. 340). If, then, we could determine where this line was, we would gain a valuable insight into the strategy of the late fifth and early sixth centuries.

Regrettably, there are alternatives: two probable, and one tentatively possible. Indeed, for the river-name itself the possibilities are legion, for *dubglas* means simply 'blue-black', a word as generally applicable to rivers as *glein*, 'pure', or 'clear'. Moreover, by a very slight verbal change, the British word 'blue-black' came to be confused with another possible river-name meaning 'black stream'. From these we get little-changed forms like Douglas, Dulais; more changed ones like Dawlish, Divelish, Devil's Brook; and even, perhaps, plain translations into English such as Blackwater. Our source may well have been aware of the proliferation of rivers called *dubglas*, and therefore added the qualifying term *in regione linnuis*. To this, then, we turn for help.

The best philological opinion is that *Linnuis* should derive from a British-Latin word like *Lindenses*, 'the people of *Lindum*' or *Lindensia*, 'land of *Lindum*'. Neither of these British-Latin words is in fact recorded, but there seems to be no doubt that such words must have existed as derivatives of the known word *Lindum*; and, furthermore, no doubt that either of them would by the ninth century become *Linnuis* by regular processes of philological development. Where, then, was *Lindum*?

The most obvious candidate is the Roman town of *Lindum*, Lincoln, with the surrounding district still known as Lindsey, from the old

English *Lindisse*, itself derived from *Lindensia*. The only snag is that no Douglas, Divelish or Blackwater river appears to be known in Lindsey. But the second century geographer Ptolemy also records another *Lindum*, a little to the north of the Clyde estuary. If this was in the area of Loch Lomond, then we have glen Douglas which runs down to that loch. This could conceivably have been the scene of an Arthurian battle against the young Scottish kingdom of Dalriada, but it seems an unlikely place for four battles. If, on the other hand, Lindsey is the correct region, then we would have to picture Arthur fighting the Anglo-Saxons in an area where they had long been established and where their strength was greatest. A chance phrase of Gildas suggests that this may be less unlikely than would at first appear.

We come now to the third possibility, which involves a minor emendation of our text. That some emendation might be justified is suggested by the fact that all the main groups of manuscripts have different readings at this point. Harley 3859 reads *linnuis*, but other manuscripts, not appreciably later in date, read *linuis* or *inniis*. Now it is notorious that in words consisting largely of *i*s, *n*s and *u*s – that is, of simple ascending and descending strokes – *n* may easily be written for *u* or vice versa; or either of them may be converted to *i*; or an *i* may be lost. The proposed emendation involves the suggestion that this is what has happened, and that the source which lies behind the manuscripts we possess actually read *lininuis*. Now just as *linnuis* derives regularly from (the unknown word) *Lindenses*, 'the inhabitants of Lindum', so *lininuis* would derive regularly from the word *Lindinienses*. These people we do know, from inscriptions, as one section of the great tribe of the *Durotriges*, who in the first to fourth centuries inhabited Dorset and much of Somerset, Wiltshire and Hampshire. The *Lindinienses* themselves were the people around *Lindinis*, usually identified with Ilchester. Some twenty miles south-west of Ilchester two Dubglas rivers form a north-south line across the North Dorset Downs. To the north the Divelish flows to the Stour, and to the south the Devil's Brook runs down to the Piddle or Trent. This is not an impossible line for a series of engagements against Saxon spearheads thrusting west. Its acceptance turns on the emendation of the text at a point where a majority of the manuscripts diverge, and where there is no evidence on which to declare that the reading *linnuis* is certainly correct.

Three other battles we can dismiss as impossible to locate in the sense that their names cannot be identified with those of any places known today. These are the sixth battle on the river Bassas, the eighth in castle Guinnion and the tenth on the shore or strand of the river called Tribruit.

There remains the twelfth battle, that of Badon; but before we examine its location it would be useful to discuss the battle which the *Historia Brittonum* omits, but which we find in the Welsh Annals, that of Camlann. There is no basis for locating this at Slaughterbridge, on the Cornish river Camel. It has been suggested that the name might derive from the British *Camboglanna*, which would give Camlann in Middle Welsh. In Early Welsh, however, the form should have been *Camglann*, and therefore if the battle had been entered contemporaneously in an Easter Table we would expect *gueith Camglann*. The fact that we have *gueith camlann* may mean either that there never was a contemporary entry in Primitive Welsh – and so the credibility of the Arthurian entries in the Welsh Easter Annals would be destroyed – or that, in the process of copying and recopying, some scribe had modernized the spelling. There is no basis, in the evidence before us, for deciding between these alternatives. There is even a third possibility, that the original form was not *Camboglanna* but *Cambolanda*. The main reason for favouring *Camboglanna* is that we do know a place of this name, the Roman fort of Birdoswald which stands above the Irthing valley towards the western end of Hadrian's Wall. The traditions which grew up around Camlann mark it out as a battle not against invading pagan Saxons, but as an internecine strife of Briton against Briton, and the terse entry of the Annals (above, p. 45), would not contradict this. *Camboglanna*, which presumably was in the kingdom of Rheged, would certainly be a suitable site for such a battle. But the identification is not unambiguous. *Camboglanna* means 'crooked bank', *Cambolanda* is 'crooked enclosure', and both place-names may once have been as common as the 'pure' (*glein*) and 'blue-black' (*dubglas*) rivers which we have noticed already.

With the battle of Mount Badon we come to quite a different category of historical evidence. Though such a view is implicitly rejected here it could be argued that all the battles which we have discussed so far, even including Camlann, are not supported by any early or trust-worthy evidence; they all represent Arthurian romance and fable rather than Arthurian history. But to reject the battle of Badon in the same way is to exhibit prejudice, not scholarship. Our witness for the historicity of Badon is of course Gildas. However much we may reject the earlier sections of the *De excidio* as a worthless muddle, we cannot similarly reject Badon, which must have been within the memory of all the senior element in Gildas's audience. Had it not been a his-torical fact, Gildas would surely have destroyed much of his position as a preacher by mentioning it. But Arthur's connection with Badon is quite another matter. This does not come from Gildas, who is silent about the British commander at the battle (above, p. 28). But if we accept the integrity of the Badon entry in the Easter Annals (above, pp. 50 f.), we have a contemporary witness that Arthur was the victor at Badon. The *Historia Brittonum* seems to provide an independent wit-ness to the same fact: independent because it omits details which the Annals contain – the carrying of the cross – and equally it provides details which the Annals lack, especially the number of the enemy slain in one of Arthur's charges.

Here a sceptic would make the point that it is physically impossible for one man single-handed to slay 960 of the enemy in a single charge; therefore this account of the battle is palpably false, and the battle-list in *Historia Brittonum* is thereby discredited. This, however, is to mistake the nature of our account. This is not an official communiqué issued at the end of a battle (even they may exaggerate enemy casual-ties, in good faith); it is from a heroic poem in praise of Arthur's prowess in battle. It belongs to the same genre as the sources from which the *Anglo-Saxon Chronicle* culled the information: 'Cerdic and Cynric slew a Welsh king and five thousand men with him.' In short, we are dealing with poetic exaggeration, and behind the sober-seeming Latin there may be a Welsh poetic phrase 'three three-hundreds and three twenties'.

If we accept that the battle of Mount Badon was certainly a historical event and that Arthur's connection with it is also probably authentic, where did it take place? It is generally agreed that Gildas saw it as a battle between Britons and Anglo-Saxons, rather than between Britons and Picts or a combination of Picts and Saxons. Whether we date it to the end of the fifth or the early sixth century, a battle between Britons and Anglo-Saxons is likely to have been fought at that period in southern England.

As it happens, the Welsh Annals refer to a second battle of Badon, fought about a century and a half after the first, in a year which may be calculated as AD 667. But the relevant part of the annal is cryptic and unhelpful in the extreme – merely saying '*Bellum badonis secundo*', 'the second battle of Badon'. It has rightly been observed that this must contain an allusion to the first battle of Badon, and it implies that the earlier battle was still remembered. It might also imply that the second Badon was fought not merely in the same place but between the same combatants as the first. We might in this case hope to find a reference to the conflict in English sources, especially because by this date the *Anglo-Saxon Chronicle* is becoming fairly detailed in matters of politico-military history. But both the *Chronicle* and Bede are silent here, and it seems that from the English point of view the second Badon was not an important battle. It is equally clear that between the brevity of the British account and the silence of the Anglo-Saxons we have no real hope of using the second Badon to help us to locate the first battle. In view of the very fluid nature of warfare in the period (below, pp. 338 f.) it would even be rash to use the recorded expansion of Wessex as a strategic guideline to help us delimit the probable area in which the second Badon was fought.

We are forced back then on place-name studies. One proposal which has won much support starts from the suggestion that the names which we have in our Latin texts – Gildas and the Annals – are represented in English by one of various Badburys. This is not a very helpful clue, because there are not less than five possible Badburys, in an arc from Dorset to Lincolnshire, and the selection of one or other of them is likely to turn on unprovable hypotheses about British and Saxon strategy. No matter; if these are genuine alternatives we must be prepared to accept the confusion which results. But first we must understand the case for the identification. The Old English form of Badbury is *Baddanbyrig* or *Baddanburg*, 'the fort of Badda'. Because there are several 'Badda's forts' it is suggested that there was a legendary Saxon hero or demi-god who had come to be associated with the hill-forts which had been built up to a thousand years earlier.

It is not thought likely that an Anglo-Saxon army, besieged in an ancient hill-fort by counter-attacking Britons (or, alternatively, besieging the British defenders), named the place 'Badda's fort'; and that this name then reached the ears of the victorious Britons and became Latinized as *Badonis*, *Mons Badonis*, or *Mons Badonicus*. Instead it is considered that the hill-fort was already known by the British name 'Din Badon', and that the Anglo-Saxons, only partly hearing this name, assimilated the Badon element to the genitive case of their own hill-fort hero – that is *Baddan* ('of Badda'), and so came to give the name *Baddanbyrig*. This explanation is only possible, of course, for the particular 'Badda's fort' which already bore the British name Din Badon.

There are two difficulties about accepting this explanation unreservedly. It is true, of course, that the names of heroes, demi-gods and demons become attached to fortifications and other monuments when their true significance has long been forgotten: various Arthur's Stones, Grim's Ditches and Devil's Dykes prove this. But the supposed hill-fort-building hero is known only from the *Baddanbyrig* place-names, and not from any independent source. Second, in the British place-name which Latin writers spelt *Badonis* the *d* was not pronounced as in 'bad' but was actually a 'th' sound as in '*th*at'. In Old English this sound has its own letter – ð. A literate English warrior would have written the name of the battle as *Baðon* rather than *Baddan*.

This suggests an alternative identification for Badon. Later Welsh tradition identified the Badon of the battles with Caer Vadon, or Bath. It is generally considered that the English gave the name Bath to a decayed Roman spa-town because traces of the Roman hot baths were still visible when the Wessex dynasty captured the area in AD 577 (below, p. 118). Certainly the English name owed nothing to a Roman predecessor, for the Romans knew the spa as *Aquae Sulis*, 'Waters of Sul'. But we do not know what the native British name for the locality was. If it had been *Baðon* it is possible that the Anglo-Saxons, after they had captured it, assimilated its British name to their own word for 'baths' because of the remains of the hot baths. Hence the *Anglo-Saxon Chronicle* tells us of the capture of *Baðanceaster* in 577, while a charter of AD 796 mentions *aet Baðum*, 'at Bath'. This suggestion seems as likely as the hypothesis that they assimilated *Baðon* with *Baddan*, 'of Badda'.

This is not to suggest, however, that the battle, or siege, of Badon may have occurred among the ruins of the Roman spa, in its swampy valley bottom. Gildas and the *Historia Brittonum*, with their expressions 'the siege of mount Badonicus' and the battle 'on mount Badon', seem to represent two independent traditions that the action took place on a hilltop. We might think, therefore, of one of the hills overlooking Bath. But we should not go so far as to identify the site with the hill-fort on Bathampton Down. There is in fact nothing in our earliest sources to suggest that the battle was fought at a hill-fort rather than on an open hilltop – the idea of a fort is a spurious element introduced into the discussion to strengthen the identification with *Baddanbyrig*, where the fort element is certain. In strategic terms, given the mobility of warfare at the time, there is nothing to exclude Bath as the site of either the first or second Badon.

Only one other feature of the account of Arthur's twelve battles needs discussion at the moment, namely, the carrying of the image of the Virgin Mary on Arthur's shoulders in his eighth battle 'and the pagans were put to flight that day, and great slaughter was wrought upon them by virtue of our Lord Jesus Christ and St Mary'. Those scholars who interpret the statement of the Easter Annals that Arthur carried the cross of Christ on his shoulders as a religious myth will take the carrying of the image of Mary in the same way. They will see it as casting grave doubt on the historicity of the eighth battle. From this position, of course, we may be rescued by the suggestion that the scribe who wrote '*super humeros suos*', 'on his shoulders', was in fact mistranslating Welsh *scuit* 'shield', as *scuid* 'shoulder'. He should have written *super scutum suum*, 'on his shield'. There is certainly nothing unlikely about Arthur's shield being ornamented in this way. We should notice furthermore that we seem to be dealing with two independent traditions that Arthur displayed Christian symbols on his shield: in the Welsh Annals it is the cross at Badon; in the *Historia Brittonum* the image of Mary at Castell Guinnion. The discrepant details suggest that we are not dealing merely with two versions of a single source, and serve therefore to buttress the central fact that Arthur was an overtly Christian ruler.

Some other potentially early evidence

There is some rather shadowy evidence that during the sixth century Arthur came to be regarded as a model of martial valour, a person to be emulated; and this may help to strengthen our belief that he had been an authentic historical person. On the other hand it may leave us thinking that someone who became an idealized figure within half a century of his death had probably never existed at all.

The key reference here is in *Y Gododdin*, in a stanza celebrating the prowess of the warrior Gwawrddur:

> *gochone brein du ar uur*
> *caer ceni bei ef Arthur*

'He glutted black ravens on the wall of the fort, though he was not Arthur.' Presumably Arthur is introduced in this particular stanza because of the rhyme-scheme. The couplet itself is a poetic way of saying that Gwawrddur was as skilled at slaying his enemies as Arthur had been – the raven being the symbol of death, especially on the battlefield, and 'feeding the ravens' being a common image for battle-slaughter. The effectiveness of the comparison depends, of course, on Arthur being a recognized symbol of martial valour at the time the couplet was written. As we have seen, *Y Gododdin* was probably composed in the late sixth century, but our actual manuscript is of the mid-thirteenth century and contains stanzas which on linguistic grounds cannot be as early as the sixth century. Some of these were probably interpolated during the long process of transmission. The best we can say about *Y Gododdin* is that the spelling of much of it suggests that our thirteenth-century copy goes back ultimately to a version originally written down in the ninth century: before this the transmission was by word of mouth. The actual reference to Arthur occurs in a stanza which was probably present in the ninth-century version.

So we can say with reasonable certainty that Arthur was accepted as a model of military prowess in the ninth century. He may well have been regarded in this light already by AD 600, but this we cannot prove. Two further points arise. Because early Welsh poetry contains no references to persons who are demonstrably legendary or unhistorical we may find confirmation that Arthur was a historical person. Second, it has been suggested that the full implication of the reference is that Arthur used to glut the black ravens with the bodies of the same enemies as those whom Gwawrddur slew – the Angles of Northumbria. In other words, just as Gwawrddur and most – though not in fact all – of his comrades were northern Britons, engaged in an attack on the nascent kingdom of Northumbria, so too Arthur had been a northerner engaged in the same exercise. Such an interpretation, however, seems to strain the natural meaning of the words.

Another set of facts may support the belief that Arthur was regarded as a great national figure in the latter part of the sixth century and early in the seventh. The name Arthur was unknown in native circles in Britain before the time of the Arthur who is our concern. But in the generations around 600, at least four royal families called one of their sons Arthur. The two who are best attested are Artuir son of Aedan king of Dalriada, and Arthur son of Petr and great-grandson of Vortipor of Dyfed. We hear of the first, under the name Arturius, in Adomnän's *Life of Columba* which was written about a century after the events which it describes. Adomnan tells how Artuir was slain in the 'battle of the Miathi', a Pictish tribe. The battle is not closely datable but appears to have been fought in the last decade of the sixth century. Artuir appears to have been quite a young man at the time, so he may well have been born about 570. Arthur son of Petr appears in the Welsh genealogies in the *British Historical Miscellany*. Even if we assume that the genealogy is completely sound, we cannot date Arthur very closely. The nearest member of the dynasty whom we can date is Vortipor, but we can only attempt this because he is one of the kings attacked by Gildas; and we have already seen that the writing of the *De excidio* can be moved up and down either side of 550. Still, a birth-date for Arthur map Petr towards the end of the century would be reasonable. This seems to have been the time when the fame of Arthur made the name briefly popular in royal families.

The Glastonbury exhumation[5]

We come now to one of the most contentious matters in Arthurian scholarship, but one which may provide us with a clue not merely to

Arthur's historicity, but also to his main field of activity: the Glastonbury exhumation. In 1191 the monks of Glastonbury Abbey [Pl.
11] claimed that they had uncovered the bodies of Arthur and his
queen Guinevere in their burial place a little south of the Lady Chapel
of the Abbey church. Reports of the exhumation are given by a contemporary chronicler, Ralph of Coggeshall; in two highly coloured
accounts by Giraldus Cambrensis, who visited Glastonbury in 1192
or 1193, and who saw the bones at that time; and by Adam of Domer-
ham, a monk of Glastonbury who wrote a history of the abbey about
1291, and who presumably drew upon oral traditions. Almost the only
agreement between these accounts is that the bodies were found
between two ancient inscribed pyramids, and were accompanied by
an inscribed cross of lead. Apart from this they differ about the cause
or occasion of the discovery and exhumation; about the character of
the coffin; and about the inscription on the lead cross. According to
Ralph, the burial was 'in a very old sarcophagus', *in quodam vetus-
tissimo sarcophago*; but in Giraldus' accounts the bodies lay in a
'hollowed oak', *quercu concava*. Ralph's version of the cross is:

> *Hic iacet inclitus rex Arturius*
> *in insula Avallonis sepultus.*

'Here lies the famous king Arthur, in the isle of Avalon buried.'
But Giraldus, who had actually seen the cross, gives a slightly different
order of words and adds after the name of Arthur '*cum Wenneveria
uxore sua secunda*', 'with Guinevere his second wife'. He adds details
about a tress of golden hair which had retained its pristine wholeness
and colour, but which crumbled to dust when a greedy monk snatched
at it. Circumstantial though these details seem, they are just the kind
of imaginative colouring which Giraldus adds to his more unlikely
anecdotes. The whole Guinevere element in his report may be held
suspect.

Whatever the actual circumstances of the exhumation, and whatever
was found, all positive evidence has subsequently disappeared. A tomb
was built in 1192–3 to hold the bones. It was opened in 1278 in the
presence of Edward I and queen Eleanor, and the bones were subsequently translated to a more elaborate tomb in front of the Glastonbury
high altar. This tomb was broken up at the Reformation and the bones

dispersed irretrievably. The cross, or what purported to be the cross, was seen by John Leland about 1542. His version of the inscription agrees with that given by Giraldus, except for the omission of any reference to Guinevere. Beyond this, the cross can be traced into the eighteenth century, when apparently it was in Wells; but thereafter it too disappeared.

Despite the loss of so much of the evidence, archaeological excavations at Glastonbury have at least been able to indicate the site of the exhumation. The careful description of the twelfth-century historian William of Malmesbury makes it clear that the two 'pyramids' which flanked the burial were in fact standing crosses, respectively four and five stages high. They stood in the ancient cemetery south of the Lady Chapel. Trenching there in 1962 disclosed firstly a pit apparently about five feet across, from which a great cross might have been removed; then, about ten feet further south, traces of an early mausoleum, which had already been demolished in the tenth century; and third, between the mausoleum and the pit, a large irregular hole which had been dug out and then shortly afterwards refilled in the 1180s or 1190s. The evidence for this precise date is the occurrence in the hole of masons' chippings of the Doulton stone which was used only in building the Lady Chapel in 1184-9. The masons' chippings can scarcely have lain around the area for any length of time. All this points to the irregular hole being the one from which the bones claimed as those of Arthur and Guinevere were exhumed in 1191. It does not guarantee the authenticity of the claim, which we must now examine.

The received doctrine on the Glastonbury burial is that the whole thing was bogus: in fact, a monkish fake. Two possible motives have been suggested for it. The first is political, and stems essentially from the statement by Giraldus that the exhumation had been suggested by Henry II himself. Henry's empire contained many diverse peoples. Late in his reign some unrest among the Celtic peoples may have been inspired by the suggestion that the great king Arthur had risen again in the person of Arthur, son of Geoffrey of Anjou and Constance of Brittany, and grandson of Henry II. It was politically expedient to demonstrate that king Arthur had not risen and never could arise, by producing his body. This hypothesis does not explain why a monastery remote in the west should be chosen for what was essentially a public relations exercise, unless it already had Arthurian associations. The second suggested motive is that the Glastonbury monks were engaged in a large programme of building to make good the damage caused by a disastrous fire in 1184. In order to raise funds it was necessary to stimulate pilgrimages to the monastery; and it was with this in mind that the monks staged the exhumation of Arthur and Guinevere. This was merely the first step on the primrose path which was to lead Glastonbury to further bogus claims about Joseph of Arimathea and the Holy Grail. Once again, the hypothesis evades any explanation as to why Arthur was chosen as the object of pilgrimage unless he already had a traditional connection with Glastonbury.

It may be admitted that medieval monks were quite capable, both physically and morally, of creating forged documents: this is a commonplace of medieval documentary studies. But this is not to say that all documents emanating from monasteries are to be treated as forgeries until proved genuine. Moreover, forgeries were normally concocted in order to provide documentary evidence for rights or privileges to which a monastery considered itself already entitled. In other words, the underlying philosophy was: 'We own this piece of land, we are entitled to this exemption from taxes; unfortunately there are no documents to prove this undoubted right, so we will produce the needful charters or whatever.' Clearly the Glastonbury exhumation, if it was a fake, was of a quite different character from the general run of monkish forgeries. Despite this, historians have gone to considerable lengths to add colour to the hypothesis of a forgery, even suggesting that the monks had dug up elsewhere a Celtic chieftain and his wife, buried over a thousand years earlier in a tree-trunk canoe or coffin, in order to 'salt' the grave. The only comment needed here is that no modern archaeologist would know where to dig up such a burial.

Most previous discussions of the Glastonbury exhumation have paid too little attention to the lead cross which was said to have been found beneath the coffin cover. We have already seen that the contemporary or near-contemporary readings of the inscription on this cross differ in detail, but this should not disturb us. It merely reflects the incompetence of medieval writers at verbatim reporting. It is worth mentioning in this connection that when in 1582 Richard Robinson published an English translation of John Leland's *Assertio inclytissimi*

Arturii Regis Britanniae, his version of the inscription differed at four points from Leland's, despite the fact that he had had Leland's printed text before him. We can therefore readily accept minor discrepancies in the transcription of the text without doubting the authenticity of the original.

Leland published the inscription in his *Assertio* in 1544 as:

HIC IACET SEPVLTVS INCLYTVS REX ARTVRIVS IN INSVLA AVALONIA

'Here lies buried the famous king Arthur in the isle of Avalon.' This agrees with the reading given by Giraldus, stripped of the reference to Guinevere for which he is the only authority, and it differs only in minor points of word order and spelling from Ralph of Coggeshall's transcription. Camden in the first five editions of his *Britannia* (1586–1600), gives a version which differs only on one point from Leland's, substituting I for Y in INCLITUS and thereby restoring the spelling of both Ralph and Giraldus. We can therefore be confident about the actual text of the inscription, but this in itself does not tell us whether the cross is part of a monkish forgery, or an authentic relic of earlier date.

Our next piece of evidence comes from the sixth edition of *Britannia*, published in 1607. Here Camden gives with a flourish a drawing of the cross: '*Sed ecce crucem illam et inscriptionem*', 'Behold the cross itself and the inscription.' The vital question here is: does this drawing depict the details of the lettering with such accuracy that we can use it to date the cross on epigraphic grounds? There are good reasons for assuming so. The early editions of *Britannia* had a small page-size, not more than seven and a half inches high. But the edition in which the drawing first appeared was in a larger format with the page now twelve and a half inches high. The cross itself is drawn six and seven-eighths inches tall. If the drawing is a full-scale facsimile it is clear that it would not have fitted on the page in the earlier editions. If on the other hand it is merely a sketch and not a full-size facsimile, why was it not drawn out small enough to fit the pages of the earlier editions?

If we accept that Camden gives us an accurate copy of the cross, what does the style of lettering tell us about its date? First, it is quite certainly not an inscription contemporary with Arthur's death in the

first half of the sixth century. Various letter forms, in particular the
*N*s, which look like *H*s, and the square *C*s, argue against so early a
date. But they tell equally against a date in the late twelfth century,
the time of the exhumation and the supposed forgery. The best comparisons for the letters are provided, in fact, by the inscriptions on
Late Saxon coins, and on epigraphic grounds a date in the tenth or
eleventh centuries would seem most likely.

6. Camden's drawing of the Glastonbury lead cross, from the 1607 edition of
Britannia.

At first sight this merely makes the issue more confused, for how
could an authentic burial of the sixth century – the date of the historical
Arthur – or a forgery of the twelfth century be associated with a tenth-
century inscription? A possible explanation is that this is one of the
less skilful aspects of the forgery. Twelfth-century monks, it is argued,
were sufficiently scholarly to know that the script of their own day

would be inappropriate for what they were passing off as an ancient burial. There is certainly evidence from forged charters that *scriptoria* sometimes attempted to imitate the letter forms of a century or more earlier. We can detect this only when their imitation was incompetent, when for instance they used a mixture of contemporary and archaic letters. Presumably a forger who was both a good epigraphic scholar and a skilled penman might escape detection even by the shrewdest of modern scholars. But we may suppose that the Glastonbury forger knew just enough to tell him that a contemporary script would not do, but not enough to be able to reproduce an authentic sixth-century script. Casting around in the monastic library for ancient manuscripts to serve as models, his hand fell upon some work of the tenth or early eleventh century, as well it might, and copying the capital letters from that he produced an inscription which was colourably ancient.

This is all plausible enough; but another explanation is also possible, which takes account of the total archaeological evidence from the area of the exhumation. This had taken place in an ancient cemetery of slab-lined graves which lay to the south of the old church of St Mary. One feature of the ancient cemetery was the mausoleum, of which traces were found in 1962. The mausoleum would have held the body or relics of some important saint and burial close beside it would have been a considerable privilege. Here, it may be suggested, Arthur was buried after the battle of Camlann. In accordance with sixth-century practice (below, p. 240) his grave would have been marked by an upright slab or pillar of stone, inscribed in Roman capitals with the words

HIC SEPVLTVS IACIT ARTVRIVS

'Here buried lies Arthur', or some similar formula.

We know that when St Dunstan was Abbot of Glastonbury in the years after 945 he enclosed the ancient cemetery with a masonry wall and raised the area itself. Excavations in 1954 and 1962 showed that the raising of the level had been done by laying down a broad low bank of clay, which was revetted on the south by Dunstan's wall, and which sloped towards the old church on the north. This clay bank immediately overlay the floor of the mausoleum, which must therefore have been demolished before the deposition of the clay. The demolition of the mausoleum may well have been part of Dunstan's work. Had there been a monument to Arthur standing just north of the mausoleum, it would have been removed at the same time. But it may have been felt that the grave of such a distinguished person should not go altogether unmarked, so a lead cross, inscribed in contemporary tenth-century letters, was placed in the grave. By that time, as we know from the 'Marvels of Britain' in the *Historia Brittonum*, legends and wonders were already attached to the name of Arthur. Consequently the tenth-century text, improving on its original in the customary manner (above, p. 4), added two phrases which could not have been on the sixth-century memorial: INCLITVS REX, 'illustrious king', and IN INSVLA AVALONIA, 'in the isle of Avalon'. These, then, were the cross and the burial which were exhumed in 1191.

The last two paragraphs are admittedly a structure of hypothesis; some would say, a work of romance or historical fiction. But two points should be noticed. First, nothing in this explanation runs counter to the motives put forward for the fake exhumation. Whether an authentic or a bogus burial was involved, the reasons for doing it at that juncture might be the same: either political, to counter the Celtic unrest inspired by Arthur of Brittany, or financial, to raise funds for a building programme. Either of these motives makes more sense if we believe that Glastonbury already had a traditional Arthurian connection. Second, the hypotheses favoured here do attempt to take into account all the available evidence, whereas the hypothesis of the monkish forgery dismisses it. In particular, the evidence of the leaden cross can only be discounted if we maintain either that Camden's drawing is not an accurate facsimile or that the master mind behind the exhumation was sufficiently learned to reproduce ancient letter forms in the inscription. In the nature of the evidence, neither of these points can be proved.

Some general considerations

We have now reviewed first, the verbal evidence which might be contemporary with Arthur himself; second, that which probably falls within three generations of his life-time; and third, in the case of the Glastonbury cross, a possible witness to his place of burial, which, if it is authentic, is quite independent of the development of Arthurian fable and romance at the hands of Geoffrey of Monmouth and later writers. On this evidence the case for the historicity of Arthur rests. No real help is provided by later stories whether in poetry or prose, or by later localizations of Arthurian activity.

At this point it must be admitted that the kind of historical figure which begins to emerge from this evidence would be largely rejected by some competent scholars. In particular, any connection between Arthur and events in southern Britain – the battle of Badon, the burial at Glastonbury – is ruled out absolutely by that school which believes that Arthur's activities were wholly confined to the north.[6] We must therefore examine the arguments on this point more fully than we have done so far. We have already noticed a strained interpretation of the couplet in *Y Gododdin*: the suggestion that Arthur's enemies had been the same as those of the men of the Gododdin, namely, the Angles of Northumbria. Even if we were to read this into the words it would only imply that some of Arthur's battles had been fought in the north, not that all of them were.

We have also dismissed the view that the reference in the Welsh Annals to Arthur at the Battle of Badon was a late interpolation. We have argued that there is no cause to see a miraculous or fabulous element in this entry, and that it would be difficult to imagine how a religious legend about Arthur could be inserted into the Annals in the later tenth or eleventh centuries. In brief, there is nothing cogent about the arguments for separating Arthur from Badon unless it has already been decided, on other grounds, that Arthur could not have fought the battle because his campaigns were wholly in the north.

In fact, the only positive evidence for an Arthurian battle in northern Britain is provided by Cat Coit Celidon. The battles on the rivers Glein and Dubglas could have been fought in the north, and so might the eleventh battle if we favour the reading *in monte qui nominatur breguoin* rather than *in monte qui dicitur Agned*. But in no instance is the location certain. In the last analysis, the case for the northern Arthur rests not on the positive identification of Arthurian battle-sites or other localities – Cat Coit Celidon always excepted – but on the analysis of the early sources of information about him: namely the Easter Annals and the list of battles in the *Historia Brittonum*.

It has been claimed that, although the *British Historical Miscellany* in which we find the information is a Welsh manuscript, none the less the actual origin of those sections which interest us lies among the Britons of the north. Their language, no less than that of the sixth-century inhabitants of Wales, was British in the process of becoming Welsh. When their lands were overrun by the Angles, and the Welsh language disappeared from the north, poems and tales about historic personages were carried to the west and preserved in Wales simply because that land was not anglicized. In this way the wholly northern poem *Y Gododdin*, and Taliesin's poems about the northern ruler Urien of Rheged, came to be preserved in Wales. All this is beyond dispute because of the clear-cut nature of the evidence. But in the case of Arthur it is by no means self-evident that his activities were northern, and that the stories about him were subsequently transferred to Wales and Dumnonia, and re-localized there. Arguments here frequently assume what they should in fact attempt to prove.

It must be stressed for a start that the earliest Welsh poetry was not composed wholly in the north about northern princes and heroes. This is demonstrated most clearly by the scraps of biography which we can reconstruct about Taliesin himself. Even if we dismiss alto-gether the traditions about his conflict with Maelgwn of Gwynedd, his poem to Cynan Garwyn of Powys, which we have already quoted (above, p. 14), makes it clear first that bards moved freely about the Welsh-speaking areas of Britain seeking patronage, and second, that the early poetry does contain historical information about a person who certainly was not a man of the north. It follows that we cannot reasonably argue that because one of our sources of information about Arthur was most probably a Welsh battle-listing poem, therefore the source itself must necessarily be northern, and so must Arthur.

Nor can we argue convincingly from the precise context in which the list of Arthur's battles occurs in the *Historia Brittonum*. As we have seen, it is preceded by a brief reference to the kings of Kent (above, pp. 35–8). A determined advocate might turn even this into a 'nor-thern' reference, because Octha the son of Hengest came to Kent '*de sinistrali parte brittannie*, 'from the northern part of Britain'. But we have also seen that in our best manuscript, Harley 3859, the battle list is separated from the Kentish reference by a coloured initial letter, from which it would appear that *Tunc Arthur pugnabat* introduces a new section altogether. The termination of the Arthurian section, on the other hand, is less easy to define, for it runs indistinguishably into a statement about Ida of Northumbria, which in turn leads on into the 'Northern British History'. The question has been asked, therefore, whether the battle list itself is part of the 'Northern British History'.

In fact no firm answer has been given, nor is one likely, but even if the question were decided in the affirmative, this would not in itself make Arthur a northern Briton. There are several grounds for this assertion. First, while the 'Northern British History' contains many references to men who were undoubtedly northern Britons it also relates the deeds of men who were not Britons at all, as well as of Britons who were certainly not northerners. Notable in this respect are Maelgwn, Cadwallon, Cadwaladr and Cadafael, all rulers of Gwynedd. Second, we have already argued the case (above, p. 36) that the core of the so-called 'Northern British History' is not British but Northumbrian Anglian. We have seen that around this Anglian core diverse British elements were added, and a particularly prominent British element comes quite certainly from Gwynedd. From all this it follows that even if the Arthurian battle-list is an integral part of the 'Northern British History' this is no proof that Arthur's military activity was confined to the north.

The evidence of the Easter Annals in the *British Historical Miscellany* may be analysed on similar lines. Supporters of the northern Arthur have claimed, for instance, that because a majority of the early entries in the Annals refer to events in the north of the island, it may therefore be inferred that Arthur was a man of the north. It is difficult to know what is meant by 'early entries' in this context, for there are certainly no northern references before the battle of Camlann, even if we allow that to have occurred at Camboglanna on Hadrian's Wall. If we analyse all the battles which are recorded during the first two hundred years of the Annals we get the following results. Year 72, Badon was in southern England. Year 93, Camlann was possibly in the north. Year 129, Armterid (or Arderydd) was in the north, near Carlisle. Year 140, a battle *contra euboniam*, 'against the Isle of Man'. Year 169 was the battle of Chester. Year 185 was the siege of King Cadwallon *in insula Glannauc*, 'on Ynys Lannog', that is Priestholm off Anglesey. The two following years saw other battles involving Cadwallon: that which

Bede appears to place at Hatfield, near Doncaster, in which Cadwallon and Penda of Mercia slew Edwin of Northumbria and his two sons; and that of Cantscaul or *Denisesburna* near Hadrian's Wall, in which Cadwallon himself was slain. It seems probable that these two battles are mentioned not because of the northern interest of the Annals, but because of their Venedotian interest. Year 188 saw *Strages sabrine* 'the slaughter on the river Severn'. Finally, year 200 records the death of Oswald king of Northumbria and Eoba king of Mercia at the battle of Cocboy, which was most probably fought near Oswestry in the northern Marches of Wales.

It seems difficult to use this list to sustain the view that the Welsh Easter Annals have a predominantly northern British interest, and quite impossible to maintain that any event appearing in the Annals must have occurred in the north. The same is true when we analyse the persons who are mentioned in the first two hundred years of the Annals. There certainly are northerners present, including for instance St Kentigern and the Scottish king Aedan mac Gabran. Curiously enough, some of the most eminent northern Britons, men like Urien Rheged and Rhydderch Hael, whom we know about from early poetry and from the 'Northern History' sections of the *Historia Brittonum*, do not appear at all in the Annals. But among those mentioned we may certainly note three Welsh bishops and four Welsh rulers. Once again the inference that Arthur, by appearing in this company, is marked out as a man of the north is seen to be indefensible.

In any case, arguments based on what are supposed to be the predominant interests of the early entries in the Annals are founded on a misconception. This is that we are dealing with a unitary document, so that if we can determine the principal area which interested its compiler we can thereby establish its source. But it is more probable that the Great Cycle of Easter Annals which we find in the *British Historical Miscellany* incorporates entries from several short-cycle Easter Tables (above, p. 40) which could have come from various *scriptoria*. This is especially true in the case of the earlier annals, and it is only the later ones which we can attribute to the single *scriptorium* of St David's. Even that *scriptorium* was highly eclectic, and a strong case can be made that one of the Easter Tables which it was able to use had been compiled at Bangor in Gwynedd in the days of Maelgwn and his successors. A case might also be made that the entries for years 1 to 80 were originally compiled at Glastonbury. This hypothesis would account for the entries about Saints Patrick and Bridget, who had special connections with Glastonbury, and it would be of special interest to us because year 72 has the entry about Arthur at Badon. But it is not pressed here, in face of the received doctrine that the information about Patrick and Bridget was copied from Irish Annals. What can be asserted, however, is that most previous analyses of the Welsh Easter Annals in terms of predominant interest and possible source have failed to comprehend the piecemeal way in which the document we possess came into being.

It may be thought that this refutation of the case for the northern Arthur has been unnecessarily laboured. But it is fair to stress first that the hypothesis is very strongly entrenched in academic circles; and second, that it forms a major obstacle to any rational consideration of the historical Arthur.

We now face another difficulty in the way of accepting Arthur as a great soldier who fought at least one battle in southern Scotland, at least one in southern England, and others at widespread places in between. This is the claim that such widespread campaigning implies a quite impossible degree of mobility. From this it is inferred that the compiler of the battle list in the *Historia Brittonum* had very little firm information about the battles which Arthur had actually fought, and he therefore borrowed from other warrior-heroes in order to make up an imposing list. From Gildas he took the anonymous battle of Badon; from a poetic source he borrowed Urien's battle of Breguoin; and he pushed the famous battle of Chester a hundred years back in time to attribute it to Arthur. We can be sure – the argument runs – that the Chester battle was borrowed in this way, because Chester lies too far west to have seen an engagement between Britons and Saxons in the early sixth century.

There is no real substance in these arguments. We might start by analysing the specific case of the battle of Chester. It is of course perfectly true that the frontier between Saxons and Britons – if we can think in such rigid political terms – cannot possibly have been as far west as Chester in the early sixth century. But when we come to study the well-documented warfare of the seventh century we shall find that battles did not necessarily occur on frontiers at all, but might be fought in the very heart of enemy territory (below, pp. 338 f.). There is nothing at all impossible in the idea of an Anglo-Saxon force raiding as far west as Chester in the years around 500. Indeed we might take a well-known phrase of Gildas about the fire which 'blazed from sea to sea' as implying that a generation or more earlier the invaders had momentarily reached the Irish Sea. It is unreasonable to assert, in face of the scantiness of the evidence, that because the only battle of Chester which we know about otherwise is that of 616, this must have been 'borrowed' to eke out the Arthurian list.

It is worth remembering here that, with the doubtful exception of Breguoin, Chester and Badon are the only famous battle sites in the list. If a person, whether poet or scribe, who was ignorant of Arthur's actual battles, had to compile or invent a list, it seems most probable that he would have chosen famous engagements to embellish his hero. But our modern difficulties in identifying the places named in the battle list reflect their real obscurity. This may well suggest that they are genuine rather than invented or borrowed.

As to the wider objection that one man could not have fought battles in both the north and in southern England, the military history of the seventh century is once again instructive (below, Map 10). The years of keenest strife between Gwynedd and Mercia on the one hand and Northumbria on the other provide indisputable examples of high mobility on the part of princes who certainly were no Arthurs. The outstanding example was the campaign in which Penda of Mercia chased Oswy of Northumbria as far north as Stirling, a distance of two hundred and fifty miles from Penda's capital at Tamworth. Penda is also known to have fought the rulers of Wessex at Cirencester. In view of this it can scarcely be maintained that Arthur could not have fought both Cat Coit Celidon and Badon.

There are, moreover, two differences between Penda and Arthur which might allow the British *dux bellorum* to be even more mobile than the Mercian king. First, we have no reason to think that Arthur was a territorial ruler, attached to a particular kingdom. It is more likely that he was either a freelance who offered the services of himself and a band of followers to whatever king would pay best, or an overall commander appointed collectively by the kings of the Britons.

If we want an example of the first possibility, we may find it in the Venedotian warriors who fell with the rest of the Gododdin at *Catraeth* – soldiers of fortune rather than mercenaries. In relation to the second hypothesis, we may recall Gildas's statement that it was not Vortigern alone but all the *consiliarii* who appointed a band of Anglo-Saxon mercenaries to combat the Picts on their behalf. This demonstrates that the Britons were capable of taking cooperative action to appoint a commander who could fight their enemies wherever they appeared. Such a role might fit both the battle list and also the opening phrase of the Arthurian section in the *Historia Brittonum*, in which Arthur was said to have fought 'along with the kings of the Britons, but he himself was *dux bellorum*'.

The second point of difference between Arthur and Penda is that Arthur's troops were almost certainly mounted, whereas Penda's were undoubtedly foot-soldiers. But to say this is not to suggest that Arthur led a force of heavily armoured cavalry, mounted on armour-encased horses. It is true that such a hypothesis has been formulated on the strength of two apparently converging lines of argument. The first is the suggestion that the medieval romances of the Knights of the Round Table reflect a genuine folk memory of a peripatetic warrior band led by the historic Arthur. The second is the argument that the late Roman army had made use of heavy cavalry, in which both men and horses were armoured; that two units of such cavalry served in Britain in the fourth century on the evidence of the army list known as the *Notitia Dignitatum*; and that Arthur created a mobile force on this model a century later.

So far as the first point is concerned, it should be stressed that we find no hint of Arthur as leader of a force of heavy cavalry in the earlier stages of the development of the Arthurian cycle. Surveying the whole of that development we can be sure that such an idea, far from being a folk-memory from earlier times, is essentially a reflection of the contemporary world of the thirteenth and later centuries. Nor is there any weight in the second argument in the form in which it was stated in the last paragraph. A close study of the Roman use of heavily armoured cavalry has shown that this was only occasional, that it was unsuccessful as a military device, and that it was confined to the eastern parts of the empire.[7] The units which the *Notitia Dignitatum* assigns to

Britain probably consisted of warriors wearing relatively light chainmail or scale armour, mounted on unarmoured horses. There is nothing inherently improbable about the hypothesis that such a cavalry force served as a model for the immediately post-Roman generations, and it is at least certain that Arthurian Britain did not create its defences out of a vacuum. But the study of the weapons and tactics used by Arthur and his contemporaries makes a whole field of research in itself. Any further discussion must therefore be deferred to Chapter 11.

Meanwhile, we can fairly ask the question: if the whole weight of reasoning and reasonable scepticism is brought to bear on Arthur, what remains as the irreducible minimum of historical fact? The answer is that we are left with a single entry in the Welsh Easter Annals: '*An* [nus xciii]. *Gueith camlann in qua arthur et medraut corruerunt.*' 'Year 93. Strife of Camlann in which Arthur and Modred perished.' There is no case for regarding this as anything other than an authentic contemporary entry in an Easter Table. It does not tell us where or why Camlann was fought. It tells us nothing about Medraut, and it is only in the light of later tradition that we identify Medraut with 'Modred' and assume that Arthur and Medraut fought on opposite sides. But it does assure us that Arthur was an authentic person; one important enough to be deemed worthy of an entry in an Easter Annal; most probably a king or prince, but if not that, then emphatically a great warrior. And even if we cannot calculate a reliable date for the battle, we can at least be sure that Arthur died in the first half of the sixth century.

Having established this small kernel of Arthurian fact, we can now proceed to examine the political and military situation which would have faced a British war leader at that time. Chapter 4 narrates the events leading up to the Arthurian age, in the years AD 367–490, while Chapter 5 traces the decline of British resistance in the century after Arthur's death.

Four

The Historical Background, AD 367-490

Introduction[1]

In our examination of the most reliable Arthurian documents we have discovered acceptable evidence that Arthur was a renowned British soldier, more probably a great commander than a king. His battles were fought principally in the first part of the sixth century AD or perhaps around the turn of the fifth and sixth centuries. It is difficult to overthrow the traditional view that his military activities extended very widely over Britain, perhaps from the southern uplands of Scotland down to Somerset or Dorset. And since no cogent case can be made for dismissing as fable Arthur's connection with the battle of Badon, we should see his major enemy, the one against whom he won his most signal victory, as the Anglo-Saxon invaders. This, then, provides the focal point for any description of the historical background to Arthur, or any discussion of the Arthurian situation.

The period from about 367 to 634 – that is, from the barbarian conspiracy which overran the Roman defences of Britain down to the death of Cadwallon of Gwynedd at the hands of Oswald of Northumbria – saw the replacement of the Romanized diocese of Britannia by a complex of warring kingdoms in which four nations – Britons, Scots, Picts and Anglo-Saxons – all played a part. The most dramatic aspect of this process was the virtual extinction, throughout eastern Britain from the Forth to the English Channel, of British speech and culture. In its place we find the vigorous growth of the English language, and in the archaeological record, a flourishing material culture with Teutonic roots. Less dramatic, though no less definite, was the implanting in western Scotland of Goidelic or Gaelic speech at the hands of a dynasty from Ireland, and at the expense of the Picts and Britons of the area. On an even more minor scale, an Irish dynasty and Goidelic speech were implanted in south-west Wales. In short, from both east and west the island of Britain received waves from the great flood of barbarians which swept across Europe in the fourth, fifth and sixth centuries AD.

The anglicization of eastern Britain at this time is an undeniable fact; but when we ask exactly how and when it came about we enter a quagmire of contention and hypothesis. The classic account is that given by Gildas in Chapters 3 to 26 of his *De excidio*. He saw that the primary enemy, the one who had most engaged the Romans' military power, was the northern barbarians, the Picts. When in 446 the Romans finally refused to provide further aid to the Britons they in their folly sought a new ally in the eastern barbarians, the Anglo-Saxons. The impression left by Gildas's account, overlaid and obscured as it is with rhetoric and biblical allusion, is that it was at a definite point in time, around the middle of the fifth century, that the Anglo-Saxons were originally recruited. The first-comers soon called over reinforcements, and before long, those who were supposed to be defending Britain revolted and overran the island with fire and slaughter. Cities were sacked, their inhabitants were massacred or forced to flee, and the whole system of culture and economy was shattered. Ultimately the citizens were rallied under the leadership of the romanized general Ambrosius Aurelianus, who initiated a series of battles of fluctuating fortune which continued up to the great victory of Badon. Shortly afterwards there began a period of peace which lasted up to the time when Gildas himself was writing.

Had this account been confined to the turgid pages of the *De excidio*, it might have exercised little influence on historical thinking. But in the eighth century it was given wide and lasting currency by one of the most renowned of ancient historians, the Venerable Bede. In his *Ecclesiastical History of the English People* Bede relied largely on Gildas for his history of the Anglo-Saxon settlement. Indeed he strengthened the apparent value of the Gildasian account, not only by improving the style in which it was written but also by adding numerous circumstantial details. For instance, he explained that the Romans could no longer aid the Britons in 446 because they were engaged against the Huns. He gave names to the Anglo-Saxon leaders, Hengist and Horsa, and to the British ruler who recruited them, Vortigern. He analysed the diverse tribal groups which constituted the English people, and he speculated on their continental homelands. Where Gildas had given no date for the first recruitment of Anglo-Saxons, Bede attempted to calculate one – or rather, two (below, p. 108). Above all, because he was writing not a simple political history but a species of hagiography, in which the English people are described in the terms which St Paul used about the people of Israel, Bede saw the coming of the Anglo-Saxons as initiating an era. He therefore several times refers to events happening so many years after the *Adventus Saxonum in Brittaniam*, 'the coming of the English to Britain'.

The *Anglo-Saxon Chronicle*, with its seemingly circumstantial reports of battles in Kent, Sussex and Wessex, reinforces the picture presented by Gildas and Bede. Not surprisingly, it makes no mention of the great English defeat at Badon; but despite this some historians have claimed to show, by manipulating a few early entries, that during the first half of the sixth century the expansion of Wessex was brought to a standstill, probably as a result of this battle. Only in 552 were the Saxons at last able to push forward to Salisbury and beyond. But the most important feature of the *Chronicle*, in corroborating the witness of Gildas and Bede, is the detail in which it reports the sites, the personnel involved and the numbers slain in the battles between British defenders and English invaders. In other words it converted a vague, rhetorical, impressionistic account of fire and slaughter into something far more circumstantial and therefore credible.

The classic account of the English invasion and settlement has three main elements. First, the settlement is seen as inaugurated by a single decisive event – the *Adventus Saxonum*. In theory this event is precisely datable, even if Bede himself is self-contradictory about the date. At least it could be agreed that the *Adventus* had taken place a few years either side of AD 450. Second, the settlement was effected by military means, even, in the eyes of some historians, by strategically planned operations. As a result, the native Britons were slaughtered in thousands. Where they were not exterminated they were forced to flee ever further westward, so that by the late sixth century eastern England had been largely cleared of Britons, while by the ninth the refugee remnant had been confined to Wales and Cornwall. Third, this process of expulsion and extermination was halted – indeed the tide of invasion was momentarily reversed – for a generation or so early in the sixth century as a result of Arthur's victory at Badon.

When we look closely, however, at the sources on which the classic account is based, we may begin to wonder about its reliability. We have seen that Gildas is useless as an authority for events in the late fourth and early fifth centuries, and that it is impossible to determine how sound he is about the crucial middle decades of the fifth century (above, pp. 25-7). In so far as Bede follows Gildas, he is no independent witness. As for the *Anglo-Saxon Chronicle*, we have seen that its chronology for the fifth and much of the sixth centuries is often artificial, and we cannot reasonably claim that it derives an essential soundness from regnal lists (above, pp. 19-20). Finally we have suggested that its emphasis on battles and slaughter reflects the heroic poetry used as source material by early Wessex chroniclers, rather than a true image of the process of English settlement (above, p. 44).

It is evident, then, that the normal historian's tool of source criticism can be used to pry some small cracks in the fire-and-slaughter image of the English settlement. But we shall also see (below, p. 104 f.) that the same tool can be used constructively, and that it allows us to formulate the hypothesis that there were at least three 'comings of the English' in the second quarter of the fifth century. Here new thoughts about the verbal evidence harmonize with newly won archaeological evidence, which has been equally destructive of the concept of a single *Adventus* – event occurring around AD 450.[2] For a start, some pagan Anglo-Saxon cemeteries contain pottery vessels closely similar to urns found in the continental homelands of the English and dated on the continent to the decades before 450 [Fig. 27*a*]. From this it appears that the English had already ceased to raid and had started to settle in Britain significantly before Bede's date for the *Adventus*. Again, the recognition on Roman military sites in south-east England of sword-belt buckles ornamented in a mixed Roman-Provincial and Teutonic taste argues for a large deployment of German troops for the defence of Britain in the late fourth and early fifth centuries [Pl. 17]. Despite the impression left by Gildas, Vortigern was not the first to recruit Germans to ward off the Picts.

In these and other ways it is becoming apparent that the English settlement was much more complex, both in its chronology and in its character, than Bede would suggest. We can no longer confine our study of it to the middle years of the fifth century. Instead, we must begin by looking back on the military problems which beset Roman Britain, and the means employed to cope with them.

Roman Britain and her problems

The military problems of the Romans in Britain arose basically from their failure to complete the conquest of the islands. In the middle years of the first century AD they had scored rapid successes against the politically sophisticated and centralized tribes of the south-east. But as they moved west and north they were faced not only with more difficult terrain, but more important, with tribes which were altogether more backward, more fluid politically, and therefore more resilient militarily. It took the legions less than a decade to reach the river Severn, and virtually a quarter of a century to consolidate their hold beyond it to the Irish Sea. Even then the absence of towns, except for Caerwent and Carmarthen, the scarcity of villas, and the intermittent reoccupation of forts throughout the Roman period all argue strongly that the Cambrian mountains and their western slopes were never fully pacified.

Further west again was an even more barbarous and loosely organized land, which was not even garrisoned: Ireland, from which came curragh-loads of raiding parties, gathering treasure and slaves from the richer areas of western Britain. The classic historical instance of these raids is the abduction of the youthful Patrick, while they are reflected in the archaeological records in Ireland by hoards of Romano-British silverware [Pl. 14b], which had apparently been chopped up to be shared out between the partners in a looting expedition (but see below, p. 254). In Britain itself the construction or modification of coastal forts such as Lancaster and Cardiff mark the Roman attempt to ward off raids in the third and fourth centuries. Among the natives, on the other hand, the reaction may have been to reoccupy the hill-top defences of their ancestors, sites like Dinorben, Degannwy, and Coygan. And, especially in the late third century, hoards of coins were buried for safe-keeping along the western coasts, and were never recovered by owners who presumably had been slain or taken into slavery.

So much for the west. In the north the problems were similar; this was a region inhabited by barbarians in the Pennines and Border country and even fiercer tribes in the Highlands – the Caledonians and Picts. The Pennine area was, like Wales, a district without towns or villas, and more or less continuously patrolled by the garrisons of auxiliary forts. But the northern raiders had the advantage over those from Ireland that they could move by land as well as by coastal voyage. So more drastic solutions were needed in the north, and attempts were made to control or keep out the unconquered tribes of the Highlands by physical barriers, the walls of Hadrian and Antoninus. The second of these had only a brief history, and was abandoned by the Romans after the Caledonians had overrun it and destroyed its forts late in the second or early in the third century. But Hadrian's Wall remained the key to the defence of the north throughout most of the Roman occupation of Britain. After the abandonment of the Antonine Wall the tribes immediately north of Hadrian's Wall were turned into buffers against the Highland barbarians by engaging them in treaty relations with the empire, though their territory was nevertheless patrolled by frontier scouts stationed in outpost forts. On the whole this system – the client tribes, the scouts, the Wall, and the Pennine forts – worked perfectly satisfactorily. According to the most recent interpretation of the history of northern Britain, the Wall and its associated forts were only twice seriously damaged by hostile action. The second of these occasions was in AD 367 when, as we shall shortly see, the barbarian attack was combined with massive defections on the part of the frontier garrison.

Among the garrisons which were thus engaged in the defence of Roman Britain some had been recruited beyond the imperial frontier on the Rhine, from the free peoples of Germany. Along Hadrian's Wall there were cavalry units of Frisian irregulars at Burgh-by-Sands and at Housesteads. At the latter fort they set up a shrine, with inscribed door jambs and carved lintel, to their ancestral gods the Two Alaisiagae, and these same gods were also worshipped there by another German unit which called itself *Numerus Hnaudifridi*, Notfried's Troop. The special interest of these dedications, which go back to the third century, is that Frisians were among the ancestors of the English people. They demonstrate that the recruitment of Germanic barbarians for the defence of Britain had a very long history.[3]

But Roman Britain had other contacts with the Germanic peoples which were more ominous for the future. In the late second century a number of unretrieved coin-hoards around the south-east coasts of Britain suggests that Saxon sea-raiding had already begun. The forts erected at Reculver and Brancaster early in the third century mark the first tentative organization of defences. But it was only in the last decade of the century that the fullydeveloped Saxon Shore system was organized, combining a channel fleet with a series of at least ten new forts from the Wash to Southampton Water [Pl. 1]. The character of these counter-measures is sufficient indication that the threat of Saxons from across the North Sea was becoming as serious as that of the Picts from the north.

In 367 the defences of Roman Britain suffered a major disaster at the hands of an utterly unexpected alliance of various barbarian enemies. From Ireland came the Scotti and Attacotti; from the Highlands came the Picts; and meanwhile Franks and Saxons assaulted the frontier and coast of Gaul. The attack on Hadrian's Wall was facilitated by the treachery of the frontier scouts, and by a breakdown of discipline among the regular troops. The Duke of the Britains, commander of the frontier garrisons, was captured, and the Count of the Saxon Shor was slain. (Incidentally these two men, the highest ranking officers in Britain at the time, both appear to have been Germans, to judge from the linguistic character of their names, Fullofaudes and Nectaridus.) As far south as London bands of deserters as well as barbarians plundered the land. Apart from the Frankish and Saxon pressure in Gaul, the Emperor Valentinian was engaged against the Alamanni at the time, and it seems that if the raiders had been intent on conquest rather than on looting, the diocese of Britannia might have been lost to the empire.

The situation was finally retrieved by the wise and forceful policy of Count Theodosius. Having won back the disaffected troops with an amnesty, in 369 he was ready to undertake reconquest and reconstruction. The damaged forts on Hadrian's Wall were rebuilt, but the outpost forts were abandoned and the treacherous frontier scouts were disbanded. But as a complement to this the pro-Roman tribe of the Votadini, who occupied extensive lands from the eastern half of the Wall to the Firth of Forth and beyond, may have been brought into closer treaty relations with Rome, with special responsibility for guarding the main approaches from Pictland (but see below, p. 129). South of the Wall the Yorkshire coast as far south as Flamborough Head was protected by a chain of signal-towers which had the duty of alerting the inland garrisons to the approach of sea-raiders, more probably Pictish than Saxon. In the civil areas of the province, town-walls were provided at various dates with projecting bastions which served as emplacements for artillery pieces capable of breaking up massed barbarian attackers; presumably small military units were posted to the towns. These military measures were accompanied by some political and administrative re-organization, so that by 370 Britain was once again a secure and prosperous diocese of the empire.

This security, however, was soon weakened. In 383 the disaffected general Magnus Maximus, who was probably at the time *Dux Britanniarum*, rebelled, and took a considerable part of the British garrison to Gaul. There, having slain the Emperor Gratian, he held the western Empire until his death in 388. It is probable that the troops whom he led to the continent never returned to Britain, and certainly we find the former garrison of *Segontium* – Caernarvon – serving later in Illyricum. It is unlikely that a competent and experienced commander would have made no arrangements to protect his rear. So far as the north was concerned, there are hints that Maximus carried out a warning campaign against the Picts and Scots in the year before his rebellion.

Down the west coast, from Galloway to Pembrokeshire, he seems to have made other arrangements, of profound importance for the future. It is thought that he handed over the responsibility for defence to native chieftains, who founded the local dynasties of the fifth and later centuries. The case for this rests partly on the fame which he acquired in Welsh folk-tale and poetry, and partly on a number of royal genealogies which trace their line back through Maximus. Among the Welsh *Mabinogion* tales, that known as 'The Dream of Macsen Wledig' begins 'Macsen Wledig (Prince Maximus) was emperor of Rome . . . the best fitted of all that had gone before him.' Most of the genealogies are relatively late, and even the earliest, those preserved in the *British Historical Miscellany*, have spurious elements such as a garbled list of Roman emperors passed off as the lineage of British princes. But from

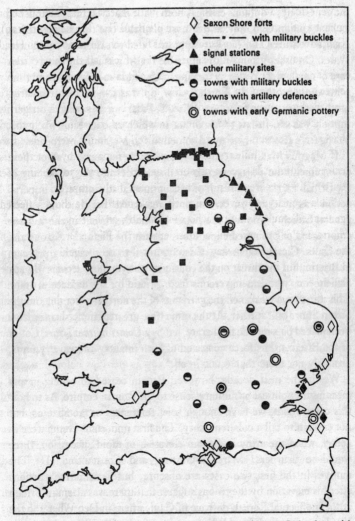

Map 3. Roman Britain in the late 3rd and 4th centuries AD. Only sites with definite archaeological evidence for the period are shown.[4]

the genealogies a dubious case has been made that Maximus established a client king in Galloway, and a more plausible one that he planted an Irish adventurer and his war-band in Dyfed to safeguard south-west Wales. On other grounds it is arguable that it was Maximus who took care of north-west Wales by moving in Cunedda and his war-band from somewhere north of the Forth (below, pp. 124 f.). Finally, the early-ninth-century inscription on Eliseg's Pillar implies that Vortigern himself was son-in-law to Maximus, in which case it seems likely that Vortigern's rise to power owed something to Maximus' patronage.

If Magnus Maximus really was responsible for some or all of these arrangements he deserves great credit; for despite the weakening of the British garrison as a result of his continental adventure, no imperial action was necessary in Britain until 396-8. At that time the Vandal general Stilicho, who was the power behind the throne in the western empire, led or promoted expeditions against the Picts, the Saxons and the Scots. Clearly barbarian raids continued to be a nagging problem in Britain, but the threat on the continent was yet more serious. By 401 Stilicho was withdrawing troops from Britain for the defence of Italy. This must have weakened the garrisons of the northern frontier and the Saxon Shore still further. At the same time greater emphasis may have been placed on a mobile field army, led by a *Comes Britanniarum*, Count of the Britains. His force consisted of both infantry and cavalry units, probably not more than 6,000 in all.

Within the next decade, however, Britain ceased to belong in any meaningful political or military sense to the Roman empire. As to how this came about, we have enough brief references to tantalize us, but not enough to tell a coherent story. The first important events were in 406-7, when the army in Britain elevated, in rapid succession, three would-be usurpers: Marcus, Gratian, and Constantine III. The motives in the first two cases are obscure; but Constantine's actions after his elevation by the troops suggest that there was alarm in Britain at the ineffectual Roman defence of Gaul, where in December 406 the Vandals, Alans and Suevi had crossed the frozen Rhine. In other words because Britain was still part of the empire the army wished to play its part in imperial defence. This, for a time, Constantine was able to do. Presumably he took the field army and much of the remaining frontier garrisons as well, and with their aid he temporarily restored the situation in Gaul and Spain. But ultimately he overreached himself, and by the end of 411 he had been defeated and executed by the troops of the western emperor Honorius.

It might have been expected that the diocese would then have been brought back within the full organization of the imperial system, as it had been after the usurpations of Albinus, of Carausius, and of Magnus Maximus. There were two reasons why it was not. The first was Roman continental commitment. Never again did the Romans have sufficient control over Gaul to free troops for action in Britain. But the second reason was purely insular: the Britons expelled the Roman administrators. Our authority for this is the Greek historian Zosimus, who was close enough in time but too far away in space to be really interested in these events. In consequence various constructions have been placed upon his brief notice, ranging from the view that a party of legitimists had expelled the administration of the usurper Constantine III in order to restore lawful officials, to the hypothesis that there was a nationalist revolution aimed at providing Britain with a more effective defence than Rome had done. We lack the evidence to judge between these and other hypotheses. But the effective outcome was made clear when Honorius wrote, not to the military commanders – the *dux* or *comes Britanniarum* – nor to the chief civilian administrator, the *vicarius*, but to the local councils, the *civitates*, telling them to undertake their own defence. This, according to Zosimus, they had already done: 'The Britons took up arms and, braving danger for their own independence, freed their cities from the barbarians threatening them.'

Those threatening barbarians were, of course, still the same Picts, Scots and Saxons who had plagued Roman Britain. The next part of our account must attempt to show how an island which retained much of the organization and culture of a Roman diocese attempted to cope with the barbarians; and how, in the process, most of that organization and culture was lost.

Independent Britain[5]

So far we have been sketching a story in which we can be reasonably sure of events and persons and dates, even if we often cannot be certain about the significance of the events. But after 410 we enter a period of nearly two centuries in which it is no longer possible to write a continuous narrative history. The principal reason for this is that the break with Rome took Britain out of the orbit of the Mediterranean writers who had provided most of our information for the earlier period. After 410 there are only occasional continental notices of happenings in the island, while the native historical sources are scarcely more numerous.

Among the earliest authentic information which we possess are accounts of the two visits of St Germanus of Auxerre in 428–9 and 445–6. Their most obvious significance is in relation to ecclesiastical history, and this we shall examine later (below, pp. 133–4), but the visits also had political implications, not least because the Pelagian heresy, which Germanus came to combat, seems to have been favoured by a wealthy and influential element in Britain. This at least is the implication of the description of the Pelagians in 428–9 as '*conspicui divitiis, veste fulgentes, circumdati assentatione multorum*' ('distinguished by their riches, resplendent in their attire, and surrounded by the adulation of the multitude'). It has been suggested that this influential element among the British Christians favoured also an independent approach to politics, and was indeed none other than the party which (on one reading of the events of 407 to 410) had preferred native self-help to Roman incompetence and corruption. It is easy here to build too much on slight foundations, and to see a polarization in British politics between a Romanophil party, orthodox in religion, symbolized by Ambrosius, and a native or independence party of Pelagian heretics, symbolized by Vortigern.[6]

Far from assenting wholeheartedly to this hypothesis, we might feel some caution about accepting the description of the Pelagians in the terms quoted above from Constantius' *Life of Germanus*. This was not written during the saint's lifetime, but sometime between 472 and 491, and therefore within living memory of him. It is likely to be sound in its broad account of the events of his life; but all its details must be additions by the biographer himself. However circumstantial they may seem, they are likely to have been put in to heighten the achievements of the saintly hero, in the common manner of hagiography. Here we might note in passing how the account of Germanus sleeping in a storm in the English Channel parallels the story of Christ sleeping in the storm on the Sea of Galilee, given in the Synoptic Gospels (Mark iv, 35–41 and parallels). This is the very stuff of hagiography.

Nevertheless, we may hope to obtain some glances into secular history, and into the social and political background to Germanus' visits. The first point which can be confidently asserted is that communications between southern Britain and Gaul were still open up to the mid-years of the fifth century, for otherwise Germanus and his colleagues could not have been summoned by the British church to refute the Pelagians. Moreover, although on the first visit the party was nearly lost in a storm, there is no suggestion that they were impeded or even endangered by Saxon pirates. Since they would almost certainly have travelled down the Seine valley to make their crossing at the eastern end of the Channel – the end closest to the Saxon coastlands – this absence of molestation is noteworthy.

In Britain itself they appear to have travelled around freely, among people who were living for the most part at peace. They were able to preach the gospel and to minister to the converted in town and country, '*per trivia per rura*'. The implication is that, at least in 428–9, town life in a recognizable Roman sense was still continuing. So too was some form of romanized administrative organization, for they were able to heal the blind daughter of a man described as '*tribuniciae potestatis*', 'of tribunicial power' – in short a magistrate, an official of one of the *civitates* to which Honorius had remitted responsibility in 410. On his second visit Germanus was again called upon to heal a sick child; but on this occasion the father is described not in the terms of romanized officialdom, but simply as '*Elafius, regionis illius primus*', 'Elafius [surely a British name], the leading man of that region'. But it would be very rash to infer from this that between 429 and 446 there had been any marked disintegration, or even weakening, of the fabric of romanized administrative arrangements.

One problem in assessing the significance of this information is that we have only one clue to the area which Germanus actually visited. The clue is provided by his pilgrimage, during his first visit, to the tomb of the martyr St Alban at Roman *Verulamium*, the modern St Albans. It follows that part of the journey took place in the south-east midlands, an area highly romanized in itself, and sufficiently removed from the east coast to have some security from Saxon raids. We cannot be certain, however, that this was at all a characteristic region. And we have no clues at all about where Germanus went on his later visit.

Into this generally peaceful scene one discordant note intrudes, a raid by Saxons and Picts. This, according to Germanus' biographer, found the Britons unprepared and panic-stricken, but they were encouraged by the saint and his companion Lupus. Finally Germanus declared himself their leader in battle, '*ducem se proelii profitetur*'. He arranged an ambush in a valley surrounded by hills, and on his signal the entire British host shouted 'Alleluia'. This so terrified the barbarians that they turned and fled, many of them being drowned in a near-by river. Though the account of this bloodless victory is inflated in the interests of hagiography, the outline presented here probably depicts a historical event. This is far from being the only occasion on which a bishop rallied his flock against the barbarians. Gregory of Tours, for instance, relates how Anianus, bishop of Orleans, inspired his fellow-citizens to hold out against Attila's Huns until the city was relieved by a combined Roman and Visigothic army.

It would be interesting to know whereabouts these Saxons and Picts were marauding in 428-9. Welsh tradition locates the battle at Maesgarmon, Germanus' Field, near Mold in Flintshire, but a valley in the Chilterns would fit the description of the ambush at least as well. Maesgarmon belongs in fact not to sober history but to Welsh folk-tale. There are, especially in north Wales, a number of place names in which Harmon or Garmon (from Germanus) forms an element, and there are also ancient dedications to that saint. In the *Historia Brittonum* several chapters are devoted to the alleged Welsh miracles of Germanus, to those of his supposed activities which led to the foundation of the dynasty of Powys, and to his conflict with Vortigern. These tales were evidently well developed by the early ninth century, when the *Historia Brittonum* was put together, but it is impossible to reconcile them with what we know about St Germanus of Auxerre. They refer at best to a Welsh ecclesiastic of that name, but it is at least as likely that they were invented to explain a number of dedications to the Gaulish saint.

We have mentioned in passing the second leading character of the fifth century, Vortigern, and to him we must now turn, though with considerable reluctance.[7] He first appears in a role of historical importance in Bede's *Ecclesiastical History*, as the British king *Uurtigernus* who called in the Saxon nation from lands across the sea to aid the Britons in their defence against the Picts and Scots. We shall see that Bede's date for this is ambiguous (below, p. 108), but that he thought it occurred around the middle of the fifth century. In the *Historia Brittonum* the doings of Vortigern feature at length: he is active both in Kent and in Wales; he is in conflict with Ambrosius, with Germanus, and with the Saxons. We have already seen (above, p. 34) that these tales about Vortigern are of very uneven historicity. There is little doubt that some of the stories with a Welsh setting, like the tales about Garmon or Germanus, were invented in order to explain place names which had 'Vortigern' as one element in them.

The issue is made more complex by two facts. First, Vortigern means something like 'high chief', and it may therefore have been a title rather than, or as well as, a personal name. Second, even as a personal name, it could have been borne by more than one person – we know at least two Irish Vortigerns, one of them buried in Co. Cork, the other in Co. Waterford. The possibility that we also have more than one Vortigern to account for in Britain may indeed help us out of a chronological difficulty, because some of the British evidence suggests that Vortigern was active a generation earlier than the date suggested by Bede. Apart from the *Historia Brittonum* and other evidence in the *British Historical Miscellany*, which will be discussed in a moment, we have the implication of Eliseg's Pillar that Vortigern was son-in-law of Magnus Maximus who was killed in 388.

At the same time we should note that Gildas, who was Bede's chief source at this point, does not name Vortigern: he refers merely to a *superbus tyrannus*, 'supreme ruler'. Was Gildas, who would certainly have been bi-lingual in Latin and British, giving a twisted translation of 'Vortigern', whether as a personal name or as a title? Or did Bede conflate one source which told of the Saxons coming at the invitation of Vortigern with Gildas's account of an invitation by an unnamed tyrant, and assume that these were the same invitation and the same person? Much scholarship and argument has been devoted to the problems posed by Vortigern, but each learned article merely makes them more intractable. The solution offered here is deliberately simplified, perhaps oversimplified. It can only be an interim solution, until much more work has been done especially on the sources of the Vortigern stories in the *Historia Brittonum*. Its chief claims to merit are that it attempts to isolate the earliest sources and it is in accordance with a growing body of archaeological evidence for the character of the Anglo-Saxon settlement (below, pp. 177–8; pp. 188–9).

It is almost certain that our earliest reference to Vortigern, and therefore our best source of information about him, is the set of chronological computations that stand at the head of the Easter Annals in the *British Historical Miscellany*. Since computations of this kind have an affinity with the calculations needed to compose an Easter Table it is reasonable to suppose that the association of the computations and the Easter Annals in our manuscript is an authentic one. The latest event in the computations, as we shall see, appears to be dated to 437. The Easter Table from which the earliest of the Annals was taken began in 447. It is therefore reasonable to suggest that the computations were calculated in 447 (or perhaps 455, see above, p. 39) as a preface to the original Table. If this argument is sound, then the computations merit the closest scrutiny.

The relevant part runs as follows:

> *Guorthigirnus tenuit imperium in brittannia theodosio & valentiniano consulibus. & in quarto anno regni sui saxones ad brittanniam uenerunt Felice & tauro consulibus quadringentesimo anno ab incarnatione domini nostri ih'u xp'i.*

'Vortigern held rule in Britain in the consulship of Theodosius and Valentinian. And in the fourth year of his reign the Saxons came to Britain in the consulship of Felix and Taurus, in the 400th year from the incarnation of Our Lord Jesus Christ.'

There is one major blunder in these calculations (as well as other minor ones in parts of the computations which are not discussed here). The consulship of Felix and Taurus was in fact in 428 AD and therefore four hundred years not from the Incarnation but from the conventional date for the Passion. We have already seen that until the general acceptance of the Dionysiac system of dating from the Incarnation, confusion between Passion and Incarnation eras was not uncommon. If therefore we emend 'Incarnation' to read 'Passion', we obtain a consistent series of dates. The first consulship of Theodosius and Valentinian was in 425 and an earlier, partly bungled calculation had

THE HISTORICAL BACKGROUND | 105

already equated the start of Vortigern's reign with that of Valentinian, again 425. So the fourth year of Vortigern's reign would be 428, which was the consulship of Felix and Taurus. So the Saxons – at least, those with whom Vortigern had dealings – came to Britain in 428. Incidentally, this date for Vortigern's accession fits well enough his relationship as son-in-law of Magnus Maximus.

Another piece of seemingly authentic information is contained in these computations:

> *a regno guorthigirni usque ad discordiam guitolini & ambrossii anni sunt duodecim quod est guoloppum id est catguoloph.*

'From the [beginning of the] reign of Vortigern up to the dissension of Vitolinus and Ambrosius are twelve years which is Wollop (?Wallop in Hampshire) that is *Catguoloph*, Battle of Wallop.'
The interest of this is three-fold. First, it is a reference to the kind of internal conflict among the Britons which cannot have helped them to organize defence against the barbarians. But, second, it is not possible to construe this particular conflict in terms of nationalists versus Romanophils, for Vitolinus, unlike Vortigern, bears a name that is as Roman as Ambrosius. Third, it demonstrates that Ambrosius was already an active soldier in 452 + 12 = AD 437. If this is correct, he can scarcely have been the commander at Badon. On the other hand, such a date is not entirely incompatible with the notice of Ambrosius in Gildas.

So far as Vortigern and the Saxons are concerned, the computations tell us nothing of the circumstances in which the Saxons came, or of their relationship with Vortigern. We may reasonably speculate that they came as allies and were given land to occupy in return for military service, for this would have been a normal late Roman arrangement. But we cannot go beyond this. All other notices of Vortigern's dealings with the Saxons are likely to have been influenced by Bede's identification of him with the *superbus tyrannus* of Gildas.

Our next apparently authentic information about Saxon activity in Britain comes from a set of terse but factual annals that were maintained in Gaul from about 380 to 452, the so-called *Chronica Gallica a. CCCCLII*, 'Gallic Chronicle year 452'.[8] Despite first appearances this is not a simple run of contemporary annals, taken perhaps from an

Easter Table. The prime reason for asserting this is that at the start of each Emperor's reign the chronicle gives the total number of years that he reigned – an item which clearly must have been entered posthumously. It then uses the regnal years for the main framework of its chronology. Moreover, in the period with which we are concerned it is influenced by, if not actually derived from, another chronicle, the *Chronica Gallica a. DXI*, 'Gallic Chronicle year 511'. The relationship is shown by the way in which these two chronicles treat the reign of Theodosius II – who was already emperor in the east – after the death of his uncle Honorius, emperor in the west. At this point, incidentally, there is a chronological dislocation of five years, which does not leave us with much confidence in the value of this source for accurate dating.

For what they are worth, these two chronicles say this:

Chronica Gallica a. CCCCLII
XVIIII *Brittanniae usque ad hoc tempus variis cladibus eventibusque latae in dicionem Saxonum rediguntur.*

'19 [th year of Theodosius – after the death of Honorius = AD 441] Britain, which up to this time had suffered manifold devastations and accidents, was subjected to the domination of the Saxons.'

Chronica Gallica a. DXI:
XVI *Britanniae a Romanis amissae in dicionem Saxonum cedunt.*

'16 [th year of joint rule of Theodosius and Valentinian = AD 440] Britain, abandoned by the Romans, passed into the power of the Saxons.'

Taken as they stand, these are very sweeping statements, which invite the counter-assertion that it is quite impossible to believe that a major part of southern Britain had fallen under Saxon dominion as early as 440. Early and factual though this source may be, we cannot accept it wholeheartedly. But it is equally impossible to reject the inference that some part of Britain had come under Saxon domination at this time. Presumably it was a region which hitherto had been in close contact with the Gaulish centre where the chronicle was put together, probably in southern Gaul.

We can be reasonably sure that the region subdued in about 440 was not Kent, because Bede preserves a tradition about the settlement of Hengist and Horsa in Kent some ten years later. In seeking evidence for his account of the English settlement in the *Ecclesiastical History of the English Nation*, Bede had two principal sources: the narrative of Gildas in the *De excidio*, and certain Kentish traditions which may have been committed to writing before Bede's day but which ultimately depended on transmission by word of mouth. He was, however, ignorant of the sources which we have just quoted – the Easter Table computations and the Gallic Chronicles – so we are justified in modifying his history in the light of other evidence. In particular, we can see that both the documents we have just examined and the witness of archaeology concur to refute Bede's view that the coming of the English, the *adventus Saxonum*, was a single cataclysmic event, datable to the middle of the fifth century.

Although it was Bede's own interest and expertise in the technique of chronology which made him think of the *adventus Saxonum* as starting a new era, to a major extent his ideas about it were derived from Gildas. Very briefly, Gildas's story was this. Faced with continued pressure from the Picts and the Scots, the Britons appealed for help to the authorities in Gaul, addressing their 'groans of the Britons' to a person who appears in most of the manuscripts of the *De excidio* as 'Agitius [or Agicius], in his third consulship'. Here at once confusion arises. Agitius is most reasonably identified with Aegidius who was the commanding general in Gaul, *magister militum per Gallias*, between 457 and 462. But Aegidius was never a consul; and Bede silently amends Agitius to Aëtius, a previous commander in Gaul, whose third consulship began in 446. It is possible that Bede's copy of the *De excidio*, which was four centuries earlier than the oldest manuscript which we now possess, did actually read Aëtius, but the weight of the manuscript readings is against this.

The appeal to Aegidius or Aëtius was not answered. There followed, according to Gildas, a great famine; a rally on the part of the Britons which for a time held back the Picts and the Scots; a period of great prosperity; and a great plague. Only after all these events, which seem to imply a considerable lapse of time, did the *superbus tyrannus* and all the counsellors, *omnes consiliarii*, decide to call in the Saxons. Thus far Gildas. Bede substitutes *suo rege Uurtigerno*, 'their king Vortigern', for *superbus tyrannus*, 'pre-eminent ruler'. He adds a lengthy analysis of the newcomers into 'three very strong German peoples, the Saxons, Angles and Jutes', and identifies their continental homelands and the areas of Britain which they occupied. This is probably a piece of historical speculation on his part. He also gives the names of the first leaders, Hengist and Horsa, with their genealogy back to the pagan god Woden, and he mentions other details about them. Since the dynasty of Kent traced its descent from Hengist, we need have no doubt that these details which Bede adds to Gildas derive from the Kentish source which he acknowledged in the preface of the *Ecclesiastical History*. Though we may think that the earliest British evidence, that of the Easter Annals, weighs against the identification of the *superbus tyrannus* with Vortigern, and suggests that Bede has conflated two different 'comings of the Saxons', yet we can also accept that at this time Hengist and his followers were settled in Kent as allies against the Picts.

But when did this happen? Bede gives two slightly different reckonings. Referring to the fourteenth year of the emperor Maurice, that is 596, he says it was about 150 years after the coming of the English. Writing of events in 627, he says it was about 180 years after their arrival. Again, writing in AD 731, he says that it was about 285 years afterwards. These three computations give us a date of 446–7 for the *adventus Saxonum*. There seems little doubt that in reckoning this Bede had seized upon the one and only chronological pointer which he could find in Gildas: the third consulship of Aëtius in 446. Ignoring the famine, the British recovery, the period of prosperity, and the plague, which all supervened before the invitation to the English, he dated that to 446–7. But he had another date too. 'In the year 449' (correctly 450), he tells us: 'Marcian, taking up the rule with Valentinian, held it for seven years. In their time the Angles, invited by the Britons, came to Britain.' This would give a date 450–57 for their arrival. It is quite independent of Gildas and the confused reckoning which Bede based on the *De excidio*. Has it any support?

The account of the settlement of Kent which appears in the *Anglo-Saxon Chronicle* is partly based on Bede, but in many of its details it is independent. Under the year 449 it says: 'Mauricius and Valentines succeeded to the throne and ruled for seven years. In their days, Hengist and Horsa . . . came to Britain at the place called Ebbsfleet.' 'Ebbsfleet' certainly comes from a Kentish tradition which owes nothing to

Bede. It is also possible to suggest that the garbled forms Mauricius and Valentines, for Marcianus and Valentinianus, reflect an oral tradition strong enough to resist the written authority of Bede. If this view is correct, then Bede may have calculated his 450–57 date for the *adventus* on the basis of information from his Kentish source. Even if the names were already garbled when they came to him, his knowledge of imperial history was sound enough for him to recognize Valentines as Valentinianus, and then to correct Mauricius to Marcianus. There is a case here, then, for the establishment of Hengist in Kent a little after 450. Such a date is not incompatible with Gildas's story, for what this is worth.

The arguments which we have deployed allow us to think of three 'comings of the English': in 428 at the invitation of Vortigern, to an unknown area; in 440, in circumstances wholly unknown; and to Kent in about 450. If this is correct, then the further 'comings' related in the *Anglo-Saxon Chronicle* might seem to fit an established pattern. We must examine this in a moment, but before we do, we must follow out the story told by Gildas.

The Saxon revolt and its aftermath

According to Gildas, the Anglo-Saxons at first won a victory over the Picts. Inspired by this and enticed by the fertility of the island and the cowardice of its inhabitants, large-scale reinforcements came from Germany. They too were given land to settle and were paid as mercenaries against the Picts. But as the strength of these Germanic settlers increased, so they became a source of danger to their British hosts. Finally, indeed, they entered into an alliance with the Picts themselves, and set out upon a campaign of devastation which brought war and destruction across the whole island as far as the western sea. We need not follow here all the details of the Gildasian account: the cities overthrown, the citizens slaughtered in heaps or driven into the mountains. All this might pass as a highly-coloured account of the final breakdown of the authority of the romanized *civitates* and the scarcely less romanized *tyranni* who had invited the Saxons to Britain, and of the consequent seizure of power by ill-disciplined and barbaric warbands.

But Gildas adds one further detail which historians have not sufficiently noticed. After ravaging the island extensively, the 'cruel
brigands' did not settle down on the lands which they had traversed.
Instead, they returned home – '*recessissent domum crudelissimi prae-
dones*'. 'Home' in this context must mean the lands in the east on
which they had already been settled. In other words the clear implication of Gildas's phrase is that this had been a looting expedition, not a
land-taking. This runs completely counter to the received doctrine that
the revolt led forthwith to a phase of unchecked Saxon land-seizure.
Can we say that Gildas is now writing of a time so close to his own that
he is worthy of belief? This is doubtful. Even if we accept the earliest
possible date for the writing of the *De excidio*, and put the battle of
Badon and the birth of Gildas about AD 490, the Saxon revolt still
took place at least half a century before he was writing, and possibly
as much as a quarter of a century before he was even born.

The reason for asserting this lies in the sequel to the revolt, as
Gildas tells it. When the plundering parties had returned to their
settlements, the remnants of the Britons gradually took heart and at
last, under the leadership of the romanized Ambrosius Aurelianus,
engaged the enemy in a victorious battle. Gildas gives us no date for
this, and the only chronological fix that we have for Ambrosius is that
provided by the *computi* at the start of the Welsh Easter Annals. This,
as we have seen, dates the conflict of Ambrosius and Vitolinus, *Catguoloph*, to 437. If Ambrosius was already an eminent general by that
date it is unlikely that he saw active service after 475. The Saxon
revolt must therefore have occurred some time before that date. There
is therefore no reason to think that Gildas is a particularly trustworthy
witness here.

We have already learned of the events which, according to Gildas,
followed Ambrosius' victory (above, pp. 26–8). In a brief sentence
Gildas takes us from that first victory, through a campaign of fluctuating fortunes, up to the siege of Mount Badon. We have argued that
the phraseology does not allow us to infer, against the weight of later
tradition, that the victor of Badon was Ambrosius rather than Arthur.
But when all allowance is made for the chronological vagueness of the *De
excidio*, it is difficult to believe that there was any long interval between
the initial Ambrosian victory some time before 475, and the triumph

of Badon. If this view is sound, then it becomes difficult to think of Badon as late as 518. In other words, a consideration of the possible dates for Ambrosius leads us to favour the alternative earlier date for Badon, namely AD 490.

Before we consider the aftermath of that battle, we must look at certain other events which were taking place beyond the range of Gildas's interests and were probably outside his knowledge altogether: the settlements of Kent and Sussex. We have said already (above, p. 41) that the *Anglo-Saxon Chronicle* gives what seems to be a circumstantial account of these events, in which both persons and places are named. We have however suggested that the chronology here is artificial, and that the general tone is biased in favour of fire and slaughter simply because historical knowledge was preserved originally through the medium of heroic poetry, namely battle poems in Old English. But this is no reason why the factual elements should be dismissed as unreliable. If we strip off from the statements in the *Chronicle* those elements which are derived from Bede, we are left with a core of Anglo-Saxon oral tradition which is worth some attention.

The story opens with the landing of Hengist and Horsa at Ebbsfleet in Kent in the reign of Marcian and Valentinian (450–57). Shortly afterwards they fought King Vortigern at an unidentified place called *Ægelsthrep*, where Horsa was killed. Hengist and his son Æsc then began to reign. From this point Vortigern disappears, not surprisingly if we are right in thinking that his correct date is considerably earlier than the coming of Hengist and Horsa, and that he had only been introduced at this point as a result of Bede's mis-identification of the *superbus tyrannus*. Hengist and Æsc then fought the Britons at *Crea-canford*, another site which cannot readily be identified. We need not believe either that four thousand Britons were slain, or that the remnant abandoned Kent and fled in great fear to London, though this would chime well enough with Gildas's picture of the Saxon revolt. We are then told of two further battles, one at the unidentified *Wip-pedesfleot*, the second unlocated. Finally, Æsc succeeded to the kingdom, presumably on the death of Hengist.

If we turn now to Sussex, we find that the *Chronicle* account begins in the usual way with the coming of three ships, this time with Ælle and his three sons Cymen, Wlencing and Cissa. They landed near

Selsey Bill, slew many Britons, and drove others into the woods of the Weald, *Andredeslea*, named after the Saxon Shore fort of *Anderida*. They subsequently fought two more battles. The first, 'near the landing-place of the [unidentified] *Mearcredes* stream', is typical of the warfare of the period: a fight at a river crossing. But the second is one of the most remarkable battles recorded in this period in Britain, and the *Chronicle* account is worth giving in full: 'Ælle and Cissa beset the fort of Anderida and slew all that were therein and not one Briton was left alive.' In other words this barbarian host had successfully stormed a Saxon Shore fort whose walls, to judge from their present condition, were still standing up to the wall-walk and battlements [Pl. 1*b*].

Nothing has been said yet about the chronology of these events. Indeed it has been argued earlier that the dates given in this part of the *Chronicle* are at best unreliable, and perhaps largely artificial (above, p. 43). But this criticism needs to be tempered. First, we have seen that the reference to Marcian and Valentinian provides a credible starting point in the 450s for the whole series of events (above, p. 109). Second, it may have been possible to calculate Ælle's dates from a regnal list, so the chronicler may have had some basis for assuming the invasion of Sussex to be around 480. Third, the chronological scheme of the *Chronicle* may gain some support from the course of events across the English Channel.

The original task of the Count of the Saxon Shore had been to resist Saxon raiding and settlement on both sides of the Channel, for the expansion of the Saxons from their homeland between the Elbe and the Weser had led them to Gaul as well as to Britain. Place-names like Quentovic, and other evidence, make it clear that some settlement of the north Gaulish coastlands did take place. But in the second half of the fifth century the growing power of the Franks had put an end to this. In the 460s the Franks, as allies of the dying western empire, had expelled Saxon settlers from around Angers. After 486, when Clovis defeated the last Roman commander in Gaul and the Franks virtually inherited Roman power and responsibilities, there were no openings for other Germanic peoples. It is thought that this deflected further Saxon expansion to the northern shores of the Channel, so that the 480s saw the settlement of Sussex, while in the 490s another Saxon dynasty established itself at the head of Southampton Water. If this is so, then there is a broad credibility about the chronology of these years in the *Anglo-Saxon Chronicle*.

Just as no record of developments in Kent, Sussex and Hampshire occurs in Gildas, so likewise the battle of Badon and the other engagements of Arthur pass unnoticed in the *Chronicle*. This is interesting, because the *Chronicle* often gives quite credible names for British leaders.

Meanwhile we should not forget that at the same time as the various Germanic nations were settling in the south and east, new peoples and dynasties were becoming established in the north and west. But we have little or no contemporary evidence for this, and the events of the fifth century are perhaps best seen from the perspective of the mid-sixth. To that we now turn.

Five

The Historical Background, AD 490–634

The aftermath of Badon

Whether it was Arthur or Ambrosius who won the victory at Mount Badon, the testimony of Gildas is clear and credible as to the outcome of the battle. It was 'not the least slaughter of the hang-dogs', and also 'almost the last'. Thereafter foreign wars ceased, but not civil war: 'cessantibus externis bellis, sed non civilibus'. The foreign wars may be taken to mean the aggression of both the Picts and the Saxons, whereas among the civil wars may be reckoned that gueith Camlann in which Arthur and Medraut perished. According to Gildas, the cities which had been ruined during the Saxon revolt remained uninhabited. As for the citizens, they were at first chastened by the disasters which they had undergone, so that all 'kings, officials, private citizens, priests and churchmen' – 'reges, publici, privati, sacerdotes, ecclesiastici' – observed their proper place in society. But as those who had lived through the Saxon revolt gradually died, there succeeded a generation who knew only the present peace, 'praesentis tantum serenitatis experta'. Then the guidance of truth and justice was overthrown, so that scarcely even the memory remained. The result was the total dissolution of church and state. It was a denunciation of latter-day decadence which formed Gildas's principal reason for writing, so at this point he concludes his historical account in order to mount an attack on five British kings. We shall see shortly the importance of this for British history (below, pp. 121–2), but meanwhile we must inquire further about the aftermath of Badon.

Gildas certainly lays stress on the peace which followed Badon, in three telling phrases: 'almost the last slaughter', 'foreign wars ceasing', 'present serenity'. Sceptical though we must feel about most of his historical account, we cannot reasonably doubt him at this point. It is none the less fair to say that there is no direct historical evidence which provides corroboration. There is no mention of Badon in Anglo-Saxon sources independent of Bede, whose own account is of course based on Gildas. But this is not surprising, for the battle poems or other sources which lie behind the early entries in the *Anglo-Saxon Chronicle* were only interested in the victories won by the English. Moreover, the geographical range of the *Chronicle* in the fifth and sixth centuries is very severely restricted, and Badon, whether it was fought at Bath or elsewhere, could easily have lain outside that range.

As it happens there are some indirect indications that the Anglo-Saxon settlers, or at least some of them, had suffered a reverse in the early sixth century. A late ninth-century continental writer, Rudolf of Fulda, has an account of Saxons arriving near the mouth of the Elbe from Britain, apparently around 530. The historical value of this story has been questioned; but the occurrence in north Germany and the Low Countries of some English-looking pottery and brooches may add substance to it. At least it seems possible that there was some back-wash of settlers from the insecurely held fringes of the Anglo-Saxon area.

Is there any corresponding evidence from England – as we may now reasonably call the eastern parts of Britain? The difficulty here is of course that we lack any large number of closely dated settlements, or even of settlements at all. Given a continuous series of datable sites or objects we might be able to say 'The English had penetrated up to such a line by the early sixth century; they were then held to that line – or even forced to pull back from it – for half a century.' If such archaeological observations could be made they would fit very well Gildas's account of the results of Badon. There is indeed good reason to hope that a refined typological study of the large numbers of orna-mented pots from pagan Saxon cemeteries will eventually provide just the evidence needed for such observations. Already it is possible to suggest, for instance, that in the upper Thames valley the sequence of pottery styles was dislocated in the early sixth century. This was an area which had received settlers very early and by the second half of the fifth century it was the centre of a flourishing Anglo-Saxon culture. But it was also sufficiently far forward to have suffered from a British resurgence under Ambrosius and Arthur; and it may be that this is what the break in the pottery sequence reflects.

The early history of Wessex[1]

In one area of great importance for the future, the victory of Badon appears not to have restrained the invaders. In 495, according to the *Anglo-Saxon Chronicle*, two *ealdormen* ('chieftains'), Cerdic and his son Cynric, came to Britain with five ships and landed apparently on the shore of Southampton Water. In 501 they were reinforced by Port and his two sons, who seized land around Portsmouth, and in 514 they seem to have gained further reinforcements led by Stuf and Wihtgar. Battles were fought in 508, 514, 519, 527, and 530. In this last one the Isle of Wight was captured. But the *Chronicle* provides no evidence that the *Cerdicingas*, the followers of Cerdic, penetrated more than twenty miles inland until 552, when Cynric advanced to Salisbury and defeated the Britons. Four years later Cynric and his son Ceawlin were fighting at *Beranbyrig*, Barbury Castle in Wiltshire, over fifty miles inland. From that date we can count the dynasty of Cerdic as firmly established in southern Britain.

The *Chronicle* account which we have just summarized can be criticized on several counts. We have already noticed (above, p. 43) that the chronology is artificial and unreliable. Despite this, the dates given in the *Chronicle* have been quoted here in order to provide a rough time table for events, without any thought that they are accurate. To take a specific point: Cynric apparently lived until 560 when he was succeeded by Ceawlin; if this date is even approximately correct it seems highly unlikely that Cynric was a warrior, let alone a chieftain, as early as 495. A possible solution of this difficulty may be found by abandoning altogether the pre-Conversion dates and recalculating the accessions of Wessex rulers on the basis of the regnal list preserved in one version of the *Chronicle*. If we accept that the dates of Cynegils, the first Wessex king to be converted, were probably entered correctly in an Easter Table, and then work backwards from his accession in AD 611, we arrive at 523 as a possible date for the landing of Cerdic and Cynric, and 571 for the succession of Ceawlin. But it scarcely needs stressing that we have no real basis for preferring our own calculations from regnal lists to those made by early Wessex chroniclers and annalists.

A second major difficulty in accepting the *Chronicle* account of the conquest of Wessex is that some of the names in it appear to have been invented to explain pre-existing place-names. Thus Port doubtless took his name from the harbour of the Solent – *port* in Old English, the *Magnus Portus* of Ptolemy, and something like *port* or *Porth* on British lips too. Wihtgar's name seems to have been invented in response to the Isle of Wight, already known as Vectis (and pronounced Wectis) by the Romano-Britons. It is even possible that Stuf and Wihtgar merely duplicate Cerdic and Cynric as a result of some blunder on the part of the chronicler. But despite these criticisms, and without putting any confidence in the detailed chronology, we can nevertheless believe that at the end of the fifth century or early in the sixth a small band of Saxon adventurers landed on the south Hampshire coast. For some decades they achieved little more than the conquest of Wight and the securing of a bridgehead on the mainland, but in the second half of the sixth century they erupted into the heartland of Wessex.

How do these events fit the idea of a signal British victory won at Badon and followed by nearly half a century of peace? One possibility is that it was the fear engendered among the English by the slaughter of Badon which held the *Cerdicingas* to their beach-head for about fifty years. But if we accept the date of 490 for Badon, and one of 495 or later for the landing in Hampshire, then it is equally possible that this group of adventurers, coming to an area remote from the main region of early settlement, were quite unaffected by the check which other Anglo-Saxon peoples had suffered. How, then, may we account for the series of Wessex battles which span the period of supposed peace? We know about the battles because of the happy accident that it was the dynasty of Cerdic which compiled a detailed history in the *Anglo-Saxon Chronicle*, and naturally enough paid most attention to its own origins. In default of other sources, we cannot know whether in other parts of England too there was continued skirmishing in the first half of the sixth century. But it seems most likely that it was the relative remoteness and insignificance of these events in southern Hampshire which allowed Gildas to remain ignorant of them.

However restrained their early activity may have been, once the *Cerdicingas* had passed north of Salisbury they began a campaign of aggressive expansion directed against both the Britons and their fellow Anglo-Saxons. Against the Britons their most important victory was the battle of Dyrham in 577, in which they slew three kings and captured the walled towns of Gloucester, Cirencester and Bath, thereby cutting off the West Wealas of the south-west from the Britons of Wales. But in 568 their enemy had been Æthelberht of Kent, whom they had put to flight. In 571, after fighting the Britons at the unidentified *Biedcanford*, they had captured four settlements with wholly English names: Eynsham, Bensington, Aylesbury and Limbury. It has been suggested that this operation, from the Thames valley along the scarp slope of the Chilterns, was aimed at the elimination of a British enclave based on the Chilterns. But the distribution of early pagan cemeteries suggests that if there was such an enclave it was centred rather on *Verulamium*, with the northern Chilterns as its north-western boundary. The Vale of Aylesbury and the upper Thames valley, on the other hand, were settled by the Anglo-Saxons at a very early date; and whatever disruption these settlements had suffered after Badon (above, p. 115), it seems possible that in 571 Ceawlin and Cutha were really engaged in asserting their control over fellow-Englishmen. In 584, on the other hand, they were once again fighting the Britons, this time in north Oxfordshire. In brief, the history of the foundation of Wessex is that of a dynasty pushing inland from the south coast to establish itself over both Britons and fellow-English in the Thames valley.

This process was not without its reverses. In the campaign of 584 Cutha was killed; and though Ceawlin captured many *tuns* and great spoils, yet he returned to his own land 'in wrath'. And in 592 there was a great slaughter at Woden's Barrow in north Wiltshire, and Ceawlin was driven out. Cryptic references like this, together with certain inconsistencies in the genealogies, suggest that there was a struggle for power in Wessex, if not within the dynasty itself. And the location of Woden's Barrow a mile south of Wansdyke [Pl. 13] reminds us that this great earthwork possibly played a part in the military struggles between the *Cerdicingas* and the upper Thames Saxons on the one hand, and between English and Britons on the other (below, pp. 349–50). But the century ended triumphantly: in 597 'Ceolwulf began to reign in Wessex, and he continually fought and contended against the English, against the Britons, against the Picts and against the Scots.'

The other English kingdoms

Only in the case of Wessex can we present a reasonably detailed and consecutive account of the history of a dynasty from the landing of its founders down to the seventh century; and that only because it was at the Wessex court that the most systematic historical record, the *Anglo-Saxon Chronicle*, was compiled. For the other kingdoms we are dependent at first on slight references in the *Chronicle* or in Bede's *Ecclesiastical History*, or on the doubtful framework of genealogies compiled principally in the late eighth century or later. Thus for Kent we have references to Æthelberht (560–616), principally because it was in his day that the mission of St Augustine arrived. For Essex we have a brief notice of Sæberht, partly because he was Æthelberht's nephew. For East Anglia we have rather fuller references to the great King Rædwald, principally because he impinged on Northumbrian history by acting as host to Edwin of Northumbria when he was in exile. In general, evidence of this kind is quite inadequate for us to trace the steps by which the kingdoms of the English – Kent, Sussex, Essex, East Anglia and Mercia, to say nothing of Lindsey and Middle Anglia – came into being.

Fortunately we are better served in the case of the most important kingdom, Northumbria – unless indeed it merely appears to be the most important because the sources for its early history are so rich.[2] Bede himself supplies a fully detailed account for the seventh century, as well as some material for the sixth. The *Anglo-Saxon Chronicle*, especially in its northern version, provides several references, though the kings that it mentions in the second half of the sixth century cannot be reconciled with an eighth-century regnal list of which we have two versions. This should warn us that all the chronology here is debatable. The northern material in the *Historia Brittonum* provides information which supplements or contradicts Bede, and finally the Easter Annals of the *British Historical Miscellany* provide a date for the important battle of Chester which Bede left undated. From all this a tolerably coherent account can be built up.

The history of Northumbria begins in 547, when Ida began to rule. From the *Chronicle* we learn that he built *Bebbanburh*, Bamburgh, which was enclosed at first with a 'hedge' – presumably an earthen

rampart – and afterwards with a wall. This is a very remarkable statement, the only reference to a defensive work built by the Anglo-Saxons
in the settlement phase. A garbled phrase in some manuscripts of the
Historia Brittonum tells us furthermore that he joined Deira and Bernicia. This statement conceals the long prehistory of Northumbria,
which archaeology is now beginning to uncover. Very briefly, we can
say that Deira, roughly the land from Hadrian's Wall to the Humber,
received some of the earliest English settlers in the form of Germanic
soldiers in the service of the Roman empire. Settlements which had
begun in the late fourth century continued, and presumably expanded,
in the fifth. Meanwhile north of Hadrian's Wall the old client kingdom
of the Votadini continued to hold eastern Britain up to the Firth of
Forth and beyond. This situation lasted for almost a century and a
half, until Ida used Deira as a springboard for an assault on his
northern neighbour, in which the first move was the establishment of a
fortified beach-head at Bamburgh.

The expansion from that beach-head was bitterly contested, as the
Historia Brittonum makes clear. Some time after Ida's landing, 'Outi-
gern fought bravely against the race of the English.' Later still four
kings are said to have fought against the Angles – Urbgen or Urien of
Rheged, Riderch 'the Old', Guallauc and Morcant. Among the
Angles, Theodric is mentioned as fighting bravely against Urbgen and
his sons. Reckoning from the regnal list, Theodric appears to have
reigned 571–8, and this is perhaps within a year or two of being
correct. Sometimes the enemy and sometimes the citizens (that is, the
Britons) were victorious – perhaps a conscious echo of Gildas. Urbgen
besieged Theodric for three days and three nights on the island of
Lindisfarne; but while he was on that expedition he was done to
death at the instigation of Morcant, who was jealous of his renown.
All this we can reconstruct from the cryptic notices, derived from
regnal lists and Easter Annals, which came to be incorporated in the
Historia Brittonum. Finally, if we regard the *Gododdin* poem as referring to an actual historical event, it shows that a military expedition
starting from the region of Edinburgh might completely by-pass the
infant kingdom of Bernicia in order to strike at the Angles in the heart
of Deira. Admittedly the expedition was disastrous; but presumably it
set out with hopes of success.

The accession of Æthelfrith towards the end of the sixth century finally consolidated the Anglian hold on Bernicia as well as Deira, and ensured that Northumbria was to be the dominant power in northern Britain. To the British he was Æthelfrith *Flesaur*, 'the Twister', but to Bede he was 'very valiant, most avid for glory'; he more than any other king of the English ravaged the Britons, and settled or conquered more of their lands, having exterminated or subjugated the native inhabitants. His first great recorded victory was over Aedan mac Gabran, king of the Dalriadic Scots, who, alarmed at his success, led an army against him. This was virtually annihilated at Degsastan in 603, and thereafter no Scottish king dared challenge Northumbria. No less important was his advance into western Britain; but this we must defer until we have outlined the early history of the British kingdoms.

Celtic kingdoms of the west and north

We have now traced something of the events which led to the formation of the English kingdoms in eastern and southern Britain. For the whole of midland England there is a blank until the appearance of Penda of Mercia in the 630s. Much of what we know about him derives in any case from his alliance with Gwynedd against Northumbria, two areas about which we are tolerably well informed. It is necessary to stress how utterly ignorant we are about what was happening over much of central Britain. It is only when we reach the west and the north that the picture clarifies a little.

Section C of the *De excidio* presents us with some information about the political organization of the west about the middle of the sixth century in the form of a diatribe aimed at five reigning kings. Their status had already been summarized by Gildas: '*Reges habet Britannia, sed tyrannos.*' ('Kings Britain has, but usurpers [or despots].') The justification of this taunt must be examined later (below, p. 320), but meanwhile we may list the five. They are: Constantinus, 'tyrannical whelp of the unclean Damnonian lioness'; Aurelius Caninus ('the Dog'), 'whelp of the lion'; Vortiporius, usurper of Dyfed; Cuneglasus, 'in the Roman tongue tawny butcher'; and Maglocunus, 'dragon of the isles'. Maglocunus is already known to us (above, pp. 22–3 and pp. 37–8) as Maelgwn of Gwynedd or north-west Wales.

Cuneglasus (whose British name in fact means 'Blue Hound', not 'tawny butcher') is found in the Welsh genealogies in the *British Historical Miscellany* as Cinglas, and has the same grandfather as Maelgwn. Gildas himself places Vortiporius in Dyfed, and, assuming that the list is arranged in some geographical order Aurelius Caninus probably ruled in south-east Wales or the lower Severn. His name has led to the suggestion that he may belong to the family of Ambrosius Aurelianus, and may be one of those degenerate descendants of Ambrosius who are referred to elsewhere by Gildas, but the case is far from convincing. Finally, Constantinus is probably to be placed in Dumnonia, though it should not be overlooked that in Ptolemy's *Geography* the Damnonii inhabited the Forth-Clyde isthmus, and doubtless formed the basis for the Kingdom of Strathclyde.

About two of these dynasties we have enough information to form hypotheses about how they came into being. In the case of Vortipor we have an inscription which is generally accepted as his epitaph [Pl. 27]. This is on a rough pillar of stone (below, pp. 243-4) which formerly stood at Castell Dwyran, on the borders of Carmarthenshire and Pembrokeshire, some three miles from the traditional court of Dyfed at Narberth. Around the edge of the stone is a name in the Irish script and the Old Irish language: *Votecorigas*, '[the memorial] of Votecorix'. On the face of the stone, below a ring cross, is inscribed in good Roman capitals: MEMORIA VOTEPORIGIS PROTICTORIS, 'the *memoria* of Votepor *Protector*'. The first and last of these words are technical terms which must be explained rather than translated. *Memoria* would normally be understood to mean a shrine or monument to a saint or martyr, but this is difficult to square with Gildas's description of Votepor as 'debaucher' and worse. As for *protector*, this was an official Roman rank or title, given to a cadre of officer-cadets who formed the imperial bodyguard. There can be no doubt that Votepor never served in this way, but there is evidence that his dynasty maintained a hazy memory that one of his ancestors had been a *protector*, and the title may have been appropriated as though it were a hereditary one.

The evidence for this comes from the genealogy preserved in the *British Historical Miscellany*, but before we examine it we must reckon with the fact that two discrepant genealogies are known for the dynasty.

An Irish tale, *The expulsion of the Dessi*, gives an account of the migration of the tribe, usually known as the Dési, from southern Ireland to Dyfed under a certain Eochaid mac Artchorp or Eochaid *Allmuir*, 'from overseas'.[3] This Irish account also includes a genealogy from Eochaid through Guortepir mac Aircol – Vortipor son of Agricola – in the fifth generation to Teuder son of Regin in the fourteenth generation. The Welsh version of the genealogy agrees with the Irish version back to Vortipor's grandfather, but before that it is garbled and even fictitious. But among the garbled or impossible names we find the three generations *Maxim guletic map Protec map Protector*, and it is not unreasonable to suggest that this enshrines a memory that Magnus Maximus (*Maxim guletic*) played some part in the founding of the dynasty, and that some early member of it had borne the title *Protector*.

When was the dynasty of the Dési likely to have been founded in Dyfed? It used to be thought that this occurred about 270, on the grounds that the events which led up to their expulsion from Ireland are dated to 265 in the Irish *Annals of the Four Masters*. This, it was claimed, could be cross-checked by dead-reckoning from the genealogy, for 'taking a generation as thirty-three years and starting with the year AD 270, a simple calculation brings us to AD 730 as the time when Teuder mac Regin must have reigned', a date which is 'fully confirmed' by that of Meredydd ap Teuder who died, according to the Welsh Easter Annals, in 796 (correctly, 798). It need scarcely be said that the Irish Annals are unhistorical in a period as early as 265; and second, that this is a naïve use of genealogical data. Even within its own terms of reference it can be shown to be wrong, because the same 'simple calculation' of thirty-three-year generations starting from AD 270 would give us a date around 435 for Vortipor – and such a date is incompatible with his mention in the *De excidio*. Once we have rejected the case that the migration took place in the late third century, we would be foolish to attempt to recalculate it from the genealogy on the basis of some other arbitrary 'generation length'.

The recent tendency has been to place the migration of the Dési at the very end of the fourth or beginning of the fifth century, and to see it as a response to the evacuation of the Welsh frontier by Magnus Maximus in 383. In other words the Irish, who had long been raiding the Welsh coasts, found that there was no longer any formal opposition to them, so they moved into the vacuum. The genealogy, however, suggests that the Romans played a positive, not a negative role here. Vortipor's father had the Roman name Agricola. Even more interesting, in both the Welsh and Irish versions of the genealogy Agricola's father was Triphun, a name which is almost certainly derived from the Latin *tribunus*. The most normal meaning of *tribunus* is 'commander' of a military unit, usually a cohort of infantry. It is very tempting to think that it could be the title appropriate to the commander of a force of Irish irregulars, a *numerus Dessorum* in this instance, recruited to guard south-west Wales. Examination of the late Roman army list, the *Notitia Dignitatum*, shows however that the commander of a unit of this kind would have been a *praepositus*, not a *tribunus*. It can also be said that the rank of *protector* would be quite inappropriate for such a command. Nevertheless the genealogy of Dyfed does suggest some familiarity with Roman military titles.

If we accept the occurrence of *Maxim guletic* in the genealogy as based on some memory of historical events, we may frame the following hypotheses. Knowing that his bid for the empire would involve the withdrawal of troops from Britain, Magnus Maximus made preparations for the defence of the most vulnerable areas. To Dyfed, an area which probably already had Irish connections, he brought the Desian chieftain, Eochaid mac Artchorp, as the leader of a *numerus* which was composed principally of Eochaid's war-band. In view of the obvious dangers in setting a thief to catch a thief, and following both Celtic and Roman precedents, Maximus took one of Eochaid's sons with him, ostensibly as one of his bodyguard, in fact as a hostage. This son would almost certainly have had the title of *protector* in Maximus' court, and he might have returned to Dyfed to the title of *tribunus* in both senses – 'commander' and 'chieftain'. Even if the whole of this hypothesis is rejected as speculative, not to say fanciful, it cannot be denied that the combined weight of the two genealogies and of Vortipor's tombstone argue for strong Roman or romanized influences in the foundation of the Irish-derived dynasty of Dyfed.

The same claim has been made about the dynasties of north-west Wales, represented by Maelgwn and Cinglas. According to the genealogies in the *British Historical Miscellany*, these two are descended through a common grandfather from a certain Cunedag or Cunedda, whose position in both genealogies is that of great-grandfather to the two contemporary rulers. One of the Venedotian entries in the *Historia Brittonum* tells us that

Maelgwn ruled as a great king among the Britons, that is in the region of Gwynedd, because his *atavus*, that is Cunedag, with his sons, eight in number, came previously from the northern part, that is from the region which is called Manau Guotodin one hundred and forty six years before Maelgwn ruled and expelled the Scots [i.e. the Irish] with a very great slaughter from these regions [presumably Gwynedd] and they [presumably the Irish] never returned again to dwell there.

Although the *Historia Brittonum* as we have it is a compilation of the ninth century, the primitive spelling *Cunedag* argues that an appreciably earlier written source underlies this passage.

At the end of the Welsh genealogies the *British Historical Miscellany* gives us further information about Cunedda and his sons:

These are the names of the sons of Cuneda of whom the number was 9. Typipaun [for Typiaun] the first born who died in the region called Manau Guodotin and did not come hither with his father and aforesaid brothers; Meriaun his son shared the land with his [i.e. Typiaun's] brothers. 2 Osmail, 3 Rumaun, 4 Dunaut, 5 Ceretic, 6 Abloyc, 7 Enniaun Girt [grandfather of Maelgwn and Cinglas], 8 Docmail, 9 Etern.

This is their boundary, from the river which is called Dubr Duiu [the Dee] up to another river Tebi [the Teifi] and they hold many regions in western Britain.

Finally, in an early section of the *Historia Brittonum*, which presents a largely fictitious account of the peopling of the British Isles, we are told that the sons of the Irishman Liethan obtained land 'in Dyfed and in Gower and Kidwelly until they were driven out by Cunedda and his sons from all parts of Britain'.

These are the documents, and in some cases early ones at that. What historical account can we make from them? It should be said at the outset that some scholars would regard the whole account of Cunedda's sons as a confection, or at best as a piece of antiquarian speculation about the origins of certain Welsh place-names. According to this view, Ceretic comes into the story to explain Ceredigion (Cardiganshire), Dunaut to explain Dunoding (the district around Tre-madoc Bay), Etern for Edeyrnion (north-east Wales), and so on. In other words, the personal names and the story connected with them are supposed to be back-formations from the place-names. But against this it can be asserted first, that names like Ceretic and Etern are well attested as personal names; and second, that Welsh territorial names were regularly formed by adding possessive or territorial suffixes, *-ing* or *-iog*, to personal names. There is nothing inherently improbable about part of west Wales being called Ceredigion after an early ruler Ceretic, nor is there any reason why the account of Cunedda and his sons should be anything other than a record of fact.

In essence, the story is one of a British warrior-chief and his *teulu*, his personal following, consisting of his sons and his war-band (below, p. 324; p. 337), who moved from one part of Britain to another in a military operation designed to expel a barbarian invader, in this case the Irish. Such movements can be readily attested in other parts of the empire in the later fourth and the fifth centuries. There is no serious dispute about where Cunedda came from. Manau Guotodin – to dis-tinguish it from Manaw, the Isle of Man – was a small district around the head of the Firth of Forth, on the northern limits of the tribal region or kingdom of the Guotodin, Gododdin, or Votadini. And it is equally clear that he obtained possession of west Wales as far south as the Teifi, and that he may even have engaged in military operations in the coastal districts of the south, if we accept the *Historia Brittonum*'s statement about the expulsion of the Irish from Gower and Kidwelly.

When this took place is a matter of dispute, because the evidence is itself contradictory. The genealogies make Cinglas and Maelgwn the great-grandsons of Cunedda. It is unlikely that 146 years should span a mere four generations. On the conventional reckoning of thirty years to a generation, Maelgwn should have flourished between 90 and 120 years after Cunedda. It can be argued that even this interval is too long, because the thirty-year generation seems quite unrealistically long in the conditions of fifth- and sixth-century Britain. Against this, other scholars have produced examples of very long generations, even in warring societies such as that of the bedouin Arabs. The apparent precision of the figure 'one hundred and forty-six years' has a strong attraction. Because it is spelt out in our source – *Centu* [m] *quadraginta sex*, not *cxlvi* – it is difficult to claim that there has been a scribal error, and then manipulate the figures, as scholars delight to do, to produce for instance *cxxi*, 121 years. On the other hand, we are entitled to ask how such a figure could have been calculated retrospectively from Maelgwn's reign back to Cunedda's migration. The answer might lie in a regnal list, but we have already seen that these must be used with caution. To some extent the figure of 146 may be defended against the genealogies by reference once again to the *Historia Brittonum*. Cunedda is described there as the *atavus* of Maelgwn. The word has two meanings: either, in a general sense, 'ancestor', or, more specifically, 'great-great-great-grandfather'. If we could believe that this second use was intended here, it would imply that two generations had dropped out of the genealogies, which is not an impossible happening. It would also make the period of one hundred and forty-six years appear very probable. If we accept this, for the moment, when does it place Cunedda?

Here we come to the final problem. From what date is the 146 to be counted? In other words, when did Maelgwn start to reign? In fact we have no evidence whatsoever to decide this, and the only dating evidence for Maelgwn is that given in the Welsh Easter Annals for his death. But we have already seen that this date, 549, cannot be reconciled with the date which the same source gives for the battle of Badon (above, p. 54), or with other evidence which suggests that Maelgwn survived into the second half of the century. If, however, we take 549 as our one fixed point, and allow Maelgwn to have ruled for twenty years before his death, and then subtract a further 146 years, we arrive at 549 − 166 = 383 as a possible date for Cunedda's migration. The figure is almost too good to be true. It would imply either that Cunedda had been brought into north-west Wales, as Eochaid *Allmuir* appears to have been planted in south-west Wales, as an act of policy by Magnus Maximus, or that he had moved into the vacuum created by the withdrawal of Roman garrisons from Segontium and other forts in that area.

Within the limits of the available dates and figures, this argument cannot readily be refuted, but it has the overriding weakness that it does not account for the traditions preserved in two places in the *Historia Brittonum*, that Cunedda expelled the Irish from the regions which he and his sons took over. It is very difficult to believe that there could have been any Irish settlement in Gwynedd as long as Segontium was held, and it is altogether more likely that the Scotti whom Cunedda drove out had arrived after 383. If, then, we reject this date, the chronology becomes completely fluid. Taking the extreme opposite position, we might think that Maelgwn began to reign about 550, and that he was preceded by three generations each of about twenty years, so $550 - (3 \times 20) = 490$ for Cunedda's migration. If on the other hand we accept that Maelgwn died in 549, then a date nearer the mid-point of the fifth century becomes possible.

These chronological problems have occupied the attention of many scholars, but no certainty has been attained or is even likely. They have been discussed at length here for a variety of reasons. First, they present a typical example of the chronological difficulties which beset the study of the period, even when we are dealing with undoubted historical figures. Second, they have important implications in the field of interpretation. If Cunedda's migration took place about 380, then it was an act of Roman policy; if it occurred around 450, it may have been organized by some sub-Roman authority like that which brought in the Anglo-Saxons as allies; but if it was as late as 490 it was certainly an act of private enterprise, perhaps inspired by Pictish pressure. Whichever of these hypotheses is correct they are all, of course, in perfect accord with the events of the Migration Period throughout Europe. Third, this close attention to the dynasty of Maelgwn is justified by the prominent place which it occupied in sixth- and seventh-century Britain.

Before we describe the later history of the dynasty we should briefly look back to the generations before Cunedda. We need not follow the genealogy back to 'Anna, whom they say was the cousin of the Virgin Mary'. What matters is that Cunedda's great-great-grandfather, and the earlier generations in so far as they appear to be historical, bear Pictish names. This is not surprising, given the position of Manau Guotodin on the southern borders of Pictland. But the three generations which are immediately ancestral to Cunedda all have Roman names: his father was Aeternus, his grandfather *Patern Pesrut*, Paternus of the Red Robe, and his great-grandfather was Tacitus. This has led to much speculation about the character of the Roman influences which had made such names fashionable in this rather remote family. In particular it has been suggested that Paternus' red robe or cloak was a mark of some romanized authority or office, or at least of recognition by the Romans. Attempts have even been made to calculate back by dead-reckoning from an assumed date for Cunedda to that of his grandfather; and then to speculate on which emperor had bestowed this recognition on Paternus, as part of what particular act of policy in the north. Two observations are necessary here. First, in view of our complete uncertainty about the date of Cunedda we have no basis for speculations about his grandfather's chronology or possible relations with Rome. Second, if we accept that Manau Guotodin was a small district around the head of the Firth of Forth, largely north of the Antonine Wall, it is difficult to believe that the Romans had any serious interest or influence as far north as this by the middle of the fourth century.

Dyfed and Gwynedd are the only two kingdoms in western Britain in which we can trace dynastic origins with any degree of confidence. It is true that the *Historia Brittonum* attributes the founding of the Powysian dynasty to St Germanus, and relates how Ambrosius gave lands further south to Pascent, son of Vortigern. The first of these is incredible, and the second at least dubious. In northern Britain, we have fitful glimpses of eminent rulers such as Coroticus or Ceretic of Strathclyde, who had been slave-raiding among St Patrick's Irish converts; or Urien of Rheged, whom we have seen besieging Theodric of Bernicia on Lindisfarne, and who is more fully known to us in the poems of Taliesin; or other princes of the British 'Heroic Age' who appear briefly and factually in the 'Northern British History', and who feature more colourfully in Welsh poetry. Mention has already been made of the possibility that the dynasty of Galloway was one of those established by Magnus Maximus on the eve of his usurpation. The evidence lies in one of the genealogies in the *British Historical Miscellany* which begins with *Maxim guletic* 'who killed Gratian King of the Romans'. Only one person in the genealogy has been identified: tenth in descent from Maximus was Mermin who, according to the *Annals of Ulster*, was slain either in Man or in Ulster in 682. Despite the absence of other points of reference, it has been suggested that the dynasty belonged originally to Galloway and was expelled thence by the Angles in the mid-sixth century. Even this shaky framework of evidence and inference is lacking for the foundation of the other northern British dynasties, though the *British Historical Miscellany* has often preserved their genealogies.[4]

North of the British princedoms lay Pictland and, from the fifth century, the nascent kingdom of the Dalriadic Scots. These areas are peripheral to our main theme, and need not detain us long. When we consider the pressure which the Picts had exerted on Roman Britain, and the part which, according to Gildas, they continued to play in the fifth century, it is quite remarkable that there is no evidence for Pictish folk-movement or territorial expansion in the Migration Period. It is perhaps equally remarkable that the evidence of history, of place-names and of archaeology should all concur to support the hypothesis that the Antonine Wall remained roughly the southern border of Pictland. North of that line the Picts may have been broadly divided into a northern and a southern group but it is not clear whether these terms used by Bede reflect merely a geographical distribution or whether they mark a political division as well. Certainly in Bede's day, and even as early as the reign of Bridei son of Maelcon in the late sixth century, the Picts appear to have comprised a united kingdom. We have shadowy scenes of them at war with the Strathclyde Britons, the Angles of Northumbria, and the Scots of Dalriada. Against the first two they could certainly maintain themselves, and they inflicted notable defeats upon their Dalriadic enemies too; but in the long term the dominion of Scotland north of the Antonine Wall was to be with the Scots.

The kingdom of Dalriada had been founded, presumably at the expense of the Picts, by migrants from north-east Ireland to the west coast of Scotland. Irish annals provide us with some possibly contemporary notices of events in Scotland, and we can check these in part from genealogies and from material which ultimately goes back to regnal lists. For one important phase of Dalriadic history we also have Adomnan's *Life of Columba*, composed nearly a hundred years after Columba's death, and more interesting as a specimen of hagiography than as a historical source.

According to early sources, the actual Dalriadic invasion of Argyll was the work of a band of only a hundred and fifty men, led by the sons of Erc: Fergus, Loarn and Aengus. It has been suggested that so small a force could only have established itself with the aid or at least the connivance of the Britons of Strathclyde and this has been taken to imply a deliberate anti-Pictish alliance between the Britons and the Scots. But two points should be remembered here. Argyll was remote from the main centres of Pictish power. And military bodies of this size are clearly implied by the invasion stories in the *Anglo-Saxon Chronicle*. Either a force like this was militarily effective, or else the figures of our texts – one hundred and fifty men, three keels, and similar figures – are literary conventions with no historical significance (below, pp. 335–6). In either case there is no real weight in the hypothesis of an alliance betseen Strathclyde and Dalriada.

The date of the invasion is in dispute. The *Annals of Tigernach* place it in 501; but the genealogies suggest that this may be forty years too late. On the other hand, given the possibility that an Easter Table may lie behind the date in the Annals, this is to be preferred to dead-reckoning from genealogies. By the late sixth century the line descended from Fergus mac Erc had come to dominance in the person of Aedan mac Gabran, the friend and patron of St Columba. His principal stronghold was the rocky citadel of Dunadd [Pl. 4*b*] on the Crinan Isthmus (below, p. 267). Aedan embarked on a policy of campaigning towards the south and east, presumably in the interests of territorial expansion, though this cannot be taken as certain, given the nature of contemporary warfare (below, pp. 340–3). He won a victory against the 'Miathi', probably in southern Pictland, but lost 303 men, including two of his sons, Artuir and Echoid Find, in the battle. Late in his reign, in 603 according to the *Anglo-Saxon Chronicle*, he was moved to challenge the rising power of Æthelfrith of Northumbria. But the result was the disastrous battle at *Degsastan*, probably Dawston in Liddesdale. Admittedly Æthelfrith's brother Theodbald was slain with all his troops; but according to Northumbrian sources Aedan lost almost all his army. Adomnan adds the information that Domingart, Aedan's son, was killed 'in martial carnage in England'. It is not surprising that Bede could add that 'from that time to this [that is, 731] no king of the Scots in Britain has dared to come against the English in battle'.

We have now outlined political events in Britain down to the end of the sixth century. At that time the arrival of Christian missionaries among the Anglo-Saxons brought a new element into society. Before we examine the situation which developed in the early seventh century we must trace the history of Christianity up to the coming of Augustine to Kent.

Early Christianity in Britain[5]

Any account of the origins and early development of Christianity in Britain must start with a paradox, or at least with a conflict of evidence. When we look for archaeological evidence there is indeed very little in the way of monuments or other remains of Christianity in the last century of Roman Britain. The available material evidence suggests rather a strongly flourishing Celtic paganism. The verbal evidence, on the other hand, favours a contrary conclusion. There is no suggestion in the *Life* of St Germanus that he had to combat paganism as well as refute heresy in Britain. In the following century, Gildas found it necessary to attack the failings of a mature church which had become decadent rather than those of a young evangelizing body. These are positive pointers, albeit indirect, and they must count for more than the negative argument from archaeology (see also below, pp. 171-2).

In fact other verbal evidence makes it clear that the spread of Christianity to Britain goes back into the third century if not earlier. Reliable traditions about the British martyrs Alban of Verulamium and Julian and Aaron of Caerleon show that there were Christian communities in southern Britain before the conversion of Constantine. Immediately thereafter three British bishops attended the council of Arles in 314, while bishops from Britain are also known to have been present at the Council of Rimini in 359. It seems likely that the three at Arles were the metropolitan bishops from three out of the four provinces into which Britain was divided at that time. The existence of bishops implies that the island had been incorporated within the normal framework of ecclesiastical organization in which each city had its own bishop. This system was admirably suited to the Mediterranean world, and also to the more romanized parts of Britain, in which there were a number of 'cities' or *civitas* capitals – though doubtless not the twenty-eight mentioned by Gildas. What is more difficult to see is how the less-romanized regions of the west and north, where towns and cities were unknown, could be fitted into the scheme. It may be the unconformity in western Britain and Ireland which facilitated the rise of a monastic organization there at the expense of the diocesan system.

How well did the diocesan system survive? In the west the presence of bishops is certainly attested in the sixth century both by Gildas and by contemporary inscriptions, but we may doubt the strength of their disciplinary powers and the rigidity of their territorial organization. In the east, the areas of English settlement, the picture is altogether obscure. It may be noticed that Germanus' *Life* makes no mention of bishops in Britain itself, nor is the issue of Pelagianism debated in a regular synod. But it is inconceivable that cities and diocese were not continuing side by side at the time of Germanus' first visit. The absence of any mention of British bishops must represent an omission on the part of Germanus' biographer rather than any authentic historical fact. In the long term, however, it does seem significant that there is no evidence for British Christianity surviving, or influencing the Anglo-Saxons in southern or eastern England. The basis for this judgement is not merely Bede's statement that the Britons never preached the gospel to the Anglo-Saxons who inhabited Britain with them. This might be dismissed as prejudice. But what seems clear is that in the area of English settlement there were no remaining congregations of British Christians to welcome either the Augustinian or the Celtic missions. Again, we hear of churches being restored in the late sixth and seventh centuries, but only once, in the case of St Martin's, Canterbury, is there even a dubious hint that worship may have been continuous from the fourth century to the seventh.

At first sight it is not easy to reconcile this lack of continuity with the belief which we shall argue later (pp. 310–13) that the English settlement was a relatively peaceful process. But it may well be that it was the character of the ecclesiastical organization itself which caused Christianity to vanish from fifth-century England. Since that organization was centred on the *civitas*, it was in the cities and towns that the strength of Christianity lay in the fourth-century empire. Conversely, the evangelization of the countryside had not proceeded very far. It is notorious that the term *pagani* meant 'countrymen' before it came to mean 'heathens'. In the late fourth century steps were being taken to preach the gospel in the countryside, but Christianity remained an essentially urban religion. If we accept that the cities of Roman Britain did not survive the fifth century (below, pp. 185–90), it was inevitable that Christianity too should disappear from England.

In the west, by contrast, monasticism became the dominant force in the late fifth and the sixth centuries. In Ireland it largely submerged the diocesan system which had been introduced in the 430s by the missions of Palladius and Patrick. Although the immediate influences in favour of monasticism came from southern Gaul, in the background lay the inspiration of the Desert Fathers. In the late fifth century that inspiration may well have been invigorated by direct contacts with the eastern Mediterranean (below, pp. 206–8). Certainly in the Celtic west we find the two leading elements of the Desert life: the monastery where men gathered together for common observances, and the hermitage where three or two or even one person of great piety practised the extremes of asceticism. Presumably this appealed to the particular religious sensibility of the Celts, just as the monastic system fitted the tribal framework of society in western Britain and Ireland. The monasteries themselves were often great seats of learning, as we can infer from the writings of Gildas Sapiens, 'the wise', or from accounts of the influential school of St Illtud in south Wales. Nor was this learning wholly a matter of religious writings. Especially in Ireland and in continental centres founded by Irish missionaries, the monasteries were the homes of secular learning and the guardians of classical writings in both Latin and Greek through the turmoil and destruction of the barbarian migrations. Finally, they were patrons of the arts and crafts, and we shall see that they fostered the production of fine metalwork in a distinctive Celtic mode (below, p. 235; p 264).

Celtic Christianity is frequently represented as having developed certain differences from Catholic Christianity as a result of being cut off from the continent by the Anglo-Saxon settlement of England. It is sufficiently clear that at the time of the first visit of St Germanus in 428–9 the British church was in close contact with that in Gaul, and was ready to summon assistance from the continent. This is equally implicit in his second visit in the 440s. Moreover the Easter Annals in the *British Historical Miscellany* demonstrate that in 455 the British church was receiving information from Rome about the proper date on which to celebrate Easter. But by the early seventh century Augustine had to admonish the clergy of western Britain for not keeping Easter at the proper time. For Bede, this was a major failing of the Celtic churches, whether among the Britons or in those regions of England which had been evangelized from Columban Iona.

What Bede does not make clear, however, is that the difference between the Celtic and the Catholic observance was not due to any change, whether revolutionary or degenerative, on the part of the Celtic church. The British and the Irish had stayed still; it was Rome which had changed. This would seem to imply that the Celtic church had not been aware of revised calculations for Easter put out from Rome after 455; and further, that this was because the Celtic west was isolated by the barrier of heathen England. This view is in fact impossible to maintain. There is sufficient literary evidence to make it clear that monks travelled freely from the lands around the Irish Sea to Brittany and Gaul. The verbal evidence is now reinforced by archaeological evidence for contacts between Britain and Ireland on the one hand, and western Gaul and even the Mediterranean on the other. A more reasonable explanation of the divergence is simply that the Celtic clergy were conservatives: defiant and self-righteous conservatives at that. They believed that they were upholding the correct, established practices against the innovations of the Bishop of Rome. When every allowance has been made for Bede's prejudice, this explanation can still be read into his account of the meeting of Augustine with the British bishops. It is implicit, too, in the slowness with which the various Celtic regions finally accepted the Catholic Easter: southern Ireland in the 630s, northern Ireland by 704, Iona in 716, and Wales not until 768.

It should be emphasized here that the Easter controversy was no mere sterile technicality about abstruse computations, nor was the issue one simply of the preservation of Catholic unity and peace. To the Roman party the Celtic practice was not merely sinful, it was heretical as well. This at least seems to be the implication when Bede calls the monks of Bangor-on-Dee '*perfidi*', for he uses the term also about the heresies of Arianism and Pelagianism. But whether we read this into the word or not, it is startling to see the hostility of the

Romanists as starkly displayed as it is by Bede when he writes with approval of the slaughter of the Bangor monks by the heathen Æthelfrith at the battle of Chester. No doubt religion had been a major divisive factor in sixth-century Britain, when it separated the heathen English from the British Christians; but it remained so in the seventh century too, as Roman Christianity spread slowly among the English kingdoms.

From Chester to Denisesburna

By the late sixth century the slaughter of Badon and the success of the British counter-attack had been forgotten. We have already seen (above, pp. 117–18) the Saxons of Wessex campaigning almost to the shores of the Severn estuary at the battle of Dyrham in 577. It is generally assumed that the reported capture of Gloucester, Cirencester and Bath at that time was an act of land-taking, which drove a wedge of Saxon territory between Dumnonia and Wales and led to the disappearance of one or more British kingdoms. Further study of the causes and strategy of warfare in the sixth and seventh centuries (below, pp. 340–3) will show that this is only an assumption, but for the present it may be allowed to stand. Early in the following century Northumbria was poised for similar action against the northern Britons and north Wales. The result was a clash between the two greatest kingdoms of seventh-century Britain, which came near to destroying Northumbria but which ultimately curbed the power of Gwynedd to lead a British resurgence.

We have already traced the early history of the Venedotian dynasty (above, pp. 124–8). Before we follow its challenge to Northumbria we should examine certain clues which reveal the special place which it held among the British kingdoms. Its prestige probably went back into the sixth century, if we can read this into the fact that the 'Northern British History' singles out Maelgwn as 'the great king', '*Mailcunus magnus rex*'. The passage continues '[Maelgwn] was ruling among the Britons, that is in the region of Gwynedd', '*apud brittones regnabat, id est in regione guenedote*'. This expression is echoed later in the same source by a reference to Cadwaladr of Gwynedd 'reigning among the Britons', '*regnante apud brittones*'. It seems from this that the dynasty of Gwynedd was regarded as being in some way pre-eminent. Of course, if at one stage in its transmission the 'Northern British History' had passed through a Venedotian *scriptorium* (above, p. 38), then it could be argued that such expressions merely reflect the bias of some later Venedotian scribe. But we have one witness to contemporary attitudes: the tombstone of Cadwaladr's grandfather Cadfan, fourth in descent from Maelgwn (below, pp. 244–5), on which Cadfan is described as OPINATISIMUS OMNIUM REGUM: 'most illustrious of all kings' [Pl. 27*b*]. This certainly reveals what the dynasty thought of itself in the mid-seventh century.

In fact it was not on Gwynedd but on Powys that the first Northumbrian blow fell, at the hands of that Æthelfrith whom Bede describes in such glowing terms (above, p. 121). According to the Northumbrian version of the *Anglo-Saxon Chronicle* this was in 605, a mere two years after Æthelfrith's overwhelming success against Aedan mac Gabran at Degsastan. Bede does not date the campaign, but the Welsh Easter Annals place it in year 170, AD 616, and there is no reason to doubt that this is within a year of the correct date. The terse entry in the Annals records simply: *Gueith cair legion. et ibi cecidit selim filii* [for *filius*] *cinan*. ('The battle of Chester, and there fell Selim [or Solomon] son of Cynan [Garwyn of Powys].') Bede supplements this with the information that Æthelfrith had collected a great army, and carried out a 'very great slaughter of that heretical [or 'unbelieving'] nation', *maximam gentis perfidae stragem*. He then adds an account of the massacre of nearly twelve hundred monks from Bangor-on-Dee who had come to pray on behalf of the Britons.

Bede's main interest in the story is that it fulfilled a prophecy allegedly made by Augustine of Canterbury to the British bishops, that if they did not preach the gospel to the English they would suffer death at their hands. Consequently he tells us nothing about Æthelfrith's purpose in collecting an army against Chester, and we are left to guess whether this was merely an extended looting expedition, or had the strategic purpose of breaking the links between Northumbria's traditional British enemies in Rheged and Strathclyde and their fellows in north Wales. Nor do we know whether Chester retained any administrative or military function at this date, or was merely a landmark. The traditional centres of Powys were in fact further south, but it seems reasonable to suggest that Selim moved up to the borders of his kingdom to meet Æthelfrith's army.

There is certainly no evidence for land-taking or settlement in the west immediately after the Northumbrian victory at Chester. It was shortly followed by the expulsion and slaying of the British king Ceretic and the seizure of his land of Elmet. The chronology here is a little confused, but the most probable course of events is this. The year after Chester Æthelfrith was slain by Rædwald of East Anglia, who sponsored Edwin for the throne of Northumbria. The 'Northern British History' tells us that Edwin drove Ceretic out of Elmet, and the Welsh Easter Annals record the death of a Ceretic, probably the same one, in 619. The conquest of Elmet was in fact no great achievement for Edwin. Place-name evidence suggests that it was a small district extending up to the Pennine watershed south-west of the Vale of York. The remarkable thing is that a British kingdom should have survived so long despite the early anglicization of the York region.

This modest step marked the beginning of a massive expansion under Edwin. The Northumbrian version of the *Anglo-Saxon Chronicle*, echoing Bede, says that Edwin conquered all Britain except for the people of Kent. It is not quite clear what degree of direct political control is implied either by the *Chronicle* or by Bede, who uses such expressions as: '*cunctis quae Brittaniam incolunt, Anglorum pariter et Brettonum, populis praefuit.*' ('He ruled over all the people who inhabit Britain, English as well as Britons.') Both Bede and the *Chronicle* relate how in 626 Cwichelm king of the West Saxons sent an assassin to Edwin's court, and how, after the attempt had been foiled, Edwin mounted a punitive expedition against Wessex. In the course of this, according to the *Chronicle*, he slew five kings as well as many of the people. It is evident from this that within Edwin's overlordship there were many persons of regal status.

The most important claim made by Bede was that Edwin's sovereignty was exercised over the Britons as well as over the Anglo-Saxons. Twice he adds that Edwin subdued the 'Mevanian isles', that is Anglesey and Man, to English rule. The claim appears circumstantial, for not only are we told that the southern of the two isles is the larger and more fruitful, but we are even given an assessment in English terms, *iuxta aestimationem Anglorum*, that Anglesey had room or resources for 960 households, and Man for 300 or more. This is an assessment for tax or tribute, and it leaves no room for doubt about the reality of the conquest. We have regrettably little information about how this was achieved: no more, in fact, than the terse entry of the Welsh Easter Annals for AD 630 or 632: 'Siege of King Cadwallon [of Gwynedd] on Ynys Lannog' or Puffin Island off the east coast of Anglesey. It can reasonably be assumed that before Edwin could launch attacks on Anglesey and Man he must have established his rule west of the Pennines, and he must also have built a fleet.

Despite the blockade of Cadwallon on Ynys Lannog, the immediate future lay with him and not with Edwin. Two years later the Easter Annals record: 'Strife of Meicen, and there Edwin was slain with his two sons. Cadwallon, however, was victor.'

This event, the first great British victory since Badon, requires some detailed analysis. Bede, looking at it from the Northumbrian point of view, presented Cadwallon's attempt to resist Edwin as a rebellion. Cadwallon's ally was Penda of Mercia, who thus appears on the scene for the first time. We can only assume that a common fear of Northumbrian expansion had united pagan Mercia and Christian Gwynedd. Bede places the battle 'on the plain called *Haethfelth*, on 12 October AD 633' (or perhaps 632 in modern reckoning). *Haethfelth* is generally identified with Hatfield Chase on the southern boundary of Northumbria, whereas Meicen is traditionally placed on the borders of Powys. The apparent confusion here has not been resolved, but a possible solution is that the Easter Annals have run two events together: an initial battle on the borders of Mercia and Powys, followed by a shattering victory over an enemy who was retreating to his own territory. The probability of this is demonstrated by the fact that the Annals have certainly conflated two events when they state that Edwin's two sons were also killed in the battle. The statement is repeated in more detail in the *Historia Brittonum*, but Bede says that only Osfrith was slain at *Haethfelth*. Eadfrith, the other son, surrendered to Penda, who later had him murdered. Bede is likely to be the more reliable source here.

Whatever the details, there can be no doubt about the effects of the overthrow of Edwin. When every allowance is made for Bede's prejudice against the Britons, it seems clear that Cadwallon and Penda embarked on a systematic ravaging of Northumbria. It was Cadwall-on's intention to wipe out the whole English race from Britain: *totum genus Anglorum Brittaniae finibus erasurum se esse deliberans.* The immediate result was that Edwin's widow Æthelburh fled with her children to Kent, and Northumbria split into its two components, Deira and Bernicia. Christianity, which had been established by Edwin's conversion, received an immediate set-back. Paulinus, who had been the original missionary to Northumbria, fled with Æthel-burh and Edwin's two co-successors, though nominally Christians, both apostasized. Cadwallon then showed his complete mastery of the situation by destroying them both. Osric of Deira besieged Cadwallon 'rashly', *temerarie* as Bede says, in an unnamed town which is frequently identified as York. Cadwallon sallied out unexpectedly and destroyed Osric and all his army. Later he slew Eanfrith of Bernicia, who had come to him on a peace mission with only twelve companions.

As it happened, the slaughter of Eanfrith led to Cadwallon's own destruction. Eanfrith was succeeded by his brother Oswald. He, according to the *Historia Brittonum*, was 'Oswald *Lamnguin*, "White-blade". He himself killed Cadwallon king of Gwynedd in the battle of *Ca[n]tscaul* with great slaughter of his army'.

This is the central fact. To it Bede adds that the battle took place at *Denisesburna*, which has been located a little south of Hexham. The battle is usually referred to as 'Heavenfield', but this name rightly belongs to the place where Oswald set up a wooden cross and sought for divine aid, probably on the night before the action, which began with a dawn attack. Writers from Adomnan and Bede to recent historians have given colourful accounts of the battle, which range from hagiography to imaginative fiction. In Bede's account Oswald came with only a small army, *cum paruo exercitu*, whereas the unspeakable leader of the Britons had boundless forces, *infandus Brettonum dux cum inmensis illis copiis.* When we recall, however, that Oswald's army was, again according to Bede, '*fide Christi munito*', 'fortified by faith in Christ', and that Oswald himself was 'chosen by God', '*Deo dilecti*', we realize that it is impossible to disentangle hagiography from historical fact.

What is not in dispute, however, is that Oswald, in destroying Cadwallon and his army, had simultaneously destroyed the hopes of a

British revival under the leadership of Gwynedd. It is true that the Britons had some further success against Northumbria, but the account of this in the *Historia Brittonum* makes it clear that it was achieved under the leadership of Penda of Mercia. By contrast, in Cadwallon's reign there can be no doubt that Penda was the junior partner. The threat to Northumbria was effectively brought to an end when Oswald's successor Oswy slew Penda himself.

The battle of Denisesburna is a significant point at which to end this outline of the historical background to Arthur's Britain. From the time when the Anglo-Saxon mercenaries and settlers first began to throw off the control of the Britons, they received only two serious checks. The first was in the fifth century campaigns initiated by Ambrosius which culminated in Arthur's victory of Badon. We can say little about the strategy, or about the political and military results, of these early campaigns. But the second great check which the English received is reasonably well documented for us by both British and English sources. Cadwallon's victories over Edwin and his successors, and his overthrow of Northumbrian suzerainty, could never have led, as Bede suggested, to the complete removal of the English nation. But they might well have confined the invaders south of Humber and east of Severn, leaving the west and north as far as the Forth-Clyde isthmus in the control of a British confederation. Oswald's victory destroyed this possibility; and later events were to prove that the destruction was final.

Six

The Archaeological Background: The Nature of the Evidence

Introduction

After considering in Chapters 1 and 2 the kinds of verbal evidence which are available for the study of the historical Arthur and the politico-military context in which he operated, we examined in detail the documents for Arthur himself in Chapter 3. From this it appeared that he was most probably a great British warrior of the late fifth and sixth centuries whose most important victory was the crushing defeat inflicted on the Anglo-Saxons at Badon. It then became necessary to ask what the Anglo-Saxons were doing in Britain, and what their relations were with the native Britons. Chapters 4 and 5 therefore outlined the circumstances under which the Anglo-Saxon settlement came about, and traced its progress up to the time when Oswald's defeat of Cadwallon ensured once and for all that the major part of Britain south of the Forth-Clyde isthmus was to become England.

This historical sketch has certainly not exhausted the resources of the verbal evidence. Many details could be added to it, while many of the details given would doubtless be modified by other scholars. None the less it can be claimed that its broad outlines are correct and that enough of the historical background has been delineated to make Arthur's political and military situation understandable. For a fuller and richer picture, we must now turn to the material evidence for the culture of Arthur's Britain. Just as it was necessary to examine the character of the verbal evidence before we attempted to make use of it, so too we must scrutinize the nature of the archaeological evidence, and evaluate its reliability, before we attempt to describe the material culture of the period.

When we turn from the evidence of manuscripts to that of archaeology, it might appear that we turn simultaneously from a history made up of half-truths and shifting inferences to one of hard substantial fact. No appearance could be more illusory. It is true and obvious that archaeology deals mostly with material objects, and that these are often big and normally solid. They can be measured individually; groups of them can be counted and their characteristics can be quantified and even – to use the jargon – processed by computer, or computerized. All this gives an immediate air of objectivity to archaeology in contrast to the admitted subjectivity of history.

In fact, the material bits and pieces which archaeology studies have as much to do with the proper subject of archaeology as leaves of vellum with ink marks on them have to do with the proper study of historians. In both cases we start with material relics of the past, which we then proceed to interpret; and from piecemeal interpretation we move on to create a network of interpretations, a synthesis which we call history.

Very frequently the first stage of interpretation in archaeology is so immediate that the experienced archaeologist is not conscious of it as such. He trowels through the earth, scraping soil and stones into a shovel and throwing them away, distinguishing as he goes fragments of bone, metal, pottery and so on, and putting them into appropriate bags and trays. That he is in fact continually interpreting every particle that passes under his trowel becomes clear enough if a complete novice is set to work beside him, for the novice will constantly ask, 'Is this anything? How do you know this is stone and not pottery? Is that a lump of dirt or some rusty iron?'

But this stage – the distinguishing in the field of the man-made, the artificial, from its natural background – is only the first step in the long process of interpretation. The novice has duly put his finds of pottery in the tray. Mostly these are fragments; can we now go on to infer what shape and size of vessel they came from, and what its function was? If so, we may be able to reconstruct it, at least on paper. Next, what was the date of the original pot? Chronology is almost wholly a work of inference, yet it is central to any historical discipline. Then, was the pot made locally or did it arrive on the site where it was found by trade or some other means? Here we begin to make inferences about social structure, possibly appealing to anthropological parallels. What was the pot doing in the place where we actually found it? Was it domestic refuse, or a ritual offering? Here our inferences become even more insubstantial.

In brief, the main business of the archaeologist is not with objective facts, but with inferences. The contrary belief, which has beguiled all too many historians, is founded on a philosophical confusion between what is concrete or material, and what is subjective. And because archaeologists sometimes succeed in beguiling themselves as well as others, it is necessary here, if we are to make sensible use of archaeological evidence in later chapters, to describe a few of the limitations of archaeological inference.

This chapter, then, is not a simple manual of archaeological field methods. It is a review of some of the methods which are most relevant to our period, and a discussion of some of the problems which arise when we attempt to use archaeological evidence as part of the total evidence for history.[1]

Preservation

It seems almost unnecessary to say that we can only learn about the past from those fragments of it which have been preserved down to the present day – whether in the form of oral traditions, written documents, or pots and pans. But it is worth saying for this reason: if we can establish what fragments have survived, and more particularly why they survive, we have some basis for estimating how much of the past we have lost, and what particular elements are missing. So we can perhaps infer more about the past than we could if we concentrated all our attention on the relics we actually possess.

The substance of which an object was made is a major factor in its preservation. We have already seen the truth of this in the case of literary documents: in western Europe vellum tends to survive, whereas papyrus emphatically does not (above, p. 3). So too with all biological remains. Except under very exceptional conditions – extreme aridity, or extreme water-logging – organic materials such as wood or textiles rarely survive. Bone may be well preserved in an alkaline or neutral soil, but will disappear altogether in an acid one – and it should be noticed here that humic acid alone is enough to reduce bone to a condition in which it can scarcely be recovered. There is evidence from literary sources that wood, flax, wool, horn and leather were all freely utilized in Arthur's day, and we may infer that gut and sinew were equally important; but virtually none of these survive.

Pottery is normally considered to be a substance with a high survival value, but this is not necessarily so on the acid boulder clays or the upland sites of western Britain. Among metals, pure gold survives perfectly; silver may be reduced to a purple stain; bronze may vary from a bright green powder to a solid object which differs only from its pristine state in having a blue-green patina in place of its original reddish or golden-yellow surface. Iron, the commonest metal of all, has suffered worst. In the first place a broken iron object could easily be reforged, so it was not customary to leave iron weapons or tools littered around domestic sites. But once iron is buried, major and irreversible chemical changes take place. In ancient times large objects were often wrought by placing strips of iron together and forging them into a whole. In the process of rusting, the boundaries between the strips are particularly liable to attack, and the object is liable to split up into numerous laminae. Nor is any wholly effective method known of stabilizing a badly rusted piece of iron after it has been excavated.

It is as well at this point to sound a pessimistic note. The Laws of Hywel Dda present us with several inventories which list the material possessions typical of a free household in western Britain. In the case of divorce, for instance, the division of household property is strictly regulated:

The husband is to have the boiler, the blanket, the bolster, the coulter, the fuel axe, the auger, the gimlet, the fire-dog, all the sickles except one, and the baking griddle. The wife is to have the trivet, the pan, the broad-axe, the sieve, the ploughshare, one sickle ...

If we were to put together all the household objects found on all the sites of the fifth to eleventh centuries so far excavated in western Britain, they would not add up to a list like this.

What is true of movable objects – that the substance used is a major factor in preservation – is also true of architecture. Buildings of mortared stone could, theoretically, survive almost unscathed, and indeed some late Roman fortifications do still stand to the level of the original battlements. More normally, of course, only the lower parts of the walls remain, but at least they pose few problems of identification.

Dry-stone walling, whether of fortifications or houses, may also remain almost undamaged in remote areas, provided that the stones have not been needed by latter-day farmers for making field walls.

Buildings of timber have rotted away completely. This is obviously a very severe restriction on our knowledge of architecture in a period when wood was the principal building material. But at least one may hope to discover the plans of timber buildings, and to infer from this something of the superstructure. This hope has been fostered by one of the major triumphs of prehistoric archaeology in western Europe – the discovery that the post-holes used for the erection of the uprights of timber buildings can be recovered by excavation. This is especially true on a dwelling site where solid rock lies close to the surface, for there the builders found it necessary to dig pits into the rock to take the posts. The stones which were then packed around the post to stabilize it can be readily distinguished from the solid rock. When the pit was dug into sand or clay, and this was then tamped around the post in such a way as to be indistinguishable from the parent sub-soil, the post itself is frequently recognizable as a dark, soft, and often damp patch, the last product of the decaying timber. An outstanding example of a group of seventh-century building plans recognized by such signs is provided by the summer palace of the Northumbrian kings at Yeavering (below, pp. 309–10).

The triumphs of the excavator in recovering the plans of timber buildings have been very real, but a note of caution must be sounded. Some constructional methods do involve the digging of substantial pits or trenches as emplacements for upright posts or wall planks; but other methods known and used in ancient times do not. A circular house can be made, for instance, by driving thin stakes into the ground at short intervals and binding them together firmly with wickerwork. A rectangular building in which the uprights are cross-braced does not need to have them deeply bedded. In both these cases the uprights would penetrate the subsoil shallowly, if at all. A combination of ploughing and weathering of the rock may then obliterate all trace of the building in the course of a millennium or more. Finally, as iron tools became more common and carpentry more sophisticated, so it became possible to erect a timber-framed house in which the uprights never penetrated the ground; instead they were mortised into a heavy cill-beam or sleeper-beam. If this was laid directly on the ground, then a large and skilfully constructed dwelling may disappear altogether.

In other words human activities – in this case the methods of the builders – may play as large a part in preservation as the material itself. This is seen most strikingly in those societies which regularly place intact artefacts in the ground as part of their ritual practices. Among many of the pagan Anglo-Saxons the normal burial rite involved the placing of material possessions – a warrior's weapons, a woman's jewelry – in the grave with the body [Fig. 26]. The first importance of this is that it provides us with complete examples of many objects which on domestic sites are either pitifully fragmentary or not represented at all. Second, since the number, variety and quality of the grave-goods differ from grave to grave, we can begin to make inferences about the relative wealth and social standing of the persons buried there. At the top of the social pyramid we have the unique treasures of the royal household of East Anglia revealed at Sutton Hoo [Pls. 23–4]; and at its broad base countless graves which contain no more than a simple iron knife. Third, comparisons of jewelry and pottery styles may make it possible to define tribal groups.

All this adds greatly to the richness in material and to the complexity of inference of pagan Saxon archaeology. By contrast the archaeology of western Britain appears strikingly impoverished. But it is not clear whether this appearance reflects a genuine poverty of material culture or whether it is rather the result of the absence of grave-goods in the west. The Britons, being nominally Christian, did not place funerary deposits with the dead. But even in a society where grave-goods are common, it remains a problem how much light they throw on the everyday possessions of the living. It seems likely, for instance, that much of the pottery used for funerary purposes among the pagan Saxons was made specially for such purposes and had no domestic function. This is particularly true of the elaborately ornamented cinerary urns.

Discovery

The tools available to the archaeologist in his search for ancient sites have been spectacularly improved in both quantity and quality over the past half century. Aerial photography brings out the character of a site, or may even reveal sites which are not visible on the ground. A great armament of electronic devices can reveal ancient disturbances of the subsoil caused by human activity – pits for rubbish or for the posts of timber buildings, hearths and ovens, even individual metal objects. Chemical analyses of the soil may reveal, by concentrations of phosphates for instance, areas of human habitation. Over the same period a great increase in the manpower of archaeology, both among professionals and amateurs, has of itself increased the rate of discovery.

But these advances are general to the whole of British archaeology rather than specific to the period of our interest. Certain sites have indeed been claimed as fortifications belonging to the post-Roman centuries, as a result of aerial reconnaissance and photography, but these claims have not been substantiated. In fact, a survey of the known or supposed sites of Arthurian date in Wales has revealed that they display no features to distinguish them from sites character-istic of the pre-Roman Iron Age, the fifth century BC to the first century AD. Only the recovery, in the course of archaeo-logical excavations, of objects datable to the fifth century AD or later made it possible to say that certain forts had been founded or at least re-occupied then. Here the evidence of excavation has been decisive.

Before we turn to this aspect of discovery the point must be made that much archaeological material comes to light as a result of chance and nothing more. This is obvious enough in the case of stray finds – odd jewels, weapons, coins, which may be turned up whenever the soil is disturbed, whether on a small scale by the gardener or on a large scale in building work, quarrying and so on. It is perhaps less obvious that all surface trace of relatively large and rich sites may vanish, so that nothing is known of them until the plough or bulldozer begins to turn up pottery, building-stones, or even human bones. Some of the most important pagan Saxon cemeteries were discovered by chance as a result of the expansion of towns and the building of railways in the nineteenth century. And the early Saxon village about which we know most, Sutton Courtenay, was discovered in the course of gravel-quarrying.

Excavation

If chance plays a large part in the field of discovery, it is in excavation that the archaeologist seems to be most in command of the situation. Here he sets out purposefully to recover the plans of ancient buildings and the material relics of their builders. These at least have been the objectives for most archaeological exploration throughout the world. It is true that there is a more sophisticated school which dismisses the quest for artefacts as 'treasure-hunting' and which sees the function of excavation as answering questions about the past. On this view, the method of the excavator consists of formulating very precise questions, and then devising excavations in order to answer them; the excavation itself corresponds with the experiment of the natural scientist. This highly intellectual form of 'question-and-answer' archaeology is only possible on monuments like Hadrian's Wall or Stonehenge, about which a great deal is already known, and where therefore precise questions can be proposed to bring refinements to our knowledge. In pioneering fields a more flexible approach is necessary and the archaeologist often has to fit his questions to his excavation rather than the other way round.

Even at its simplest, excavation involves something much more than the recovery of structures on the one hand and portable objects on the other – it involves also the discovery and analysis of the association or connections between the two. The simplest and most obvious form of structure in our period is the grave pit of a pagan Saxon burial. What matters here is the association of human bones – of a person male or female, old or young – with certain weapons, jewelry or other objects; and perhaps in a distinctive type of grave. The totality of this evidence demonstrates the burial rite in use. The association of particular grave goods in one grave shows that they were all contemporary, and this provides one basic link in the chains of reasoning by which we construct chronological schemes. This is archaeological association at its simplest, and its observation requires neither a developed philosophy nor an elaborate technique of excavation. Despite this, the associations of grave-groups were frequently recorded in a hopelessly inadequate manner, or even not recorded at all, by the nineteenth-century archaeologists who dug up the majority of the pagan Saxon objects now in our museums.

An altogether more sophisticated form of association is that summed up in the word 'stratification'. The layman who has some acquaintance with archaeology knows that stratification or stratigraphy has to do with 'layers' or 'levels' on a site – but 'layer' and 'level' are themselves technical words which have a special archaeological meaning. In essence, stratification provides the evidence for the whole history of a 'site' – another technical term – from the time when the natural soil or rock was first disturbed by man up to the present day. And the term 'whole history' includes both human action – for instance the erection of buildings – and inaction – their abandonment; and also natural processes – for instance, changes in the soil due to the percolation of water, or the displacement of objects by burrowing animals.

It is the analysis of stratification which tells us that pottery of type X comes from underneath rampart A, and is therefore earlier than the rampart, whereas pottery of type Y came from a rubbish pit dug into rampart A, and is therefore later than the building of the rampart. Pottery of type Z, by contrast, came from a hearth built with stones pulled down from rampart A, and is therefore later than the destruction of the rampart. If we can date the rampart, for instance by historical references to its construction and destruction, we could date our three types of pottery in relation to it. If, on the other hand, we had no first-hand evidence for dating the rampart but could date the pottery, we could then apply the ceramic dates to the building and throwing down of the rampart. All this depends of course on the stratification having been correctly observed, recorded, and applied to the association of finds and structures. Suppose, however, that the excavator had failed to notice that the Y pottery was in a pit cut into the rampart, his records would merely show that such pottery was present in the rampart, and he would conclude that it was lying around the site as refuse before the rampart was built and had been scooped up with other material in the make-up of the rampart. This reverses the chronological relations of pottery and rampart, to the general confounding of the chronology of the site.

It would be optimistic beyond all reason to suggest that this failure to observe stratification never occurs. At first sight this statement might seem to be an unprovable assertion – once a particular block of stratified levels has been dug away the evidence is destroyed, and no one can say that it once existed. (The fact that the excavator necessarily proceeds by destroying his primary evidence is in itself one of the most disturbing aspects of archaeological research.) Nevertheless the assertion can be justified on two main grounds. First, any normally competent excavator finds that when his colleagues visit his excavations, they observe features which he himself has not noticed; and he hopes that the complementary process will be true when he visits their excavations. Second, it sometimes happens that the evidence from a particular site places it quite out of line, especially in terms of dating, with other sites of the same class. It is then a reasonable inference that there has been a major failure to observe the stratification correctly.

Scholars in other disciplines, such as historians who make some use of archaeological evidence, may wonder, if they have not taken part in excavations, how this kind of observational failure comes about. For a start, we should recognize that archaeological excavation is a form of research in which there is a very large – perhaps excessively large – human element. The primary evidence is being won – and simultaneously destroyed – by volunteer workers, for many of whom the only contact with excavation is a month's digging each summer. Some of these are very competent – they have great manual dexterity, keen senses of vision and touch, a feel for how stratification comes about and how it should be dissected, and often wide experience. Others are the reverse – ham-fisted, colour-blind, insensitive to anything in the soil. Yet such people are not necessarily complete beginners; they may have taken part in well-conducted excavations for many years. We welcome them to our excavations, place them in situations which demand skill and experience, and find out too late that an important piece of stratification has been irretrievably mangled.

What is true at the level of pick and trowel is no less true all the way up the hierarchy of command. Most professional archaeologists must have seen workers, who in their opinion could only safely be employed to shift dumps, rise to the position of supervisor on other excavations. And every honest director is aware that he himself has blind spots, and tries to bring in assistants to cover them for him. But presumably we are least aware of the places where we are blindest.

Metaphorical blindness apart, the whole problem is compounded because for the most part we are digging blind. Except in the coarsest or simplest fashion no air photograph, no geophysical instrument, can tell us in advance what lies beneath the soil, still less what the sequence of layers is going to be. One method of minimizing our blindness is to make exploratory cuts across a site, sacrificing to a large extent the stratification within the cut itself in the interests of obtaining on its side walls a clear picture of what the relation of layers and structures actually is. We can then follow in turn, over the rest of the site, the individual layers which have been revealed in this way in the exploratory cut. Given, for example, a defensive rampart 1500 metres long, it seems reasonable to sacrifice several cuttings each about 3 metres wide by digging them with a mechanical excavator, so that we have a preview of the sequence of rampart construction, which we can then dissect in detail by hand. In the same way, given a masonry building, it may be useful to obtain a literal cross-section of its history by means of an exploratory trench or trenches dug as the first stage of an excavation.

But it is now being realized that this time-hallowed excavation method may sacrifice not only the exploratory cut itself but any hope of understanding the site. In the first place, the sides or sections of any one trench may not reveal all the stratification. It is a common experience, for instance, in excavating gravel floors or road surfaces, that one may peel a later floor off an earlier underlying one with complete confidence, yet in the section the two may be indistinguishable. In the second place, the last score of years has brought the realization that whereas the plan of a timber or dry-stone building may be sufficiently clear if the whole of it is revealed at one time, no single part of it would be recognizable without all the rest. In other words, exploratory trenches could cut through such a building without ever recognizing its existence; and even an excavation laid out in a series of boxes would fragment the traces of the building beyond all recognition. Consequently, the only hope of discovering certain types of building is by means of an open, overall excavation.[2]

It so happens that this is crucial to the evaluation of the archaeological evidence for one of the key problems in our period. Did the incoming Anglo-Saxons make use of the towns and farms of their Romano-British predecessors? If they did, then it is possible that they constructed timber buildings, some of them quite flimsy, over the collapsed walls of the Roman period. Such buildings could only be discovered by the open-area technique of excavation. But Romano-British sites have normally been excavated by the fragmenting techniques which involve the layout of boxes or even exploratory trenches. So the fact that traces of post-Roman buildings have not normally been found overlying Romano-British ruins may reflect an inappropriate excavation technique rather than the absence of such buildings. This is not mere hypothesis. Within the last few years the use of the open-excavation technique at the Romano-British town of Wroxeter has revealed clear evidence of post-Roman buildings which though flimsily built were yet of a good size (below, pp. 187-8).

One further point about excavation demands consideration here. Archaeological excavations are not primarily carried out to enrich the cabinets of collectors, whether public or private, nor for the mere delectation of those who take part in them. Although they are often conducted as though these were their true aims, in fact the purpose of excavating is to acquire knowledge, with the further implication that the knowledge so won should be disseminated. With this in mind, it has been well said that the date of a discovery is the date of its publication. This is true also at a deeper level: it is only when the excavator disciplines his eyes, his hands and his mind to the task of drawing and writing up his finds for publication, and using them as foundations for historical inference, that he himself really knows what he has found, in all its manifold implications and equally manifold limitations. In this sense, the publication *is* the discovery.

Meanwhile, no doubt, the conscientious excavator has issued numerous interim statements. The very brevity of these has made it possible for him to evade the inconsistencies and limitations of his evidence. The statements he has put out have been at best half-truths; some he will find, when he examines the whole of the evidence, to be false. But until the excavation is fully published, other scholars have to make do with these possible falsehoods and undoubted half-truths. It is therefore a deplorable aspect of archaeology as a form of research that some of our major sites are excavated by people whose readiness to dig is only equalled by their reluctance to publish. In no period is this more true than in the one which concerns us.

Typology

After objects or structures have been discovered, whether by chance or by controlled excavation, various mental processes are set in motion to convert the material remains into historical hypotheses. The most important of these processes is that of typological study. At its simplest this involves comparing remains of broadly the same kind, and sorting them out into groups in which all the members are related one to another through sharing common characteristics. Obviously this can be done with types of house or fortification as well as with types of pottery or jewelry; but it must be admitted that the more plastic an object is, the more refined its typology can be. This is a major reason why ceramic typology seems the be-all and end-all of some archaeological research.

Considered in this simplest form, the most important use of typology is that it enables us to relate objects from different geographical areas. For instance, in pagan Saxon graves in eastern England we find pottery vessels which are closely similar, not only in the character of the clay from which they are made but also in their shape, colour and ornament, to vessels found on the continent in the Jutish peninsula or between the Elbe and the Weser. It is unlikely that the resemblances are accidental, and we must face the possibility either that the pots were exported from one area to the other, or that the potters themselves migrated, either as wandering craftsmen or as one element in a migrating community. In this case our historical knowledge allows us to infer that the typological similarities are the result of the Anglo-Saxon migration.

Again, in western Britain we find certain red bowls and dishes with stamped or rouletted ornament, which can be compared in every way with dishes from Greece, Asia Minor, the Levant and north-east Africa. The direction of movement of the pottery is clear: it is a product of sophisticated Late Roman and Byzantine technology, not of the broken-down Romano-British pottery industry. No folk movement is known which could account for the appearance of such pottery in the west, so we can infer that it was imported. This need not necessarily imply an organized commerce between the east Mediterranean and the Irish Sea, and indeed the restricted numbers of vessels present rules out any such inference (below, pp. 206–7).

Sometimes scientific analysis can validate typological comparisons, which may have a large subjective element in them. For instance, trace elements or impurities in the metal of two implements or ornaments might demonstrate that both were made of ore from the same region. Again, the clay from which pots are made in relatively simple technologies generally contains grits or other particles which prevent the clay from shrinking during the drying and firing of the pot. These grits are often geologically diagnostic, and make it possible to say where the pot was manufactured. Obviously for this kind of inference to be made the grits must be unique to a closely defined geological region, and not such as might be found very widely.

The kind of typological comparison we have been considering is quite unexceptionable, but there is another aspect of typological study which is altogether more dubious, namely that which uses typology as a basis for inferences about dating. The assumption here is that objects are comparable because they are contemporary; the closer the comparison, therefore, the closer the date of one object to another; conversely the greater the difference, the greater the divergence in date. So a number of pots or brooches may be arranged in a series in which each stage diverges only slightly from the stage on either side of it, but progressively from all other stages. This seriation, or arrangement of types in a series, is relatively objective, and for any one class of objects closely similar series would be arranged by a scholar familiar with the objects; by a scholar from another discipline who was familiar with the principles of typology; and by a computer.

What follows, however, is a leap into the realm of hypothesis. It is widely assumed that the typological series is a sequence, in which one end of the series is early and the other late. If we make this assumption, then sometimes the series appears to contain its own chronological pointer. In a series of brooches, for instance, one end is florid, the other is simple; so we equate the simple with early, and the florid with decadent and late. A clearer case is provided when one end of the series is related to another, technologically less advanced, type of object. This can easily be exemplified by a modern instance: given a typological series of steamships we could immediately fix which was the early end because of its relation to sailing ships. So our typological study may give us a relative sequence of objects, in which C is later than A

and B and earlier than D and E. If by one means or another we can put absolute dates to one or more stages in the series, then we can infer dates for all the other stages.

The use of such typological series as a basis for dating is fundamental to much of the superstructure of history which has been built upon archaeological evidence. The last paragraph will have made clear how far such a use is a matter of piling inference upon inference. It may be true that with objects of utility there is a trend to increasing efficiency, so that a series arranged on such a basis should be a time series. Our steamships illustrate this very well, but with the warning that the greatest development of the preceding technological stage, the sailing ship, took place in the half-century after the steamship was invented. But much of the material that we use for seriation – jewelry, or the decorative aspects of pottery – is governed not by efficiency but by fashion. And common experience suggests that here we should no longer expect a linear series; it is as likely to be cyclical. Finally, who can say of a crude, ill-decorated pot that it represents the end stage of a craft in decline rather than the first faltering steps of a new industry, or the fumbling of an apprentice in a mature stage of an established one, or even the blunder of a highly competent craftsman with a hangover?

Chronology

It is self-evident that before we can use archaeological material for historical purposes we must be able to date it; and the precision with which we can use it depends absolutely on the accuracy of our chronology. This in fact is not easy in the period with which we are concerned. For a start, none of the chronometric techniques developed by the natural sciences are applicable. Even the method of dating by the decay of radioactive carbon is too coarse. Essentially this is a statistical technique, based on counting the emission of radioactive particles from carbon – charcoal, for instance – found on archaeological sites. The dates calculated by this method are correctly expressed as probability statements, in a form such as AD 500 ± 70, where the ±70 implies that there is a 2:3 chance of the true date falling within a bracket of 140 years. If we want to narrow the possibility to a 19:20 chance, then we must double the bracket. In other words, the date AD 500 ± 70 could be expressed as 'very probably in the range AD 360–640'. On the whole we can normally provide a more precise date than this by archaeological or historical methods, without the large expense of a radio-carbon analysis.

One obvious class of archaeological material carries its date with it, namely coins. It should be stressed that in our period coins do not bear *anno domini* dates, but nevertheless they can normally be dated by reference to our historical information about the ruler who struck them. This is certainly true of Late Roman and Byzantine issues, but we should recognize that there is a continuing debate about the chronology of Merovingian coins. It must also be noted that what we are dating is the minting of the coin, not its incorporation, accidentally or deliberately, in an archaeological deposit. None the less, the chronology of Germanic pottery and jewelry in the fourth and early fifth centuries can reasonably be inferred on the evidence of coins placed in graves.

In England, however, the position is less satisfactory. No coins were minted or circulated during the Arthurian period. Late Roman issues continued to circulate in the early decades of the fifth century. The terminal date for their currency may still be debated, but it can hardly be later than 430. Thereafter the Britons neither struck nor used coins, while effectively the use of coins by the Anglo-Saxons did not begin until the seventh century (below, p. 318).

It is true that coins are found in pagan Saxon graves, but it is impossible to use them to determine the date of the graves. In 1913 it did indeed seem possible to assign a grave from Chatham, Kent, to the period 450–500 because it contained a silver coin of the emperor Anthemius, AD 467–72. But it is now recognized that this date cannot be reconciled with the probable chronology of the jewelry in the grave, which can hardly be earlier than 500. In other words, the coin of Anthemius was at least a generation old when it was buried, while the other datable coin, one of Valentinian, was more than a century old. This indeed is normal with the coins in pagan Saxon graves: they were not in circulation, but had been perforated for use as pendants. The date of their minting has no relevance to the date of the grave.

That ancient coins may be placed in a grave introduces another problem of pagan Saxon chronology: are all the objects deposited in one grave contemporary, and can we therefore apply the date established for one piece to all the others found associated with it? Sometimes indeed there is clear evidence to the contrary: in a grave from Finglesham in Kent, for instance, along with brooches and other jewels in a near-perfect condition was placed a brooch with corners rounded and ornament worn smooth by years if not decades of wear. This is an obvious case; but elsewhere it may be suggested, if not proved, that family heirlooms, a generation or more old, were taken in nearly new condition from a jewel casket, to be placed in a grave along with the latest fashions.

Another of the main props of pagan Saxon chronology has collapsed in recent years. This was the belief, based essentially on Bede's *Ecclesiastical History*, that the coming of the English, the *Adventus Saxonum*, was a unique and closely datable event which took place about 450. If Bede was correct in thinking this, then no pagan Saxon material in this island could be earlier than the *Adventus*; and any typological sequence could be given a starting date of 450, and could run on from there by guess and by dead-reckoning. Moreover, this date could be transferred back to the continental homelands of the Anglo-Saxons. Any continental pots or jewels which were closely comparable to English examples must, on this reckoning, be later than 450. But continental scholars have found it increasingly difficult to accept a date in the second half of the fifth century for some of this material. At the same time several lines of argument have converged to show that many Germanic elements had settled in England before 450 (below, pp. 117–18). Consequently we no longer have this as a fixed point for the start of our pagan Saxon type series.

It is fair to warn those readers who are not themselves practising archaeologists that there is no intrinsic or internal evidence to date Anglo-Saxon material before the late seventh century. On the whole, the chronology of the pagan Saxon period depends on comparisons between English pieces and continental ones, which have themselves been dated with greater or lesser security by coin evidence or by their connection with historical – especially royal – personages. In other words we have here a chain of inferences which is normally tenuous and frequently elastic as well.

The position is no better in western Britain. We shall see in the next section some of the problems raised by the attempt to date sites by their associations with historical or legendary personages. A cautionary example of the use of historical evidence for dating is provided by the royal residence of Lagore crannog in Ireland. When this was excavated in 1934–6 the earliest known mention of Lagore was in the year 785. This was not even a statement on the lines that Lagore was founded in that year, but nevertheless this was assumed to be the foundation date and therefore the earliest possible date for any of the objects found there. This date was then applied to comparable objects found on other sites, and by extension to the sites themselves. Later documentary research, however, uncovered a reference to Lagore as early as 651. But again, this is not an account of the founding of the royal residence there. The evidence of the pottery suggests indeed that the site may well begin in the sixth century; and if that is so, we may have to push back the date not only of Lagore, but of the other sites dated from it, by half a century or more.

So far as the dating of British jewelry and fine metalwork is concerned, we can see a starting point in late Roman pieces of the fourth century, and we can begin to establish sound historical dates at the very end of the seventh century. In between, we must use such aids to dead-reckoning as art history and seriation may provide.

In recent years, however, it has seemed that we have within our grasp a chronology for the lands around the Irish Sea which is quite independent of local arguments based on shaky British or Irish historical associations. This chronology appears to be provided by the east Mediterranean pottery which has been recovered in increasing quantities over the past thirty years from both monasteries and princely strongholds. Since this pottery had been manufactured in literate, coin-using areas of the Near East it seemed reasonable to believe that it could be closely dated there, and that the dates could then be applied directly to sites in Britain and Ireland.

This hope has still to be realized. The difficulty is partly that some at least of the relevant oriental sites have not been excavated as critically as British standards would demand; partly that the pottery from them has not been fully published; partly again that the Near Eastern evidence, such as it is, is not always self-consistent. But the overriding problem is that it is difficult to find a scholar who is a master of both

Near Eastern and Irish Sea archaeology. Until one appears, it will be necessary for western archaeologists to take the best available Mediterranean evidence on trust, and to consider how far it conforms to chronological schemes based on their own fragile historical evidence.

Topography

Some brief consideration should be given finally to topographical studies, because this is the field in which archaeological methods are most directly applied to literary evidence. In both Biblical and classical studies much exploration has been devoted to the identification on the ground of cities, battle-fields and other places mentioned in the texts, whether those texts are dealing with historical, legendary or purely fictitious events. In principle the topography of Arthurian Britain could be studied in just the same way, and with equal profit.

In practice, however, this is only true in a minority of cases. Many of the battles listed in the early years of the *Anglo-Saxon Chronicle* can be located in the sense that the Old English name can be identified with a modern village name. This is potentially useful in strategic terms even though the actual field of battle, and the tactical reasons which governed it, elude us. But only one of the thirteen battles attributed to Arthur in our earliest sources can be located with confidence; and even then only in a general area – Cat Coit Celidon, the battle of the Caledonian Forest, was fought in southern Scotland (above, pp. 61–2).

A spectacular success in the identification of a royal site is the excavation of the summer court of the seventh-century kings of Northumbria. Bede refers to the place where Paulinus preached to King Edwin as *Adgefrin*. Large-scale excavations at the foot of the Iron-Age hillfort of Yeavering Bell in Northumberland have revealed a complex of timber halls, temples, and even the amphitheatre in which Paulinus preached (below, p. 309). Equally certain is the identification of Dunatt, mentioned in the Irish Annals, with the rocky fortress of Dunadd [Pl. 4*b*] dominating the Crinan isthmus in west Argyll (below, p. 267).

Moving from certainties to probabilities, we have the case of the dynasty of Gwynedd and its seats. Tradition – principally a reference to 'the long sleep of Maelgwn in the court of Rhos' – points to the vicinity of Degannwy [Pl. 4*a*], despite the fact that this is on the east bank of the river Conway and therefore outside the Snowdonian heartland of Gwynedd. But the rugged twin summits of Castell Degannwy look ideal for a citadel; the name *Vardre* attached to them shows that this had been a *maerdref* or administrative centre; and the discovery of appropriate pottery in recent excavations clinches the matter (below, p. 213). But Degannwy can never have been anything other than a frontier fortress for the dynasty. Their principal seat is known to have been at Aberffraw on the west coast of Anglesey. All the resources of place-name studies and field archaeology have been deployed in the search for this important site – so far without success.

Consideration of the topographical problems raised by the Tristan-Iseult-Mark stories is illuminating. The Tristan romance seems originally to have been told about a member of the Pictish royal family, and in Welsh literature Tristan is always known as Tristan ap Talorc, who is certainly Pictish. In south-west Scotland we find Trusty's Hill and Mote of Mark. How far we can talk about Picts in Galloway is itself a matter of dispute, but at best we can say, on archaeological grounds, that Mote of Mark was occupied at broadly the right time for Tristan (below, p. 218), and Trusty's Hill has a secondary fortification which could be contemporary. In the developed versions of the romance, however, the setting is in Cornwall or Brittany. Relevant here is a memorial stone just north of Fowey to *Drustanus filius Cunomori*: 'Tristan son of Cynfawr'. Already by the ninth century Cunomorus was being equated with Mark, and by the twelfth century the area north of Fowey – St Sampson in Golant – was made the setting for the romance. As part of the same process, the near-by Iron-Age hill-fort of Castle Dore (below, p. 212) has come to be identified as King Mark's Palace, despite the fact that the most likely candidates for the historical Mark are Welsh or Breton. We can at least affirm that the Cornish Tristan was historical – indeed the Tristan memorial stone is the only strictly contemporary evidence for any Tristan. His father Cynfawr was historical too; and excavation at Castle Dore has revealed a large timber building which may well have been his feasting hall.

The case of Tristan and Mark, then, discloses a perplexing mixture of romance, legend, and history. The case of Arthur is similar in kind but far worse in degree. We may begin by inquiring into the location

Map 4. Places associated with Arthur and Tristan in folk-lore and romance.

of Camelot and of other courts or strongholds attributed to him. The French poets were vague – perhaps deliberately vague – about the topography of Camelot. Malory in the *Morte d'Arthur* always identifies it with Winchester. But when Caxton came to print the *Morte d'Arthur* he referred in his preface to 'the toune of Camelot, which dyvers now lyvyng hath seen' in Wales, meaning perhaps by this the Roman walls of either Caerleon or Caerwent. Leland rejected both these attributions and identified Cadbury Castle [Pl. 5] as 'Camallate, sumtyme a famose toun or castelle'. It is not clear whether he did this because he found some genuine folk memory of Arthur preserved locally, or because having just passed through the villages of Queen Camel and West Camel he saw the massive defences of Cadbury towering before him, and the derivation Camelot > Camel leapt to his mind. This is indeed quite likely, because he then corrupted the local place-names to suit his identification, referring to Queen and West Camallat. However that may be, his identification was a happy one. Repeated by generations of antiquaries, it formed one of the inspirations of the recent excavations which revealed at Cadbury Castle a major fortification of the Arthurian period.

The truth is, however, that attempts to identify Camelot are pointless. The name, and the very concept of Camelot, are inventions of the French medieval poets. 'Camelot' first appears in the variant manuscripts of the *Lancelot* of Chrétien de Troyes, suggesting that it was invented around the end of the twelfth century. Before that, Geoffrey of Monmouth had established one of Arthur's chief courts at Caerleon, others being at London and Winchester. There is no archaeological or historical justification for any of these suggestions. Our earliest traditions, as preserved in the Welsh *Mabinogion*, make no attempt to localize Arthur's court, despite the fact that it plays a central part in some of the tales. Finally, the Welsh Triads locate it at Celliwig in Cornwall. This has been identified with Callington, or more probably with Killibury. At the latter, there is a circular double-banked fortress which is doubtless an Iron-Age foundation, but excavation may yet reveal a later re-use comparable with that at Castle Dore.

So far we have examined only the simpler cases of Arthurian topography. The real problem arises from the scores of archaeological sites, of many kinds, to which the name of Arthur has come to be applied over the past fourteen centuries. Some of them may indeed be genuine sites of Arthurian date, comparable in that respect with Mote of Mark or Castle Dore, but others are certainly bogus. We are not likely to be deceived by the various King Arthur's Round Tables, because the whole concept of the Round Table is a medieval invention. So we are not surprised that the Round Table at Caerleon is a Roman amphitheatre, while that near Penrith is a ritual site of the late third or early second millennium BC. Some of the sites known as Arthur's Stone are spectacular examples of chambered tombs of the Neolithic period. But what are we to make of Arthur's Seat in Edinburgh [Pl. 2]? This is in an area where the historical Arthur may well have operated, and the hilltop has traces of a defensive scheme which may belong to the post-Roman rather than the pre-Roman Iron Age. None the less we must recognize that, even if excavation should reveal pottery or other relics of Arthurian date within the defences of Arthur's Seat, this would still fall far short of proving any personal connection.

Here is the nub of the problem of Arthurian topography. Early antiquaries went to considerable lengths to establish Arthurian connections. The memorial stone from Slaughterbridge, Camelford, one reputed site of the battle of Camlann, is instructive here. The stone is still clearly legible in the double sense that the inscription is scarcely

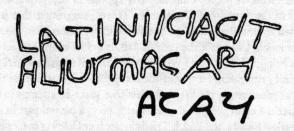

7. The inscription on the stone from Slaughterbridge, Cornwall, with a suggestion as to how Carew mis-read it.[3]

weathered and the letter forms are fairly good Roman capitals. It reads LATINI [H]IC IACIT FILIUS MAGARI: '[the monument of] Latinus. Here he lies, son of Magarus'. Carew, writing of it in the sixteenth century, refers to it as bearing the name of Arthur, though now corrupted to ATRY. One can only conclude that the last five letters had been read, wishfully, as the Gothic letters 𝔄𝔗𝔕𝔜.

The simple fact is that no contemporary inscription to Arthur is known, nor is there any contemporary literary reference to his principal seat. Moreover, there is no archaeological site which can be irrefutably associated with Arthur in a personal sense. But this is a result of the essential and ineluctable limitations of archaeological evidence in a barely literate period. The point can be emphasized by comparison with two better documented periods. Our historical sources tell us of the personal interest which Hadrian took in the planning of the great frontier work which bears his name. Knowing this, we can picture him striding the crags and fells of northern England to decide the best line for it; and we imagine that we can detect the very stamp of Hadrian's character upon it. But without the specific reference to Hadrian's interest in the Wall we would never have been led to make this personalized interpretation. Again, in north Wales there is a series of great castles which we call Edwardian, and in which we detect the personalities of Edward I and his architect, Master James of St George. We are able to do this because of the very full historical evidence that we have for the building of the castles. Without this it is questionable whether we would even attribute these castles to one and the same reign, so wide is the typological range which they exhibit.

The implication of this is that it is altogether unlikely, on the nature of the evidence, that we will ever be able to identify a fortress, or other site, with Arthur in a personal sense. On the other hand every excavation of a British site of the fifth and sixth centuries helps to enrich our picture of the material circumstances in which Arthur lived and fought.

Seven

The Culture of
Roman and
Sub-Roman Britain

We are now equipped to delineate the material culture of Arthur's Britain. More correctly, we should think of 'cultures', for though the Britons and the Anglo-Saxons were on a very similar technological level, and though both owed much to Mediterranean civilization, yet the Celtic and Teutonic transmutations of that civilization were quite dissimilar. This chapter and the next, then, depict the culture of Britain from the time when it was a diocese of the Roman empire menaced by barbarian attacks, up to the mid-seventh century. The following chapters examine the culture of the barbarian attackers themselves, first the Celtic barbarians in Chapter 9, then the English in Chapter 10.

The material culture of Roman Britain[1]

Archaeologists are accustomed to divide Britain into two major geographical zones: to the north and west a region of older, harder rocks, often barren, in general elevated, and called therefore the 'highland zone'; and to the south and east an area of softer, younger rocks, often very fertile, of lower altitude, and hence known as the 'lowland zone'. As a basic concept of physical geography the division is useful, provided first that we apply it subtly, remembering that the highland zone is fringed by coastlands and penetrated by river-valleys; and second, that we do not use it to explain human developments on a determinist basis. The folly of such explanations is well demonstrated in the Arthurian period, when the highland zone was shared between the Britons, the Picts, the Scots and the Angles. But in the Roman period the division was more significant, because it corresponded very broadly with the line between the frontier or military zone and the settled or civilian area of Roman Britain. In the north and west were fortresses and forts, whereas towns and villas were rare; in the lowland zone, on the other hand, military installations were confined to the Saxon Shore forts, whereas civilian – and civilized – forms of building abounded.

In part, the highland zone was the military zone because the ruggedness of the terrain in itself made it difficult to pacify; but more to the point, to the north and the west were unlimited reservoirs of hostile manpower, the Picts and the Scots. The lowlands by contrast had been rapidly overrun and pacified, and it was only the seamanship of the Saxon barbarians which brought the coasts of the south and east back into the military sphere. There were major economic differences too. South-eastern Britain was already exporting corn to the continent before the Roman conquest. In the following centuries increased demand, tighter organization and improved equipment all helped to increase the production of corn. The rearing of sheep for wool, and the concomitant weaving industry, formed another source of prosperity in the lowlands; and to this were added specialized industries like the potteries of the east Midlands. In the highland zone, by contrast, enough grain was probably grown to meet local needs, and there is even some evidence for an increase in arable farming to meet the demands of the army; but such prosperity as there was must have depended largely on the raising of cattle for meat and hides. Another potential source of wealth lay in the mineral deposits of the older rocks, lead and its by-product silver, copper, tin, and even gold. But these were exploited under state control and therefore created no local prosperity.

In brief, the lowlands were pacified and prosperous, the uplands were not. This is immediately reflected in the distribution of towns. The Dumnonian peninsula had one only: *Isca* – Exeter. Wales and the Marches had four: *Moridunum* – Carmarthen; *Venta* – Caerwent; *Magnis* – Kenchester; and *Viroconium* – Wroxeter. North of York, which was a military base, there were four: Aldborough, Carlisle, Catterick, and Corbridge. South and east of these areas there were thirty-five or more *coloniae* (settlements of retired legionaries), cantonial capitals, lesser walled towns and spas. We are not here concerned with the administrative implications of the towns, though we have already seen that it was the *civitates*, the cantonal capitals, which inherited the imperial authority in 410 (above, p. 99). Our present interest lies in the towns as material embodiments of the Mediterranean idea of civilization, deliberately created with this in mind. It is difficult to assess the population of the British towns, but in terms of area they range from a great commercial centre like London at 330 acres through large cantonal capitals like Cirencester (240 acres) to small capitals such as Caerwent at forty-four acres and down even to a mere five acres. A town of any size would have as its focus a group of imposing public buildings: a *forum* or market place, a *basilica* or town hall, public baths, a theatre and an amphitheatre, and several temples. Compared to similar buildings in the towns of Italy, these would have seemed indifferent in the quality of their architecture and ornament; but compared, as they should be, to the similar structures of the pre-Roman Iron Age and of the early post-Roman centuries they represent a high degree of sophistication. In addition to these public buildings the towns contained shops and private houses. Some of the latter were large affairs, arranged around a central courtyard, and the largest of them are often interpreted as inns. Finally, Roman towns were provided with a public water supply, and probably with some public system of sewerage as well. For their time, then, they reflected a high degree of both material comfort and civic organization.

In terms of a romanized way of life, the rural equivalent of the town was the villa. There was probably a direct link between the two, in that many villas were the country residences of the members of the official class, the magistrates, who dominated the towns. In terms of size and luxury they display such a great range that it is often possible to dispute, at the lower end of the scale, whether or not a rural building deserves to be classed as a villa. But in general they exhibit certain features which mark them off in material terms from anything before or immediately after, namely masonry walls – even if these were only foundations supporting a timbered superstructure – heated rooms, and decorative mosaic floors. In such an architectural setting it would have been possible to lead a gracious life. But the villa was also the centre of an economic unit, normally dependent on farming, but sometimes exploiting the natural resources of the land – stone for building, clay for potting, or wool for weaving. Much of the work was doubtless carried out by slaves, and a large establishment would have quarters for them. But on a farming estate some of the real wealth must have come from tenants who, it seems, were becoming increasingly tied to the villa organization. We should also notice that the last century of Roman Britain saw the fullest development of the luxury villa, though the economic reasons for this are still in dispute.

While the villas with their solid walls and floors are the most readily detectable element in the Roman countryside, they certainly do not constitute the only one. In those parts of the highland zone where unmortared stone was the natural building material there are homesteads which seem to form the local equivalent of villas. Among the best known are the enclosed homesteads of the area which was to become Gwynedd.[2] These range from enclosures with straight sides, containing both romanized rectangular and native circular houses, to those where the enclosing bank is oval and all the houses circular. They are frequently associated with terraced fields, but their wealth may also have come from local mineral resources. The more imposing ones, like Din Llugwy in Anglesey [Fig. 17a], must have been the residences of men at the same social level as the owners of the luxury villas.

But in the lowlands we find Celtic-looking homesteads scattered among the villas. The classic examples of these, in Cranborne Chase, appear to have contained native-style timber round houses. But the homes were sometimes embellished with painted wall-plaster in the Roman fashion, they might possess corn-drying kilns of Roman type, and their inhabitants owned Roman pots and bronze trinkets. It is not easy to define the social status of these homesteads or of others which are being detected in increasing numbers on the gravels of the Thames and the Warwickshire Avon, or in the Fenland. Some may be the homes of the tenants of the villa-estates, but others may be those of peasant proprietors. Whatever their precise social or tenurial position, the most significant feature historically speaking is the recent recognition of the occurrence of low-lying, even valley-bottom, farming and settlement.[3] It used to be thought that Celtic agriculture and settlement, whether of the pre-Roman Iron Age or the Roman period, was largely confined to the chalk downs, and that the exploitation of the lower, richer, but more difficult soils was the work of the Anglo-Saxons. It is now seen that this view was based on the easy recognition of ancient field systems on the downs, where early field boundaries have often been spared from obliteration by ploughing because the land has been marginal in recent centuries. It was probably marginal in earlier times too, and the focal areas of Romano-British farming may not have differed greatly from those of the Middle Ages. This hypothesis is of great moment for the question of continuity of settlement from Roman Britain into Saxon England (below, pp. 192 f.).

One other monumental feature of the lowlands should be mentioned here, namely the temples. Architecturally these were often elaborate buildings, and they formed the focus for other manifestations of Roman culture ranging from statuary and inscriptions to the trinkets and coins offered up by humble devotees. The actual cults included the divine emperors, the Olympic pantheon, various oriental deities including Mithras whose worship required a special form of building, and the pre-Roman Celtic gods. These last were often assimilated with Olympic gods. During the fourth century, and especially after 350, there seems to have been a great upsurge of devotion to the Celtic divinities.[4]

The most striking architectural evidence for this is provided by the great temple complex, dedicated to the Celtic god Nodens, which was erected within the ramparts of an Iron-Age hill-fort at Lydney about 367. But this is only one example of the re-use of hill-forts as centres of pagan Celtic worship at this time. There were probably two motives for this. In the first place it reflects some continuity of tradition from pre-Roman times when the great hill-forts certainly had a religious or ritual function. Second, this tradition was reinforced by the need, in an empire which was officially Christian, to remove pagan worship from public scrutiny in the towns. This was how *pagani*, a term which (as we have seen) originally meant 'countrymen', came to mean 'heathens'. The fourth-century pagan Celtic revival has sometimes been represented as the birth of a quasi-nationalist movement which was to be potent in both art and politics in the fifth century. But a recent close examination of the coins which had been offered at Celtic shrines makes it clear that the revival scarcely lasted down to 400, let alone into the succeeding century. None the less a phrase in the *De excidio* of Gildas suggests that pagan cult-images were still to be seen in his day, towards the middle of the sixth century.

Compared with the monumental evidence for pagan cults, that for Christianity is extremely tenuous. At Silchester there was a church

42 feet long by 33 feet wide across the transepts. It had an eastern porch or narthex, and a western apse at the back of the altar. Its minute size makes it clear that this can never have been the seat of the bishop of the *civitas* of the Atrebates, whose capital was Silchester. At Caerwent a room about 21 feet long by 17 feet wide had an apse crudely inserted in its east wall and a wide shallow narthex added on the west,

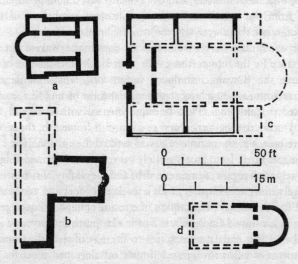

8.*a* The Romano-British church at *Calleva Atrebatum* – Silchester, Hampshire; *b* the supposed church at *Venta Silurum* – Caerwent, Monmouthshire; *c* early seventh-century church of SS Peter and Paul, Canterbury, Kent; *d* St Mary's, Lyminge, Kent, founded after 633.[5]

at some very late Roman date. Since these are the only two churches known in Roman Britain it has often been felt that, despite official recognition, Christianity must have remained an extremely feeble religion in fourth-century Britain. We have already seen, however, that this would be difficult to reconcile with the literary evidence (above, pp. 132–3). Recent work has stressed, moreover, that even in richer parts of the empire a fourth-century church may be indistinguishable in plan from a large town house. Its identification as a church may be based on continuity of religious tradition, or on the survival of specifically Christian paintings or inscriptions – conditions which do not occur in Romano-British towns. In other words, the seats of the fourth-century bishops of Britain may be lurking among the undifferentiated houses which appear on the plans of British cantonal capitals. Our only evidence for Christian paintings comes in fact not from a town but from the Lullingstone villa, where a suite of upper rooms, with its own access, had been turned into a house-church. To judge from the overtly or implicitly Christian symbolism of their mosaics, other villas were also centres of Christian worship.[6]

One other class of Roman religious monument was of greatest importance for the future. Along with other kinds of inscription carved on stone the Romans introduced tombstones, which combined a religious formula with a brief statement about the name and age of the deceased person. This might be supplemented with details of title, military service, tribal origin and so on, and it frequently ended with some reference to the persons who had erected the epitaph. The stone itself might range from an elaborately carved monument showing the deceased in full regalia, to a simple slab; and the quality of the lettering might also vary considerably, with a marked tendency to carelessness by the fourth century. The custom of erecting epitaphs, though pagan in origin, continued among Christians in the fourth century, and gave rise in the fifth and later centuries to the so-called Early Christian monuments which provide such important documentation for our main period of interest (below, pp. 238–48, pp. 262–3).

We turn now to the military zone. Here the main architectural evidence for the Roman presence lies in the legionary fortresses – especially those at Caerleon, Chester and York; the auxiliary forts; the roads between them; and the two northern walls. The fortresses, forts and roads formed a linked system, in which the forts held the forward units, normally cohorts five hundred or a thousand strong of men recruited from the conquered provinces, while the fortresses at the rear of the system held legions of a nominal strength of about five thousand. In fact much of the legion was often away from base on detachment duties. From the second century the fortresses had stone defensive walls, and both the administrative buildings and the barracks were also of mortared stone. The auxiliary forts in plan were scaled down versions of the fortresses. From the mid-second century they normally had a stone defensive wall and masonry administrative buildings, but the barracks were more likely to be of timber. The system was largely laid out during the phase of conquest and pacification, but thereafter the individual forts had a chequered history which, it is now being realized, allows of no simple generalization. Some forts of the conquest period later became towns; some were soon abandoned altogether; perhaps a few were continuously occupied, but the most normal pattern was one of intermittent abandonment and reoccupation as the Roman authorities shifted their inadequate resources of manpower to meet threats now of barbarians from the north, now of revolts in Wales. From our present point of view, the most important feature of their history is their final abandonment. For Wales as a whole, this appears to have taken place when Magnus Maximus removed troops in 383. Some of the forts in the Pennines and on Hadrian's Wall may, however, have been garrisoned down to 400 and beyond.

The two northern walls need not detain us long. Their chief interest for us is their prominence in the historical section of Gildas, and the large degree of muddle on his part which is thus exposed. Both walls were sited to take advantage of the indented coast of Britain, but they had the great difference that the Forth-Clyde line of the Antonine Wall largely coincided with the southern border of Pictland, whereas the Tyne-Solway line of Hadrian ran across the territory of the great tribe or confederation of the Brigantes. The Antonine Wall had only a short history, but Hadrian's Wall, with its attendant forts both to front and rear, retained its importance in controlling the northern tribes and in defending Britannia against yet fiercer enemies from the Highlands. The major element in this scheme was a physical barrier in the form of a masonry wall, normally fronted with a ditch if not with natural precipices. In itself the barrier would have been useless without some means of patrolling it, and without the provision of garrisons both to screen the wall and to sally out against hostile bands. The precise way in which this patrolling and garrisoning was arranged varied from time to time, in ways which do not concern us here. But the very fact that such activities were necessary provides an instructive comment on the defensive barriers erected in later centuries (below, pp. 349–50).

In themselves, of course, the walls, forts and roads did nothing to civilize the people of the highland zone, except possibly by enforcing a precarious peace. But a degree of commerce sprang up between the soldiery and the natives in whose territory the forts were planted. As a result, civil settlements were founded outside the fort walls. Some of these, like that at the legionary fortress of Caerleon, contained houses which were as good as any in the towns, and temples were also a regular occurrence. In other cases there was little more than a bazaar of wooden shops. But even here, the natives had the opportunity of obtaining minor objects of Roman culture – pottery and bronze trinkets, for instance – in return for their own products. Even more important, here was the meeting place of auxiliary soldier, whether provincial or barbarian in origin, and native women, which was to breed the future garrison of the fort. Here too the retired soldier most probably settled to live out his days. So in the military zone, these civil settlements were the main focus of romanization.

Throughout Roman Britain, in villas and homesteads, towns and forts, certain by-products of Roman culture are almost universal. The most ubiquitous is commercially produced pottery. In the pre-Roman Iron Age some areas already had a flourishing pottery industry, and this contributed much, in both shape and decoration, to early Roman styles. Other areas, notably parts of the highland zone, had no native pottery tradition but none the less they were happy to use the pottery which became available in the second and later centuries. By the late Roman period a range of very efficient utility vessels could readily be purchased – vessels for cooking, eating, drinking and storage. Some of these were attractively decorated with applied, impressed or painted ornament. Production was highly industrialized at a limited number of centres. A significant number of these exploited the boulder clays of eastern England, which must have made them vulnerable to Saxon raiding, just as their commercial and industrial organization was vulnerable in the economic collapse of the western empire.

The warrior-aristocrats of pre-Roman Britain had patronized a flourishing metal industry. In so far as this was producing arms and armour it was of course entirely suppressed in areas under Roman control. But the blacksmith had also produced efficient tools and implements for the craftsman and the farmer. These underwent some minor improvements during the Roman centuries, but they are not sufficiently characteristic to detain us here. More interesting are the brooches of bronze, sometimes inlaid with other metals or with the vitreous paste known as enamel. Following on from Celtic models, these were made in a variety at once fascinating and bewildering for a century or more after the conquest, but gradually the repertory dwindled, until by the fourth century we need single out only those types which have some significance for the future. Certain plate or disk brooches, ornamented in relief or with enamel, preserved some of the motifs dear to Celtic artistic taste, and may therefore have formed one of the starting points of the Celtic artistic revival. Another was undoubtedly provided by the most characteristically British brooch – the penannular [Fig. 22]. On the turned-back terminals of this the Irish saw birds' heads and the Britons saw animal heads, from which sprang the splendid series of decorated zoomorphic penannulars which graced both men and women in Arthur's Britain (pp. 236–8). The third type, the crossbow brooch, was popular on the continent as well, where it passed into Germanic hands and initiated an important series of cruciform brooches, which came back to Britain on the dresses of Anglo-Saxon women [Fig. 26c].

Finally, it is worth stressing that Romano-British culture was based on a money economy. In south-eastern Britain coins were indeed already in use before the conquest, but the Romans were responsible for spreading their circulation throughout the island. The extent to which currency permeated the whole commercial life of the country, down to the smallest transactions, may be gauged from the occurrence of coins on the humblest Romano-British sites and in the remotest part of the province. Moreover, whenever there was a shortfall in supplies of coin from official sources, local production took place; for instance, in the second quarter of the fourth century, local imitations of the imperial coinage, mostly of inferior style and weight, enjoyed wide circulation. The importance of coinage is also indicated by the promptness with which usurpers like Carausius organized the production and circulation of coins appropriate to their regime. But it should also be noticed that the overwhelming bulk of the currency in use in Britain was imported from Italy or even Gaul. There was from time to time a mint at London, but this was closed early in the fourth century and only briefly revived in the 380s by Magnus Maximus.

Change and continuity

By the fourth century the material culture of the Romans, in both its military and its civilian aspects, must have appeared firmly established in Britain. But already certain developments were taking place in the field of defence as a response to barbarian threats. We must first examine these, and then turn to the fifth and later centuries to see what in the way of things Roman survived the political events of 410 and later.

The first development to notice is the appearance of new types of fortification. The normal auxiliary fort had consisted initially of an earthen bank, with straight sides and rounded corners; to this a masonry wall was usually added, and this would be furnished with towers which did not project in front of the wall-face. Such forts were essentially protected bases, from which the garrison moved out to control the country. But in the forts of the Saxon Shore, built in and after the late third century (above, pp. 95–7) the emphasis was all on the wall [Pl. 1]. This might be straight or curving, its angles might be sharp or rounded, but invariably it was high and thick. Projecting from it were round or rectangular bastions, which probably served as artillery platforms and which certainly provided flanking-fire along the wall-faces. These forts were evidently strong-points, concentrations of fire-power, intended to receive and to slaughter bands of attackers. This new tactical concept marked also a new strategy – that of an empire on the defensive. At the same time, the siting of the forts on estuaries or by the coast implies that they were also bases for naval patrols which provided an element of mobility in the scheme.

Inland, too, it seems that forts at critical river-crossings might be provided with massive walls and used as bases for large cavalry units whose main advantage must have lain in their mobility. In the late fourth century, as troops were withdrawn from Britain either to support usurpers or to defend the empire against the Germanic hordes, so the number of forts that were actually garrisoned must have dwindled progressively. At the very end of the century or early in the fifth, it seems likely that the system of frontier defence based on the forts was replaced by one in which the main element was a mobile field army commanded by a *comes Britanniarum*, Count of the Britains. Presumably such a force would have had one or more bases, but we have no evidence about their location or character.

Meanwhile a new element altogether had been brought into the scheme of defence: the towns. Most if not all of the towns had been provided with defensive ramparts and walls at dates which vary from the first to the third century. The purpose of this was to protect them against rebellions within Britain itself as much as against marauders from outside. But after the great barbarian conspiracy and the disaster of 367, as part of the programme of recovery and restoration under Count Theodosius (above, p. 96) most town walls were provided with projecting bastions like those of the Saxon Shore forts. At the same time the original town ditch would be filled in and a new, very wide ditch would be dug further out. The bastions were designed as artillery platforms and the ditch was now sited so that it confronted hostile marauders with a serious obstacle just as they came into range. The towns were therefore capable of vigorous self-defence, a military fact that should be borne in mind as the background to Honorius' instruction, nearly half a century later, that the cities should look to their own defence. Given this degree of protection in a troubled age, it is not surprising that the British towns appear to have prospered in the fourth century.

The towns shared something more than bastions with the Saxon Shore forts; they seem to have had the same kind of troops operating the *ballistae*, artillery pieces, which were mounted on the bastions. Despite the supposed incompetence of Germanic barbarians at handling engines of war, it has been inferred that Germans formed an important element among the artillery men. In cemeteries outside both towns and forts in eastern England there occur pottery urns, holding the cremated ashes of the dead, which can be closely compared with vessels from across the North Sea. Frisian connections are especially strong [Fig. 27a] recalling the Frisian elements which we have already noticed on Hadrian's Wall (above p. 94). Some at least of this pottery would be dated before 400 on the continent, and it seems therefore to imply the settlement of Germans in the vicinity of the cemeteries in the late fourth century. Furthermore, forts and towns in southern and eastern England produce military buckles and belt-fittings which have parallels in Germanic warrior-graves along the Rhineland frontier (below, p. 286). Some scholars maintain that the ornament on this metalwork is specifically German in taste, but others would consider that it is characteristic of the provincial Roman taste current along the frontier. The earliest buckles are very close to the continental examples, but they are few in number. It is thought that they represent the equipment of troops brought in by Count Theodosius. More numerous, later examples seem to have been made in Britain itself, perhaps to equip further Germanic troops recruited either before or even after 410 [Pl. 17]. These later pieces are spread as far west as Cirencester and even Caerwent, and also up into the midlands at Leicester.[7]*

In the case of the Saxon Shore forts, we know from the late Roman army list, the *Notitia Dignitatum*, that the normal garrison was a *numerus*, commanded by a *praepositus*. In some cases, it was the kind of irregular unit which we have already seen in the *Numerus Hnaudifridi* at Housesteads (above, p. 94) or which we have inferred in Dyfed (above, p. 124). It seems possible that similar units or, more likely, detachments from them were manning the artillery bastions of the towns as well. But our knowledge of late Roman military organization is too slight to tell us what kind of man a *praepositus* might be at this date – whether he was a noble of the tribe from which the *numerus* was recruited; or a senior warrant-officer from a regular unit; or a Roman gentleman on some kind of career ladder. Clearly the character of its commander might well influence the extent to which a unit became romanized. Nor can we readily determine whether a whole tribal group – warriors, women and children – was brought over and planted on the land, or whether only the menfolk were recruited. The occurrence of Frisian pottery probably implies Frisian women to make it, and this is likely in the case of the troops whom the Romans called *laeti*, a term which originally meant 'serfs'. These can have absorbed very little Roman culture. Finally, we might ask how many of these Germanic troops, recruited to Britain in the late fourth century, went

*Since this was written an important note has appeared on Germanic warrior-graves in what was otherwise a normal fourth-century cemetery a quarter of a mile outside the north gate of the Roman town of Winchester – *Venta Belgarum*: Clarke, G., 'Lankhills School' in Biddle, M., 'Excavations at Winchester, 1969', *Ant. J.* 50, 1970, pp. 277–326, especially pp. 292–8.

back to the continent with Magnus Maximus in 383, or with Constantine III in 407. The answer would clearly be significant for our understanding of the early phases of Germanic settlement; but regrettably it is unattainable.

The developments in defence which we have considered so far were largely confined to the lowland zone. In the highland zone, it has been inferred that forts of Saxon Shore type were built along the shores facing Ireland, but the only examples actually known are a fragment at Lancaster and a type-specimen at Cardiff. It has also been thought that, faced with Irish raiding and no longer adequately protected by Roman forces, the natives turned to self-help by reoccupying the hilltop fortifications of their ancestors. The evidence for this hypothesis is clearest in Wales, where the excavation of hill-forts frequently produces rich relics of the third and fourth centuries, especially pottery and coins. Some of these sites, notably Dinorben, Castell Degannwy [Fig. 15, 6], Dinas Emrys [Fig. 15, 7] and Coygan,[8] have also yielded pottery or other finds of the Arthurian period; so we are faced with the possibility that we have, already in the third century, an anticipation of the pattern of the late fifth and sixth. The possibility gains added weight when we recall the legendary importance of Dinas Emrys as the scene of the conflict between Vortigern and Ambrosius (above, p. 34), and the historical significance of Castell Degannwy as a citadel of Maelgwn Gwynedd [Pl. 4a]. In fact, however, the coin evidence does not support the hypothesis that hill-forts which had been reoccupied in the third century continued to be military and administrative centres into the sixth. The latest recorded coins are as follows: from Coygan, an imitation of a Constantinian coin, dated 337–41; and from Dinorben and Castell Degannwy, coins of Valens, 364–78. Since later coins are known in some quantity in Wales, notably at Caerwent, it is reasonable to believe that the end of the coin-series at these hill-forts also marks an effective break in their occupation.

The supposed intention of the third- and fourth-century reoccupations as a defence against Irish raiders may also be called into question. First, not all the reoccupied forts are near the threatened coasts: the Breiddin, which overlooks the flood-plain of the Severn where it debouches from the hills is a clear example of an inland fort. Second, in no instance has it been shown that the defences were refurbished in the late Roman period;* on the contrary, third-century refuse often laps over the ruinous back of the principal rampart. Admittedly, the siting of these forts is enough to make them defensible, even with their ramparts in decay; but the evidence of the successive ramparts on pre-Roman hills-forts like Maiden Castle and Cadbury Castle makes it clear that if a fort is to be re-used for a military purpose it would be normal to rebuild or at least refurbish the defences. We have already noticed activity in the hill-forts of lowland Britain in the third and fourth centuries, but there the purpose was religious, not military. It seems likely that this was true in the west as well. At Cadbury, Devon, for instance, a ritual shaft was found to contain votive bracelets, rings and beads. Among the sparse finds of bronze from Dinorben were a bronze wand or staff of office, ox-head mounts from a ceremonial vessel, and bracelets comparable with those which formed votive offerings at the Lydney temple, which was itself built in a hill-fort.

Even if this hypothesis that the late Roman re-use of hill-forts was ritual rather than defensive should prove to be mistaken, yet it is fair to re-emphasize that the defences of the forts were not refurbished at this time. This generalization points up the contrast with the one native site where wholly new defences are known from the fourth century:

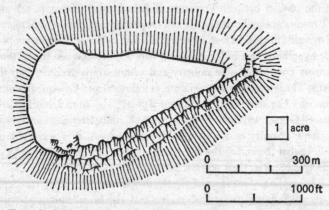

9. Traprain Law, East Lothian; plan of the defences of the Votadinian stronghold in their final, fourth-century phase.

*Excavations carried out at the Breiddin since this was written suggest that there at least elaborate timber defences were erected in the late fourth century.

Traprain Law, the great stronghold of the Votadini.[9] From the middle of the first century AD this rugged hill-top had been crowned with a stone-walled fort some forty acres in extent, which itself replaced a succession of earlier defences. The forty-acre fort was twice rebuilt, the last occasion being about AD 300. Some time later the northern defences were retracted from an advanced line part way down a very steep slope, and realigned at the brow of the hill. The defences now enclosed only some thirty acres, but the readily habitable area within them remained about the same. There is no direct evidence for the date of the new defensive wall, which was an unusual structure consisting of a turf core with stone facing, measuring twelve feet in overall width. It has been suggested that this last defence belongs to the time, about 370, when Count Theodosius is supposed to have converted the Votadini into a treaty state; but since this hypothesis depends firstly on confusing Manau Guotodin with the territory of the Votadini, and secondly on putting dates to the genealogy of Cunedda (above, pp. 128–9), it may be discarded. It is none the less likely that the final defensive work belongs to the fourth century, and later rather than earlier in the century. A close study of the relics looted over the years from Traprain Law, and especially of the coins and brooch types, makes it clear that it was a flourishing defended town at the very end of the fourth century and into the first decades of the fifth, but its occupation did not last beyond 450 at the very latest. There is therefore no reason for dating the construction of the last defence to the fifth century. If Traprain Law were to be adequately excavated, the last generation of its existence would provide a rich picture of life among the northern Britons on the eve of the Arthurian period. But it remains a curious fact, without explanation at present, that by Arthur's day it was wholly abandoned.

The early fifth century

From this consideration of native forts we must turn back to strictly Roman sites, and ask what befell the forts and towns and villas after 407. How far did they continue into the fifth century and beyond? The problem has two aspects, the structural and the institutional. The first is the province of the archaeologist, the second has rather to be examined in the light of verbal evidence, and of this there is all too little. If we take the military sites first, it is clear that as structures they remained standing for centuries. Bede, writing in 731, describes Hadrian's Wall as plain to be seen, and twelve feet high. Several of the Saxon Shore forts have walls which are still eminently defensible: those at Burgh Castle are fifteen feet high even today, while the walls and bastions of Pevensey – *Anderida* stand even higher. At Portchester, and again at the legionary fortress of Chester, the Roman wall served as the basis for medieval castle- and town-walls. Indeed, given the quality of Roman masonry, there is no reason why these walls should have undergone much collapse or destruction until the time when their stone was robbed to make churches and castles. But the survival of the outer walls of a fort is no guarantee that its internal buildings survived more than a generation of neglect. Once the garrisons had gone, as the last of them probably had by 407, these places might soon have become empty shells.

But perhaps the story is not as simple as this. We have already noticed the buckles and belt-fittings, allegedly ornamented in Germanic taste (above, p. 178). The earlier series of these was imported, perhaps in 367, whereas the later examples were manufactured in this country over an unknown period which could well extend into the fifth century. A very rich collection of the earlier type comes from the Saxon Shore fort of Richborough – *Rutupiae*, but the later class is also represented there. In itself this need not take us beyond 407. But Richborough has also produced in some quantity pottery vessels which look like degenerate versions of Romano-British jars, and which had been modelled by hand in a domestic context rather than manufactured industrially on the potter's wheel. Some specimens occur in the top-soil, but others are found in rubbish pits along with well-known types of late Roman wheel-thrown pots. It seems inconceivable that the wheel-thrown and the hand-modelled vessels were being manufactured at the same time, and the most reasonable explanation is that the hand-modelled ones represent the degenerate continuation of Roman forms after the pottery industry itself had broken down. Unfortunately we have no basis for saying when this took place. It was presumably part of a general process of economic decay, for which the clearest evidence is the collapse of the money economy, which seems to have taken place in the decade 420–30 (below, p. 198). So the hand-

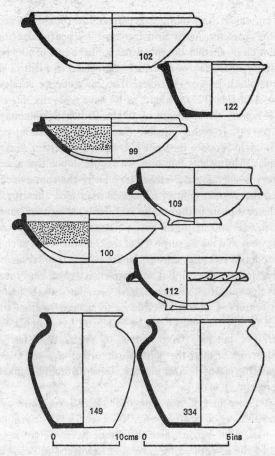

10. Some of the pottery from Pit 1, Temples Site, *Rutupiae* – Richborough, Kent. Vessels 99, 100, 102, 109, 112, 122 are standard wheel-thrown products of the highly organized Romano-British pottery industry, but 149 and 334 are the crude hand-modelled products of cottage industry. There are ten vessels comparable with 149.[10]

modelled pottery, which we may reasonably call sub-Roman, could well belong to the period 430–50. It has no Germanic features about it, and it argues for a purely British community residing within the walls of Richborough down to the coming of Hengist and Horsa. It is perhaps curious, if this hypothesis is correct, that the site has produced none of the characteristically British zoomorphic penannular brooches.

It is not clear whether the sub-Roman inhabitants of Richborough were military, or civilian, or a mixture – perhaps even a British *numerus* with its families. It is at least clear that this evidence is relevant to events at Anderida [Pl. 1*b*] where, as we have seen, the *Anglo-Saxon Chronicle* reports the massacre of all the British inhabitants in 491 (above, p. 112). It seems possible that skilled excavation, properly reported, might produce the same sub-Roman pottery at Anderida as at Rutupiae. Meanwhile, however, we should notice that a very different story is emerging at Portchester.[11] There the coin evidence has suggested that regular military use ceased in or soon after 367. Structurally the next phase in the interior is represented by a sunken-floored house characteristic of pagan Saxon peasant villages. On historical grounds, we would not be surprised at the construction of such houses in an abandoned fort after Cerdic's landing – that is to say after 495 at the earliest (above, p. 116). But an ornamental disk of gilt bronze, and distinctive pottery from the house, have been dated to the first half of the fifth century. Can this be evidence for a *numerus* from the Low Countries (where the pottery can be matched), living not in Roman-style barracks, but in a German type of house? And if so, was it recruited before or after the political rupture of 407–10? Clearly we are only on the eve of discovering how Roman Britain became Anglo-Saxon England.

At Portchester the evidence of pagan and later Saxon pottery demonstrates continuous occupation, even if we cannot yet determine what form it took. But we can infer that other Saxon Shore forts were deserted by the seventh century, because Reculver and Bradwell both had churches built in them before 700. Bede also gives us a circumstantial account of how King Sigeberht of East Anglia granted the Irish missionary Fursa a site to build a monastery in the fort of Burgh Castle [Pl. 1*a*]. The ecclesiastical aspects of this we will consider later (below, p. 326); for our present purpose it is enough to notice that there is no suggestion that either soldiers or civilians had to be turned out to make way for the monks. Elsewhere we have no clear evidence about the state of Roman military buildings by the fifth and later centuries. In lowland England, of course, the forts of the conquest phase would have been reduced to grassy banks long before 407; but in the military zone, as we have said, their walls may have remained as strongpoints in time of need. We may speculate that in 616 the walls of Chester had been a magnet to Æthelfrith, even if the battle itself was fought in the open.

In the same way, the walled towns[12] would still have formed strongpoints and places of refuge, whether or not they had troops to man the bastions or town councils to organize the defence. Despite the lurid picture which Gildas gives us of the sack of towns, archaeological evidence for this has been claimed at only one site, Caistor-by-Norwich. Caistor, *Venta Icenorum*, was a small walled town thirty-five acres in extent possessing the usual civic amenities of public buildings, metalled roads, and piped water-supply. In the late fourth century the intensity of occupation diminished, and there may have been some economic decline. Despite this, it appears that a body of Germanic soldiers and their families were settled at *Venta*, as we may infer both from military buckles found there, and also from Germanic pottery of around or before 400 found in a cemetery outside the walls. Excavation has also revealed that a large town house was burned down about AD 400, after at least thirty-six people had been massacred. This is interpreted as implying that the German soldiery had got out of hand, and certainly the fact that the bodies had been left unburied suggests that civic life had come to an abrupt end.

Several comments are necessary here. If we accept these hypotheses, this particular massacre took place half a century before the Saxon rebellion reported by Gildas. But can we in fact accept them? No adequate report has yet appeared on the extensive excavations carried out over many years at Caistor. But from what little has been published it appears that the evidence for massacre and burning was confined to a single house. There is nothing to show that this disaster affected the town as a whole or to suggest that such events were common to Roman towns throughout Britain, as the fire-and-slaughter interpretation of the English settlement demands.

If any significant number of towns had been brought to an end by sack and burning, archaeologists could expect to find burnt debris – one of the most easily recognizable of archaeological deposits – as a regular feature. It might occur either as the latest level on those sites which were permanently abandoned, or overlying ruined Roman walling and cut into by Saxon and medieval pits and foundations in towns which were later reoccupied. The great revolt of Boudicca in AD 60 provides an excellent parallel here, for clear traces of a Boudiccan burning-level occur at London, *Verulamium* and *Camulodunum*, the three towns which she sacked. But nothing of the kind has ever been claimed for the fifth century AD. Its absence is most noticeable in the case of *Calleva* – Silchester – for this is the town which has been most completely excavated. In other town sites, it is common for the stumps of Roman walling to be covered not by a burning-level but by an accumulation of humus, suggesting decay and abandonment rather than any dramatic catastrophe. In other words archaeology provides no evidence in support of the view that the end of romanized urban life in Britain came as a result of the military activities of rebellious Saxon mercenaries.

It is even necessary to analyse and discuss how far urban civilization did perish. The case is plain enough when, as at *Calleva*, or at *Viroconium* – Wroxeter – the Roman town had no medieval or modern successor. Even the mention of a town-name in an early source is no guarantee for the continuity of urbanized occupation, or even of occupation at all. That Chester should be a battle-site in 616 might suggest that town life, fostered originally in the suburbs of the fortress, might have lingered on within the protection of the walls after the garrison had left in the later fourth century. But in 893 Chester was '*anre westre ceastre on Wirhealum*', 'a deserted fort in the Wirral', which provided temporary refuge for a Viking army on the run. Consistent with this record, intensive excavations there have failed to produce any body of relics to bridge the gap between the end of the fourth century and the beginning of the tenth, when Chester was reoccupied and refortified as a defence against the Vikings. In the meantime, *Legaceaster* and *Cair legion* had been the Saxon and British names respectively for a mere heap of ruins.

This is relevant to a discussion of the fate of Bath, Cirencester and Gloucester. We have seen (above, p. 118) how the *Anglo-Saxon Chronicle* records that in 577 Ceawlin of Wessex slew three kings in the place that is called *Deorham* (Dyrham), and took three 'chesters': *Gleawanceaster*, *Cirenceaster* and *Bathanceaster*. This annal has widely been held to imply that here in the west an enclave of Romano-British urban civilization had survived undisturbed until 577. It was considered that the fact of survival could not be denied, even if the quality of romanization and urbanization might be suspect. *Corinium* – Cirencester – was certainly a *civitas* in the Roman period, while *Glevum* – Gloucester – as a *colonia* ranked even higher in the administrative system. Both, therefore, were political units of the kind to which power was delegated in 410. It might even be suggested (below, p. 321) that the men whom the English called 'kings', *cyninges*, would have been called *magistratus* [Pl. 28] by their fellow Britons. But the example of Chester warns us that the place-names alone are not enough to prove urban survival; other evidence is needed. Cirencester has produced some late Roman military buckles, so it seems that it was provided with a protective detachment of soldiery in the late fourth century. On the other hand, it is one of the towns where a sterile layer is said to intervene between the late Roman and the Saxon or medieval layers, suggesting a period of abandonment. Moreover, not one of the three towns has produced specimens of the imported pottery which was widespread in western Britain from about 470 to 600 or later. Such pottery certainly came into the Severn Sea, and it has been found in quantity at Congresbury, only a score of miles from Bath. Its absence from Gloucester, Cirencester and Bath suggests that these towns had not retained enough urban organization to engage in commerce. There is no other archaeological evidence to sustain a case for continuity.

There are nevertheless other towns where continuity or survival of a kind can be clearly demonstrated. In discussing the available scraps of evidence it should be said at the outset that they must be given a weighting out of all proportion to their quantity. This is firstly because, on those town-sites where occupation lasted through the Middle Ages into modern times, the digging of foundations, wells, cess-pits and cellars has fragmented the remains of fifth- and sixth-century structures even where it has not obliterated them completely. Second, even the more elaborate buildings of the time are likely to have been of timber, and we have seen already that these are the structures least likely to be recognized in the trench and box excavations of an earlier generation of archaeologists (above, p. 153). There is ironic significance in the fact that such buildings have been best recognized at *Viroconium*

– Wroxeter – a town which appeared to have been deserted completely from the fifth century. The *Viroconium* houses were long narrow structures 10 metres or so long by three metres wide, with doors in the long sides opening into a through passage which divided the house into dwelling-room and byre. At present the finds only allow us to say that these houses are later than the fourth century and earlier than the eleventh. It would therefore be premature to assign them either to Germanic soldier-peasants – *foederati* or *laeti* – settled by the Romans, or to Mercian farmers moving in on their own initiative, the *Wrocen Saetan*, 'dwellers around the Wrekin', which itself takes its name from *Viroconium*. On either view, this is scarcely a case for the survival of urbanization. Its real significance is as a warning of what may have been lost from other town-sites.

Three towns, *Verulamium* – St Albans, Canterbury, and Dorchester-on-Thames, have indeed yielded particularly relevant evidence. *Verulamium* is frequently considered to figure in the historical record as the scene of Germanus' triumph over the Pelagians in 428–9. This is not fact but inference, based on the statement of Germanus' biographer that after the successful refutation of the heretics Germanus and Lupus 'repaired to the blessed martyr Alban to give thanks'. This tells us only that the shrine of Alban, the first British martyr, was celebrated, not that Germanus' confrontation with the Pelagians had taken place at St Albans. If it had done, then Germanus would have found there a reasonably flourishing romanized town as the archaeological evidence makes clear. Shops and houses were certainly being altered or repaired in the early fifth century; and about or even after AD 450 piped water, one of the great amenities of romanized urban life, was still available. Around 400 the presence of a detachment of soldiery is suggested by a military buckle. It seems likely, too, that this was one *civitas* which looked to its own defence with considerable success, for from *Verulamium* up to the scarp of the Chilterns there is a marked dearth of pagan Saxon cemeteries.

At Canterbury and Dorchester-on-Thames, on the other hand, the evidence is for the establishment of Germans, perhaps at first as soldier-allies, and later as free settlers, but in either case within the structural framework of the town. In both places, the earliest Germanic buildings are sunken-floored houses of the kind we have already noticed at Portchester. At Canterbury, six of these were roughly aligned, parallel with a Roman street and about ten metres back from its edge. If the hypothesis is adopted that these pit-houses were the out-houses of more substantial dwellings built at ground level (below, p. 303), then there would be room for the latter alongside the road itself, but there is no positive evidence for this. At Dorchester a similar sunken building, apparently a kitchen or bakery, was entered by a crude flight of steps from a Roman street. Later it was filled in and overlaid by a large rectangular building. This was at right angles to the road and had one row of its wall-posts dug through the metalling, suggesting that the street grid was still extant even if building frontages were not being maintained. Both towns have yielded Germanic pottery of early Anglo-Frisian type, and from outside Dorchester comes an important group of late Roman military buckles and belt-fittings. The Germanic pottery continues through the fifth and sixth centuries.

This evidence suggests, then, how the settlement of German soldiers and their families may have eased the transition from Roman Britain to Saxon England in an urban context. Of course these people were not living in Roman-style houses, and there must have been a considerable architectural decline, especially in the case of public buildings. But when Canterbury and Dorchester appear again in the historical record on the evangelization of the English, each is referred to as a 'city', *civitas*. Thus Bede tells us that in Canterbury, the metropolis of the Kentish realm, '*quae imperii totius erat metropolis*', Augustine received his episcopal see, '*in regia civitate sedem episcopalem . . . accepit*'. It seems reasonable to infer from this that Augustine, timid and conservative as he was, none the less saw in Canterbury something that he could recognize as a *civitas* in Mediterranean terms, however watered down. It may be argued here that Canterbury is a special case because the geographical proximity of Kent to Gaul and the political links which developed in the sixth century had made it the most civilized of the English kingdoms. But this cannot be argued in the case of Wessex, whose apostle Birinus, having been consecrated at Genoa, was given 'the city called Dorchester to make there his episcopal see', '*civitatem quae vocatur Dorcic ad faciendam inibi sedem episcopalem*'.

It is possible, indeed, to compile from Bede's *Ecclesiastical History* a significant list of former Roman towns which he thought fit to describe as *civitates* when, on the conversion, they became the seats of bishoprics. Besides Canterbury and Dorchester, it includes Rochester, York, Lincoln and Winchester. The most interesting example is that of *Lundonia civitas*, London, for Bede tells us not only that this is the metropolis of the East Saxons, but that it is 'a market-town of many people coming both by land and sea', '*multorum emporium populorum terra marique venientium*'. All this suggests that at least the pale semblance of a Mediterranean town survived in these and other cases; and that so far as London was concerned the commercial basis of urbanization was strongly present.

Against this view it might be urged that *civitas* is a normal term for an episcopal see. It is used, for instance, in a charter of 679 to describe Reculver, where the church had been set up in the ruins of a Saxon Shore fort. But it is noteworthy that Bede himself does not use it of Aidan's seat: 'The King gave him an episcopal seat on the island of Lindisfarne, as he himself had requested,' '*rex locum sedis episcopolis in insula Lindisfarnensi, ut ipse petebat, tribuit.*' In fact Bede only uses it of those sees which were placed on Roman sites. We have seen conspicuously at *Verulamium* that a survival of Roman town life, architecture and amenities can be demonstrated far into the fifth century, and *Verulamium* cannot have been alone in this. We have seen from the verbal evidence that some former Roman towns were acceptable seats for bishops in the seventh century, and thereafter their urban existence has been continuous. Since the ancestral continental Anglo-Saxons were certainly not town-dwellers it is altogether unlikely that their descendants would have breathed new life into the towns of Roman Britain if they had really found them dead. It is altogether more likely that certain of the towns survived in a weakly condition; that they proved capable of absorbing some of the English immigrants; and that they were gradually revived by the needs of trade, ecclesiastical and civil administration, and defence until they became the flourishing towns of late Saxon England. It is equally true that some never revived at all; but this is as true beyond the range of barbarian raiders, for instance at Caerwent, as it is in the east at Silchester. It may be suspected from this that economic factors were more potent than barbarian raids.

As we have seen, the other important class of romanized structure and institution comprised the villas. These rich dwellings, standing isolated in the countryside, were as tempting to raiders as the towns and obviously more vulnerable. Since military buckles are found on some villa sites, it appears that occasionally they enjoyed the protection of detachments of Germanic soldiers. In view of the close economic and social links between villas and towns it is tempting to wonder whether in these instances a town magistrate had sent a squad to look after his country seat. It has frequently been claimed, from the evidence of excavation, that despite such protection particular villas were burned down by raiding parties in the late fourth or even in the fifth century. There were certainly plenty of occasions when this might have happened: in the barbarian conspiracy of 367; in Saxon or Irish raids of various dates; or at the hands of a discontented or actively rebellious peasantry in the first decades of the fifth century. But a critical examination of all the evidence makes it very doubtful whether more than a handful of villas suffered a violent end.[13] The traces of burning are normally confined to one or two rooms, and are most likely the result of accidental fires. The corpses which earlier excavators believed had been left scattered and unburied on the sack of the villas are now seen as regular burials made long after the buildings had fallen into decay. It is only when we find corpses and masonry thrown down a well that we can believe in deliberate destruction. Even this, in its very wantonness, smacks more of social upheaval than of looting activities.

None the less the villa buildings, or even the villa sites in a slightly wider sense, appear not to have survived to the point where they were taken over and used by Saxon proprietors. It is sometimes argued that this appearance is due to the destruction of the latest or uppermost levels by ploughing, or to the failure of excavators concentrating on masonry walls and mosaic floors to notice the flimsy timber buildings of the fifth and later centuries. But it cannot be said too firmly that it is quite impossible to believe that all the material objects of a hypothetical Saxon occupation could have been destroyed by ploughing. Some fragments of pottery, some jewelry at least, should have remained for discovery by the archaeologist. So we can accept that in general villa sites were not occupied after 450, that relatively few remained in use after 400, and that many were already abandoned in the 360s. But the reasons for this are economic, and linked to the economic decline of the towns. Indeed, simply because the more elaborate villas were luxuries, they showed that decline earlier than the towns themselves. Thus in the later fourth century we find reception rooms put to industrial or agricultural purposes by the insertion of furnaces or corn-drying ovens. The more luxurious suites may be left derelict and only the humbler rooms used for habitation. This may suggest that the villa owners kept to the security of the walled towns, leaving only a factor or bailiff in residence.

There is, however, one instance, Shakenoak,[14] near Wilcote in Oxfordshire, where excavation seems to present a very different picture, for there early Saxon domestic pottery is found in quantity as well as very late Roman pottery. These excavations are still in progress, and the full significance of the discoveries cannot yet be assessed. Nevertheless it seems very probable that at Shakenoak the villa site, if not the actual buildings, was taken over by a people using Saxon pottery. We cannot at present say at what social level the take-over occurred, whether by a noble Saxon landowner or by a peasant community. But thinking beyond the immediate evidence of Shakenoak we must realize that even if we had absolutely no signs of the English immigrants using villa sites as such, we could not infer from this that the landed estates of villas were never taken over. This could only be proved, of course, if we had documentary evidence of ownership, which is impossible. An attempt has been made to demonstrate that at Withington in Gloucestershire the known boundaries of a Saxon estate coincided with those of a villa estate, but since the villa's boundaries are wholly inferential there can be no proof of this.[15] But it must also be recognized that, as a result of recent research, the terminal date for villas has been placed later, while the initial date for Saxon settlement has been pushed earlier, so that the two now touch even if they do not overlap. It becomes increasingly probable therefore that in some areas the incomers found villa estates still in being, and took them over as going concerns.

This hypothesis is relevant also to a consideration of those Romano-British rural settlements which we have seen to stand below the villas in the social scale. In general there is no evidence that Saxon peasants took over these so-called 'native' or 'Celtic' settlements and the associated fields. They do not survive. Instead, it has long been suggested that there was a 'valley-ward drift' from the poor soils of the chalk downs, where traces of 'Celtic' fields are most prominent, to the rich soils of the valley-bottoms where we find the nucleated villages of the Anglo-Saxons established by the time of the Domesday Book. Putting the matter more positively, it was believed that the Anglo-Saxons with their iron axes initiated the clearance of virgin oakwoods, and began to cultivate the fertile clay-lands with a heavy plough. In doing this they laid the foundations of the settlement pattern of medieval England, a pattern which was quite different from that of their British forerunners. As a proof of this, it was claimed, there is no trace of British village-names over most of England. The names of our villages, their origins, plain to read in the pages of Domesday or in Saxon charters, are English names because the villages themselves are Anglo-Saxon foundations.

This account of the relations of Roman Britons and pagan Saxons in the countryside is widely accepted, but it is almost wholly fictitious. For a start, such evidence as we have of the agricultural tools and practices of the ancestral English on the continent shows that they were no better equipped to deal with dense forest and heavy clay-land than the Romano-Britons had been. The villa owners at least probably had the advantage in terms of capital. While it cannot be doubted that in the six or seven centuries preceding the Domesday record the area of forest clearance was greatly expanded, it is probable that the earliest English settlements were on land already cleared and cultivated by the Britons. In Cheshire and Shropshire, for instance, it has been possible to show how the clearance of forest spread outwards from certain nuclei.[16] It is in these nuclei that early Anglian place-names are mostly found, but the Celtic place-names are clustered in just the same areas, making it evident that the first English settlers were taking over clearances made by their Celtic precursors. Furthermore, as we have already mentioned (above, p. 169), there was some low-lying farming and settlement in the Roman period. This has been well demonstrated, for instance, in the valleys of the Welland and the Warwickshire Avon, which were both areas of early English settlement. Confirmatory hints are accumulating from Wiltshire as well. It is becoming increasingly difficult to believe in the 'valley-ward drift' and correspondingly easy to think that many of our Domesday villages had not merely pagan Saxon ancestors but Romano-British ones going back earlier still. Finally, the early dating now proposed for the English settlements, combined with a fuller knowledge of vegetational history, makes it certain that, even where British farmers had abandoned their fields, heavy forest could not have sprung up by the time the Anglo-Saxons moved in. There must have been every incentive for the immigrants to start by clearing the scrub from British fields where they were too late to take those fields over as going concerns.

The failure of British village-names to survive remains to be considered.[17] Here it is necessary to stress the transmogrification which Celtic names are known to have undergone on British lips. On the north coast of Kent was a town whose name, meaning 'the bridges of the stronghold', was latinized as *Durobrivae*. Bede knew this, presumably from Latin sources, as *Dorubrevis civitas*, but he adds 'which the English call *Hrofaescaestrae*, [that is, 'Hrof's fort', modern Rochester] after one of their former chiefs named Hrof.' The history of the name between the Roman period and Bede's day appears to be this: on British lips, in Primitive Welsh, the original form was probably clipped to *D'robriw*. The Anglo-Saxons heard this as something like *Hrofri*, which they assimilated to their own word *Hrof*, 'roof'. To this they added the *caestrae* or 'chester' element in reference to the walled town. Later still, Hrof the chieftain was invented to explain the place-name. The lesson to be derived from this is clear. If we did not know the British-Latin name from a Roman source, the Antonine Itinerary, and if all we had were variants on *Hrofaescaestrae*, we would believe that the name of Rochester was purely English, and that the British name had been lost. We might further infer from this that there was no continuity on the site. It is only because we do have a Roman source that we can see how the English name derives from a garbled form of the British name. But with the overwhelming majority of minor Romano-British settlements we have not a shred of evidence for their British names. It follows that if a mangled Primitive Welsh word underlay the first recorded version in Old English, we could not hope to detect it. Very many English place-names have the form 'personal or kin name' + 'village, town, or settlement'. It is then very tempting to believe that the person or the kindred founded the settlement, and since the person or kin name is English, so must the settlement be. The example of Hrof and his fort or walled town warns us that this need not be so. It may well be that apparent absence of settlement names derived from Primitive Welsh is proof only that the Englishman's traditional inability to pronounce a foreign language correctly is a trait of very long standing.[18]

Finally, we must examine briefly the evidence for the survival of religious monuments. We have seen that the pagan Celtic revival of the mid-fourth century had lost its impetus by the end of the century (above, p. 170). Gildas mentions briefly that the 'devilish monstrosities' of pagan cult-idols were still occasionally to be seen in his day 'intra vel extra deserta moenia', 'both within and without the deserted walls [or enclosures]'. It is not clear whether moenia has its customary meaning of town- or fort-walls, or whether it refers to temple enclosures. Around 500, dressed stone was being used to refortify Cadbury Castle (below, pp. 222–3) and one source for this was a ruined Romano-Celtic temple on the hill-top. In general, then, we should think of the pagan temples as abandoned and starting to collapse in the fifth century, to serve as quarries for worked stone in later ages. On the other hand, in the sixth or seventh century an elaborately ornamented glass jar, a rare and costly object, was deposited at a depth of about thirty-four feet in the well of the Roman temple on Pagans Hill, near Chew Stoke in Somerset. It is difficult to resist the idea that this was a ritual offering, implying some continuity of sanctity in the site, however ruined its buildings may have been.

In the case of Christian structures, it seems that the house-chapels of the villas fell into decay along with the other villa buildings in the late fourth and fifth centuries. But it is interesting to see that at several villas, notably at Llantwit Major in Glamorgan, Christian burials were deposited in the period between the collapse of some of the buildings and the establishment of churchyard burial as the normal practice. This may suggest that some villas continued to be meeting places for Christian communities. As for churches, the only structure which we might possibly place in the fifth century is that at Caerwent (above, p. 171). But its stratigraphical position, above the carefully demolished colonnade of the Roman baths, does not necessitate a post-Roman date at all, while the absence of pottery of the late fifth and sixth centuries from Caerwent argues that the town, and with it the church, was deserted long before 500. The suggestion has been made, very tentatively, that a minute building of basilican plan at Lydd in Kent may be of Roman or sub-Roman date, but there is no evidence to substantiate this. In fact, it is only from some remarks of Bede that we have any indication of Roman churches still standing at the time of Augustine's mission in the late sixth and early seventh centuries. The clearest instance is that of St Martin's, Canterbury, 'a church built of old . . . while yet the Romans inhabited Britain' in which Bertha, the Christian queen of Kent, used to pray. Scanty traces of the original masonry can still be seen embedded in later work (below, p. 308). Furthermore Bede tells us that when King Æthelberht himself had been converted Augustine and his followers 'were allowed to build or restore churches', '*ecclesias fabricandi vel restaurandi licentiam acciperent*'. That churches had to be restored suggests that they had fallen into disrepair as part of the fifth- and sixth-century decline of civic life.

To sum up, it would seem that it was only the decayed vestiges of Roman material culture which the Britons of Arthur's age had inherited. The decay itself was due more to economic decline and social distintegration than to barbarian ravages. And in some of the towns, and at field and village level in the countryside, it was a qualified not an absolute decay. Nevertheless it is clear that romanized influences were feeble in Britain around 500. It is time now to examine the culture of the Arthurian period in its Celtic rather than its Roman aspects.

Eight

The Culture of
the Britons,
AD 450–650

Dating evidence, AD 450–650[1]

In describing the material culture of the Britons in the period 450–650 our first problem is to define and to discover the sites on which it is represented. This is basically a chronological problem, namely, to say which sites can be dated to the period. Very occasionally we have direct verbal evidence to help us here. The dangers of legendary or traditional connections, especially with figures in the Arthurian circle, have already been pointed out (above, pp. 161–5). But when Bede, referring to Alcluith or Dumbarton Rock [Pl. 3], calls it '*urbs*' or '*civitas Brettonum munitissima usque hodie*', 'a town or city of the Britons, strongly defended up to the present day', we can be sure that this was one of the principal strongholds of the northern Britons in the centuries before 731 when he was writing. But convincing references of this kind to British sites are all too rare. In any case they serve only to pinpoint one moment in the history of the site; they cannot help us to date its development – for this we need a series of datable artefacts. In the Roman period, apart from verbal evidence, we have coins, metalwork and pottery to help us establish a framework of chronology. How far are these available after 450?

For a start we have no currency.[2] It used to be believed that certain very minute coins bearing barbarous Roman designs represented a typological degeneration from true Roman coinage. On this basis they were placed in the post-Roman centuries, and some were even published, perhaps rather frivolously, as 'King Arthur's small change'. Now, however, the opinion of numismatists is that these *minimissimi* are contemporary with the fourth-century issues which they copy in miniature, and since they occur very frequently on temple sites they may even be token coins struck for votive purposes. There is general agreement that there was no fifth-century British coinage. The import of Roman coins, minted principally in Gaul, fell off sharply after 400, and historical as well as numismatic considerations would suggest that it ceased altogether in 410 if not in 407. The state of wear of some of the latest issues suggests that coins continued to circulate as late as 430, or perhaps even 450. Thereafter Britain as a whole ceased to have a money economy, until in the late seventh century the English kings began to mint coins. In western Britain, indeed, there are no coins until the Vikings reintroduced them to coastal markets in the late ninth century. The economic implications of this are of course profound, and all that has been said in the previous section about economic decline should be considered in the light of this absence of currency. For our present purpose we should note that we can no longer date sites with the kind of precision which coins may provide.

We have, however, a certain amount of metalwork, occurring either as actual objects or as the moulds or other apparatus used in the manufacture of jewelry. One class of ornament, the penannular brooch [Fig. 22], stems from a type current in the fourth century, so this provides a starting date for its typological development. Some penannular brooches and related pins have decorative motifs which are also used on the elaborate vessels known as hanging bowls. One stage in the development of the decoration appears on a set of three hanging bowls in the Sutton Hoo ship burial, which may be dated on numismatic and historical grounds to the years 620–60. So we have a broad span of two and a half or three centuries which embraces some of our decorated metalwork. It is doubtful whether we can break this down into smaller units on the basis of typological dead-reckoning, so the metalwork is not very helpful for establishing a detailed chronology. Of course, we should not think of the decorated metalwork simply as so many type-fossils, useful for dating archaeological levels. In terms of material culture it represents the highest artistic achievement of the Britons in this period, and in due course we will have to consider it in this respect (below, pp. 233–8).

Meanwhile we must examine the chronological evidence provided by pottery. It is well known that the changing styles of shape and ornament of pottery vessels provide some of the most important clues for archaeological dating. This is because, first, pottery is made from a highly plastic substance, clay, which can be fashioned in an almost infinite variety of ways, each of them characteristic of its own period and cultural group. Second, although pottery vessels are very fragile, actual sherds are almost indestructible, so that the inhabited sites of a pottery-using culture are likely to be littered with quantities of pot-sherds for the archaeologist to collect, classify and date. Unfortunately the Britons of our period were not prolific manufacturers of pottery. Perhaps their ancestors had become too dependent on the mass-produced wares of the Romano-British pottery industry. We have seen that a little hand-modelled pottery was being made in eastern Britain in the early fifth century [Fig. 10]. In Wales and the Marches some shapeless vessels, with thick walls which contain almost as much grit as clay, have been claimed as fifth century, but it is impossible to dis-tinguish them from certain crude pots of the pre-Roman Iron Age, so they are no help for chronological purposes.[3] In and around the Cots-wolds some rather better hand-made sherds are being recognized in post-Roman contexts, but their study is still in its infancy. Another possibility which requires further research is that a class of wheel-thrown jars and bowls, rather crudely fashioned in a fabric containing large white calcite grits, may continue from the fourth into the fifth century. Versions of this class are common in late Roman contexts, but some particularly lumpish examples are known from Castell Degannwy, which was certainly occupied in the fifth century, and cal-cite-gritted jars also occur in a deposit with Saxon cooking pots at Shakenoak.

All the examples we have quoted so far are no more than pointers. We are still a long way from writing a coherent account of British ceramics in the fifth and sixth centuries, or from establishing a dated sequence of development. The rarity of these pointers must mean that very little pottery was being made. Only in Cornwall is there any sign of a vigorous industry. It is likely that the reason for this is that the Celts of the south-west were already producing good pottery in great quan-tity before the Roman conquest, and even after it they may have con-tinued production at cottage-industry level without becoming too dependent on the mass production of a commercial industry. What-ever the explanation, in the fifth and later centuries they certainly produced very serviceable cooking pots and dishes, based ultimately on Romano-British models but now without the use of the fast potter's

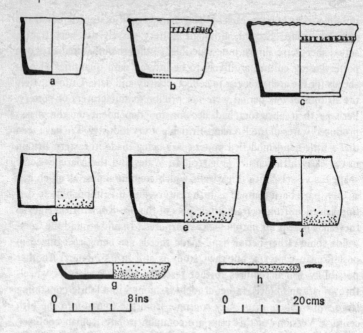

11. *a, b, c* Souterrain pottery from Ulster (below, p. 258); *d–h* grass-marked bowls and dishes from Cornwall.

wheel. About 500, however, a new class appears along the north coast of west Cornwall: rather lumpish straight-sided dishes, which often have 'pie-crust' or finger-pinched ornament along the rim. The most distinctive feature, however, is that the bases and lower exterior are pocked with tiny holes where bits of grass have burned out during firing, hence the name 'grass-marked' pottery[4]. This distinctive marking comes about because before the pots were fired they were placed to dry on a surface which had been covered in chopped grass to prevent them sticking. Curiously enough this simple technique is not used very widely, and in the British Isles it is largely, but not entirely, confined to the Cornish 'grass-marked' series and to some rather similar straight-sided dishes with pie-crust ornament from north-east Ireland. The Irish examples cannot be closely dated, but some probably belong to the middle centuries of the first millennium AD. This has led to the suggestion that the pottery was introduced to Cornwall by folk-movement from Ireland. The hypothesis may be reinforced, albeit shakily, by the occurrence in the same parts of west Cornwall of churches dedicated to Irish saints.

This very fragmented evidence for pottery of British manufacture can now be reinforced with the much more coherent evidence for imported pottery. Since the late 1930s it has been recognized that certain fine dishes found on British sites had such close parallels in the Mediterranean that they must have come from that area, and second, that certain rather coarse kitchen vessels from sites all round the Irish Sea exhibited such homogeneity of form and fabric that they must all come from a common source, probably outside the Celtic West altogether. From about 1955 the study of these imports has gathered momentum.[5] They have been recognized on an ever-increasing number of sites in Britain, Ireland and Scotland. The classification of these western examples has been systematized as a basis for typological comparison with examples from the Mediterranean and the Continent. Attempts have been made to locate the sources by petrological examination of the grits in the fabric. Above all, parallels have been sought in Mediterranean contexts dated by coins or historical references, so that a precise dating might be transferred to sites in the Celtic west. This last study, so important for us, has been made difficult by the lack of attention to pottery, or even to modern techniques of excavation, on many Mediterranean sites. None the less, the broad pattern is now clear. For the present account it seems best to begin with a description of the four leading classes of this pottery before considering the wider aspects of its importation.

Class A consists of dishes and bowls in a fairly fine brick-red fabric, coated with a slightly glossy red or reddish-brown slip. The commonest form has a wall-sided rim, frequently decorated with simple rouletted patterns. Other rim forms also occur, and some bowls have a flange part way down the side. The base normally has a very shallow footring. Some vessels have a cross stamped inside the base, and a dish from Dinas Powys has very stylized animals, probably leopards, in a haphazard arrangement. All these features of form, fabric and ornament can be paralleled precisely by vessels from Athens, and less

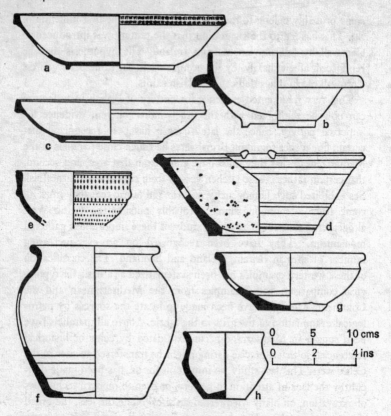

12. *a*, *b*, *c* Class A red ware bowls from Tintagel, Cornwall and Dinas Powys, Glamorgan; *d*, *e* Class D grey ware mortarium and bowl from Dinas Powys; *f*, *g*, *h* Class E cooking pot and bowl from Dinas Powys and beaker from Buston, Ayrshire.

exactly on sites in Asia Minor, the Levant, and North Africa as far west as Carthage. The parallels belong to a broad class of Late Roman and Byzantine stamped wares. Those which are closest to the Class A imports are datable from about 460–70 to 600. Their main distribution in the Celtic West is confined to south-western England, south Wales, and southern Ireland.

Class B comprises a range of large handled jars or amphorae, among

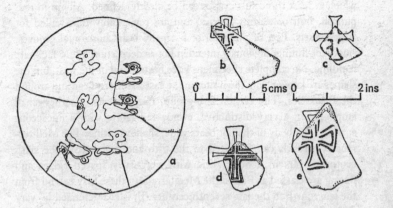

13. Stamped designs on Class A bowls; *a* Dinas Powys; *b, d, e* Tintagel; *c* Cadbury-Camelot, Somerset.

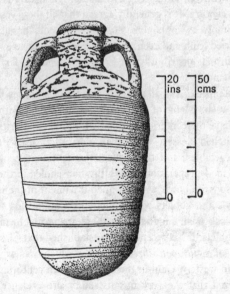

14. An amphora from Asia Minor, comparable with the Class B vessels found in fragments in Britain and Ireland.

which at least three sub-classes can be clearly defined. All are in red, pinkish, buff or creamy fabrics, and are remarkably thin-walled for large vessels. Part of the exterior normally bears horizontal grooves, ridges, or fluting, obviously intended not as decoration but to facilitate handling. No complete specimens have been found in the west, but the shapes are known from town sites in the east Mediterranean and around the Black Sea. The earliest sub-group, B*iv*, consists of rather small amphorae in a very distinctive, evenly red fabric with a micaceous sparkle. The body of the pot bears wide, shallow fluting. The Mediterranean parallels can be dated to the fifth and first half of the sixth centuries. Jars in a buff fabric with irregularly spaced ridges and fluting are classed as B*ii*. In the Mediterranean these may extend from the late fourth to the late seventh century. B*i* is characterized by very deep, close-set grooves, sometimes straight and sometimes wavy, which spiral around the upper part of the jar leaving the lower two thirds plain. The fabric is pinkish, and marked by yellow inclusions. Examples are known from kiln sites in Romania.[6] Its dating is late fifth to late seventh century. It is generally agreed that all these vessels came to the West simply as containers, holding wine, oil, possibly also dry goods like dried fruit, and even, to judge from Romanian evidence, iron nails. The insular distribution of Class B extends as far north as St George's Channel.

Class D comprises a small group of bowls in a soft grey fabric with a blue-black wash. Many of the bowls are furnished with a pouring spout, and have their interior studded with projecting grits. These are *mortaria*, kitchen vessels of Roman derivation used for mashing fruit and vegetables, and they reflect the continuance of romanized methods of food-preparation in wealthy households in the West. But there are also large bowls with stamped ornament in the interior, and smaller bowls and goblets with rouletted decoration on the exterior. The blue-black wash suggests that these are meant to imitate silver or pewter goblets. It has recently been established that Class D belongs to a group of *sigillé paléochrétienne grise* which was widespread in southern and western Gaul in the fifth and sixth centuries.[7] It should be emphasized that the very unsatisfactory site-evidence from Gaul allows only a vague dating. The best parallels for the British material come, appropriately, from the Bordeaux area. Insular examples are thinly scattered from Tintagel in Cornwall to Dunadd in Argyll, but none have been reported from Ireland.

The most widespread of the imports, Class E, is in some ways the least understood. It consists of kitchen vessels: cooking pots, pitchers, bowls and small jars or beakers. At first sight these appear to be rather crudely made, for their surfaces are normally rough, corrugated and pimply. In fact the pottery is extremely competent, for the vessels are often thin-walled and the fabric is invariably very hard, approaching stoneware. Indeed Class E would not be out of place in a modern kitchen. In these islands it occurs principally in princely strongholds and aristocratic homesteads both sides of the Irish Sea, spreading as far north as Skye and County Down. It is agreed that the homogeneity of Class E throughout its insular distribution implies a common source, and it is further inferred that the source was outside these islands, but no positive indentification has proved acceptable. The Continent seems more likely than the Mediterranean, and for some years the Rhineland was a favoured candidate. The fifth- to seventh-century ceramics of the Rhineland are well known, and it is true that Class E has a broad resemblance to them, but the comparisons are not so exact as to allow the inference that this was the source. Examples of E-ware are known from Brittany, but it seems more likely that this represents another area of distribution rather than the place of manufacture. Recently, the prolific grits from a number of Class E sherds have been compared petrologically with sands from the Paris Basin and from Aquitaine. The comparisons are not exact, but for what they are worth they appear to favour Aquitaine.[8] Such a source, like that in the Bordeaux region for D-ware, would be compatible with the insular distribution of Class E; but it must not be regarded as proven. And until datable sites in a source-area have been located, we will have no external evidence for dating this kitchen ware. The insular evidence suggests that it was not introduced before 525–50, and that it continued until about 700.

Several other groups of wheel-thrown vessels have been claimed as post-Roman imports into the Celtic West, basically on the grounds that they are not recognizably Roman or medieval. The argument is sometimes circular: these pots occur on a site which may, on shaky historical or other grounds, be post-Roman, therefore the pots are post-Roman; because the pottery from the site is post-Roman, there-fore the site itself must be. The only group worth singling out for mention here consists of flanged bowls in a very distinctive hard-fired fabric from Castell Degannwy, Coygan and Dinorben. These bowls admittedly have a Roman ancestry, but so do all the acceptable post-Roman imports. All three sites have late Roman material, but Coygan and Degannwy have Class A and B imports respectively, and Dinorben has a fragment of Teutonic metalwork datable to the sixth or early-seventh century. And at Dinorben the bowls in question can certainly be distinguished typologically from the late Roman flanged bowls which are also prolific on the site.

Having described this pottery in detail, we must consider its wider aspects. The first recognition that pottery was being imported from Gaul and the Mediterranean to these islands occasioned some surprise. Despite the clear literary evidence of contacts in the religious field between western Britain and Ireland on the one hand, and Gaul, North Africa, and even Egypt on the other, it was generally held that the Anglo-Saxon invasions had cut the Celtic West off from Mediter-ranean civilization: hence the pecularities of the Celtic church (above, p. 134). We now see that in archaeological as well as in religious terms the concept of the isolation of the Celtic West is a myth, or at best only a very partial truth. At the same time we must not exaggerate the significance of the imports. Even when every allowance is made for the comparative novelty of their recognition, the total quantity known is very small. Now that we see the imports as ranging over more than two hundred years it is no longer possible to suggest that they might have come as a single ship-load, but we should probably think of occasional ships, arriving irregularly with long intervals between each visit, rather than any regular, organized and intensive trade. Nor can the cultural impact of the imports have been felt very widely. Their distribution is predominantly coastal or near-coastal, with Cadbury Castle and Ballinderry representing exceptional inland examples in Britain and Ireland respectively. It could be argued that the British distribution merely reflects the coastal spread of good habitable land in western Britain, but of course this explanation is irrelevant in Ireland.

Socially, too, the distribution of the imports is very restricted.

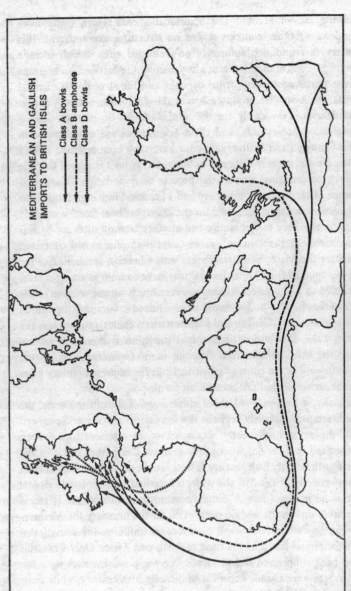

Map 5. Possible routes by which pottery of Classes A, B, and D was imported from the Black Sea, the east Mediterranean and western Gaul.

MEDITERRANEAN AND GAULISH
IMPORTS TO BRITISH ISLES

Class A bowls
Class B amphorae
Class D bowls

Leaving out of account the occasional sherds which come from middens, or other contexts where no structures are apparent, this pottery is found predominantly on defended sites, which include crannogs – one of them at least a royal site – the fortified homesteads of the minor aristocracy, tribal capitals, and the strongholds of royal dynasties. A smaller group embraces religious sites, normally Celtic monasteries. Very rarely are the imports found on peasant sites or undefended homesteads, and these occurrences are concentrated in west Cornwall and Scilly. Only once have they been reported from a Roman town, namely Ilchester in Somerset. Now it is agreed that the church played some part in the process of importation. The cross-stamped Class A dishes may have had a liturgical function, though the suggestion that they were used for the *agape*, or 'love-feast' is unlikely because this very early practice had almost certainly died out by this time. Some, perhaps many, of the Class B amphorae had contained wine for the Mass. Some fragments with Christian symbols, like the *chi-rho* roundel from Dinas Emrys, may have come in as actual sherds, intended as religious relics. But however much weight we give to the role of the church – and it should be recognized at once that the church had the necessary Gaulish and Mediterranean contacts to organize the trade – the distribution pattern makes it clear that secular princes were the chief beneficiaries. Aneirin, in *Y Gododdin*, sang of the wine flowing in the court of a British king; the imported pottery gives us the archaeological documentation for this.

Finally, a further word about chronology. Taken in the mass, the Mediterranean parallels begin in the late fourth century and run well into the seventh. Recently, examples of B*i* amphorae have been recognized in London, where they seem to come from levels of the late fourth or early fifth century. These are the only pieces known from south-eastern Britain. In the west, the earliest closely dated imports are some of the Class A dishes, beginning about 460–70. It seems probable that in the middle decades of the fifth century the Mediterranean was effectively closed to east-west traffic by the activities of Vandal pirates based on the coast of north-east Africa. Only when this had been suppressed did the trade become possible. Sites with B*iv* amphorae were already occupied in the later fifth century, while those with Class E kitchenwares may have been occupied well into the seventh. Further refinements on this chronology may be expected when details of the Mediterranean parallels have been published. Meanwhile a study of the sites which have produced imported pottery will give us a sound introduction to the material culture of Britain in the period 450–650.

Secular sites, principally with imported pottery

When we take all classes of imported ware into account, we find that about fifty sites in Britain and Ireland are known to have yielded fragments in greater or lesser quantity. Thirty of these lie in the area of our immediate interest, Britain south of the Pictish border which may roughly be equated with the Antonine Wall across the Forth-Clyde isthmus. Out of the thirty, as many as five may be religious, and these are dealt with below (pp. 249 f.). Another five sites are represented by sherds picked up among shifting sand-dunes or in other circumstances in which no buildings were revealed, so they are not described here. The remainder range from the Roman town of Ilchester, through princely strongholds, to peasant hovels. Apart from the structural evidence for types of dwelling and fortification, these sites have yielded very varied quantities of pottery, metalwork, utilized bone and stone, and other occupation debris from which some picture of material culture and human activities can be built up. But before this composite picture is attempted, it would be best to give individual descriptions of some representative sites.

We may conveniently begin at the western tip of Dumnonia, with Chun Castle.[10] This is a rather unusual chieftain's fort of the pre-Roman Iron Age, which was reused around the sixth century A.D. The fort, which stands on open moorland about 700 ft above sea-level, consists of two concentric dry-stone walls. The inner one, enclosing an area nearly 180 ft in diameter, is about 12 ft in width and is said to have stood 15 ft high as recently as the seventeenth century. Although the outer wall is slighter, the total effect is of a formidable stronghold. Originally the entrance arrangements consisted of two simple passageways, more or less in line through the two walls, but subsequently these were modified to give a narrow twisting approach, which exposed the shieldless right side of an attacker. There is no

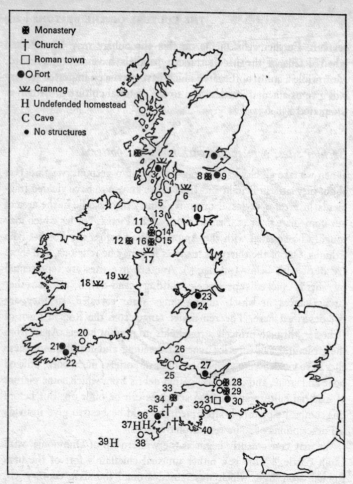

Map 6. Sites where imported pottery of Classes A, B, D, and E has been found:
1, Iona (A); 2, Loch Glashan (E); 3, Dunadd (D, E); 4, Little Dunagoil (E); 5,
Kildalloig Dun (E); 6, Buston (E); 7, Clatchard Craig (E); 8, Abercorn (E); 9, Craigs
Quarry (E); 10, Mote of Mark (D, E); 11, Langford Lodge (E); 12, Armagh (E),
13, Nendrum (E); 14, Ballyfounder (E); 15, Spittle Ballee (E); 16, Downpatrick
(E); 17, Lough Faughan (E); 18, Ballinderry 2 (E); 19, Lagore (E); 20, Garryduff
(E); 21, Garranes (A, B, E); 22, Ballycatteen (E); 23, Castell Degannwy (B); 24,
Dinas Emrys (B, E); 25, Longbury Bank (A, B, E); 26, Coygan (A, B); 27, Dinas
Powys (A, B, D, E); 28, Cadbury-Congresbury (A, B, D); 29, Glastonbury Tor
(B); 30, Cadbury Castle or Camelot (A, B, D); 31, Ilchester (B); 32, High Peak (B);
33, Tintagel (A, B, D); 34, St Constantine's (B); 35, Trevelgue (B); 36, Gwithian
(A, B, E); 37, Porthmeor (A); 38, Chun (B); 39, Tean (B, E); 40, Bantham (B, E).[9]

evidence for the date of this modification, but it is reasonable to relate it to the second phase of use, that is, the sixth century AD. At this same time, a zone about 30 ft wide inside the inner rampart was divided into compartments which contained roughly built houses, one of which yielded a typical grass-marked cooking-pot, and a fragment

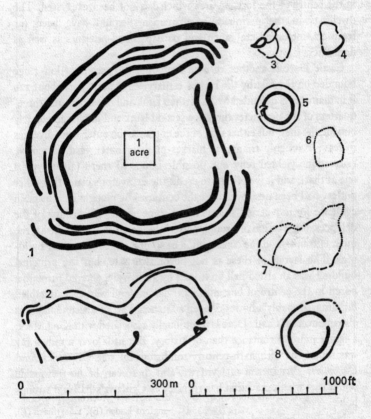

15. British secular sites with imported pottery: (1) Cadbury-Camelot, Somerset; (2) Cadbury-Congresbury, Somerset; (3) Dunadd, Argyll; (4) Dinas Powys, Glamorgan; (5) Chun, Cornwall; (6) Castell Degannwy, Caernarvonshire (dotted line shows circuit of hilltop where defences have not been uncovered); (7) Dinas Emrys, Caernarvonshire; (8) Castle Dore, Cornwall.

from the handle of a Class B amphora. Another yielded a 12 lb. lump of tin ore, and near by was a furnace which had been used for smelting. It seems very likely that control over the mining and working of tin provided a main source of wealth. Nothing that could be thought of as a chieftain's hall has been discovered, but it is probable that this stood in the centre of the fort, an area which has not been excavated. The dwellings in the peripheral compartments would have been for retainers, including craftsmen and perhaps bond-peasants as well as domestics.

Castle Dore is another re-used Iron-Age fort, set on a low ridge bounded on the east by the Fowey estuary.[11] An inner area about 220 ft in diameter is defended by an earthen bank and ditch. Around three-quarters of the perimeter there is a second bank and ditch immediately outside the first, but either side of the entrance the outer bank diverges to leave a roughly triangular market place or outer yard. Extensive excavations yielded only one possible imported sherd (an untypical one at that), and it is not easy to credit the excavator's claim that other pottery had been destroyed over the centuries by ploughing. The main evidence for our period is structural: some slight refurbishing of the defences, the erection of a rough porter's lodge, 24 ft by 18 ft, inside the inner entrance, and the construction of several large rectangular build-ings. The layout of these is not beyond dispute, but the principal building was an aisled hall 90 ft long by 40 ft wide, entered through a porch in the centre of one side wall. To one end was a small gabled building, probably a bower or even a kitchen. Part of a second hall was also uncovered. Castle Dore is traditionally associated with King Mark, a figure more of romance than of history. But little over a mile away was found the fifth/sixth-century tombstone of one *Drustanus filius Cunomori*, Tristan son of Cynfawr, and there can be no reasonable doubt that what excavation has revealed is Cynfawr's hall and strong-hold.

No such historical associations are attached to Dinas Powys in Glamorgan,[12] which has produced one of the richest collections of imported pottery, including Classes A, D and E, and three sub-classes of B. The sixth/seventh-century site was discovered by acci-dent in the course of excavating a formidable little earthwork castle of the late eleventh century, and had to be disentangled from the latter.

The excavator's interpretation was that in the late fifth or sixth century the north end of a steep and occasionally craggy hill was cut off by a feeble bank about 10 ft wide by 5 ft high, with an external rock-cut ditch of comparable dimensions. The area enclosed was some 100 ft wide by 190 ft long. Within this a number of carefully built hearths could be dated to our period, especially at the north-east corner where iron-smelting ovens and metalworkers' furnaces took advantage of a strong natural draught from the prevailing winds. This evidence for industrial activity, and other signs of high-class craftsmanship, permit the inference that Dinas Powys was the fortified court of a petty chief. But no actual remains of buildings appropriate to such a princeling were found. In the rock of the hilltop however, two pairs of drainage gullies had been dug, marking the outline of two buildings with bowed sides and rounded ends. The eleventh-century rampart was constructed partly of a freshly quarried rock, but partly of weathered slabs intermingled with great quantities of sixth/seventh-century rubbish, and it is a reasonable inference that this weathered rock had been obtained from the ruined buildings of the prince's court. In other words, these must have had thick dry-stone walls, probably supporting a thatch roof. The larger building enclosed a hearth towards one end, and though it could not be proved stratigraphically that the hearth was contemporary with the building, it is probable that it was. This building may be interpreted as the hall. Architecturally it is unpretentious compared with that at Castle Dore, and by comparison with the Glamorgan villas of a couple of centuries earlier it is positively squalid.

Lesser quantities of imported pottery have been found in other Welsh forts which occupy extremely craggy hilltops.[13] None of them has produced acceptable evidence for dwellings in our period, and the date of the defensive works is sometimes in doubt, but even fragmentary evidence can help to build up a composite picture of the period. Castell Degannwy [Pl. 4a], traditional seat of Maelgwn of Gwynedd, lies across the natural boundary of the kingdom on the river Conway. The medieval castle incorporated a pair of very craggy hillocks, but it is probable that Maelgwn's citadel occupied only the larger of the two hills, with a fairly level top measuring 230 ft by 160 ft. The crag-free eastern slope of this was defended with a dry-stone wall, but given the

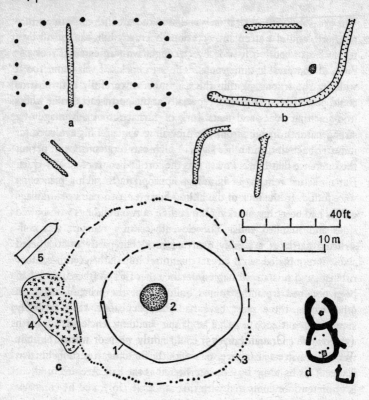

16. Some excavated British buildings: *a* post-holes and wall-trenches of hall and ancillary building at Cadbury-Camelot; *b* drainage gullies around hall and lesser building at Dinas Powys; *c* reconstruction of Buston crannog – (1) house wall of upright posts, laid stones and timber beams, (2) main hearth, (3) palisade marking limits of terrace around house, (4) midden opposite door of house, (5) dug-out canoe; *d* Gwithian, Cornwall. On plans *b*, *c* and *d* stipple indicates hearths.

total evidence from the hill this might date anywhere from about 100 to 1100 AD. Between the two hills is a broad saddle which may have held a bond settlement subordinate to Maelgwn's court. An even more craggy hilltop is that of Dinas Emrys, 'the fort of Ambrosius', a famous citadel in Welsh folk-lore because of the confrontation of Vortigern and Ambrosius which took place there. No historical weight is to be attached to this, but excavations have yielded a sherd from a Class E cooking-pot, fragments of B*iv* amphorae, an amulet with *chi-rho* and *alpha-omega* symbols, and evidence of metalworking, all of which point to Dinas Emrys as a prince's stronghold. The hilltop itself, an irregular area 500 ft long by 300 ft wide at the most, was defended by a feeble dry wall which at its maximum was only 10 ft wide. The entrance, on the east, is defended by two outworks, short lengths of walling which fill gaps in the crags. Unfortunately the defences cannot be dated by closely stratified finds and may go back to the third/fourth centuries, but it is probable that some kind of rough walling stood at the head of the crags in our period.

Some of the pre-Roman hill-forts which had been reoccupied in the third and fourth centuries (above, pp. 179–81) also produce slight evidence for the late-fifth and sixth. Dinorben in north Wales is a small but massively defended fort set on the end of a spur which drops 200 ft to the coastal plain. We have seen that it was reoccupied, but not refortified, in the third century. This occupation probably lasted down to about 400, to judge from the occurrence of coins of Valens (367–78) and Gratian (367–75) in a slightly worn or worn condition. We have suggested (above, p. 206) that the characteristic Dinorben flanged bowls may be imports of the post-Roman period, and a fragment of Teutonic metalwork, inexplicable in itself, none the less suggests occupation in the late sixth/seventh century. Partial excavation of the five-acre interior has revealed many post-holes, and the claim has been advanced that some of them mark an aisled house of post-Roman date. But this lacks the coherence of either Castle Dore (above, p. 212) or Cadbury Castle (below, p. 226) examples, and it would be unreasonable to say more than that Dinorben may have been the fortified homestead of some important family in the sixth or seventh century. A clearer case of re-use is provided in south Wales by Coygan. This is a three-acre fort on what was at the time a coastal headland. Again its defences were not refurbished in either the third or the sixth centuries, nor are there any structural remains of internal buildings in the latter period. But a slight occupation at that time is proved by the discovery of fragments from two or three Class

A dishes and a tiny sherd from a B*i* amphora. None of the metalwork or other finds need be later than Roman.

Another group of Welsh sites deserves mention here, despite their lack of imported pottery, because one of them has produced a more or less datable brooch. This is the large silver penannular, with flattened undecorated terminals, from Pant-y-saer in Anglesey.[14] The brooch has been dated variously from about 450 to 700 or later, but its best parallels are the silver penannulars found with fragments of an early

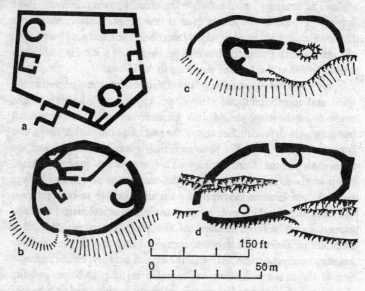

17. Enclosed hut-groups and minor forts in Gwynedd: *a* Romano-British homestead, Din Llugwy, Anglesey, after *Ancient Monuments of Anglesey, Ministry of Works Official Guide*; *b* fifth-century homestead, Pant-y-saer, Anglesey; *c* fortified house, Carreg-y-llam, Caernarvonshire; *d* small fort, Garn Boduan, Caernarvonshire (see also Fig. 30).

hanging bowl at Tummel Bridge in north Perthshire, and others in a sixth/seventh-century hoard of Pictish silver from Norries Law, Fife. These northern parallels recall Cunedda's migration from the southern border of Pictland to Gwynedd, and the family connections between Maelgwn and the Pictish dynasty (above, p. 128). Pant-y-saer itself consists of a low oval wall between 5 and 9 ft thick which encloses two circular houses, two rectangular buildings which are secondary, and a kiln or oven. The whole plan closely resembles that of other enclosed homesteads which we have seen to be characteristic of Gwynedd in the Roman period (above, p. 169). But whereas these produce Roman pottery and other finds in abundance, Pant-y-saer yielded only three worn scraps. The site cannot therefore be Roman in date but the close resemblance in plan to undoubted Roman buildings suggests that its construction cannot long post-date the fourth century. The brooch might be consistent with an occupation running into the fifth century, but some very crude pottery which belongs to the earliest phase of the homestead cannot be dated on external grounds.

Although Pant-y-saer itself can scarcely be classed as a fortified site, it seems to be the typological precursor of other sites in Gwynedd which are true forts, but which cannot of themselves be dated. Carreg-y-llam is another more or less oval enclosure, 110 ft by 40 ft with a single round house built back into the wall after the manner of the enclosed homesteads.[15] But whereas Pant-y-saer is built at the edge of a cultivable plateau, Carreg-y-llam was on top of a craggy ridge overlooking the sea. Its main enclosure wall was 10 ft thick, and this was reinforced by outer works which added significantly to both its impressiveness and its defensibility. A further typological stage seems to be represented by the small fort 220 ft by 80 ft set within the large pre-Roman hill-fort of Garn Boduan [Fig. 30], for here the internal buildings are no longer set back into the enclosure wall.[16] As at Carreg-y-llam, the wall is about 10 ft thick, and again the situation is a craggy summit. Scraps of pottery from these two sites tell us nothing about their date, and there is no metalwork. It is therefore on typological grounds alone, on the assumed devolution from the enclosed homesteads of the third/fourth centuries, that we claim Carreg-y-llam and the Garn Boduan small fort as defended homesteads of the minor aristocracy in the post-Roman period.

If we turn now to northern Britain, the key sites are Dumbarton, *Dun Breatann*, 'the fort of the Britons', in Strathclyde, and Mote of Mark in Rheged. Dumbarton, under the name of *Alcluith*, 'Clyde-rock', was referred to by Bede as a 'strongly fortified city of the Britons', *civitas Brettonum munitissima*.[17] The site is a volcanic plug of basalt on the north bank of the Clyde, and its natural strength is obvious [Pl. 3]. No trace of early fortifications has been discovered and no finds of our period have been recorded, but judicious excavation might still reveal something of its earliest history. Mote of Mark, by contrast, has no known history, and the legendary association with Mark may be discounted, but it has produced both imported pottery and good evidence for metalworking in the sixth and seventh centuries.[18] The site was so badly dug that nothing useful can be said of its internal buildings, and it is not even clear whether it was an original Iron-Age fort re-used or a new foundation of the fifth or sixth century. For what it is worth, it may be described as a low hill on the Kirkcudbrightshire coast, falling craggily on the seaward side, but more gently inland. The relatively level top, 200 ft long by 130 ft wide, was defended on the inland side at least by a rampart which seems to be of two phases. The earlier had used a combination of dry-stonework and timber-framing or lacing, and the firing of the timber – whether by accident or hostile action – had vitrified much of the stonework. Subsequently, it would seem, the defences were refurbished by piling rubble against the vitri- fied wall. It may well be that the vitrified fort is Iron Age, and the secondary rubble represents work of the Arthurian period, but with- out further excavation this cannot be decided.

The dozen sites examined so far do not exhaust the potential list of fortifications used by the Britons in the age of Arthur, but they include all the securely dated examples and a fair sample of others as well. The only one of any size is Dumbarton, the capital of Strathclyde, and even there a large part of the interior is virtually uninhabitable because of crags. It is worth drawing attention to the contrast between the small fort on Boduan, only about one third of an acre in area, and the twenty-eight-acre Iron-Age fort which surrounds it [Fig. 30]. It seems clear that we have here a change in the unit of defence as between the pre-Roman and post-Roman centuries. The sociological implications of this will be explored more fully in Chapter 11. For the moment, we may accept the generalization that the forts of the Arthurian period are the defended homesteads of chiefs and princes.

There are, however, two forts which produce significant quantities of imported pottery but which cannot be brought within this generali- zation because of their size: Cadbury above Congresbury and

Cadbury Castle, which both lie towards the eastern boundaries of Dumnonia. Congresbury is now four miles inland, but it is possible that in the fifth/sixth centuries the sea came up to the limestone ridge on which the fort stands.[19] The defences themselves, enclosing eight and a half acres, originally go back to the pre-Roman Iron Age, when the steep edges of the hill were defended by one or more ramparts, walls and ditches. Within the enclosure are traces of hut-circles which are probably Iron Age. At present it appears that the defences were refurbished on a major scale about AD 450, though Roman pottery was still available. This point will be clarified by the excavations which are now in progress. What is certain is that the defences were already decayed when a considerable quantity of pottery was imported: Classes A and B, and also, perhaps, a little of Class D. This pottery was associated with a flimsy rectangular building, about 27 ft by 10 ft, and a near-circular structure about 35 ft in diameter with a curious and unparalleled screen of posts across the entrance. It has been well observed that these two buildings are quite unlike the timber halls of Castle Dore or Cadbury Castle, but no great implications should be read into this at the present stage of the excavations.

One possible interpretation is that Congresbury is indeed a princely stronghold, but that the buildings so far uncovered are those of re-tainers. The evidence of Pant-y-saer, Carreg-y-llam and Garn Boduan makes it clear that circular dwellings were still in use in our period, and this evidence will shortly be reinforced by that from Buston (below, p. 227) and Gwithian (below, p. 228). But there is another even more likely explanation. Congresbury is 'the fort of Congar', and though this name now applies to a village at the foot of the hills, the 'bury' element makes it clear that it must originally have belonged to the hill-fort itself. Congar was a Welsh (or British) saint, roughly datable on the evidence of rather late genealogies to the sixth century, the time of the imported pottery. The practice of founding monasteries within abandoned Roman or prehistoric forts is well attested, and it is quite likely that Congar placed a monastery here simply because there was a pre-existing defence, however decayed, which might serve as the *vallum monasterii*. Congresbury would then belong with the other monastic sites which have produced imported pottery (below, p. 249).

By contrast there need be no question of the secular character of

Cadbury Castle [Pl. 5], conveniently distinguished from the other Cadburys as Cadbury-Camelot on the strength of the identification first recorded by John Leland in 1532 (above, p. 163).[20] Cadbury-Camelot is an intensively excavated hill-fort, but the impact of the excavations has been somewhat diffused through the sheer size of the site and the duration and variety of its human occupations. Since these form the background to the Arthurian refortification, they must be lightly sketched in. A steep-sided, free-standing hill was first inhabited by Early Neolithic farmers before 3000 BC, and again on a slighter scale in the Late Neolithic around 2000 BC. Characteristic pottery and flints are known, but no coherent structures have been uncovered. There was then a long period of abandonment until the eighth or seventh century BC, when another farming community established itself on the broad summit ridge and cultivated the gentle upper slopes of the hill. This community had an indigenous Late Bronze Age culture, but this was soon enriched by continental elements brought in by trade or folk-movement. By this time the inhabitants were Celts, ancestors of the Britons of Arthur's day. By the fifth century BC the community had expanded and risen to the status of a large village or town, which was now fortified with a rampart and ditch set just at the head of the steepest hill-slope. The hill-fort in turn waxed in richness of culture and intensity of occupation, until on the eve of the Roman conquest it was defended by four massive banks and ditches, and contained a shrine and armourer's workshop as well as domestic buildings.

There is evidence that Cadbury-Camelot was not stormed immediately after the Roman invasion of AD 43, but that this fate was deferred until the 70s, when the inhabitants were slaughtered, and the defences were partially dismantled. Thereafter the fort lay derelict for two centuries, though a remnant of its inhabitants continued to live in the valley outside the north-east entrance. In the late third/fourth centuries, coins and pottery mark renewed activity, which was most probably in the form of pilgrimages to a Romano-Celtic temple. Since the latest known coin is one of Honorius, dated AD 393–402, it is clear that this activity continued to the very end of the fourth century, if not indeed into the early fifth. The next phase of occupation is marked by import wares of Classes A, B*iv*, B*i*, and D. This grouping suggests that occupation recommenced about 470, while a silver ring with

Germanic animal ornament shows that the fortifications were repaired after AD 550. The subsequent abandonment was broken briefly from 1010 to 1017 when Æthelred the Unready established a mint at *Cadanbyrig*, fortified it with twelve hundred yards of masonry wall and two monumental gates, and began to lay out internal buildings including a church. Æthelred's successor Cnut removed the mint and demolished the defences. There are shadowy hints of a subsequent medieval phase, but for many centuries the hilltop has been given over to intensive cultivation.

From Leland's day or earlier the hill has attracted the full repertory of Arthurian folk-lore, aided in this by a geological structure which suggests that it could indeed be the hollow hill in which the sleeping king lies. The excavations of 1966–70 attempted to uncover the entire history of Cadbury-Camelot, but in the present account we must obviously concentrate our attention on the relatively brief reoccupation in the late fifth and sixth centuries. Relevant structural discoveries have been made on two fronts: in the defences, and on the summit plateau. Trenching at five places across the innermost rampart revealed at least seven structural phases. Ramparts A to D belong to the pre-Roman Iron Age, A being the first earth-and-timber defence of the fifth century BC, and D the dry-stone wall assaulted, captured and slighted by the Romans. On the back of rampart D is a deep plough-soil which probably marks cultivation of the hilltop in the first two centuries of Roman rule. Bedded on this is rampart E, a rather roughly built dry-stone bank, which incorporates Roman masonry – blocks of hammer-dressed and sawn stone and tufa as well as stone and pottery roofing tiles – in its make-up. Lying directly on rampart E in some places, and in others separated from it by a humus layer, is rampart F, the mortared wall of Æthelred. Above this is rampart G, the medieval work, tenuous everywhere except at the south-west gate where it is represented by crude but massive walling.

Rampart E, then, is pre-Æthelredan, and there are no historical grounds for attributing it to any earlier Saxon ruler. It is certainly later than a fragment from a Class B amphora which was found stratified beneath it. For more precise dating we must turn to the evidence of the south-west gate. Two successive road surfaces could be related to rampart E and the later of these sealed a silver ring or buckle. As an object this is without parallel, but it bears a familiar style of Germanic ornament, namely fragmentary chip-carved animals such as appear on Anglo-Saxon brooches in the second half of the sixth century [Pl. 19*d*]. It is idle to speculate how this Germanic piece came into a British stronghold, but its chronological significance is plain. The gate had been refurbished sometime after 550, and most probably in response to that westward aggression of Wessex which led to the capture of Gloucester, Cirencester and Bath in 577. There is no direct evidence to date the first phase of the gate and the original construction of rampart E, but they must lie earlier in the sixth century or even back in the late fifth. That being so, it is reasonable to think of rampart E as the defence-work of the settlement which was importing pottery of Classes A, B and D from about 470 – in other words, it is a fortification of broadly Arthurian date.

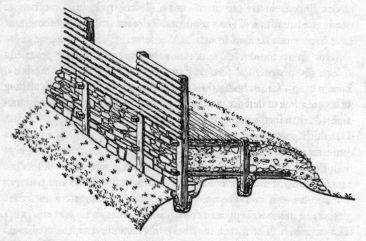

18. Cadbury-Camelot, sketch reconstruction of the Arthurian-period defences.

We must now examine the character of this defensive scheme. Wherever it was well preserved, rampart E took the form of a bank of rubble, of varying height and width but nowhere of impressive dimensions. At the rear stones were piled up untidily to make a crude revetment, while at the south-west gate and on part of the perimeter the lower courses of a rough outer revetment were also found in position. Vertical gaps between the stones showed that stout wooden posts had risen up the face to support a breastwork on top of the bank. The most interesting feature was that in the core of the rampart, where a complete jumble of rubble might have been expected, there were in fact lines of stones running both parallel to the wall face and at right angles to it. These marked the positions of thick timber beams, which had of course decayed over the centuries. Internal collapse of the rampart core, caused both by the decay of the timberwork and by burrowing animals, had destroyed any possibility of recovering the full pattern of the timbers. It is nevertheless clear that the main feature of the fifth/sixth-century defence was a framework of vertical, longitudinal and transverse beams jointed together and then anchored down by the rubble which was piled around it. We can only know about this framework where the rubble has preserved casts of it, and we have no evidence to show what rose out of the bank, but it is reasonable to suggest that it was some kind of elevated fighting platform.

Apart from minor modifications to the gates at Castle Dore and Chun, and pending the results of further excavations at Congresbury, no site except Cadbury-Camelot exhibits such a complete refurbishing of its main line of defence, amounting to nothing less than the construction of a new fortification. In character the work is utterly un-Roman. One of the most interesting pointers here is that although the builders had used large quantities of dressed masonry robbed from derelict Roman buildings, they had lost the art of laying masonry with mortar. Consequently, the entire defensive scheme, including, as we shall see, the gate-towers, was executed in a mixture of dry stonework and timber. In this it looks like a reversion to prehistoric Celtic techniques of fortification. There was, however, no means by which a knowledge of these techniques might have been transmitted over the centuries, and we are really dealing with a case in which similar materials dictate a similar solution to similar problems. A more valid comparison would be with the hilltop fortifications, often using a combination of timber and dry stonework, which sprang up along the continental frontiers of the Roman empire as a response to the barbarian migrations.

Finally, the sheer size of Cadbury-Camelot should be stressed. The configuration of the hilltop would have made it possible to fortify a much smaller area, more comparable with that of the other forts we have examined. Instead, it was decided to refortify the whole Iron-Age perimeter of about twelve hundred yards, enclosing about eighteen acres. It is evident that the unit of defence here is quite different from that of other contemporary strongholds. The military and sociological implications of this must be discussed later (below, pp. 347–9).

It is probable that there were two entrances through these defences, at the south-west and north-east corners, where the collapsed Iron-Age gates were still marked by dips in the rampart. Traces of the south-west gate were recovered by excavation, in the form of stains in the soil and breaks in the road surfaces where timbers had rotted away [Pl. 6a]. The principal members were four stout upright posts, set roughly in a square, and joined across the front and rear of the gate by massive sill-beams. At either side of the passage the rampart was shored up with sturdy planks. In the light of our knowledge of the character and development of military gateways, we can use these scanty remains to put forward a reconstruction of the Arthurian-period

19. Cadbury-Camelot: an artist's impression of the Arthurian-period gate-tower. Drawn on site by Bryan Whitton.

gate. This had two pairs of doors, each five feet wide, hanging from the uprights and closing against the sill-beams. The strength of the uprights and the depth to which they were bedded suggest that they rose to a good height and supported a considerable weight. It is therefore reasonable to imagine a look-out and fighting platform elevated above the rampart walk which would have been carried right across the passage. The whole structure would have been tied into the timber framework of the rampart itself to provide greater rigidity.

This gate-tower has considerable historical interest, both in its own right as the first Arthurian gate which can be reconstructed and also for the place which it occupies in the evolution of military architecture. Roman gateways, whether urban or military, had generally taken the form of twin towers flanking the actual gate and passage-way. But the minor gates of Roman forts, like Hod Hill and Fendoch, and the entrances of mile-castles on Hadrian's Wall and of other small fortifications, normally had a single tower raised, either in timber or in mortared masonry, above the gate and passage-way. A fortlet at Richborough shows that the type continued into the third century. Much later, the single-unit gate-tower was a common feature of eleventh- and twelfth-century castles both in Britain and on the Continent. It has been possible to trace its ancestry back through the tenth century, and perhaps even as far as the early ninth, in north-western Europe, but the further link through the immediately post-Roman centuries has not previously been found. The sixth-century gate at Cadbury-Camelot provides it, but with a difference. Most timber gate-towers, whether Roman, Carolingian or later, have three pairs of major uprights, whereas the Cadbury gate has only two. Nevertheless it represents a distinctly romanized element in a defensive scheme which, as we have seen, is essentially non-Roman in character.

Within the defences no traces of structures were visible before excavation, and it was largely a matter of chance whether or not buildings of Arthurian date were uncovered. Indeed, the large area involved, eighteen acres in all, made the possibility of discovering significant buildings seem remote. Fortunately, however, extensive clearance of the summit plateau led to the location of a sizeable timber structure which could be securely dated [Pl. 6b]. One feature of it had been an internal partition set in a continuous rock-cut trench, and among the earth and small stones tamped into the trench around the posts of the partition were sherds of a B*i* amphora. Now it is at first sight conceivable that the trench might be eleventh century rather than fifth/sixth century in date, on the grounds that the amphora sherds and other refuse could have been lying on the surface when an Æthelredan building was erected, and so came to be incorporated in its wall-trench. But the amphora sherds, despite the softness of their fabric, had sharp, unabraded edges, and there can be no reasonable doubt that they were buried in the trench-filling shortly after the vessel from which they came had been shattered. The wall-trench itself formed part of a palimpsest of Iron-Age, Arthurian, Æthelredan and medieval pits and gullies, and it was not easy to establish which other features belonged with it. Some parts of the palimpsest could readily be attributed to other periods because of their character or associated finds. From the remainder, it is possible to select those post-holes which form lines parallel to the screen-wall or at right angles to it, and which make up a coherent and rational plan [Fig. 16a].

The attribution of individual holes may remain a matter of discussion, but what has clearly emerged is a building roughly twice as long as its width – 63 by 34 ft – divided by a screen about one third of the

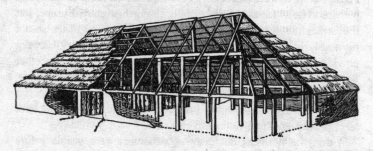

20. Cadbury-Camelot: an artist's impression of the Arthurian-period hall (plan, Fig. 16a). Drawn on site by Bryan Whitton.

way from the east end. There was probably a door in each of the long sides immediately adjacent to the screen. Although the roofing arrangements must be conjectural, the wide span of the building implies that the walls could not have carried the whole weight of the roof. Consistent with this, there are clear traces of a northern row of aisle posts and lesser evidence for a southern row. In general all the post-holes are shallow, and this implies that the building took its strength from a well-carpentered and jointed timber framework rather than from its individual earth-fast posts. In other words this building, like the contemporary defences and gate-tower, implies a very competent knowledge of carpentry.

The actual skeleton of the building can thus be described with some confidence, but it is more difficult to be certain about how it functioned. It is most probable that the larger compartment, almost square in plan, was a hall. Indeed, in view of its size and the central and dominating position of the building itself within the defences, it can reasonably be described as *the* hall: the social and administrative focus of the stronghold. The smaller compartment might then be a private chamber, or alternatively the service rooms, buttery and possibly kitchen, divided from the hall by a screened passage. This second alternative is of course the layout of a medieval hall, and it is probably too formal for the period. Our interpretation would be helped here if it had been possible to locate the hearth or hearths, but these had been obliterated by ploughing. It is certain that the hall would not have stood alone, but no other building plans can be assigned to this period with complete confidence. Some 12 ft to the north of the hall, however, there was a pair of parallel wall trenches, 13 ft long and 6 ft apart. A distinct concentration of imported pottery in the vicinity suggests that this small rectangular building may be contemporary with the hall. If so, it could have been a kitchen or other ancillary building.

The princely strongholds and fortified homesteads which have been described so far are scattered over the whole of western Britain. We turn now to another class of large homestead whose distribution is strictly limited by geographical conditions: the crannog, or artificial island, which demands lakes or at least marshes for its construction. In Britain crannogs are largely confined to Scotland, especially western Scotland, where they occur in the Roman period both sides of the Antonine Wall. Some continue into the post-Roman centuries, but attention will be concentrated here on an example at Buston in Ayrshire which belongs wholly to the sixth/seventh century.[21] This was discovered in the 1870s in the course of reclaiming the bog in which it was situated. Many cartloads of timber had already been removed before it was subjected to scholarly examination, and the character of the investigation itself leaves much to be desired. None the less a generalized description is possible [Fig. 16c]. Even in the late nineteenth century Buston Crannog was recognizable as a mound surrounded by swamp in summer and by water in winter. In other words it had been built originally in a shallow lake which had silted up over the centuries. The published plan shows a roughly circular raft or island made up of layers of tree branches and stems, stabilized by rings of piles. These were linked together by horizontal beams arranged both radially and concentrically. This, of course, merely formed a foundation, and most of the evidence for the house itself had perished. But it seems to have been oval, a little over 50 ft in diameter, and centred on a massive hearth about 10 ft across. The wall had been constructed of courses of stones and timber, but nothing is known about the roof. The door opened on to a sort of terrace or platform running round the house, and immediately across this was a large and rich refuse heap where domestic rubbish had been tipped straight into the lake. The quality of the finds suggests that the inhabitants may have been well-to-do, and it is interesting to see a large circular house, not unlike those of the pre-Roman Iron Age in southern Britain, occupied by such a household in the post-Roman centuries. It should not be overlooked that the surrounding water was a very effective defence.

A quite different social level seems to be represented by the undefended homestead of Gwithian, in the valley of the Red River within half a mile of the north Cornish coast.[22] There the remains of two drystone buildings have been recovered, datable to the sixth century by native, imported, and grass-marked pottery [Fig. 16d]. They were irregular in plan and very small, 7 ft 6 in. by 8 ft 6 in. and 10 ft by 11 ft respectively. Since each contained a built hearth, it is likely that they were residential. In the area around the houses were outdoor hearths and rubbish pits, and fragmentary traces of other dry-stone structures. It is impossible to think of these two buildings as anything more than peasant cottages. Yet the finds suggest that the community as a whole was not impoverished, for metal tools and even ornaments were plentiful and the imported pottery was both abundant and varied.

The occurrence of a contemporary midden about fifty yards from the houses suggests that there is still much of the settlement to explore. What we know from literary sources about early Welsh social structure, and what we infer about its British antecedents, suggests that the houses at Gwithian are those of bondmen on the outskirts of a *maerdref* or royal administrative centre.

It is relevant here to remark that verbal evidence gives us many hints which have not yet been realized through archaeological discoveries. We know for instance that the *tref* or settlement of bondmen was a major element in early Welsh society and economy. The bondmen were largely engaged in arable farming, and their settlements were normally located on the best land. We can infer that the pattern of settlement was not the dispersed one normal in Wales today, but one of nucleated hamlets or villages. This is deduced from regulations in the Welsh Laws about the payment of compensation if a house caught fire and the fire then spread to neighbouring dwellings, for the clear implication is that houses were close enough for fire to spread in this way. But although we know the approximate whereabouts of these nucleated settlements, not one has been located and excavated. At the other end of the social scale, we know that the principal seat of the dynasty of Gwynedd was at Aberffraw, on the west coast of Anglesey; but the precise location of this important court has defied topographical and archaeological research.

Artefacts and activities

So far this account has necessarily concentrated on the structures of the fifth to seventh centuries: defences and buildings. Now that a characteristic range of sites has been described, it is possible to examine the objects which have been found in them, and the activities which may be inferred. A double warning is necessary here. First, most of the sites produce very few finds at all, and of the excavations which have yielded a good range of artefacts only one has been adequately published. Second, the verbal evidence provides a standard by which we can judge the deficiencies of the archaeological record. As we have seen (above, p. 145), the Welsh Laws contain several lists of household goods, craftsmen's tools and farming equipment. For instance, in the event of a legal separation, the husband is to have a pail, a dish, the cart, all the liquor vessels and tubs, the boiler, the coulter, fuel axe, auger, gimlet, fire-dog, all except one of the sickles, and the baking-griddle. The wife is to have the remainder of the dishes and pails, the trivet, pan, broad-axe, sieve, ploughshare, one sickle, and all the precious objects excepting gold or silver, which should be equally shared. This is only an extract from the list, and all the objects

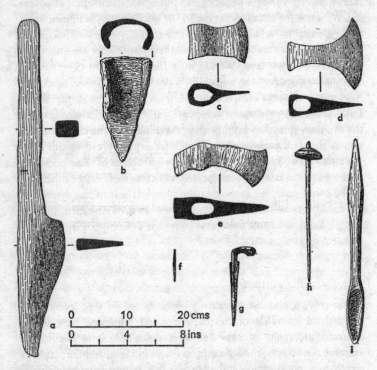

21. Iron tools and implements: *a* plough-coulter, White Fort, Co. Down; *b* ploughshare, Dundrum Castle, Co. Down; *c* axe, Buston Crannog, Ayrshire; *d* axe, perhaps a weapon rather than a tool, from a warrior-grave at Petersfinger, Wiltshire; *e* axe-hammer, Cadbury-Camelot, Somerset; *f* awl, possibly for leather-working, Buston; *g* spring from a barrel padlock, Buston; *h* iron spindle and bone whorl, Sutton Courtenay, Berkshire; *i* spoon bit, Buston.[23]

made of perishable organic materials have been deliberately omitted; in other words, all the objects quoted here might be expected on archaeological sites. From the sixteen sites listed in the previous section we have handles and handle-attachments from pails, fragments from bill-hooks or sickles, a number of awls or gimlets, the occasional axe, and some trinkets which might pass as precious objects; but this entire collection falls far short of what the Welsh Laws assign to a normal free household.

With these warnings in mind we can now attempt a synoptic picture of the way of life and material culture of the Britons. Except where acid soils have destroyed them, the most abundant relics from all classes of site are animal bones, representing the food of the community. On occasion these are of wild animals – stag or boar – or birds of song-bird size, or salmon, but on the whole it would seem that relatively little fish or game was taken whether by princes or peasants. On the other hand a wide variety of shell-fish occurs on coastal and near-coastal sites. Predominantly, however, the bones are of domestic animals: mainly cattle, with pig and sheep occurring in variable proportions. At Dinas Powys, however, pig was certainly the most common.

These domestic animals, then, provided a significant part of the food supply, and not merely flesh, but milk, butter and cheese from both cows and ewes, and lard from the pigs. They also provided the raw materials for domestic crafts and industries for both home consumption and export. The craft-products which have been recovered are limited to leather shoes, preserved only in the favourable conditions of water-logged peat, and bone objects including double-edged combs [Fig. 31], pins and needles, spindle whorls and ornamental strips for decorating wooden boxes and the like. But a very widespread use of leather is implied by the occurrence of highly polished stones used in leather-dressing, and of iron awls and heavy needles for piercing and stitching it. Horn, gut and sinew were no doubt also used, but have perished. So too has the woollen cloth implied by spindle whorls of pot or bone. It should be added that there is no evidence for the form of loom.

The evidence for stock-raising is evidently very strong, but that for arable farming is more tenuous. The enclosed homestead of Pant-y-saer belongs to a group of sites which are regularly associated with terraced fields, and there are traces of terraces immediately below the homestead. At Gwithian a field apparently 90 ft wide and between 120 and 300 ft long was cultivated with a plough which turned proper furrow slices, and was manured with refuse which included pottery of the sixth to ninth centuries from the peasant settlement already described.[24] No other fields are known from the period, nor have plough-shares or coulters been discovered. Indeed, the only clearly agricultural implements are some iron sickles from Gwithian. But it is notorious from the archaeology of other arable-farming communities that large iron objects like plough-parts are very rare finds, presumably because if they broke in use they would be reforged rather than discarded. Undoubtedly many of our sites produce evidence that grain was being ground on handmills, and at Dinas Powys certain round sandstone slabs are best interpreted as griddles for baking the thin bread known from literary sources. On the whole, then, the evidence suggests a mixture of arable farming and stock-raising.

In addition to the domestic crafts which have been described, that of the carpenter is witnessed by drill-bits, saws and files, as well as by worked timber preserved in the water-logged conditions of Buston. This includes squared and jointed timbers in abundance and a dug-out boat some 22 ft long. But the most important industries were those connected with metalworking. These began with the actual exploitation of local ores – tin, as we have seen, at Chun, and iron very widely elsewhere. Consequently lumps of iron ore, slags, cinders and blooms of iron are all commonly found, sometimes in association with primitive bowl furnaces. There appears to be no direct evidence, however, for the extraction of copper, and at Dinas Powys we have the curious fact that scrap jewelry of Teutonic origin was being melted down for its bronze and gold content. Even the scale of iron-working is pathetically small when compared with the Roman period. Roman furnaces might be 3 ft in diameter, but the blooms from Dinas Powys suggest a furnace little over 8 in. across. And whereas a single lump of iron cinder from a Roman site might weigh 80 lb., the sum total of ore, slag, cinders and blooms collected in five seasons of excavation at Dinas Powys amounted only to 50 lb. Here is a measure of the degree to which material culture and technology had declined since 400.

Although no blacksmith's tools or anvils have been reported from sites, it is reasonable to suppose that the blooms of iron were being worked up on the spot to produce tools, implements and weapons. Some of these have already been mentioned. The most widespread single class consists of iron knives with straight, thick-backed blades two to six inches long, and heavy tangs which doubtless served a handle of bone, antler or wood. We shall find very similar knives in both Ireland and pagan England [Fig. 31], and they belong to the distinctive Migration-Period class distributed from Galway Bay to the Black Sea. In Germanic circles they occur with both men and women even in poorly furnished pagan graves, and it is reasonable to believe that every adult carried one. Other ironwork includes a sturdy axe-head with a three-inch blade from Buston, an essential implement for the tree-felling required to construct the crannog; the spring of a barrel padlock from the same site; fish-hooks from Dinas Powys; and a range of staples, eyes, cleats and nails. Weapons are very rare, but Buston yielded a socketed spearhead 8 in. long, and three formidable arrow-heads, whose significance must be discussed later.

The craft of the jeweller or trinket-maker is also well represented, both in its finished products and in its technical processes. In addition to the elaborate jewelry in gilt and enamelled bronze, which will be discussed shortly, we find bone, boar's-tusk ivory, jet and shale all used for beads, pin-heads, and ornamental appliqués. Glass beads were imported apparently from both Mediterranean and Germanic sources, and glass bangles and beads were also manufactured locally. Scraps of characteristic Germanic glass have been found sporadically on British sites, and it has been assumed that these represented the actual vessels from which imported wine as well as local mead was drunk. But the more copious evidence from Dinas Powys suggests that the glass had never been present on western sites in the form of complete vessels. Instead, scrap glass was imported to make bangles and beads, and to serve as a major constituent of the enamel inlays for fine brooches. The technological explanation of this is that while it is relatively easy to mould glass or convert it into a vitreous paste, it is quite another matter to produce glass from its mineral constituents.

Some small defended sites – notably Mote of Mark and Dinas Powys – have produced evidence of the actual processes of jewelry-making. It seems likely from both archaeological and literary evidence that the craftsmen were peripatetic, and sought out the patronage of chiefs and princes at their fortified courts. There the jewellers cast decorative bronzes in open moulds made of fine clay, in which patterns had been impressed either by using existing ornaments, or by carving new designs on stamps or dies of lead, bone or wood. In addition to scrap glass they imported sticks of coloured glass, or millefiori patterned rods, from which slices were cut to serve as inlays. Several sites have produced crucibles, ranging in size from a large thimble to a small tea-cup, in which bronze and even gold were melted. The great variety of crucible-shapes suggests that this was a period of technological experiment. A favourite form, furnished with a built-in lid to help conserve heat, occurs both in Britain and in Ireland. From this we can reasonably infer that there was some movement of craftsmen across the Irish Sea.

In terms of skill and artistry the most important products of British bronzesmiths in the period are the decorated hanging bowls.[25] These are circular vessels of thin beaten bronze, fitted with three or four suspension loops [Pl. 15]. The hook which holds the loop is frequently bird- or animal-headed, and springs from a circular escutcheon which may be ornamented in openwork or with coloured enamels or patterned millefiori glass inlays. Vessels ancestral to these were being manufactured in Roman Britain, and it is likely that the earliest of the hanging bowls, those with the openwork escutcheons, go back to the fourth century. The earliest decoration is rather formal and classical in inspiration [Pl. 15a], but later examples have a varied repertory of Celtic scrolls [Pl. 15b], often ending in birds' heads, which glisten in golden bronze against a background of sealing-wax-red enamel. By far the most elaborate bowl is the largest of the three from the Sutton Hoo ship burial. It is tempting to think that this had been manufactured for the East Anglian court, and certainly the craftsman who made it had picked up from an Anglo-Saxon jeweller the idea of fashioning animals' eyes out of disks of garnet backed with crinkled gold foil. If, as some scholars think, the Sutton Hoo treasure is that of Rædwald, the great king of East Anglia who died in the 620s, this bowl must have been made shortly after 600, because it was already worn and repaired before it was buried. An alternative view is that the Sutton Hoo bowls had been made by monastic craftsmen in the monastery which the Irish missionary Fursey founded within the ruined Saxon Shore fort of Burgh Castle [Pl. 1a] in the 630s.[26] In that case, the bowls might have been made around 640 and buried towards 660. The coins from the Sutton Hoo treasure do not really allow us to decide between these two dates, because competent numismatists cannot agree on a date within a span of some thirty years. Taking account of the stages of development represented by both the Celtic bowls and the Anglo-Saxon jewelry in the treasure, I would prefer the later date.

The uncertainties about the precise chronology of hanging bowls are surpassed by the doubts about their function and place of manufacture. The ornament on some of the bowls includes Christian elements, with both the cross and the fish as symbols of Christ. So some of the bowls had a religious use, perhaps specifically in the liturgy. But this need not apply to the great majority which carry no Christian symbolism. Presumably they served as containers, and it has been suggested that they may have held oil and so, with a floating wick, have acted as hanging lamps. But the great bowl from Sutton Hoo contained a fish standing on an ornamental pedestal. Apart from the Christian implications the fish suggests water, but again it is disputed whether this was simply for drinking, or whether it was holy water for ritual sprinkling or cleansing. The debate here is endless, and may never be settled.

The dispute about the source or place of manufacture, however, can now be answered in archaeological terms. Most of the bowls come from Anglo-Saxon graves, but the ornamental designs make it quite certain that they were made not by Anglo-Saxon craftsmen but by Celts. Some of them may actually have been made for the Englishman in whose grave they were found, as we have suggested about the Sutton Hoo bowls. But most of them are likely to be loot, from churches or wealthy households. This still leaves open the question as to where they were made. It used to be asserted that the necessary techniques of enamelling and millefiori inlays could only be demonstrated on sites in Ireland, and that therefore the bowls found in Britain must nevertheless have been imported from across the Irish Sea – this despite the fact that bowls, or even fragments of them, are excessively rare in Ireland, and normally differ in shape from those found in Saxon graves. But the evidence of millefiori and enamel work from Dinas Powys has proved that British craftsmen were masters of the same technical skills as their Irish counterparts. Granted this, the plain evidence of distribution is in favour of the view that the bowls found in Britain had been produced by local craftsmen.

Apart from the hanging bowls, however, it is difficult to attribute any great range of fine metalwork to the craftsmen whom Arthur might have patronized. In the later Roman period British bronzesmiths had made a variety of brooches and pins, of which the leading types were pins with a crook shank and a disk or ring head; straight pins with a 'zoomorphic' stylized animal head; and zoomorphic penannular brooches. This last type consisted of a pin swivelling on a hoop which had a gap flanked by stylized animal heads. In use, perhaps to hold a cloak, the pin was pushed through the folds of cloth, and then passed through the gap in the hoop, which was then turned until in effect it locked behind the pin. Pins and brooches of these types seem to have developed in the fourth century, and occur both in native forts like Traprain Law and in Roman forts, towns and temples. Their manufacture probably continued for about a century, with minor developments which are more apparent to the modern typologist than they would have been to a fifth-century Briton. Meanwhile the idea was taken to Ireland and to Pictland, perhaps in the minds of craftsmen carried off as slaves. In the west and the north they stimulated the creation of quite new varieties, richly embellished with enamel or glass inlays like those on the hanging-bowl escutcheons, which by the eighth century had developed into elaborate masterpieces of jewelry.[27]

Little of this development is seen among the Britons, however. There are a very few enamelled zoomorphic pins and crook-shanked pins. Britain has also some barbarous versions of an Irish type of pin ornamented with a freely swivelling ring, the loose-ring pin. Dinas Powys produced a lead die or trial casting from the manufacture of an enamelled zoomorphic penannular brooch, showing that these were made in Britain, but no finished examples have been found. Pant-y-saer in Anglesey yielded a silver penannular comparable with some from Perthshire and Fife, which probably represent a fashion of the Picts brought to Gwynedd by the dynasty of Cunedda (above, p. 216).

The apparent poverty of British craftsmanship, which is so marked when we contrast the numbers of penannular brooches manufactured

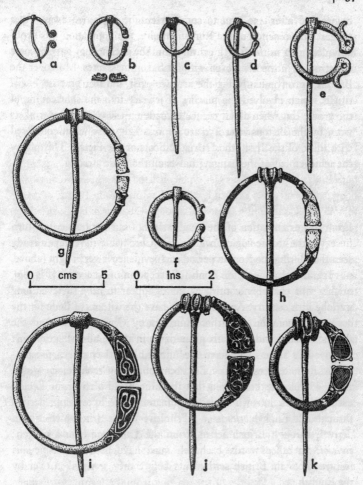

22. Penannular pins and brooches: *a* Iron-Age type with coiled terminals, Glastonbury, Somerset; *b* first-century example with crimped terminals, Cadbury-Camelot, Somerset; *c, d, e* Irish omega pins developing into ornithomorphic forms; *f* fourth-century ornithomorphic example, Lydney, Gloucestershire; *g* fourth-century Romano-British zoomorphic penannular, Caerwent, Monmouthshire; *h* similar brooch from Ireland; *i* sixth-century zoomorphic penannular embellished with champlevé enamel, Dinas Powys, Glamorgan; *j, k* comparable decorated zoomorphic penannulars from Ireland.

before and after 450, can to some extent be explained away. As a general phenomenon of the Roman empire, the population was probably declining in the fourth century, and the decline may have become catastrophic in the fifth, even without Saxon massacres. Moreover the Britons, inconveniently for the archaeologist, did not practise burial rituals which involved the placing of jewelry into the safekeeping of the grave. But when all allowance is made on these lines, the trinkets worn by the Britons after 450 are depressingly poor when compared with those of the Irish, the Dalriadic Scots or the Picts.* This makes the achievement of the hanging bowls all the more striking.

Religious monuments

From this examination of the secular sites of our period we now turn to survey the archaeological evidence for Christianity. We have already seen that during the Roman period such evidence is very slight (above, p. 171), and that, with the doubtful exception of Caerwent [Fig. 8b], neither villa chapels nor town churches appear to have survived long into the fifth century. Against this we have the witness of Bede for the use and restoration of earlier churches by Queen Bertha and the Augustinian mission. Certain place-name evidence also suggests that the invading Saxons may have encountered British churches, presumably of Roman ancestry, far more commonly than archaeology would allow. Philologists are agreed that the widespread place-name Eccles, used either on its own or in combinations like Ecclesham, derives through Old English ecles from a Primitive Welsh egles, which in turn derives, through British Latin, from the Latin word for a church: ecclesia. In other words a church must have been a conspicuous feature of certain British settlements before they were taken over by the English.[28]

Despite this, churches figure only very rarely in the archaeological record even in the westernmost parts of Britain. Instead, the largest group of religious monuments is that of the inscribed and carved stones which are usually described simply as Early Christian monuments.[29] These are classified in three broad groups, of which only two concern

*The quantity and ornamental richness of the moulds from Mote of Mark suggest, however, that this assessment may be unreasonably derogatory.

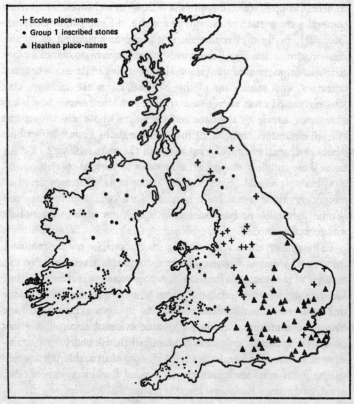

Map. 7. Place-names indicative of British Christianity and Anglo-Saxon heathenism, together with Ogham stones in Ireland and contemporary monuments in Britain. For Eccles, see note 28; for Group I stones, note 29; for heathen place-names, Stenton, F. M., 'The Historical Bearing of Place-Name Studies: Anglo-Saxon Heathenism', *Transactions Royal Historical Society*, 4th series 23, 1941, pp. 1-17, reprinted in Stenton, D. M. (ed.), *Preparatory to Anglo-Saxon England*, Oxford, 1970, pp. 281-97.

us here. Group I, which dates to the fifth, sixth and seventh centuries, comprises memorial stones with an epitaph in Latin and/or Goidelic. Group II, partly overlapping the first group and running on to the ninth century, consists of slabs with crosses incised or carved in low relief. Inscriptions are rare. Group III, beginning in the ninth century or earlier, and continuing to the Norman Conquest, includes elaborately carved cross slabs and even free-standing crosses, which are sometimes datable by the names of the rulers who had them set up. We are interested, then, in all the monuments of Group I, totalling nearly two hundred, and also in the earlier examples of Group II, in so far as these simple cross-incised stones can be divided on a chronological basis. It should be emphasized at the outset that considered as monuments these stones are very crude. Little was done to shape the natural slab, pillar or even boulder on which the cross or inscription was pecked or incised.

The formulae used on the earliest inscriptions are not far removed from those of pagan Roman memorials, and this gives a clue to the ancestry of the memorial form itself. A good example is the stone from Llanerfyl in Montgomeryshire.[30] This is one of the very few stones that were erected in an inland region, and it seems likely that it owes more to a remnant of Roman Christianity surviving around *Viroconium* (Wroxeter) than to any new influences coming by sea to the western coasts. The Llanerfyl stone [Pl. 25*a*] is a roughly rectangular slab, with a Latin inscription written in good Roman capitals, set out in evenly disposed horizontal lines. It reads:

HIC [IN]	Here in
TVMVLO IA	the tomb lies
CIT. ROSTE	Rustica
ECE. FILIA. PA	daughter of
TERNINI.	Paterninus.
ANI XIII. IN	Aged thirteen. In
PA [CE]	peace.

Now this is a very romanized inscription. The two people named, Paterninus and his daughter Rustica, both have good Roman names, even if the spelling of Rustica is shaky. The statement of the age of the deceased is a regular pagan practice which gradually died with the spread of Christianity, though it does occur on good Christian epitaphs in Gaul and Spain. Two features mark Rustica's memorial as Christian: the absence of the opening pagan formula, *D [is] M [anibus]*, 'to the divine shades', and the expressly Christian termination IN PACE, 'in peace'. In terms of its style and epigraphy, there is no reason why this monument should not have been erected in the fourth century, but a cautious date would be early fifth.

At the opposite pole stands the stone from Eglwys Gymyn, Carmarthenshire,[31] a pillar with a bilingual inscription in Irish written in the Ogham script along the vertical edges of the stone, and a Latin inscription which is also written vertically on the face of the stone [Pls. 29a, b]:

Latin: AVITORIA FILIA CVNIGNI
         Avitoria daughter of Cunignos
Ogham: AVITTORIGES INIGENA CUNIGNI
         [The monument] of Avittoriga daughter of Cunignos

This inscription has nothing specifically Christian about it. Indeed, in the light of the injunction to 'Call no man thy father but he which is thy Father in heaven', the emphasis on the paternity of Avitoria has been considered as positively un-Christian. This 'filiation formula' is rightly at home in a pagan tribal society, where descent was a major factor in a person's status. We shall see that statements of descent achieve their fullest elaboration in Ireland (below, p. 262) and it has therefore been claimed that the filiation formula was imported from Ireland to Britain along with the Irish language, the Ogham script, and the pagan idea of setting up rough stone memorials. The immigrant tribe or dynasty of the Dési would have had the chief responsibility for the introduction of these Irish customs.

It is true that filiation stones are most common in those parts of Britain where Ogham and vertical inscriptions are to be found, and where there is other evidence for Irish elements. But it is easy to exaggerate the extent of Irish influence. In so far as a statement of descent is appropriate to a tribal society, we should remember that British society had the same Celtic tribal roots as Irish, even if it had been subjected to more modification through Roman influences. We have seen the clear Roman ancestry of the Llanerfyl stone, and it seems reasonable to suggest that both the Ogham stones of Ireland and the Early Christian monuments of Britain derive in parallel from pagan Roman epitaphs. Nor will it have escaped notice that the name of Rustica's father is given on her memorial. Parallels for this can· be quoted from both pagan and Christian inscriptions on the Continent. Nevertheless, a simple filiation formula without any Christian elements at all is distinctive of the lands bordering the Irish Sea.

Between the two poles of Llanerfyl and Eglwys Gymyn lies a range of formulae which normally contain two elements: the name of the deceased, and the statement HIC IACIT, 'here he lies'. Along with the name there may be the statement of descent, or more rarely something about rank, status or profession: PRESBYTER, 'priest' [Pl. 26a]; ELMETIA-COS, 'native of Elmet'; VENEDOTIS CIVES, 'citizen of Gwynedd' are examples of this [Pl. 28]. Occasionally the *hic iacit* is qualified, sometimes in execrable Latin: IN HOC CONGERIES LAPIDUM, 'in this cairn of stones' [Pl. 30a]; IN TUMULO, 'in the tomb'. A statement about the age of the deceased, which had been customary on pagan epitaphs, is exceptionally rare, and it is generally considered that the rarity reflects a Christian indifference to the length of this worldly life.

It has already been suggested that an inscription which stands close to pagan Roman forms, like that from Llanerfyl, might be dated early in the fifth century. Another stone which could be very early comes from Whithorn in Wigtonshire.[32] Written in quite good Roman capitals set out in regular horizontal lines, the stone records the ages of the deceased, Latinus aged thirty-five and his unnamed daughter aged four [Pl. 25b]. Pagan inscriptions frequently state that the widow or other relative of the deceased had been responsible for an epitaph, and here we are told that Barrovadus the grandson (or nephew – the Latin could have either meaning) had set up the monument. But the Christianity of the inscription is not in doubt, for the opening words are TE DOMINVM LAVDAMVS, 'We praise thee Lord', a reference to the 146th psalm and the Roman office for the dead. We have here evidence for an early Christian community, at a site which can be identified as the *Candida Casa* of St Ninian.

There are very few inscriptions which we might date before about 450 on the grounds of their closeness to pagan formulae. Thereafter any precise dating becomes impossible, except in the rare cases where we can identify the person named on a memorial with someone known from the historical records and datable on that basis. For such dating to be sound, there must be no doubts about the identification: if the name is a common one or can be shown to be repeated periodically in a dynasty, the argument is obviously weakened. And for the chronology to be accurate the historical dating should be based on something better than genealogical dead-reckoning. No single inscription satisfies all these conditions; but in default of first-rate evidence of this kind, attempts have been made to place the stones in a dated typological series on the basis of their epigraphy, that is, the actual shapes of the letters used on them.

The background to this epigraphic chronology is a well-known development in the scripts used both for writing in books and for carving or incising on stones. This was the change from rather stiff and formal Roman capital letters to more flowing, rounded scripts, suitable for writing books on parchment, and known therefore as book-hand. So far as Latin manuscripts are concerned a fully developed book-hand, the script known as uncial, emerged in the fourth century, but did not at once supersede the use of capitals which continued until the early sixth century. As Christianity, with its need for psalters, gospels, and other religious books, spread in the Celtic west, so insular variants of the uncial script were developed, especially in Irish *scriptoria*. These had already reached a fairly mature stage by the end of the sixth century, as we can see from the Irish psalter known as the *Cathach*, 'Battler', of St Columba.[33] This evolution of book-hand should be reflected in the epigraphy of the monuments, and should serve as a basis for dating them.

To some extent this proposition can be checked. From Penmachno in Caernarvonshire comes the one stone which can be precisely dated [Pl. 29c], for it carries the inscription IN TE [M]PO[RE] IVSTI[NI] CON[SULIS], 'In the time of Justinus the Consul'.[34] This is to be equated with the sole consulship of Justinus in AD 540, and this must be the date of the inscription, which is in good Roman capitals. Perhaps slightly later is the stone of Voteporix [Pl. 27a], MEMORIA VOTEPORIGISPROTICTORIS, 'the memorial of Voteporix Protector'.[35] This man is generally identified with *Demetarum tyranne Vortipori*, 'Vortiporius usurper of Demetia', whom Gildas attacked in the *De excidio*. He was certainly alive, therefore, in 535, which appears to be the earliest possible date for the *De excidio* (above, p. 55), and he could well have survived until 550 or later. Broadly speaking, then, a date in the mid-sixth century seems appropriate for his *memoria*, which again is in Roman capitals without a trace of book-hand.

The earliest datable inscription which displays any appreciable use of letter-forms derived from uncials is the memorial to Catamanus or Cadfan, king of Gwynedd [Pl. 27*b*], which is now built into the wall of Llangadwaladr church in Anglesey.[36] This reads:

catamaNus	Cadfan
rexsapIeNtisi	King, wisest
mus OpINatIsIm	most renowned
us OmnIumreg	of all
um	kings

An attempt has been made here by the use of lower- and upper-case type to reproduce the curious mixture of half-uncial and Roman capital letters of the inscription. In other words, the full influence of book-hand has still to be felt. The date of Cadfan's death cannot be established exactly, but it must lie between 616, when the death of his father Jacob is recorded in the Welsh Easter Annals, and 633-4, when his son Cadwallon was slain by Oswald of Northumbria. It is in fact usually placed around 625. But it is possible that the memorial was not actually set up until Cadfan's grandson Cadwaladr founded the church at Llangadwaladr late in his reign, which ended either in 664 or 684 (above, pp. 54-5). The most we can say is that sometime between about 625 and 660 Roman capitals were still occasionally in use for inscriptions on stone.

Moreover, the three stones just mentioned are the only ones which can be dated with any sort of confidence. It follows that, even if a typological series of inscriptions could be established, there are not enough fixed points to calibrate the series and so use it for close dating. It is even doubtful whether a satisfactory series can be established. The one usually propounded runs from inscriptions in good Roman capitals, through those with a mixture of capitals and half-uncials like the Cadfan stone, to those inscribed entirely in book-hand letters. But apart from the customary warning that typological development is not biological evolution, it is necessary to observe here that the primary epigraphic developments were not taking place on the inscribed stones, which borrowed letter forms from the manuscripts. Moreover, if we take the Cadfan inscription and, say, the Book of Durrow as being broadly contemporary, it is clear that the borrowing was only partial, rather than wholesale, and that the stones continued to use archaic letter forms. A principal reason for this was simply that capitals are more suitable than book-hand for carving on stone. The choice of an up-to-date half-uncial letter or of a time-hallowed capital must in each case have depended on the whim of the individual mason, and it is clear that we cannot seriate personal whims. But a broad chronology is still possible. Inscriptions using nothing but Roman capitals may run throughout the fifth century and up to the middle of the sixth, if not beyond. Those using entirely book-hand forms belong at the earliest to the late seventh. In between, some mixture of letter-forms may be expected.

Apart from its importance for epigraphic chronology, the Cadfan stone is also important because it gives us the first dated example of a true cross among the British stones. Crosses of any kind are rare on the Group I stones, but when they occur with inscriptions in Roman capitals they are frequently monogrammatic crosses, that is, formed out of the *chi-rho* monogram for Christ [Pl. 30a]. It has been suggested that this is because the early Christians felt a repugnance to the cross which had been the instrument of capital punishment in the empire before the peace of the church. Despite this repugnance, the true cross as well as the monogrammatic cross was already prominent on church mosaics in the fifth century, and by the end of that century it was certainly known in Britain on imported dishes of Class A [Fig. 13]. These have been found in quantity at Tintagel, and once also at Cadbury-Camelot. So it is rather strange that the true cross should not appear on inscribed stones before the mid seventh century. There are, it is true, earlier stones with crosses on them, for instance, one from Llanfyrnach in Pembrokeshire [Pl. 30b], which has an almost unreadable Ogham inscription down one edge, and what appears to be a processional cross pecked on the face.[37] If the cross and the inscription are contemporary then the cross should belong to the fifth or sixth century. But we certainly know cases where a cross is secondary to a

Group I inscription, for it either cuts across the letters, or the stone has been turned upside down to accommodate it. Moreover, when a simple cross occurs with an inscription, the inscription is normally in half-uncials. We must conclude, then, that the inscribed crosses belong on the whole to the later seventh and subsequent centuries.

Within western Britain the distribution of the stones which can reasonably be dated to our period is curiously restricted. Taking the Latin, Goidelic and bi-lingual inscriptions of Group I, there are ten from northern Britain between the walls of Hadrian and Antonine. Five of these form two close groups at Whithorn and Kirkmadrine, while the remainder are scattered singly. There are two in the Isle of Man, but none from the opposite coastlands between Hadrian's Wall and Flintshire. Wales has the overwhelming bulk, some 140 concentrated in Gwynedd, Dyfed and Brycheiniog, but not entirely lacking from the south-eastern coastlands. Dumnonia has about forty, of which more than two dozen are in Cornwall, while the Devon total has recently been increased by the discovery of four on Lundy. Two curious features of Dumnonia are the virtual absence of stones from Somerset, despite the closeness of the south-Welsh coastal group; and an unexplained cluster preserved at Wareham in Dorset, which is the easternmost find-spot in southern Britain. It might be thought that the Wareham stones are relics of an original eastward distribution embracing at least Dorset, western Wiltshire, Somerset, parts of Gloucestershire and Monmouthshire, and that over all this area stones had been broken up to use for field walls, farm tracks and so on. But the occurrence of stones in the agricultural lowlands of Glamorgan is a sufficient refutation of this view.

The distribution as we have it probably reflects the original spread of the stones fairly faithfully. But to say this leaves unexplained the absence of stones from areas which were certainly in British hands in the fifth and much of the sixth century. If the practice of setting up such memorials were simply a legacy from Romano-British Christianity the virtual absence of stones east of a line from Chester to Exeter would be incomprehensible. A handful of early examples has led us to postulate a Roman element in the ancestry of the Group I stones, but their overwhelming distribution pattern is away from the lowland heart of Roman Britain, and lies instead in the Irish Sea zone. This pattern reveals new influences, and some of the formulae of the inscriptions make it clear that these came from Gaul and the Mediterranean. In broad archaeological terms – but only in broad terms – they demonstrate the same contacts and the same routes as the imported pottery, especially that of Classes A, B and D. And historically speaking, the distribution of Group I stones reflects the travels of the Celtic saints, both around the Irish Sea and beyond it to Gaul and the Mediterranean.

The siting of the stones in detail has less interest than their overall distribution. The reason for this is that some stones are known to have been moved from their original location, perhaps in the first instance to serve as a gate-post or even a footbridge. Later when their Christian significance and historical importance came to be recognized they might be moved into a churchyard, or even within the church itself, for protection. But it can be said that stones were scarcely ever erected near the secular settlements of the period. Some, as we shall see (below, pp. 248–9), formed part of a cemetery which might in time acquire a church, and in this way some of those which now stand in churchyards may be on their original site having served as a focus for religious activity.

Equally certainly some were erected in the open countryside, even in elevated positions on the moors of Dumnonia and Morgannwg which served as summer pastures for neighbouring communities. A few in Wales lie close to Roman roads, and this may be a continuance of the Roman practice of burial alongside the roads leading out of a town. It also suggests that the roads themselves were still known and in use, even if the weight of traffic had diminished. The example of Maen Madoc is instructive here.[38] The stone, which reads DERVACI FILIUS IVSTI IC IACIT, '[stone] of Dervacus. Son of Justus, here he lies', stands near the southern border of Brycheiniog, by the road from the auxiliary fort at Coelbren to that at Brecon [Pl. 31]. The pit in which the stone was erected was dug through the metalling near the verge of the road. This may have been done inadvertently because the metalling was already partly overgrown, or deliberately in order to give a secure bedding for the stone. Some ten feet from the monument, a pit about eight feet square and two feet deep had probably contained the body of Dervacus, laid beneath a setting of pitched stones. But the pit had been much disturbed, and this, together with the acid soil, had destroyed all trace of human remains. This is the greater pity because the grave of Dervacus is one of the very few which have ever been investigated.

The relatively few Group I stones which bear more than the filiation + HIC IACIT formula are a precious addition to the contemporary verbal evidence for our period. Occasionally they refer to kings or other secular ranks, and such inscriptions will provide clues when, in Chapter 11, we attempt an analysis of British society. For the moment our interest lies with those examples which tell us about religious organization. Several stones mention *sacerdotes*, a term which in this context is usually translated 'bishops'. At Kirkmadrine a roughly rectangular slab bears a monogrammatic cross in a circle, surmounted by an *alpha* and *omega* [Pl. 26*b*]. The main body of the slab is a memorial to the 'holy and eminent bishops Ides, Viventius and Mavorius', and it demonstrates the existence of an episcopal organization in south-west Scotland in the fifth century.[39] From Aberdaron in Caernarvonshire comes the memorial of 'Senacus, priest. Here he lies with a host of the brethren', CUM MULTITUDINEM FRATRUM [Pl. 26*a*]. This is a contemporary witness to a monastic community at the remote tip of Gwynedd.[40]

The memorial of Senacus now lies in a garden shed at a mansion near the site of its discovery, but if the spot at which it was first erected could be located exactly, traces of the monks' cemetery and monastic buildings would doubtless be discovered. Apart from the isolated burials like that of Dervacus son of Justus, evidence for cemeteries with associated memorial-stones or other structures is steadily accumulating as a result of planned fieldwork and excavation. A simple example has long been known at Kirkliston in Midlothian, where a cemetery enclosed by an oval bank contained also a low mound with the memorial of Vetta son of Victus. The burials themselves were protected by stone slabs in what are known as 'long-cist graves'. Not all of these followed a Christian orientation, and it is almost certain that the ancestry of such enclosed cemeteries goes back to pagan practices in late-Roman Britain. Sometimes the focal point of a cemetery might be a special burial, as at Kirkliston, or at Cannington in Somerset where a cemetery containing perhaps a thousand burials had two foci:

the grave of a young person covered by a stone cairn, and another grave near the centre of a circular rockcut trench.[41]

Elsewhere, however, a built shrine or reliquary may have formed the central feature of a cemetery. This seems to have been so on the small tidal island of Ardwall, Kirkcudbrightshire.[42] There the shrine had been largely obliterated by subsequent structures, which were of great interest in themselves. The shrine was superseded by a minute rectangular building of timber, 11 ft by 7½ ft, of which three corner posts were recovered. A number of burials were laid out parallel to the timber building, which was probably an oratory or chapel. This in turn was superseded, perhaps in the eighth century, by a dry-stone chapel on a slightly different axis, again with parallel burials. The Ardwall sequence could only be recovered because the eighth-century chapel was never overlaid by a major ecclesiastical structure, but there is reason to think that it is typical. We shall see parallel developments represented in Ireland at Church Island, Valencia (below, p. 264). In Britain, however, hints must suffice. At Whithorn, the *Te Dominum* stone was found among a cemetery of long-cist graves which cluster around a small oratory of stones bedded in clay. Since the walls of the oratory were covered with white plaster, this was probably the *Candida Casa*, 'White House', traditionally assigned to St Ninian. At Clynnog Fawr in Caernarvonshire the chapel or oratory of the seventh-century St Beuno measured only 18 ft by 9 ft 9 in., had walls of rough boulders set in clay, and burials set close against the walls.

These however are minor sites, and when we seek the remains of a major religious monument in Celtic Britain we find only the monastery of Tintagel.[43] This, of course, has been a major setting for Arthurian romance since the days of Geoffrey of Monmouth, but there is no basis for a secular Arthurian connection, or for attempts to recognize pre-Norman, and therefore potentially Arthurian, fortifications of mortared masonry. So far as the late fifth/sixth centuries are concerned, the remains are unequivocally those of a Celtic monastery [Pl. 10]. The date is given by the occurrence in quantity of imported pottery of Classes A, B and D, while the absence of Class E may suggest that the monastery was abandoned in the latter part of the sixth century. The chapel of the castle, which was erected in the twelfth century, was

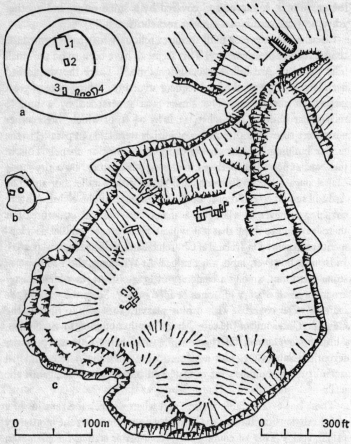

23. Celtic monasteries: *a* Nendrum, Co. Down – (1) enclosed graveyard,
(2) church, (3) school, (4) monks' cells; *b* Church Island, Valencia, Co.
Kerry; *c* Tintagel, Cornwall – (1) monastic *vallum*, cutting off the approach
along a narrow ridge of land. Later structures have been removed from all
plans.

dedicated to St Ulitte, identified with St Juliot, who probably flourished around 500, but the most that can be said for this tenuous
historical evidence is that it is compatible with the archaeological
dating.

Tintagel occupies a dramatic headland on the north Cornish coast,
and it is possible that the location was originally chosen as a deserted
spot suitable for a hermitage. The nucleus of the main group of
buildings on the headland may even have been the cell of Juliot, but it
is certain that Tintagel ceased to be a hermitage 'in the desert' and
became a monastery with some degree of architectural sophistication.
The headland was cut off by a *vallum monasterii* in the form of a broad
ditch and a bank 8 ft high and 30 ft across. On the fairly level summit
of the headland were several groups of buildings, for which functions
can be suggested from our knowledge of the life and practices of a
monastery. They should include a guest-house, a treasury and a
sacristy, as well as cells for the monks. A tomb-shrine, perhaps
containing relics of St Juliot, stood beside walling which has been
identified as that of an oratory. A corn-drying kiln in another building
hints at the economic activities of the community. Where the headland
drops away to sea-cliffs, terraces have been quarried into the slopes,
and here stand some of the cells, as well as other buildings identified as
a library, *scriptorium*, refectory, and sweat-house. This represents a
degree of elaboration without parallel in these islands. One other
architectural feature must be stressed: without exception the buildings
at Tintagel are rectangular, not circular as they normally are in Irish
monasteries.

Compared with Tintagel, other British monasteries are regrettably
uninformative. One problem is to find sites where a traditional early
date is confirmed by the discovery of imported pottery. Glastonbury
Abbey [Pl. 11], for instance, has a legendary connection with St
Patrick in his later years, and certainly his cult was observed there.[44]
We have also seen the possibility that Glastonbury was the scene of
Arthur's burial (above, p. 80). Extensive excavations have revealed a
monastic *vallum* as massive as that at Tintagel, and there are traces of
timber buildings which may be early, but not a single sherd of imported pottery has been found to support a date in the fifth and sixth
centuries. On the other hand, the summit of the remarkable pyramidal

hill of Glastonbury Tor has produced some quantity of amphora sherds, associated with metalworkers' hearths and undecipherable traces of timber buildings.[45] It is a matter of dispute whether we are dealing here with a chieftain's eyrie or with a small monastic settlement in a wild deserted spot. In my view, the shape of the hill is inconvenient for a stronghold, and the absence of defences tells conclusively against the interpretation as a chieftain's citadel. On the other hand, the occurrence in quantity of the bones of food animals has been held to be incompatible with the ascetic practices of a Celtic monastery. The debate has not yet been settled, and Glastonbury Tor must remain, like Congresbury (above, p. 219), a site yielding imported pottery, which may be either secular or religious.*

*These ambiguities are not resolved in the definitive account of the excavations, which appeared after this section was in print: Rahtz, P., 'Excavations on Glastonbury Tor, Somerset, 1964–6', *Arch. J.* 127, 1970, pp. 1–81.

Nine

The Enemies of
the Britons
1: Picts and Scots

Now that we have examined the history and archaeology of Roman
and early post-Roman Britain as one element of the Arthurian situation,
we may turn to survey the enemies of the Britons, since they formed the
other element. We have to deal here with a wide range of nations or
peoples, in two major groups: to the west and north the Celtic barbarians of Ireland and of Britain beyond the Forth–Clyde line; and to
the east, Germanic peoples from the Rhine to the Baltic. Essentially
we are concerned with these peoples only in so far as their attacks on
Britain and their settlements in the island helped to create the Arthurian
situation. We can therefore deal with them in a relatively summary
fashion. In particular, we cannot enter into matters of deep controversy. We must ignore disputes altogether and treat certain hypotheses
and interpretations as though they were the only ones in the field.

The Scotti in Ireland[1]

So far as the inhabitants of Britain were concerned both in the late
Roman period and in subsequent centuries, the people who lived
across the Irish Sea were known as the *Scotti*, and this is the term which
we shall use when we want to talk about them collectively rather than
by kingdoms, tribes, or cultural areas. It is a term which blurs local
differences, but this fault may be forgiven because of its aptness in
other ways. Latinized though it is in the form in which our documents
have it, *Scotti* is very probably related to an Irish verb meaning 'to
raid' or 'to plunder'. And this, no doubt, is how the Irish appeared
to the Britons. The well-known and doubtless historical story of the
kidnapping of the future St Patrick by Irish raiders is a case in point.

It is usually considered that archaeological evidence for Scottic
raids is provided by Roman counter-measures in the form of forts at

Lancaster, Cardiff and possibly elsewhere (above, p. 93). A more negative reaction was the burying of hoards of coins, in the late third century and through much of the fourth, in areas which seem particularly exposed to raiding such as the coastal lowlands of Wales. The idea here is that these hoards were deposited for safety when danger, in the form of Irish raiders, threatened, and were never recovered because death, kidnapping or other misfortune had befallen their rightful owners. In Ireland itself the profits of raiding have been seen in deposits of Roman silver, both bullion and chopped-up tableware, especially in spectacular hoards from Balline in Co. Limerick [Pl. 14b] and Coleraine, Co. Derry.[2] It is usually considered that the richly-worked silver vessels in these hoards had been looted from wealthy villas near the exposed western coasts of Britain, perhaps in Somerset or the Cotswolds, in the late fourth or early fifth century. They had then been chopped up in order that the members of a raiding party might share the loot. But another explanation is possible. The deposition of hoards of this kind is a widespread occurrence among the barbarians on the fringes of the Roman empire. Within these islands an exceptionally rich one was found in the hill-fort of Traprain Law, a metropolis of the Votadini, a tribe which was almost certainly a client kingdom of the Romans. It is unthinkable that the Traprain treasure is loot, and it is most reasonably interpreted as a payment in bullion either to secure friendly relations, or to pay for the services of Votadinian mercenaries. In the same way the Balline and Coleraine hoards may be either diplomatic gifts – bribes – to keep off Irish raiders, or payments to tribal chiefs for the services of their warriors in *numeri* of the Roman army in Britain. That either of these explanations is more likely than the loot hypothesis is confirmed by the presence at both Balline and Coleraine of officially-stamped silver ingots of a kind which were given to Roman troops on the accession of an emperor.[3] These must mark the hoards as officially sanctioned payments.

Important as the hoards are in revealing one facet of the relations between Roman Britain and the *Scotti*, they are of no relevance to the dating of Irish sites. Here the failure of the Romans to invade and occupy Ireland, and the absolute dearth of readily datable coins and pottery which resulted from that failure, have created a very serious problem for the archaeologist. There is good reason to think that a

1a Burgh Castle, Suffolk: Saxon Shore fort beside the Waveney estuary and site of Fursey's monastery in the 630s.

1b Pevensey, Sussex: curtain wall and towers of the Saxon Shore fort of *Anderida*, with the medieval castle top centre.

2 Castle Rock, Edinburgh: site of *Din Eidyn* and base for the warriors of
Y Gododdin. Arthur's Seat in the background.

3 Castle Rock, Dumbarton: *Alcluith*, Fort of the Britons, chief centre of Strathclyde, with the hills of Pictland in the background.

4a Castell Degannwy, Caernarvonshire: the twin hills of Maelgwn Gwynedd's stronghold.

4b Dunadd, Argyll: the rocky citadel of the kingdom of Dalriada, rising above the Crinan isthmus.

5 Cadbury-Camelot, Somerset: air view of the excavations in 1970.

6a Cadbury-Camelot: the Arthurian-period roadway through the south-west gate, showing slots where the timber beams of the gate had decayed. Ethelredan wall top right.

6b Site of the Arthurian-period hall, with white markers standing in the original post-holes.

7 Cahercommaun, Co. Clare: stone-walled ring-fort with outer enclosures, set on the edge of a ravine.

8a Lismore Fort, Smarmore, Co. Louth: a simple earthen rath.

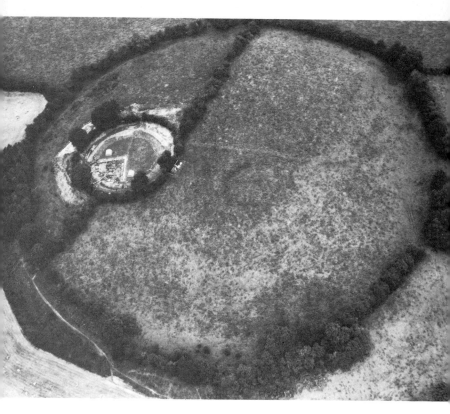

8b Emain Macha or Navan Fort, Co. Armagh: excavations at the seat of the kings of Ulster.

9 Tara, Co. Meath: two double raths enclosed by an earthen bank; Rath of the Synods in the middle distance, and other raths in the background.

10 Tintagel, Cornwall: the medieval castle and Celtic monastery. For a plan of the monastery see Fig. 23.

11 Glastonbury, Somerset: ruins of the monastery bottom right, with Glastonbury Tor in the background.

12a Illauntannig Island, Co. Kerry: monastic cashel with rectangular oratory and circular monks' cells.

12b Carlungie, Angus: Proto-Pictish souterrain with roof missing.

13 East Wansdyke, Wiltshire, looking east between Easton Down and Tan Hill.

14a Broighter, Co. Derry: gold model of boat with sail and oars. Length 7·2 in.

14b Balline, Co. Limerick: part of a silver treasure, including both fragments of Roman table ware and officially stamped ingots. Length of the smaller ingot 4·2 in.

15a Baginton, Warwickshire: bronze hanging bowl with enamelled scroll and openwork ornament of Roman inspiration. Diameter 12·7 in.

15b Loveden Hill, Lincolnshire: bronze hanging bowl with developed Celtic scrolls, one of which is shown in detail. Diameter 9·5 in.

16a Ireland: bronze 'latchet' with Ultimate La Tène ornament, originally picked out in red enamel. Overall length 5 in.

16b Lagore, Co. Meath: bone 'sketch-pad' with Hiberno-Saxon animal and interlace patterns. Length illustrated 6·5 in.

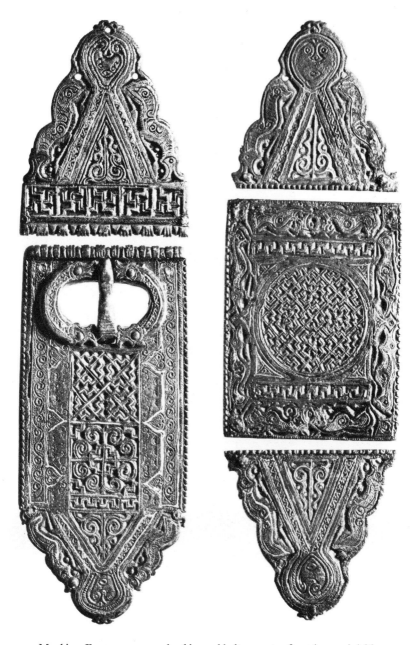

17 Mucking, Essex, grave 117: buckle- and belt-mounts of cast bronze inlaid with silver. A developed English example of Provincial Roman military gear with border animals, scrolls and fret patterns. Overall length 6·3 in.

a

18a Mucking, grave 90: gilt-bronze equal-armed brooch, comparable with brooches from the Elbe-Weser region. Width 2·3 in.

b   *c*

18b, c Gilt-bronze button brooches from the same grave. Diameter of larger brooch 0·7 in.

a   *b*

19a Oxfordshire: bronze saucer brooch with chip-carved running spirals, of continental Saxon type. Diameter 1·7 in.

19b Faversham, Kent: gilt-bronze saucer brooch of English type with Style I animals. Diameter 1·7 in.

d

19c Kempston, Bedfordshire: bronze small-long brooch. Length 2·5 in.

19d Cadbury-Camelot: silver brooch or buckle decorated with chip-carved animal legs in Style I, from the south-west gate (see pp. 221–2). Diameter 1·0 in.

c

20 Sleaford, Lincolnshire: group of bronzes from a woman's grave, comprising a cruciform brooch, pair of annular brooches, pair of wrist-clasps, and shoe-lace tag. Length of cruciform brooch 3·1 in.

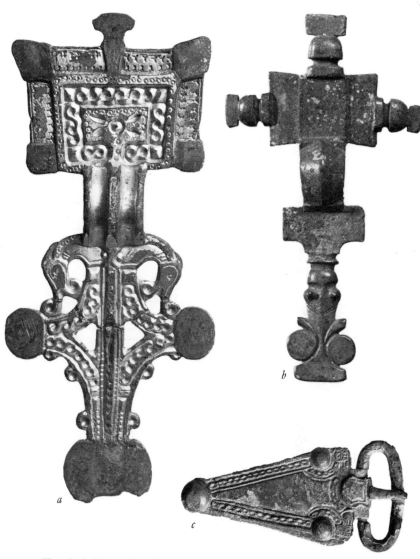

21a Kenninghall, Norfolk: gilt-bronze great square-headed brooch. Length 5·9 in.

21b Sleaford: bronze cruciform brooch with zoomorphic foot. Length 4·4 in.

21c Faversham: bronze buckle. Length 2·8 in.

22a Breach Down, Kent: silver-gilt disk brooch with central garnet and keystone garnets divided by chip-carved couchant animals in Style I.

22b Faversham: silver-gilt disk brooch set with garnets and white paste inlay.

22c Faversham: silver-gilt composite brooch, with garnets and lapis lazuli set in wire cells backed with gold reflectors, interspersed with gold filigree. Diameter 1·6 in.

23 Sutton Hoo, Suffolk: great gold buckle, ornamented with snakes, birds' heads and quadrupeds in Style II. Length 5·3 in., weight 14·5 oz.

24a Sutton Hoo: one of a pair of shoulder clasps for military dress, ornamented, in cloisonné garnets and millefiori glass, with interlaced boars and
other Style II animals, and geometric 'carpet' patterns. Length 4·9 in.

24b Reconstruction of the lid of a military pouch ornamented in cloisonné
garnets and millefiori. Length 7·4 in.

a

b

25a Llanerfyl, Montgomeryshire: *Rustica* stone (see p. 240). Height 4 ft.

25b Whithorn, Wigtownshire: *Te dominum* stone (see p. 242). Height 4 ft.

a

b

26a Aberdaron, Caernarvonshire: *Senacus* stone (see p. 248). Height 3 ft.

26b Kirkmadrine, Wigtownshire: *sacerdotes* stone (see p. 248). Height 6 ft 7 in.

27a Castell Dwyran, Carmarthenshire: *Vortipor* stone, with inscription in Latin and Ogham, and incised ring-cross (see p. 243). Height 6 ft 11 in.

27b Llangadwaladr, Anglesey: *Cadfan* stone, with inscription in Roman capitals and half-uncials, and true cross (see p. 244). Height 4 ft.

28 Penmachno, Caernarvonshire: *magistratus* stone (see pp. 242, 321). Height 2 ft 11 in.

a   *b*   *c*

29a, b Eglwys Gymyn, Carmarthenshire: inscription in Latin and Ogham to Avitoria (see p. 241). Height 3 ft 4 in.

29c Penmachno: fragmentary stone with consular date (see p. 243). Height 3 ft 4 in.

30a Penmachno: stone with monogrammatic cross (see p. 245). Height 2 ft 5 in.

30b Llanfyrnach, Pembrokeshire: stone with processional cross and illegible Ogham inscription. Height 4 ft 6 in.

31 Ystradfellte,
Brecknockshire: Maen
Madoc, standing beside the
Roman road from Coelbren
to Brecon Gaer (see p. 247).
Height 11 ft.

32a Dunnichen, Angus: Pictish symbol stone.

32b Ballyvourney, Co. Cork: stone with incised cross and figure of bishop.

major class of site, the ring-fort, was invented in the third millennium BC, became prolific in the first Christian millennium and continued spasmodically into the seventeenth century. But in default of Roman objects in stratified contexts, it is sometimes impossible to date such sites within a millennium. Until lately, this has had the further effect that there has been no control over the dating of the fine metalwork which, as we shall see (below, pp. 260–2), occurs in abundance. Consequently, estimates or guesses for the age of particular pieces, or even of whole phases of development, have differed from scholar to scholar by a matter of several centuries. Recently, however, the recognition of imported pottery of the same types as that found in western Britain – Classes A, B, and E – has brought rather more precision into the chronology of the fifth and subsequent centuries. For the preceding centuries, the discovery of stratified Roman coins at the hill-fort on Freestone Hill, Co. Kilkenny, and at the so-called Rath of the Synods, Tara, will have ever-widening repercussions.

By far the largest class of site in the first millennium AD is that of the circular enclosures, known usually as *raths* when they are surrounded by an earthen bank with external ditch [Pl. 8], and as *cashels* or *cahers* when the enclosure is a dry-built stone wall [Pl. 7] usually without a ditch.[4] It is estimated that there may be thirty to forty thousand of these 'ring-forts' scattered more or less throughout the island, but this figure must be set against the long period of time during which they were being built and occupied. In size they vary from raths as little as 60 ft in internal diameter to the great triple-banked forts, 150 ft internally and perhaps 400 ft overall. A well preserved cashel may have walls 15 ft high with flights of steps leading up to the wall-walk and chambers built in the thickness of the walls. The simple appearance of an earthwork rath may conceal dry-stone revetments and timber palisades. Very occasionally dry-stone buildings are still visible, and traces of small timber buildings have been recovered by excavation. The great majority of ring-forts must be thought of as defended homesteads, but the largest ones must have fulfilled a communal purpose, perhaps as tribal capitals.*

*To the references given in n. 4, add now: Proudfoot, V. B., 'Irish Raths and Cashels: Some Notes on Chronology, Origins and Survivals', *Ulster Journ. Archaeol.* 33, 1970, pp. 37–48.

As an example of a large rath which has been relatively fully excavated we may cite Garranes in Co. Cork.[5] In common with many such forts it is situated not in a commanding or naturally defensible position but on gently sloping ground. The interior, about 200 ft across, is surrounded by three close-set banks and ditches which do not appear very formidable today, but in their pristine state, with near-vertical walls rising out of the rock-cut ditches, they would have formed quite a strong obstacle. The entrance was protected by a series of three or four timber gates. No building plans could be detected in the interior, which was chiefly remarkable for the evidence that it yielded of metalworking including some thousands of fragments of crucibles. This, together with a dearth of domestic equipment such as weaving apparatus, led to the suggestion that there had been no regular domestic occupation. Instead, it appeared that Garranes had been a tribal centre, used as a place of refuge in moments of peril, and otherwise merely as a shelter for a group of artisans. But a wider knowledge of these sites and of the debris which they produce suggests that the scarcity of weaving equipment and other domestic apparatus is not in itself an argument for the absence of regular occupation. The metalworkers would most probably be under the patronage of a tribal king. Both the size and strength of the defences, and the presence of metalworkers, suggest that Garranes was a tribal capital. The occurrence of imports of Classes A, B and E serves to date it from the late fifth into the seventh century.

Compared with the great numbers of ring-forts in Ireland, true hillforts are rather rare, and perhaps for this reason have only recently begun to attract serious archaeological attention. The only closely dated example is that on Freestone Hill, a fairly steep-sided hill rising to a gently rounded plateau at 464 ft above sea level.[6] Here an area of about five acres was enclosed by a single stone wall and ditch, apparently in the fourth century AD, to judge from a coin dated AD 337–40. Freestone Hill belongs to a group of about a score of single-ramparted hilltop forts, ranging from one to thirty-seven acres in size, which occur principally in eastern Ireland. These include the royal capitals at Downpatrick, Dun Aillinne, Tara [Pl. 9] and Emain Macha, though it should be added that certainly at Emain Macha [Pl. 8b] and Tara the large single-banked fort encloses one or more smaller earthworks belonging to the rath class. None of these forts compares in the strength of its defences or the complexity of its entrance arrangements with the general run of British hill-forts, and the date of Freestone Hill makes it very difficult to place them in relation to either the British or the continental sequence of fort-building. More obviously related to west European and British examples are the promontory forts or cliff castles which occur, often in spectacular situations, around the coasts of Ireland. Again, very little research has been carried out in cliff castles. Some of them are known to have served as strongholds in recent centuries, but Larrybane at least was occupied during the currency of 'souterrain' pottery (below, p. 258) in the first millennium AD.[7]

Another class of site occupied then was the crannog or artificial island. The earliest Irish examples go back to the Late Bronze Age, perhaps the seventh or sixth century BC, but the early crannogs seem to have come to an abrupt end as a result of flooding, which was probably caused by a widespread climatic deterioration.[8] Thereafter it is difficult to find evidence for the building and occupation of crannogs until the middle of the first millennium AD, when they become quite common. Inevitably their location is determined by the distribution of suitable lakes, so they are commonest west and north-west of the central plain. They are really defended homesteads, the equivalent of raths in a marshy or watery terrain, but at least one of them, at Lagore in Co. Meath, is known to have held a royal homestead.[9] The finds from Lagore are correspondingly richer than those from other crannogs, especially in evidence for metalworking. Lagore, Ballinderry No. 2 and Lough Faughan[10] all produce rare sherds of Class E pottery, suggesting occupation in the sixth/seventh centuries, but several crannogs are known to continue into the Viking period or later. None has produced evidence as good as that from Buston (above, p. 228) for the kind of house that was raised on the island.

One other major class of monument was certainly built and used in our period, namely the souterrain. These are artificial caves or underground chambers. Frequently they occur in ring-forts, having an entrance either inside or outside one of the principal dwellings, and sometimes also having an exit outside the defences. In this last very rare case, a souterrain might have served as an escape route from a fort which was under attack. But the suggestion that they were normally used as a place of refuge, especially for non-combatants, is scarcely sensible. The roofing slabs and the entrance would frequently have been visible, and it would have been an easy matter to smoke or burn out anyone sheltering in the souterrain. On the other hand, Irish souterrains so frequently have internal twists, constrictions or other obstacles that it is unlikely that they were merely cellars. The truth is that no convincing explanation has been put forward. We shall encounter the problem of souterrains again in Pictland (below, pp. 274–5) but it can be said at once that the Pictish or proto-Pictish souterrains are very different structurally from the Irish ones.

With the exception of the ring-forts of the western peninsulas most Irish sites are relatively prolific in finds, even if these are unspectacular. Imported pottery, especially of Class E, occurs widely, but only in very small quantities. Until recently it had seemed that the only native pottery, the so-called 'souterrain' ware, was confined to the north-east. The implication of this would be that wooden and leather vessels were normally used in place of pottery, but the evidence from crannogs, where organic materials are well preserved, does not lend much support to this. A new type of pottery, classifiable as 'Freestone Hill ware' has recently been recognized on hill-forts in counties Kilkenny, Tyrone, Armagh and Down. Characteristically this consists of coarse, hand-modelled bucket-shaped vessels with simple rim forms. The only ornament, if it can be called such, is a row of perforations beneath the rim. In Britain such pottery might date to the Bronze Age, and in Ireland too its ancestry may go well back in the first millennium BC, but at Freestone Hill it is considered as firmly dated to the fourth century AD. As for the 'souterrain' ware of the north-east [Fig. 11a, b, c], that consisted of deep, straight-sided bowls, decorated if at all with a band of applied 'pie-crust' a little below the rim, and perhaps with finger-tip ornament on the rim itself.[11] The bases, and less frequently the lower walls, are pitted by impressions of chopped grass, picked up while the clay was wet and then burned out in the firing. We have already met this 'grass-marking' in Cornwall (above, p. 200), and have noticed the suggestion that it was introduced there from Ulster about AD 500. At this point it is appropriate to notice that 'souterrain' ware is most abundant on sites of the tenth and later centuries, even into the thirteenth. Its occasional occurrence alongside rare Class E imports may permit the inference that it was developed in earlier centuries, but there is at present no Irish evidence to take it back to a date before 500, as the hypothesis of a movement from Ulster to Cornwall would demand.[12]

Apart from pottery, which is rare, crannogs, hill-forts and ring-forts all commonly yield artefacts of bone and stone. In view of the enormous quantities of animal bones from food refuse – 14,600 pounds weight at Ballinderry No. 2 and about 50,000 pounds at Lagore – the actual quantity of utilized bone is small, but in terms of function the range is wide. Objects of utility include knife-handles of bone and antler, and spindle-whorls which may bear simple ornament. Plain or ornamental pins, and double-edged bone combs [Fig. 31e], are both very common. The lighter aspects of life are represented by bone dice and by simple pegs which may have been intended for a board game. Stone objects include rare millstones, and large numbers of pebbles with smoothed or even polished surfaces. Some of these were whetstones, but the most highly polished examples had been used either in the preparation of leather or as linen smoothers. Flints sometimes occur in such numbers that they cannot be regarded merely as survivals from an earlier age, but must reflect the contemporary use of flint for scrapers and especially for strike-a-lights. Finally, where organic materials have been well preserved by the water-logging of crannogs the great range of wooden objects is fully revealed: lathe-turned and stave-built vessels, boxes, scoops, pins, pegs and spindles, mallets, paddles and canoes. Surprisingly, however, the only identifiable leather objects are fragments of shoes.

Metal artefacts, both utilitarian pieces in iron and ornamental objects in bronze, are relatively common on Irish sites. Even though they do not match the lists given in the Welsh Laws (above, pp. 229–31), they nevertheless give us a fair idea of the equipment of a household among the *Scotti*. Weapons are rare, except for simple forms of iron spearhead [Figs. 28 and 29]. For swords, shield-bosses and horse-bits for the mounted warrior we have to turn to royal residences like that on Lagore crannog. By far the most prolific iron objects are the knives, which like their British (p. 233) and Saxon (p. 305) counterparts normally have a thick straight back and a strong tang [Fig. 31c]. Personal items include buckles and especially pins, which are often simple copies of bronze pins with ornamental heads or with loosely swivelling rings. For the household there are barrel pad-locks and the keys for them; ladles and pans; and iron handles and other fittings for wooden buckets. Iron strike-a-lights would be used with the flints which we have already noticed. For the farmer there were bill-hooks, sickles and shears. Plough-parts, including share tips and coulters, occur on sites datable broadly to the second half of the first millennium [Fig. 21*a*, *b*]. Awls may have been used either by the carpenter or the leather-worker, and there are also saws, chisels and other carpenter's tools. A rare object is a small portable anvil, probably for fine metalworking, from Garryduff I.[13]

Fine objects, occasionally in gold and commonly in bronze, are also found on sites, and the repertory can be augmented with pieces, especially ornamented brooches, which have been found casually, for instance in the course of turf-digging. The range runs from quite simple pins, through pins with swivelling rings and the related penan-nular pins and brooches, to very elaborate brooches and other orna-ments with enamelled decoration, and finally to masterpieces like the Tara brooch with both cast and applied filigree decoration and inset jewels [Fig. 22]. There is good site evidence that elaborate jewelry was being manufactured at royal residences like Lagore, tribal centres like Garranes, and even quite small strongholds such as Garryduff in Co. Cork. Crucibles used in the casting of metal are found with bronze and even gold dross or waste still adhering to them. Sticks of chequered millefiori glass occur, and also sherds of probably Teutonic glass which provided the raw material both for glass and enamel inlays and also for manufacturing beads and bangles. Rarely, glass studs or roundels were lost before they could be fixed to a brooch or other setting. Finally, pieces of bone or stone were used as sketch-pads for the more elaborate designs before these were given effect in metal [Pl. 16*b*]. All this is relevant, of course, to the problem of the place of manufacture of the enamelled hanging bowls found in Anglo-Saxon graves. But we have already seen that comparable technological skills were at the disposal of the Britons (above, p. 235), whereas Ireland has produced only one object which really matches the hanging bowls.[14]

Within the repertory which we have just summarized there is a process of development, but the chronology of this is much disputed.

The idea of champlevé enamelled ornament, in which the design is formed by red or other coloured enamels filling grooves cast in the surface of a bronze object, goes back to the La Tène phase of pre-Roman Celtic art.[15] Some of the motifs, especially spirals, C-scrolls and trumpet-like patterns, are also found both before and after the Roman centuries. The art-style of our period is sometimes classed as 'Ultimate La Tène' in consequence. But it is questionable whether there really is a continuous series of objects and patterns, either in Roman Britain or among the free Celts of Hibernia and Pictland. The question can best be examined in detail in relation to the penannular brooches with zoomorphic terminals and enamelled or inlaid patterns on the animals' heads: how early do they begin? A date as early as the third century has been suggested, but this is impossible. The large series of zoomorphic pins and penannular brooches from Traprain Law includes none with enamelling, and the clear implication is that this begins later than the abandonment of Traprain in the early fifth century.

This does not leave Ireland bereft of brooches in the first four centuries AD. Characteristic of this period is the penannular pin or brooch with simple everted terminals, known as the omega-brooch from the Greek letter Ω [Fig. 22c, d]. This is closely comparable with the early forms of Romano-British penannular, but where they develop animal-headed terminals in the fourth century, the Irish ones grow birds' heads [Fig. 22e]. The dated hill-fort of Freestone Hill adds confirmatory evidence for the state of Irish metalwork in the mid-fourth century, for its inhabitants made use of provincial Roman bracelets, and ornamented a romanized openwork mount with incised patterns in an utterly debased La Tène style. If the Freestone Hill mount is typical, the Celtic artistic revival had certainly not begun by 350.

The probable development of Ultimate La Tène art in Ireland may now be outlined. The zoomorphic penannular brooch which evolved in Britain in the fourth century was carried to Ireland on the garments worn by abducted Britons or in the minds of kidnapped or migrant craftsmen, and ousted the ornithomorphic omega pin. Other provincial Roman enamelwork, ornamented in feeble champlevé with stiff scrolls, trumpets and so on, was similarly transmitted. These motifs were then transformed into the more vigorous, free-flowing designs which appealed to barbaric Celtic tastes and were applied to the enlarged heads of the animals on the brooches. This is the genesis of the Ultimate La Tène style, which is clearly distinguishable from pre-Roman La Tène art both in the details of its motifs and in the objects on which they occur [Pl. 16a]. In the sixth century, contacts with the Mediterranean and with Gaul, forged originally by the church, brought in glass for inlays, especially millefiori, by the same trade routes as the imported pottery. In the seventh century new elements were introduced as a result of contact with Teutonic metalwork in Merovingian Gaul and Anglo-Saxon England. Again, craftsmen accompanying missionaries were probably responsible. They brought in new styles of animal ornament, interlace of various types, and the techniques of filigree, cast 'chip-carving', and glass inlays modelled on the patterns of cloisonné garnet-work. The climax of this development, the Hiberno-Saxon style of the Tara brooch or the Ardagh chalice, is an achievement of the late seventh century, and lies therefore outside our survey.

As for religious monuments, the commonest are the memorial stones inscribed in the Ogham script. These occur, in the form of slabs, pillars and boulders, throughout the island, but they are commonest in the southern and south-western counties of Waterford, Cork, and above all Kerry [Map 7]. Unlike their counterparts among the Group I Early Christian monuments of Britain, the Irish Ogham stones do not have bilingual inscriptions, and Latin inscriptions are almost wholly absent in our period. In compensation, the Goidelic inscriptions of Ireland have a far richer variety of formulae than those of Britain. From the simplest, which bear merely the name of the person commemorated, they range through those which add the name of father, grandfather or uncle, to those which record family descent from a remote tribal ancestor who may even have been a pagan god. This leads us to the points that the whole series certainly begins with pagan memorials, and that specifically Christian formulae are almost unknown. Sometimes, as in Britain, the original memorial was subsequently christianized. A particularly interesting example of this is the stone at Arraglen in Co. Kerry, on which Ronann the priest, son of Comogann, left his name together with a monogrammatic cross and a cross in a circle. Before doing so he flaked one face off the stone to a depth of six inches, presumably removing an original inscription in the process.[16]

In addition to crosses in secondary positions on Ogham stones we also find, from an early date, slabs with incised crosses somewhat comparable with those of the British Group II. These are normally true crosses, rather than monogrammatic crosses. The stem sometimes rises from a C-scroll or other ornament, but the motifs are not sufficiently specific for us to use them for dating. There is, however, a slab from Ballyvourney, Co. Cork, inscribed with a compass drawn cross, which must belong to the early seventh century [Pl. 32b]. For in addition to the cross it has a delightful sketch of a bishop, clad in a chasuble, holding a crozier, and clearly tonsured from ear to ear in the Celtic manner which, in southern Ireland, would have been abandoned along with the Celtic calculation for Easter in AD 633. Late in the seventh century, to judge from the interlace and other Hiberno-Saxon ornament which they bear, free-standing high crosses appear in several regions of Ireland, especially where, as in the Slievenamon mountains, the local rock lent itself to carving. The high crosses, and the simple cross-incised slabs before them, probably served as praying-stations and centres of worship for a countryside where churches were still extremely rare.[17]

Indeed no remains of churches reliably dated to our period are known from Ireland.[18] Nevertheless it seems likely that the minute dry-stone, corbelled-roof oratory of Gallarus in the Dingle Peninsula, Co. Kerry, gives a fair idea of an oratory of the seventh century in the stone-building areas of the west. Elsewhere the verbal evidence suggests that churches would be built of wood, or even turf, with a thatched roof. Early monasteries are also well known in Ireland, especially in remote [Pl. 12a] and often spectacular locations, but again, none of these may convincingly be dated as early as the sixth or seventh centuries. Two monasteries have, however, yielded sherds of Class E imported pottery. Of these, Nendrum was a triple-ringed cashel [Fig. 23a], and Armagh was a rath, before they were made over to religious use.[19] At Nendrum the existence of a mortared stone church and of a round tower demonstrates that the monastery had a long history, which was not elucidated by excavation. But it seems likely that the monks' cells were in the form of circular dry-stone buildings, probably with beehive roofs, set against the middle cashel wall. The occurrence of crucibles and stone 'sketch-pads' among the objects found there shows the importance of fine metalworking, to make chalices, reliquaries, book-covers and so on, among the activities of a monastery.

Finally, the rocky islet of Church Island, Valencia, Co. Kerry [Fig. 23*b*], provides an interesting parallel to the Ardwall Island sequence.[20] At Church Island an original wooden oratory with oriented skeletons was replaced by a much larger dry-stone building, again with associated burials. But the central feature of the island was domestic: a circular dry-stone house only 15 ft in diameter, which presumably housed at most a hermit and two or three disciples. After refuse from this cell had accumulated, a rectangular building was set up on the very edge of the island. When later still an enclosure wall was built around the cliff, the rectangular building lay outside, suggesting that it was a guest-house rather than a building for the community itself. A slab-lined tomb-shrine and a cross-incised slab also formed part of the layout which is strikingly reminiscent of Bede's description of St Cuthbert's hermitage on Farne Island.

The Nendrum monastery produced several iron *styli* for writing on wax tablets, reminding us that teaching and writing were both functions of a monastery. The task here was primarily a practical one: the copying out, in a culture which had no printed books, of the psalms and gospels which were needed for the service of the church. To these would be added penitentials to ensure the correct rule of the brethren, homilies to encourage them, and other writings of a religious character to instruct and edify. We have already seen how the book-hand used for writing Latin from the fourth century onwards came to be developed into the characteristic insular half-uncial, a clear and beautiful script, in the sixth and seventh centuries. And practical though the purpose was, an element of decoration crept in. Before 600, the initial letters of verses in the *Cathach*, or Psalter, of St Columba were being enlarged to the depth of three ordinary lines, and then ornamented in an Ultimate La Tène style with spirals, trumpets, S- and C-scrolls, and even animal-heads. These are the faint beginnings of manuscript ornamentation in these islands, which reach their climax in the Hiberno-Saxon masterpieces of Durrow, Lindisfarne, Kells and Lichfield.

The Scotti *in Britain*

We have already seen something of the contacts between Britain and the *Scotti*, at both official and personal levels, in the late Roman and early post-Roman periods. But apart from raiding and looting on the one hand and bribing on the other, there is evidence that an important element in these relations was the actual settlement of *Scotti* in Britain, followed by their expansion, absorption, or expulsion. The actual historical evidence is scanty and sometimes dubious, and attempts have therefore been made to supplement it by the witness of personal- and place-names, and of archaeology. Here it seems necessary to give a warning against the tendency to see an Irishman under every bush, or at least beneath every stone. Sites of our period, especially raths and crannogs, are readily recognizable in Ireland, they have been much excavated or at least dug into, and they are frequently prolific in finds. In consequence there is a very large body of Irish material to provide comparisons with the scantier relics found, for instance, in Wales. To the layman, or to the historian unpractised in archaeological thinking, the statement that an iron knife from Llareggub has good parallels at Ballybunnion and Ballyhoo may seem to imply at least trade, possibly even folk-movement, from Ireland to Britain. This is not necessarily so. We may be dealing simply with the common forms of western barbarian culture, or with the movements of a single crafts-man at a time when craftsmen, monks and bards were all peripatetic. At the same time we must admit that the tendency of some scholars to multiply Irish influences in Britain is a useful corrective to those who would see Romano-British influences as ubiquitous in Ireland.

Before we examine the evidence for the settlement of *Scotti* in Britain, and the results of that settlement, we might reasonably ask whether they came as raiders or invaders. A Dalriadic document, which we will have to examine more fully later (below, p. 335), tells us that 'three times fifty men passed over in the fleet with the sons of Erc', that is, in the invasion of Dalriada. It also makes it clear that in Scotland at least the Dalriadans were organized for military purposes into groups of houses, with 'twice seven [rowing] benches to each twenty houses, their sea muster'. Such an organization perhaps lay behind the raiding parties as well. But when we ask about the ships

which carried them we immediately find ourselves beset with ignorance. The only direct archaeological evidence is for dug-out canoes,
which are frequently found on crannogs, but these seem as unlikely
for crossings of the Irish Sea as the paving-slabs which feature as sea-
transport in some of the saints' lives.

There is, however, a carving of a boat on a pillar from Bantry, Co.
Cork, which has been ascribed to the eighth century. The stone is
very weathered, but shows a rowing boat with four pairs of oars plus a
steering oar. The lines are those of a curragh, or skin-covered boat, and
the construction of such a vessel is described in the ninth-century
account of the voyage of St Brendan. Allowing two men to each pair of
oars, the crew of the Bantry boat can scarcely have been more than ten,
so a large fleet would have been needed for a raiding party. An
altogether larger boat is suggested by a gold model of the first centuries
BC/AD from Broighter in Co. Derry, for this had eight pairs of oars in
addition to t he steering oar, and a mast as well [Pl. 14a]. It has been
calculated that this is a representation of a boat about 50 ft long. It
seems likely that this was the kind of vessel with which the sons of
Erc colonized Argyll.[21]

Whatever the means by which the *Scotti* came to Scotland, they left
remarkably little trace of themselves in the archaeological record. They
changed the language from British or Pictish to Irish, but they did so
without introducing any general practice of setting up memorials in
the Goidelic language and the appropriate Ogham script. There are
only two Goidelic/Ogham inscriptions in Scotland, both from Argyll.
This in itself can be explained away by the extreme scarcity of Ogham
stones in Irish Dalriada. On the other hand, that same area is rich in
two groups of distinctive archaeological object – the rath-type of
defended homestead, and the 'souterrain' pottery which may go back
to the fifth century. Stone ring-forts of the same generic class as the
cashels of Ireland are certainly common in Scotland, including the
west coast, but their ancestry goes back to long before the Dalriadic
invasion and must be independent of it.[22] In any case a series of these
Scottish *duns* would be readily distinguishable, as a group, from a series
of raths or cashels.

So far as the 'souterrain' pottery is concerned, none has been discovered in excavations in the relevant part of Scotland. Several expla-

nations are possible for this. It may be that, despite arguments to the contrary (above, p. 201), 'souterrain' pottery had not developed at the time of the invasion. Indeed, since contacts between north-east Ireland and western Scotland were maintained and even strengthened by missionary activity like that of Columba in the later sixth century, we would have to suppose that it was not developed for some centuries, a hypothesis which would agree with its occurrence in Ireland on sites of the tenth and later centuries (above, p. 258). An alternative explanation for its absence in Scotland is that the original migrants consisted simply of a chief's family and war-band, without any women to make pottery for them. Coming to a part of Scotland which had possessed no native pottery in the Roman centuries, they may well have abandoned its manufacture altogether, relying on imported wares for luxury and vessels of wood and horn for everyday use. Certainly Dunadd, the principal stronghold of Dalriada, was well supplied with Class D *mortaria* and with bowls, cooking-pots and pitchers of Class E, but had no locally made pottery.

Dunadd itself is set on a craggy hill [Pl. 4b] dominating the important trade route across the Crinan isthmus at the root of the Kintyre peninsula.[23] The summit is occupied by a sturdy little citadel, about 100 ft long by not more than 45 ft wide, defended as much by crags as by a 12 ft wide dry-stone wall [Fig. 15, 3]. Looping out from this are lesser walls, which use natural terraces to form a series of pendant enclosures, so that the site overall is as much as 400 ft across. Its plan belongs to a recognizable class of 'nuclear' forts, of which the best example, Dalmahoy in Midlothian, cannot possibly be Scottic. A strong case can be made that Dunadd is a British or Pictish construction of uncertain antiquity, which was taken over by the Dalriadans and used from the fifth to the eighth centuries. The method of excavating this key site would have done little credit to a potato-digger, so we are forced to rely on typological comparisons to determine which finds belong to the early Scottic period. Apart from the imported pottery, they include abundant evidence of metalworking in the form of crucibles, moulds, and stone 'sketch-pads', and a great range of ironwork, including spearheads, tools and ornaments. Stone objects include a large number of millstones.

Turning from the north to western and south-western Britain, we find the best evidence for Irish settlement is provided by place-names containing Goidelic elements, which occur to some extent in Galloway as well; by Group I monuments with Goidelic/Ogham inscriptions; and by Latin memorials to persons with Irish names.[24] In Gwynedd not more than two or three Ogham stones are known, and Latin inscriptions written vertically as a result of Ogham influence are also rare. The greatest concentration of Ogham inscriptions and of vertical Latin inscriptions is certainly in Dyfed, where the influence of the ruling dynasty of the Dési was obviously responsible [Pls. 27a, 29a, 30b]. There is another important cluster in the upper Usk valley and along the southern boundaries of the kingdom of Brycheiniog, whose rulers also claimed Irish descent. Irish personal names are even more widespread than Ogham stones, and from as far inland as Wroxeter comes a memorial in partly Latinized Primitive Irish to *Cunorix macus Maquicoline*, 'Hound-king, son of Son-of-the-holly'.[25] But for all this, Goidelic never supplanted British as it did in Dalriadic Scotland.

Other traces of Irish settlement are absent from Wales. It is true that in Dyfed there are numerous small circular embanked sites, often built on gently sloping ground, which are known as 'raths', and which do superficially resemble the raths of Ireland. Some of these yield a few very weathered sherds of Romano-British pottery when they are excavated, and this has been held to suggest that they should be dated to the post-Roman centuries, and attributed to the Dési. Other raths, however, quite certainly have Roman buildings of masonry or timber within them, and that at Walesland in Pembrokeshire is securely dated to the early first century AD or earlier. All this evidence demonstrates that the circular earthworks of Dyfed begin independently of the historically recorded migration of the Dési. It means too that the Dési would have found certain familiar elements in the Demetian landscape when they came across in the late fourth century.[26]

In Dumnonia the principal evidence for Irish settlement is a group of six or more Ogham-inscribed stones, concentrated in east Cornwall and west Devon. Vertical inscriptions and Irish names are, however, more widespread. The distribution of Ogham stones roughly coincides with that of parish dedications to the supposed 'children of Brychan', who was himself traditional founder of the kingdom of Brycheiniog. It is possible in this case that the genealogies preserve some folk-memory of a secondary Irish movement from south Wales to central Dumnonia. Further west there are no Ogham stones, but Irish folk movement has been deduced from the occurrence of grass-marked pottery in the sixth and later centuries (above p. 201).[27] Now that we have seen the evidence for the dating of 'souterrain' pottery in north-east Ireland, and have noted its absence from Argyll (above, pp. 266–7), it is not necessary to emphasize again the tenuousness of the alleged link between Ulster and west Cornwall.

At the very end of the period in which we are interested, Irish connections are firmly attested for other parts of Britain, the result now not of raiding or migration but of the dynamic missionary enterprise of the Irish church. Bede provides us with the most accessible account of the mission of Fursa to East Anglia in the 630s. King Sigeberht gave him the derelict Saxon Shore fort of Burgh Castle for his monastery. If we accept a late rather than an early date for the Sutton Hoo ship-burial, it can very reasonably be suggested that the Celtic hanging bowls found in it were made at Fursa's monastery, and that there too was the source of the millefiori glass used by the Sutton Hoo jeweller (below, p. 300). Northumbria was also penetrated by Irish influences in the generation from the accession of Oswald in 634 to the Synod of Whitby in 664. Oswald himself had been in exile at the monastery of Iona, which had been founded from Ireland by St Columba. When he gained the Northumbrian throne he promptly sent to the Irish for a bishop, receiving the saintly Aidan, who founded a monastery on the tidal island of Lindisfarne. Aidan's successor Finan, who also came from Iona, is said to have built a church at Lindisfarne *more Scottorum*, 'in the Irish manner, not of stones but of hewn oak and thatched with reeds'.

Contacts between the Irish and the English, mediated in this way through the church, must have led to much cultural interchange. In particular they must have been largely responsible for that exchange of artistic techniques and motifs which produced, in the later seventh century, the great flowering of Hiberno-Saxon art especially in the form of manuscript illumination. But the historically documented examples which we have just quoted also serve to remind us of the contacts across the Irish sea between the British and Irish churches. These are revealed, for instance, by the history of St Patrick, and by linguistic borrowings, in an ecclesiastical context, between British-Latin and Primitive Irish.[28] The free movement of men of religion, often deliberately seeking exile among a strange people, would have been paralleled by the movement of craftsmen in the service of the church or of lay patrons. And this in turn can account for distinctive types of metal tool occurring in Glamorgan, at Dunadd, and widely in Ireland, or for the occurrence of closely similar crucibles at Dinas Powys and Garryduff. The detectable cultural connections between Britain and Ireland were due as much to wandering monks and peripatetic crafts-men as to the migration of peoples.[29]

The Picts

When we turn to the second of the enemies of Roman Britain, the northern Celtic barbarians, we find ourselves faced with what has been well called the 'problem of the Picts'.[30] There is no doubt that at the end of the fourth and beginning of the fifth centuries *Picti* was a general term for the inhabitants of the whole area north of the Antonine Wall. But the meaning of the term is in dispute; so is the language which the Picts spoke; and in much of the Pictish area we know virtually nothing about material culture. Geographically speaking the area falls into two well-differentiated provinces. The west coast, with the Western and Northern Isles, and northern Scotland as far south as the Dornoch Firth, may be referred to as the Atlantic Province. It is an area of peat moors and acid grasslands with much high ground, where occupation is largely confined to the coastal strip, and movements are most natural by sea. South from the Dornoch Firth to the Firth of Forth there is still much high ground in the interior, but there are also wide lowland valleys, and much fertile land. In this North-eastern Province we shall find a concentration of the most distinctive features of Pictish material culture.

The Picts first appear by name as one of the enemies of Roman Britain in 297, and thereafter they feature frequently in Roman writings along with the *Scotti* and the *Saxones*. While it is possible that *Picti* is a Latinized form of some native word which has been lost to us, its most natural meaning is 'The Painted Men', referring no doubt to their practice of tattooing their faces and bodies with woad. It is clear that the name embraces a number of tribes, as indeed do the terms *Scotti* and *Saxones*. Ptolemy's map, based on first-century information, lists a dozen tribes in the area. Since there is no evidence for major folk-movements or population changes, it is reasonable to regard these tribes as 'Proto-Pictish'. By the early third century they appear to have coalesced into two large units, the *Maeatae* close to the Antonine Wall, and the *Caledonii* who lived beyond them, but this may be an oversimplification based on the ignorance of the classical writers who are our only informants. Even when in the second half of the fourth century we are told specifically that the Picts are divided into two peoples, the *Verturiones* and the *Dicalydones*, we must remember that for a Roman writer they were very remote barbarians. In particular we may be sceptical of attempts to see this bi-partite division as fore-shadowing the division into 'northern' and 'southern' Picts mentioned by Bede, or as echoing the geographical and cultural divisions into Atlantic and North-eastern Provinces.

Late Roman measures against the Picts – coastal signal stations, large cavalry forts, and the settlement of Germanic mercenaries – are concentrated in Yorkshire (above, p. 96; p. 176), which suggests that the main threat came not from the western islands and highlands, but from the fertile north-east. That a serious threat continued into the fifth century is of course central to Gildas's account of the first introduction of Anglo-Saxon allies in order to repel the attacks of the northern nations. We need not believe for a moment what Gildas says about the Picts dragging the Britons down from the wall-walk of Hadrian's Wall with grappling irons, although his account of the Scots and Picts alighting from their curraghs rings true enough. But this was in the same century as that in which the Scots themselves obtained a foothold in western Pictland, from which they were ultimately to establish the kingdom of Scotland. From this time it seems that the aggression of the Picts was on the wane, and that they were no longer a menace to nations beyond their own borders. Accounts of the struggle between the Picts and the Dalriadic Scots figure largely in the annals and litera-ture of the invaders. But very little trace of hostile relations between the Picts and the northern Britons has been preserved in early Welsh literature. Nor did the Picts trouble the nascent Anglian kingdom of Bernicia. Indeed, by the middle of the seventh century Bede was able to claim that King Oswiu of Northumbria had subjected the greater part of the Pictish people to the rule of the English. Admittedly Oswiu's successors were to overreach themselves in this direction. But the central fact remains: there is no evidence that the Picts presented any serious threat to the other nations of Britain after the middle of the fifth century.

Our survey of the material culture of Pictland must begin in the later stages of the pre-Roman Iron Age, about the time of the birth of Christ.[31] The division into Atlantic and North-eastern Provinces was particularly strongly marked. The Atlantic Province was dominated by the broch-and-wheelhouse cultural complex, rich in pottery, bone and even metal objects. Architecturally its most obvious feature was provided by the brochs themselves, cunningly built circular towers of dry stonework, which represented an extreme specialization of the stone forts of northern Britain. The specialization was clearly in the interests of defence, for the brochs were almost impregnable refuges. It was obviously a matter of great politico-military significance when brochs ceased to be needed for defence and their stonework was robbed to build undefended wheelhouses.[32] This process began early in the second century AD, and two different historical explanations have been offered for it, depending on whom we see as the enemies of the broch-builders. If the brochs were a refuge against Roman slave-raiders, then their abandonment suggests that the initiative in northern and western waters had slipped from Roman into Proto-Pictish hands. In other words, the events of 297 and 367 were already foreshadowed.

But it may be that the enemies were really the fort-dwellers of the North-eastern Province, and that they now found their martial energies fully engaged against the Romans on their southern borders. The North-eastern Province exhibits none of the cultural richness of the islands and highlands. If pottery exists, it is crude stuff which continues a tradition going back to the earliest phase of the Iron Age, perhaps in the seventh century BC. A varied range of forts, all more or less small in dimensions but strong in relation to their size, characterizes the area, but they are nothing like so numerous as the small forts situated between the Antonine and Hadrianic Walls. Many of the north-eastern forts are vitrified, that is, part of the stonework has become fused into a glassy mass as a result of intense heat, and though this phenomenon is not confined to the Proto-Pictish area, still it deserves special consideration here. It used to be thought that vitrifaction had been brought about deliberately by the inhabitants in order to cement the stonework together. This view is now abandoned, and it is held that a vitrified fort is one in which the ramparts had contained strengthening timber beams, which may even have protruded into the interior to form a framework for tenement dwellings. At some point in its history the timber work was set on fire either deliberately – the Romans being a favourite candidate here – or accidentally, perhaps even by some housewife's carelessness. The burning timbers created flues through the rampart, leading in turn to the intense heat required to melt the stones. It is now realized that vitrifaction, and the timber-lacing which is its pre-condition, are neither cultural nor chronological indicators. In particular, the use of timber strengthening goes back to the earliest phases of fort-building in pre-Roman Iron-Age Britain, and we have seen it again in the late fifth/sixth century AD at Cadbury-Camelot [Fig. 18]. Each vitrified fort must be considered in the light of all the evidence available before we can say when it was built and when it was destroyed.

By far the most interesting of the timber-laced forts of Pictland is that of Burghead on the south shore of the Moray Firth, for we have

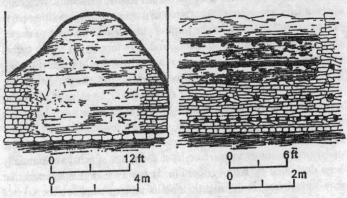

0   12 ft

0   4 m

0   6 ft

0   2 m

24. Section and elevation of the defences of Burghead, Morayshire, as excavated in 1890. Where the longitudinal timbers pass over the transverse ones, they were found to be nailed together.

radio-carbon dates for some of the timber used in its construction.[33] Like all radio-carbon dates, these are no doubt subject to modification as physicists develop their ideas on the decay-rate of Carbon 14, but they may reasonably be quoted as: probably in the range AD 120–560 (two samples), probably in the range AD 400–820 (one sample). In other words Burghead was probably constructed in the Proto-Pictish period. It was certainly occupied in the period of the historical Picts, as the discovery of large numbers of Pictish bull-symbol stones (below, p. 276) has demonstrated. It is therefore all the more regrettable that the site has been largely destroyed or built over. But it has been said that 'in point of size and strength its defences probably transcended those of any other Scottish fort,' and there can be no reasonable doubt that it was one of the principal strongholds, if not the capital, of Pictland. One other Pictish fort should be mentioned because it has yielded imported pottery of Class E: Clatchard Craig in Fife. This is a complicated structure with a long history, part of it as a multiple-ramparted fort measuring about 550 ft by 300 ft overall. The Pictish fort was somewhat smaller, but still measured 300 ft by 200 ft within the rampart which, like that at Cadbury-Camelot, made use of Roman masonry.[34]

Another type of monument which can certainly be assigned to the Proto-Picts is a sub-class of souterrains, namely, the distinctive group of about fifty which are concentrated in Angus and neighbouring parts of Perthshire.[35] These take the form of curving subterranean passages, about 80 ft long, with paved floors, and dry-stones walls which corbel inwards to carry a heavy slab roof at a height of 6 ft or more [Pl. 12b]. The inner end of the passage may be wider than the general width, while the outer end has a narrow entrance-way up to 12 ft in length, separated from the main passage by a lintelled doorway. These are quite unlike the souterrains which we have already noticed in Ireland (above, p. 257), and it is very reasonable to suggest that they were underground stores for surface-level dwellings which have normally been destroyed by later agriculture. It has even been suggested that they were byres, built with their walls underground for the sake of strength, but the absence of drains from most Angus souterrains rules out this explanation.

The most important result of recent excavations is the discovery of

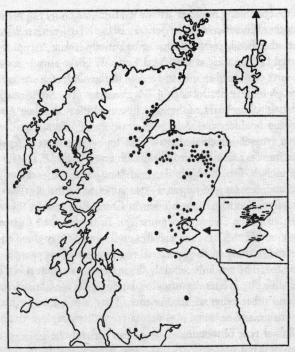

Map 8. Pictish monuments and sites. ●Pictish symbol stones. ─Angus souterrains. B, Burghead. C, Clatchard Craig.

the ground-level dwellings to which the souterrains were ancillary. These were small buildings of irregular shape, with low walls formed of large split boulders. Rather scanty finds have led to the conclusion that the two best known of the Angus souterrain-settlements were founded in the late first or second centuries AD; that the souterrains themselves were demolished and filled in during the early third century, and that the reorganized settlements then lasted into the fifth century without any change of population. In other words, it was probably from dwellings like these that some at least of the Picts went out to harry Roman Britain.

When we follow the archaeology through into the later fifth and subsequent centuries, we find the wheelhouse culture of the Atlantic

Province continuing in rather attenuated form, its pottery in particular lacking the exuberance of earlier periods. In the North-eastern Province, on the other hand, pottery seems to be entirely lacking except for the imported kitchen ware at Clatchard Craig. We have already seen that some forts continued in use, and a date in the ninth century has been suggested for the destruction of Burghead by fire. Archaeologically the distinguishing mark of the early historical Picts was their practice of incising boulders and slabs with drawings of animals, and with a range of symbols which are mostly abstract but occasionally represent combs, mirrors and other recognizable objects [Pl. 32a].[36] The animals, which include fish, birds, bulls, boars and deer, are executed with vigour and economy of line in a style common to the northern barbarians from Scotland to the borders of China. Presumably, the stones are related to the Group I memorials of Britain and the Oghams of Ireland, and in this case the pictures and symbols may stand for the names and possibly ranks or personal relationships of the persons commemorated. The symbols certainly begin in a pagan context but there was no difficulty in later centuries in adapting them for Christian cross-slabs and other religious monuments. They also occur on massive silver chains, and on some pins decorated with champlevé enamel in the Ultimate La Tène style.

The problem of the Picts has been seen variously in terms of their origins, the meaning of the name *Picti*, and the linguistic family of their undecipherable language. But from our particular view-point there is one central and pressing problem. According to our historical sources, and especially according to the account given by Gildas and canonized by Bede, Pictish raiding was a principal cause of the break-up of civilized government and social order in fifth-century Britain, and thereby a main cause of the invitation to the Anglo-Saxons. In other words it was a prime factor in the Arthurian situation. But when we look north of the Antonine Wall to study these formidable raiders on their home territory, all we seem to find are peaceful dwellers in wheelhouses and souterrain-settlements. We know nothing of the boats in which the raiders came, nothing of the weapons which they carried. And until the emergence of the symbol stones, which may be as late as the seventh century, there is nothing distinctively Pictish about the most fertile regions of Pictland. The suggestion seems scarcely surprising that 'the Picts never existed outside the imagination of Roman panegyrists'. Even in the early 1960s such a view would have had much to commend it. But it is not too much to say that the new recognition of Proto-Pictish and Pictish fortifications of a formidable character, at Burghead and Clatchard Craig, has revolutionized our picture of the military archaeology of Pictland. Further discoveries on these lines seem likely to demonstrate why Roman panegyric poets thought it worth mentioning the Picts at all, and why Gildas regarded them with such horror.

Ten

The Enemies of the Britons
2: The English

The ancestral English[1]

Historical notices of raiders coming across the North Sea to attack Roman Britain mention only the *Saxones*. But by the time that raiding passed into settlement, Bede tells us that 'three very powerful German peoples' were involved, 'that is Saxons, Angles and Jutes'. Archaeology and place-names studies would add other names to these, including Franks, Frisians and *Suevi*. Broadly speaking, we have to deal with ethnic and cultural elements coming from as far apart as the Lower Rhine and the tip of the Jutish peninsula. In so far as it is legitimate to generalize about all these diverse nations, it is convenient to have one term to include them all. I therefore propose to use the term 'ancestral English' to embrace all those Germanic peoples who contributed to the settlement of England. This usage will be confined to them in their continental homes, but once they have migrated and settled in Britain they will be regarded as 'early' or 'pagan English'. Because the intensity, permanence and long-term significance of the English settlement of Britain gave it a character altogether different from that of the Scottic settlements, we are necessarily more concerned with the English in Britain than with their ancestors. The ancestral background must none the less be sketched in, especially because of its relevance for the Saxon raiding of the third and fourth centuries.

Bede's classic statement about the original homelands of the Anglo-Saxons has set the pattern for much historical research and interpretation. He tells us that the 'race of the English or Saxons', *Anglorum sive Saxonum gens*, came 'from three very strong tribes of Germany', *de tribus Germaniae populis fortioribus, id est Saxonibus, Anglis, Iutis*. He explains that the Saxon homeland was the region 'now known as Old Saxony', while that of the Angles was the 'land called *Angulus* ... between the provinces of the Jutes and the Saxons'. *Angulus* must correspond broadly with the modern Angeln towards the base of the Schleswig-Jutland peninsula; the territory of the Jutes lay in the northern part of that peninsula; and Old Saxony was the land between the Elbe and the Weser. We have no means of knowing what mixture of oral tradition and pure speculation lay behind Bede's analysis, but for more than a century archaeologists have been collecting material to confirm and amplify it.

The study began in 1855 when the great Victorian scholar J. W. Kemble drew attention to the similarities between pottery cinerary urns found at Strade on the Elbe and others from Suffolk and Cambridgeshire. It is no part of our purpose here to follow the development of these studies in detail. It is enough to indicate that close parallels can now be quoted, in both pottery and metalwork, between England and the three areas mentioned by Bede.[2] In addition there are very important resemblances in pottery between the earliest cemeteries in England and those of the Frisian Islands and the adjacent coastlands. And in the upper levels of society, close connections can be shown with metalwork and jewelry from the Frankish regions along the Rhine and from Scandinavia, especially Sweden. Connections by folk-migration, dynastic interchange, and trade are all represented, and it is clear that what England owes to the ancestral homelands is rich, complex and varied. Nor was the movement of peoples and ideas always westwards; England had its own contribution to make to continental culture. Perhaps the most interesting result of continental studies has been the recognition that, immediately before the first migration of the fifth century, a cultural amalgam was forming in the ancestral homelands as a result of minor folk-movement and culture contact between the coastlands, the region of the lower Elbe, and most of the Jutish peninsula. To this amalgam the term 'Anglo-Saxon' can well be applied – or, as Bede would have said, *Anglorum sive Saxonum gens*.[3]

Our evidence about the material culture of these ancestral English comes largely from three sources: their cemeteries, their villages, and a small group of ritual deposits. Typical of the last category are the bog deposits at Thorsbjerg in the heart of Angeln, and Nydam a little to the north.[4] These deposits consist of large numbers of objects which had been sacrificed by throwing them into marshy pools or meres, a ritual practised by both the Celts and the Germans. The sacrifices at Thorsbjerg and Nydam were deposited over a period of some centuries, covering much of the Roman Iron Age and continuing into the period of the migrations. The votive offerings include pots containing food; metal ornaments, including spectacular gold armlets and disks, some of them imported from the Roman world, and others of them copying such imports; Roman coins which may have come north either as bribes or as loot; large quantities of weapons and armour, most of it native but including some splendid Roman imports such as two parade-helmets; and finally, at Nydam, three ships which formed the centre-piece of the whole deposit. The woodwork of the ships, and the wooden parts of the weapons, had been preserved in the peat which formed as the meres silted up, and the one Nydam boat which was recovered has been claimed as the main evidence for the character of the vessels in which the Saxons raided Britain.

The Nydam boat was a great rowing boat, a little over 70 ft long, about 10 ft wide, and with a draught of about 4 ft. It was built up of five oak planks either side of a keel which was too flimsy to bear a mast. There is no possibility, therefore, that the Nydam boat ever carried a sail, and it was driven simply by fifteen pairs of oars. In addition there was a steering oar on the starboard side. A complement of between forty and fifty seems likely. It is difficult to see how such a rowing boat could have menaced the coast of England. If we assume that the Saxon raiders coming from the mouth of the Elbe coasted along the Frisian islands as far as Texel before crossing the North Sea, they would still be faced with a voyage of over one hundred nautical miles before making a landfall. Since it has been suggested that the most likely speed would be about three knots, almost a day and a half of continuous rowing would be involved. It seems unlikely that even the hardiest of sea-raiders would have been much of a match for the Saxon Shore garrisons after such a crossing. On the other hand if the raiders had used a shorter crossing and then coasted along the British shores the dangers of interception by the *classis Britannica*, the British fleet, would have been multiplied. Clearly there is an absurdity here. It can be removed if we recall that Nydam is close to the Baltic shore and if we think of the Nydam boat as designed for that tideless sea. It is probably irrelevant to the question of the vessels used by the ancestral English whether as raiders or immigrants, and we must return later to the problems which they pose (below, p. 301).

The weapons and armour in the Thorsbjerg and Nydam deposits are varied both in kind and in the cultural connections which they display. Among defensive armour they include rare coats of chain-mail, some of them probably of Roman manufacture but others perhaps of a native type which goes back to the pre-Roman Iron Age. Circular wooden shields with metal bosses may also be of either native or Roman type. The Roman parade-helmets have already been mentioned, but native helmets do not seem to have been recovered from the bog-deposits. Offensive weapons are present in enormous quantities – Nydam, for instance, yielded over five hundred iron spearheads, some from lances, that is, thrusting spears, others from javelins for throwing. Swords with short broad blades of iron may be either of Roman origin or native copies, and Roman scabbards and harness fittings also occur. Bows of ash up to 5 ft long were found, and with them quantities of iron arrowheads. Altogether we can derive from these sacrifices a vivid and detailed picture of the armaments of the ancestral English at the time when they were raiding across the North Sea as well as over the Rhine frontier of the Roman empire. No doubt some of the Roman arms and armour had been won on such raids, but much of it, especially the finer and more ornamental pieces, had probably gone north as diplomatic gifts.

These deposits are of course altogether exceptional, and the major part of our evidence comes from cemeteries. A variety of burial rites were practised, and we shall find most of them occurring again west of the North Sea. Along the Rhine among the Franks, bodies were normally placed unburned in the grave, and were often accompanied by rich grave goods: jewelry and household objects with the women, weapons and military gear with the men. In the Elbe-Weser region and in Angeln on the other hand, cremation was the normal rite, and the ashes were frequently placed in a pottery cinerary urn. Grave goods here are less frequent, and may consist only of a fire-distorted brooch, but unburned jewelry might also be placed with the urn. In north Jutland we find inhumation-burials again, often accompanied by grave-goods, and sometimes placed in a stone chamber. It is fair to say that in the area of the Anglo-Saxon cultural amalgam there was by AD 400 considerable variety of practice, including mixed cemeteries with both inurned and urnless cremations, and inhumation burials, some of them with the body laid east/west. Two other points deserve special emphasis. The first is the very large size of the cemeteries, some of which yielded between one and two thousand urns in the course of rather casual nineteenth-century excavations. The second is that the urns themselves and the jewelry from the burials can often be paralleled very closely in England. The cemeteries are indeed our best source for comparison between the early English and their continental ancestors.

The weapons in the bog deposits and in the warrior-graves inevitably leave a strong impression of the martial aspects of Germanic society, but another aspect of it is also represented in the archaeological record, in the village settlements, which show us a prosperous society of yeoman farmers.[5] In Frisia, between the sea and the sandy heaths of the interior is a coastal belt of pasture-land which was densely inhabited throughout the Iron Age. Partly because of the need to raise dwellings above the danger of flooding, partly because villages continued on the same sites over a period of centuries, the characteristic settlement appears today as a low mound, rich in human refuse. Excavation shows that these '*terp*'s or '*wurt*'s were compact nucleated villages, containing a number of houses which show differing degrees of wealth and different groupings of industrial and agricultural activity. In those which have been thoroughly excavated it is possible to suggest that the social organization was changing with the passage of time. Pottery evidence makes it clear that the Frisian coastland area was one of the homes of the ancestral English, and it may be that the increasing expansion of these prosperous communities combined with the encroachments of the sea to make migration inevitable. Further north, in Jutland for instance, the village mounds are unknown, but nucleated villages are still normal except in some of the Baltic islands, where a dispersed pattern of isolated farmsteads has been observed.

The dominant house-type in these settlements was the so-called aisled long-house. The term 'long-house' is not simply descriptive, but is a technical term, translated in fact from the Welsh *tŷ-hir*. It refers to buildings which fulfil the dual function of house and byre under the same roof, the cattle at one end and the human beings at the

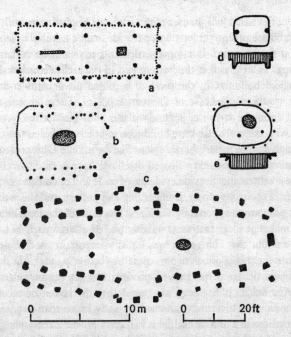

25. Continental and English houses: *a* Ostermoor bei Brunsbüttelkoog, Schleswig-Holstein, second-century aisled long-house, with post and wicker walls, hearth at one end, central drain at other; *b* Linford, Essex, partly restored plan of fifth-century house with aisles or buttressed walls; *c* Warendorf, Westphalia, eighth-century long-house with buttressed walls; *d* Linford, sunken-floored house of standard plan with axial post-holes; *e* Bourton-on-the-Water, Gloucestershire, partly-restored plan of sunken-floored house with small peripheral post-holes, hearth and loom-posts.

other, normally separated by a through passage between doors in each of the long walls. Archaeologically such an arrangement may be detected by the occurrence of a large hearth in one half of the building, and perhaps a drain or other evidence of cattle-stalling in the other. The aisled long-house is one in which the main roof support is provided by a double row of stout columns dividing the floor area into a central nave and two narrower side aisles. The walls themselves may be of turf or dry-stone, or of wicker screens between relatively light posts.

Some of the aisled long-houses of the ancestral English were both large and elaborate: over 75 ft long by 15 ft wide, with a number of separate stalls at the byre end. But some settlements have smaller rectangular buildings as well, and at the bottom end of the architectural scale are very small buildings in the form of a roofed pit or sunken-floored dwelling: the *Grubenhaus* of German scholars. These appear to be absent from the *terpen* or mound-villages, but they certainly occur, along with the more elaborate buildings, in other villages of the ancestral English. And in peripheral regions like the middle Elbe, settlements consisting solely of sunken-floored dwellings have been discovered.

These settlements provide evidence of trade and of cottage or village industries such as weaving, ironworking and pottery, but the mainstay of the economy was certainly farming. The form of the long-house in itself makes it clear that stock-raising played a large part, but there is little doubt that cultivation was equally important. Archaeological evidence for this is often hard to come by (below, p. 305), but in Jutland in particular it has proved possible to plan the boundaries of Iron-Age fields. It has been suggested that the layout of the field-divisions implies that land was owned privately, rather than communally by the village as a unit. Some fields had certainly been cross-ploughed, that is to say, in two directions at right angles. This implies the use of an ard, a light plough which was already in use in the area as early as the Bronze Age. On the other hand it has been claimed that there is evidence for an advanced type of heavy plough with a wheeled carriage in the Roman Iron Age. Recent scholarship has, however, assigned the Tømmerby wheeled plough to modern times, while still admitting that a heavy plough, capable of cutting a wide furrow-slice, was in use for instance in Schleswig-Holstein in the Roman Iron Age.

Imports from the Roman world have been mentioned several times. In the centuries before the migrations, the principal source of these imports to Germany was Gaul in general and the Rhineland in particular, with the eastern part of the empire playing a more nebulous role. In addition to arms and armour we find metal and glass vessels, pottery, especially the fine red table-wares manufactured in Gaul, beads and brooches, and coins. Because of the prestige which lay behind them these imports had much influence on the development of

Germanic arts and crafts. At a lowly level, the Saxon fondness for stamped ornament on pottery was possibly inspired by provincial Roman pottery decorated with stamped designs. Altogether more important was the influence on fine metalwork, for the realistic animals which were so common on Roman table-ware, whether of metal or pot, were the inspiration of the more or less stylized animals of Germanic art. An early phase of this influence is represented in the third century on certain ornamental silver disks from the Thorsbjerg bog, but the main influence came rather later, when the Germans made a wholesale borrowing from Gallo-Roman metalwork of animals round the borders of objects and scroll-ornament filling the interior [Pls. 17, 18a, 21a]. These were executed in the sharply ridged relief known as chip-carving. Another important influence around the Baltic in the fifth century derived from the vast quantities of gold coins of the eastern empire which poured in as bribes. These provided both the raw material for spectacular gold ornaments, and also the inspiration for the designs, in which transmogrified human faces are prominent.[6]

Among the early forms of metalwork which occur both in the ancestral homelands and in England, two leading classes are the circular 'saucer' brooches decorated with chip-carved spirals [Pl. 19a], and the H-shaped 'equal-armed' brooch with spirals and border animals [Pl. 18a]. The equal-armed brooch belongs to the broad class of bow-brooches, in which a fold of cloth or the overlap of two garments can be taken up in a semicircular bow in the upper member of the brooch, while the pin passes through the cloth. The bow-brooches of the period of the migrations derive from simpler versions with an ancestry going back through the Roman Iron Age into the earliest phases of the Iron Age in temperate Europe. The simplest form in the fourth and fifth centuries AD is the cruciform brooch, which has a cross-shaped head to accommodate the spring or hinge for the pin, and a zoomorphic foot in the form of a stylized horse's head. In Jutland, and later elsewhere, the cruciform head is sometimes replaced in the fifth century by a large rectangular plate which serves as a field for elaborate scroll- and animal-ornament, while the horse on the foot disappears under a menagerie of border animals and human masks. Another important development of the fifth century is the introduction from eastern Europe to Gaul and the Rhineland of 'polychrome' jewelry, in which spectacular effects are achieved by the clash of coloured stones and glass against a background of gold or at least gilt-bronze. The stones may be set as carbuncles or in carefully shaped wire cells – the cloisonné technique. All these developments had repercussions in England in the late fifth, sixth and early seventh centuries.

There is one further aspect of Roman contact with the German peoples which deserves mention here, namely the employment of bands of Germans as mercenaries. We have already seen the *numerus Hnaudifridi* on Hadrian's Wall (above, p. 94), and there must have been many such units on the Rhine frontier. The archaeological evidence for them is found in a number of warrior-graves datable by coins to the late fourth and early fifth centuries. The practice of placing weapons with the dead man appears in this context to be Germanic, and some of the weapons, such as throwing-axes, seem specifically German. But these are accompanied by buckles and belt-fittings which are Gallo-Roman rather than Germanic. The stylistic boundaries are rather nebulous here, for we have already seen the influence of chip-carved Gallo-Roman motifs on German metalwork further north. Nevertheless it can be accepted that the general assemblage of equipment of these warriors is Roman-provincial rather than German. Literary sources show that in the fourth century the frontier lands of Gaul, which had been ravaged by earlier Germanic raiding, were being settled by new Germanic tribes who were given land in return for military service. There was much variety of practice here. In some cases a tribe was brought across the frontier and settled on depopulated land both to cultivate and to defend it. In other cases the grant of land was really an acknowledgement of the *de facto* possession of territory which had been gained by conquest. Literary sources distinguish between *foederati*, who held their land by virtue of a *foedus* or treaty, and *laeti*, who were settled in return for military service, but the archaeological evidence cannot be interpreted in terms of such legal and tenurial distinctions. From our point of view the chief importance of these warrior-burials on the frontier of Gaul is that some of the buckles and other military gear found in them have close parallels in Britain, where, as we have seen, they may be attributed to troops brought over by Count Theodosius in 368–9.

This introduction of Germans from the Gaulish frontier to Britain is of course a minor event compared with the folk-movements from further north. Now that we have sketched the material culture of the Anglo-Saxons in their ancestral homelands, we can examine its transplantation to Britain.

The pagan English: the evidence of the cemeteries

Our evidence for the pagan English – their material culture and the early history of their settlement in England – comes principally from their cemeteries, so that we appear to know far more about them in death than in life. On the whole, scholarly examination of the material from the cemeteries has tended to concentrate on typological studies of the grave goods, which are often very well preserved.[7] But before we turn to these studies, we should briefly consider the evidence of the cemeteries as such.[8] The two rites of cremation and inhumation are both present in England, and in general the larger cemeteries are those in which both occur. It used to be considered that cremation was the universal rite in the early generations of the settlement. Furthermore it was supposed that the occurrence of inhumation burials, either in mixed cremation/inhumation cemeteries or with no mixture, represented a 'flight from cremation' which took place in this country under the influences either of the inhuming – and possibly Christian – Britons, or of the church itself after the conversion. These hypotheses are in fact unnecessary, for as we have seen several groups of the ancestral English already practised inhumation. None the less it is true that cremation is in general early, whereas cemeteries in which the bodies are regularly laid with the feet to the east can often be shown, on the typological evidence of the jewelry which accompanies them, to belong to the seventh century. It is also true that cremation is dominant in the areas which Bede assigns to the Angles, whereas the Saxons (and perhaps the Jutes) favoured inhumation.

In the cremation rite, the body was burned at about 900° C, hot enough to distort bronze jewelry or to fuse glass beads if they had been placed on the pyre. Such burned grave-goods are however rare, and more common is the occurrence of unburned toilet articles, usually bone combs or iron shears which are too small to be functional, but which hint at some ritual of shaving the body. The ashes were normally

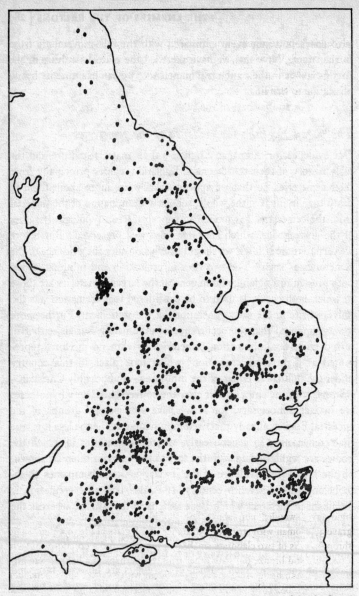

Map 9. Pagan cemeteries and barrows, showing the extent of Anglo-Saxon penetration in the 5th–7th centuries.

placed in a pottery urn, which was probably made specifically for the burial ritual. Very rarely a bronze bowl, even a Celtic hanging bowl, may have been used as the container. A very curious ritual is that in which a fire was lit in the grave-pit at the time when the corpse was placed in it, so that part of the body was consumed by fire.

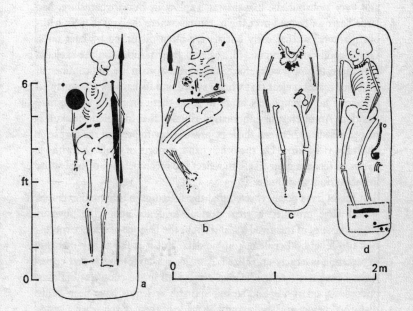

26. Four characteristic Anglo-Saxon graves: *a* Petersfinger, Wiltshire, grave 20, warrior with sword and spear at left side, belt-fittings and knife at waist, shield at right shoulder, other minor objects; *b* Shudy Camps, Cambridgeshire, grave 36, warrior with spear, battle-knife (*seax*) hanging from elaborate harness including a pouch, knife and strike-a-light near waist, rim-binding of wooden cup above left shoulder; *c* Holywell Row, Suffolk, grave 37, woman with string of 150 amber and 8 glass beads round neck and through bows of two elaborate small-long brooches and a cruciform brooch, iron knife and bronze pin with other trinkets (perhaps in a bag) at left hip; *d* Burwell, Cambridgeshire, grave 121, woman with collar of silver pendants, bronze work-box suspended by chain, food-offering of lamb-chops, wooden box at feet containing bone comb, chalk beads or whorls and other oddments.[9]

In the normal inhumation rite the body was laid out in a shallow grave-pit either stretched out on its back or on its side with the knees slightly flexed. Very rarely the presence of iron nails or clamps shows that the corpse was in a coffin, and sometimes it was partly protected by blocks of stone. Small mounds were raised over the graves in Kent, and very rich burials, like that at Taplow in Buckinghamshire, had large barrows heaped over them, but elsewhere the graves were without markers, so that early burials are often disturbed by later ones. Grave-goods are common [Pl. 20], and their position on the skeleton may indicate how jewelry, for instance, was worn in life, but continental evidence makes it clear that when a sword and its harness accompanied a warrior no attempt was made to strap them on in the appropriate position. An interesting inhumation ritual is that in which the skull is placed beside or between the legs, presumably to prevent the corpse or ghost from walking. On the other hand, reports of skeletons without hands or feet are more likely to reflect the incompetence of excavators in recovering small bones.

It might have been expected that the skeletons in inhumation graves would have provided a great deal of evidence about the physical characteristics of the invaders, and about the balance of sexes, expectation of life and other demographic data. But it is fair to say that this expectation is largely unrealized. A major reason for this is that cemeteries have most frequently been discovered in the course of building operations, quarrying and so on, and the skeletons have been badly disturbed before any study could be made of them. Even when a systematic and unhurried research excavation has been possible, the skeletons have often been badly decayed or disturbed, largely because of the shallowness of the original grave. Add to this a current mood of scepticism about the possibility of establishing sex and age from skeletal material except under ideal conditions, so that judgements about these features made by the nineteenth-century excavators and their medical friends are no longer trusted. In face of all this, it is not surprising that there is no collection of data about our pagan Saxon population. Nor can anything useful be said about racial characteristics. It has been suggested that the early English were tall and robust, and that when short and slender skeletons are found they are the remains of Romano-Britons who had perhaps intermarried with the invaders, but at present no weight of scholarship defends the suggestion. There is also a little evidence about injuries, disease and dietic deficiencies among the Saxons. On the whole, however, it would be true to say that there is a large potential field for research here.

Another still unharvested crop of statistics is represented by the actual size of cemeteries, for this should have some relation to the size of communities. Some figures are available for the upper Thames valley. There the two largest mixed cemeteries, those at Abingdon and Long Wittenham, produced 203 and 234 burials respectively. These could be the burial-grounds of small villages, but what are we to think of cemeteries only a tenth that size, for these are in fact the commonest? If we turn to eastern England, a very few cremation cemeteries are known to have produced 300 or more urns, but only Caistor-by-Norwich is believed to have topped the thousand. The size of the English cemeteries invites immediate comparison with those of the continental homelands, where cemeteries commonly produce between one and two thousand urn-burials. The cemeteries provide our only evidence for assessing the Anglo-Saxon immigrants in quantitative terms, and they seem to lead to the conclusion that the actual numbers involved were surprisingly small (below, pp. 310–11).

When we turn to the grave-goods themselves our first question must be what they imply in terms of religious belief. We can find evidence for well-developed beliefs in an after-life among other pagan Germanic peoples, notably the Vikings, but there appears to be no literary evidence for this among the pagan English. It might be thought that the very practice of depositing grave-goods demonstrated that the warrior and his lady were being equipped for the next world, but anthropological parallels make it clear that this is not necessarily so. Intimate personal possessions such as weapons and jewelry may be rendered unclean, taboo, by the death of their owner, so they are placed in the grave to take them out of circulation. Or social prestige may demand the display not merely of a costly funeral wake, but of the sacrifice of precious objects, with no thought that the objects deposited will have any future use. Even within a single village, the anthropologist warns us, individual families may have different customs in the matter of grave-deposits.[10] Consequently we cannot necessarily use the varying richness of graves to argue for differing degrees of wealth – social stratification, in fact – among the living. But whatever implications we may draw from it, the fact that there is a graded series of graves is not in dispute. The most poorly furnished male grave will have only an iron knife; more elaborate is one which adds a spear; to this may then be added a shield; very rare is the grave which has a sword as well; while only two graves in England have yielded helmets. Among female graves, where grave goods take the form of assorted jewelry and household objects like keys, needle-cases, or ornamental buckets, it is less easy to establish such a graded series. But apart from the jewelry, certain objects appear to establish the status of an important woman, the clearest being the iron weaving-sword or beater, used to close up the weft threads on a vertical loom, and symbol of a noble matron's authority over the servile weaving-maids.

The grave-goods also provide a basis for assessing the major national or tribal elements among the immigrants.[11] A preliminary clue is provided, of course, by the tribal names of the kingdoms or districts of the East Saxons, South Saxons and West Saxons, and of the East Angles and Middle Angles. To this Bede adds that the Mercians and the whole Northumbrian race came from the country of the Angles; and that *de Iutarum origine sunt Cantuari et Uictuarii*, 'of Jutish origin are the men of Kent and Wight', as well as certain elements on the Wessex mainland opposite the Isle of Wight, who up to his own day were called *Iutarum natio*. In view of what has already been said (above, p. 279) about the coming together of diverse cultural elements to form an Anglo-Saxon amalgam in at least one region of the continental homelands, it is interesting to notice that there is a definite polarity between Anglian and Saxon grave-goods. In the early pottery, for instance, stamped ornament is characteristically Saxon, and so are elaborately moulded bosses [Fig. 27c], whereas simple vertical bosses, horizontal grooves [Fig. 27a], and an absence of stamps are equally characteristically Anglian. In metalwork, cruciform brooches and the dress-fasteners known as 'wrist-clasps' are found especially in Anglian areas [Pl. 20], whereas saucer brooches are concentrated in Saxon regions [Pl. 19a]. Some of these differences go back to the time of the first settlement, but others appear to have developed in the subsequent generations. And whatever we make, with the aid of typological studies and distribution maps, of this polarity between Angles and Saxons, it is always worth remembering that Bede uses the two terms as though they were interchangeable equivalents: *Anglorum sive Saxonum gens.*

The problem of the Jutes is altogether more difficult, if only because Bede's attribution of them to Kent, Wight, and the adjacent part of Wessex is so circumstantial that we might expect to find incontrovertible traces of Jutish culture in these clearly defined areas. In fact the overwhelming impression given by both the pottery and the metalwork from graves in Kent is of connections with the Franks of the Rhineland, whom Bede does not mention at all among the settlers of England. Particularly relevant among the goods from the Kentish cemeteries are the wheel-thrown pottery bottles [Fig. 27*b*] which represent one element – albeit only a very small one – in the Frankish repertory, and also sophisticated jewelry ornamented with garnets either as carbuncles or in cloisons. Until recently a very small quantity of crude pottery and a few early cruciform brooches appeared to be the only marks of an early non-Frankish element, more Frisian than Jutish in character. On this, it was believed, a Frankish element was imposed, more probably by invasion than by trade connections, during the first half of the sixth century. In the second half of the century a distinctive Kentish culture blossomed forth, strongly fertilized by commercial and dynastic contacts with the Franks of Merovingian Gaul. The most recent trend in scholarship, however, has tended to emphasize the north German, and specifically Jutish, contribution to Kent. In metalwork, the occurrence of the gold ornamental disks known as 'bracteates', and of square-headed brooches with distinctive animal ornament, demonstrates close connections between Kent and Jutland at the beginning of the sixth century. And for the initial phases of settlement half a century or more earlier there are now satisfactory parallels between pottery from Kent and from a dozen places in Jutland.

Thus far Bede is vindicated, but in mentioning Frankish elements in Kent we have already suggested that archaeological evidence demonstrates the existence among the invaders of national groups which he ignored. In fact the problems posed by alleged Frankish connections with Kent and other areas of southern England are too controversial to be dealt with here. It is enough to say that there is very real dispute about what material is Frankish, how early it may be, and whether it was brought by trade or invasion. Altogether more profitable for us is the case of the distinctive pottery known as Anglo-Frisian for this introduces us to a continental element in England, which was not mentioned by Bede but which was already present before his conventional date for the 'coming of the Saxons'. Anglo-Frisian pottery comprises well-made bowls and jars with simple grooved ornament above the shoulder [Fig. 27a], which are found in Frisia and also in the cremation cemeteries of eastern England from Yorkshire to Kent. Some of these cemeteries stand close to Roman forts, fortified towns, and roads, while sherds of Anglo-Frisian pottery have even been found inside towns such as Dorchester-on-Thames and Canterbury. Such contexts, and a continental dating in the late fourth and early fifth centuries, imply that the users of Anglo-Frisian pottery had been settled by Roman or sub-Roman authority as mercenary defenders of Britain.

In this case, then, the archaeological evidence has added a new chapter to early English history, one which could never have been written from the verbal evidence alone. This may encourage us to hope that the witness of pottery and metalwork may make possible a thorough-going amplification or even correction of the scanty account of the English settlement given by Gildas and Bede, or the circumstantial but chronologically uncertain narrative of the *Anglo-Saxon Chronicle*. There is indeed one kingdom for which this hope is partially realized – that of Wessex. Whereas the story in the *Chronicle* is of a band of adventurers landing in Southampton Water and battling their way inland over some three generations, archaeology demonstrates that the nucleus of Wessex was a peasant settlement in the mid- and upper Thames valley, going back a generation before the *Chronicle* date for Cerdic's landing. It seems very probable that the cause of the discrepancy here lies in the chronicler's interest in dynastic affairs rather than in folk-movement, and that a balanced interpretation would see the dynasty of Cerdic imposing itself by force on farming communities of quite independent origin.

But the attempt to rewrite the *Chronicle* on the basis of archaeological evidence must not be carried too far. Granted that the dates in the *Chronicle* are shaky: there are no dates at all for the jewelry or the pottery, or the graves which contain them, before the 610s or 620s. This statement will be hotly contested by some archaeologists of pagan England, and equally warmly welcomed by others.[12] The simple truth is that the dates applied to grave-goods in England are short-hand statements for chronological hypotheses based on the comparison of English material with continental objects. Some of the latter may be dated by the Roman or Byzantine coins found with them in graves. Their dating might therefore seem beyond reproach were it not notorious that ancient as well as recent coins may be buried in graves. A clear case of this is provided by a well-known Kentish burial (above, p. 157), which cannot be earlier than 467–72 because it contains a coin of Anthemius, but which also contains a coin of Valentinian I or II, datable 364–92. In other words a coin in a grave can only give the earliest possible date for the burial. It is true that a system of coin-dated graves can be built up, but its joints are elastic. It provides no framework at all for a narrative history of pagan England. For that purpose we can only use our verbal sources, applying to them the normal canons of historical criticism, and admitting that for the sixth century the chronology is unreliable in detail, while for the fifth even the sequence of events is open to dispute.

Granted that there is no precise chronological framework for the archaeological material, it is none the less true that broad trends of development are clear and that objects can normally be assigned to their proper century. Among the cremation urns, for instance, those which are closest to continental types are assigned to the fifth century. These include the Anglo-Frisian bowls and jars already mentioned; large urns with elaborate, even grotesque bosses and other swellings [Fig. 27c], and jars with dimples arranged in the form of rosettes. Within certain broad patterns there is an enormous range of individual variation among the designs on the early pots, and there is no doubt that these are domestic products. But in the Fenlands in the sixth century a high degree of standardization appears on jars decorated principally with stamps arranged in horizontal rows and in pendant triangular panels [Fig. 27f]. It is not merely that the overall appearance of these vessels is closely similar. Identical stamps have been detected on pots from different cemeteries, and this can only mean that they have been made by one and the same potter. In other words, we have evidence here for craft specialization and for trade, albeit over a radius of less than ten miles – a day's walk to market and back again. In the seventh century stamped designs went out of favour as bossed orna-

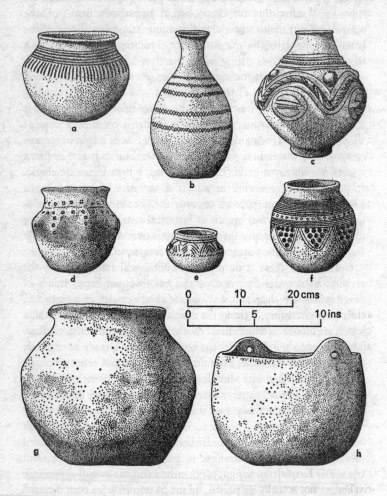

27. Pagan Saxon pottery: *a* Anglo-Frisian bowl with simple grooved decoration; *b* Frankish bottle-vase from Kent; *c* Saxon urn with elaborate bossed designs; *d* stamped and bossed urn from Wallingford, Berkshire; *e* incised bowl from Petersfinger, Wiltshire, grave 26; *f* stamped urn made for trade by the Illington-Lackford potter; *g, h* two cooking pots, the second with pierced lugs for suspension over a fire, from Sutton Courtenay, Berkshire.[13]

ment had in the preceding century, and by the end of the century sophisticated wheel-thrown pottery was being manufactured in East Anglia. This was the first production at a fully commercial level since the collapse of the Romano-British pottery industry in the late fourth/ early fifth century.

The development of fine metalwork and jewelry can similarly be traced in broad outline. Among the earliest, with close continental parallels, are the equal-armed brooches with chip-carved spiral ornament [Pl. 18a], the saucer brooches with similar decoration [Pl. 19a], and various simple bow brooches [Pl. 19, 21b] including cruciforms decorated only with a horse's head. The equal-armed brooches had no progeny, but the saucers and cruciforms gave rise to elaborate developments during the course of the sixth century. Another early group, concentrated in Kent, consists of circular brooches in silver, ornamented with realistic animals which are sometimes picked out in gold leaf. These and allied brooches look magnificent when illustrated at two or three times their original scale, but in actuality they are rather undistinguished, and they have no place in the mainstream of Anglo-Saxon metalwork. The early sixth century saw the addition of square-headed brooches to the repertory of forms [Pl. 21a], and of disintegrated animals in Germanic Style I [Pls. 19b, 18b] to the ornament of all classes of brooch. Rather later in the century, garnets begin to appear in Kent, doubtless under Frankish influence. The most interesting use of garnets was in combination with chip-carved Style I animals on circular brooches often made of silver [Pl. 22]. The earliest of these brooches have only three garnets, in the shape of key-stones, but by the early seventh century Kentish craftsmen were producing elaborate composite disk brooches which had garnets in cloison settings, and which were further embellished with lapis-lazuli, white paste bosses, and filigree animals in Germanic Style II. Rather poor imitations of this Kentish jewelry appear elsewhere, but it was only seriously rivalled, if not actually surpassed, by the Sutton Hoo jeweller, whose work will be described shortly (below, p. 300).

In addition to the pottery and the jewelry, the cemeteries provide well-preserved examples of many other Saxon objects. Some of these appear domestic in character, but it seems likely that they are not truly representative of normal household goods, either because only the best was fitting for a burial, or because objects were made specially for ritual purposes. This last hypothesis is certainly suggested by the pottery, for the elaborate cinerary urns do not occur on dwelling sites, and it is reasonable therefore to interpret them as specifically funerary vessels. So when we find the bronze bindings, handles and handle-fittings for wooden buckets, or bronze bowls with iron handles, or even work-boxes [Fig. 26d] and needle-cases in the graves, we are left uncertain whether or not these are ordinary everyday objects. The graves, especially in Kent, also provide us with many well-preserved examples of glass vessels.[14] The leading types were all intended for drinking – conical beakers, beakers with minute foot-stands and elaborate ornament, even drinking-horns of glass. All these were probably imported from factories in the Rhineland or elsewhere in northern Gaul. But there are also certain squat jars and rather baggy beakers which are distinctively English, and which may have been manufactured at Faversham in Kent.

The climax, in every sense, of the pagan graves, comes in the seventh century with the Sutton Hoo treasure and ship-burial.[15] We hinted at the problems of dating this when we discussed the Celtic hanging bowls. In brief, apart from art-historical arguments derived from both Celtic and Germanic metalwork, the best hope of dating it is provided by a curious collection of Merovingian gold coins, one from each of thirty-seven different mints. As an assemblage, these cannot be earlier than 625 and may be as late as 650–60, and of course the coins merely provide the earliest possible date for the treasure-burial itself. If those indicators which favour an early date are pressed to the utmost extent, then the claim could just possibly be substantiated that the treasure represents grave-goods for the great king Ræd-wald of East Anglia, who died in the early 620s if not before. In the 640s and 650s there are four kings who might be claimants to the treasure, three of whom met their death in battle.

But the whole question of identification is befogged by ambiguities. No body was discovered in the course of skilful excavation, but slight chemical traces may indicate a human body, a funeral feast, or a set of chessmen. Assuming that there had never been a body laid alongside the treasure, the possibilities are either that this was simply a treasure deposit, like the barrow-treasure described in the poem *Beowulf*, or that we have here a cenotaph. The fact that the treasure was placed in a ship, under a barrow, in a cemetery of funerary barrows implies by analogy that this too was a funerary deposit, but one without a body. The absence of a corpse may be either because it had been lost in battle or because on the shadowy frontiers between pagan and Christian England a king might be buried in a churchyard while his treasure was deposited according to the rites of his pagan ancestors, in a ship-barrow. And here we uncover yet another layer of ambiguity: is the treasure that of a pagan or a Christian? Pagan elements are sufficiently clear in the great ceremonial whetstone, symbol of the god Thunor, and in the bronze stag, probably a symbol of Woden. No Christian significance need be inferred at Sutton Hoo itself from the cruciform pattern which occurs on a set of silver bowls of eastern origin. A stronger case can be made that two silver spoons inscribed ⌈ΑΥΛΟC and πΑΥΛΟC, Saul and Paul, bear such a clear reference to conversion that they must be regarded as baptismal presents to a convert from paganism. But the relatively crude lettering of the 'Saul' spoon has suggested that the inscription is no more than a bungled copy of that on the other spoon, and this takes much of the force out of the argument.

There is obviously a strong temptation to overlook these ambiguities in the interests of creating a coherent historical narrative, but in the present state of Sutton Hoo studies any such narrative is as likely to be fiction as fact. Leaving these aspects aside, we can still find in the Sutton Hoo treasure a most remarkable testimony to the material culture of an English royal court in the seventh century. Apart from its overall wealth and magnificence, the burial contains direct tokens of royalty, such as the whetstone, symbol of the king as giver of swords, and a wrought-iron standard which recalls the *thuuf* carried before the great king Edwin of Northumbria. That the contacts of the East Anglian court stretched as far as the Byzantine empire is demonstrated by a great silver dish, while a Mediterranean, and most probably eastern source is also likely for other pieces of Classical or Byzantine silver. The dominating tone of the treasure is martial and virile – even the great drinking-horns of aurochs horn were symbols of valour to the Germans. But the gentler aspects of courtly life are also represented, for instance by a board game and a richly ornamented lyre.

The metalwork ornamented in Germanic styles naturally claims most of our attention. Two main groups are present. The helmet and the shield have good, but by no means perfect, parallels in Sweden, and they hint at an oblique connection between the East Anglian dynasty and Sweden. The bulk of the garnet-ornamented jewelry, on the other hand, has features special to Sutton Hoo, and there can be no doubt at all that it was produced by a master-jeweller at the East Anglian court. It includes shoulder-clasps [Pl. 24a], buckles and strap-unions from military dress and sword harness; other sword-fittings; and the decorative fittings of a purse or sporran [Pl. 24b]. All these are ornamented in exquisite cloisonné garnet-work with patterns which include animals, both interlaced and semi-naturalistic, in Style II; stepped crosses; cable patterns; and various geometric designs. Among the Sutton Hoo specialities are the use of chequered millefiori glass; the setting of large areas of red garnet against equally large areas of gold to produce an effect akin to that of champlevé enamel work; and the arrangement of minor elements of design to produce a sophisticated overall organization.

Now the champlevé enamel which was imitated in cloisonné garnet-work at Sutton Hoo was Celtic, not Germanic, and the use of millefiori may also hint at Celtic influences. The three hanging bowls from the Sutton Hoo treasure show that fine Celtic metalwork was available at the royal court. Moreover, it passed through the hands of local – that is, Germanic or English – craftsmen, for when the great hanging bowl was damaged it was repaired with a silver plate ornamented with eagles' heads in Germanic Style II. In such a way knowledge of millefiori and of champlevé enamel came to English craftsmen. But the interchange of ideas went both ways. One of the Sutton Hoo hanging bowls bears an escutcheon ornamented not with trumpet-scrolls or Celtic birds' heads but with four long-jawed animals which are Germanic in inspiration. The rather cautious contacts between Celtic and Germanic art-styles and techniques which we see at Sutton Hoo anticipate the full and glorious fusion and cross-fertilization of Hiberno-Saxon art in the later seventh and eighth centuries. We next find interlaced animals, stepped crosses, and the overall organization of design along with trumpet-scrolls and hair-coil spirals in the pages of the Book of Durrow, a decorated gospel-book, which may have been written in Northumbria and illuminated there by an

Irishman or by an Englishman trained on Iona. Hiberno-Saxon art lies beyond the confines of this book, but Sutton Hoo brings us to its very threshold.

One other aspect of the burial has still to be examined: the ship itself. This was preserved only as an arrangement of heavily rusted iron clench-nails, and lines of staining in the sand which had filled the burial-pit. From this evidence the ship has been reconstructed as an open rowing boat, almost 90 ft long, 14 ft at its greatest beam, and driven by thirty-eight oarsmen. It will be recalled that the Nydam boat was also a rowing boat (above, p. 280), and the evidence from other boat-burials of the sixth and seventh centuries in England is also for rowing vessels unsuited for a mast. In sum, then, all the available archaeological evidence is for rowingboats, not sailing vessels, among the early English and their continental ancestors. Using the calculation that such boats might have travelled at three knots, and allowing for wind and tides in the North Sea, it has been argued that the English migrants must have journeyed down the European coast to make a short crossing, and then back up the English coast; that such journeys are likely to have taken weeks rather than days; and that there would have been much opportunity for cultural interchange at various havens down the coast of Germany and the Low Countries. It is indeed possible to think that when families and friends came to join established settlers their travels were as protracted as this. But it is inconceivable that the raiders of the fourth and early fifth centuries had voyaged in such a leisurely fashion, just as it is inconceivable that the idea of the sail, known in the Bay of Biscay before the Christian era, had not been diffused to the North Sea by the time of the migrations. Fortunately we are saved from the conclusion that the archaeological evidence has not given us the full range of Anglo-Saxon ships by the latest, authoritative reconstruction of the Sutton Hoo ship which shows it under sail before a following wind.

The evidence of settlements

We have seen that in the continental homelands of the English, evidence about material culture can be gathered from ritual deposits, from cemeteries, and from village settlements. Nothing comparable

with the great bog deposits is known in England. We have skimmed
the evidence from the cemeteries, so now we can turn to the settlements. But first a general observation is necessary. Since the English
settlement, there has been no major ethnic change in rural England,
nor, until the improvements of the eighteenth century was there any
significant change in farming techniques. Consistent with these two
conservative factors, the well-documented history of villages from late
Saxon England through Domesday Book into the Middle Ages
reveals a very stable settlement-pattern. If we project this back into
the period of the migrations, we should reasonably expect the villages
of the first English settlers to be occupying the same sites as those of
their descendants. If this were so, then they would of course be virtually unavailable for archaeological examination, buried if not actually
destroyed by later building down to the present day. This hypothesis
is not disproved by the evidence of hundreds of deserted medieval
villages standing now in the open countryside, for a majority of these
were the products of the short-lived maximum extension of arable
farming in the twelfth and thirteenth centuries. In so far as an English
village of the fifth and sixth centuries is now available for excavation
it is because it failed to become a permanent settlement, and this of
itself should warn us that it may not be typical.

The classic example of a pagan Saxon village is at Sutton Courtenay
in Berkshire, where in the 1920s and 1930s evidence of some thirty-five
sunken-floored dwellings was rescued from the greedy maw of gravel-
digging.[16] It has been fashionable to decry the Sutton Courtenay
excavation as incompetent, and to devalue the evidence it provided.
But it is becoming increasingly clear that we do not need to excuse the
director, Mr E. T. Leeds, on the grounds that he lacked all the organization for rescue excavations which is now so lavishly provided by
the State. No excuse is needed, for recent excavations have made it
abundantly clear that the sunken-floored dwellings discovered at Sutton
Courtenay represent a leading type – perhaps the leading type – of
pagan Saxon dwelling. In summary terms, Sutton Courtenay yielded
sub-rectangular pits, normally 10 to 13 ft long by 8 to 10 ft wide, sunk
through the top-soil and into the underlying well-drained gravel to a
depth of 1 ft 6 in. to 2 ft. A majority had axial post-holes, either one at
each end or one at each end plus a third close to one end. This pattern

is repeated at other sites such as Linford in Essex[17] [Fig. 25*d*], and any discussion of pagan Saxon buildings must therefore take the Sutton Courtenay type of plan as its starting point.

From the time of their discovery it was felt that these buildings were disgustingly mean and squalid – small in area, lacking in headroom, their interiors filled ankle-deep or worse with ashes, food refuse, and other human detritus. This impression has been reinforced by the recognition that among the ancestral English, farmers lived in large ground-level dwellings – even if they shared them with the cattle – to which sunken-floored buildings were subsidiary. It was therefore suggested that the Sutton Courtenay pits were really industrial, or that if they were inhabited then they were the dwellings of serfs or the very lowest class of free peasant. Furthermore it was postulated that they were peripheral to a village of ground-level structures which inadequate excavation had failed to reveal. It is indeed true that some of the pits were industrial: one was a clay-puddling hole, and a second may have been a potter's workshop; one certainly had a loom, and two others were possibly weaving sheds; two have elaborate ovens which are scarcely domestic. This, however, represents only 20 per cent of the total excavated.

We may next consider how squalid these buildings really were. It is frankly incredible that people moved around with a complete ox-skull or the rotting body of a dog lying in the middle of the floor. It is altogether more reasonable to suggest that the refuse had been shot into convenient pits after they had been abandoned as dwellings. The suggestion is reinforced by the rather nebulous evidence of stratification at Sutton Courtenay, pit XII, and at Linford, and is finally clinched by the discovery of fragments of one and the same pottery vessel in adjacent pits. Nor were the sunken-floored dwellings quite as inconveniently lowly as has been suggested. If the spoil dug from the pit was piled around the edge and revetted internally with the turf dug from the area, the headroom could be increased by up to two feet. Again, the inconvenience of a small floor area would be diminished because hearths are rare in the pits, and cooking was apparently done out of doors. Finally, now that we know a complete village of sunken-floored dwellings in north Germany, it appears less unlikely that this is what we have at Sutton Courtenay.

Other evidence, published only briefly as yet, suggests that some sunken-floored dwellings may have been both larger and architecturally more sophisticated than those at Sutton Courtenay. At West Stow in Suffolk, wooden floors and plank walls have been recorded.[18] Nor should we overlook their occurrence in towns like Canterbury and Dorchester-on-Thames, and even in the Saxon Shore fort at Portchester. But the problems posed by the dominance of ground-level structures in the ancestral homelands remain unresolved. No aisled long-house of pagan Saxon date has yet been uncovered in England. Maxey in Northamptonshire has produced both large and medium-sized rectangular timber buildings, associated with pottery which is predominantly middle-Saxon but which could begin in the sixth century.[19] Only from Linford in Essex has the plan of a pagan Saxon ground-level building been published [Fig. 25b]. The evidence for this was salvaged from the gravel-diggers' bucket and dragline under very unsatisfactory conditions. It was about 20 ft wide overall, and not less than 30 ft long. The side walls were marked by double rows of post-holes, about 2 ft 6 in. apart, with the outer holes being rather more massive than the inner ones. The separation is distinctly narrow for an aisle, and the possibility remains that the inner row of post-holes marks the wall-line, while the outer row held buttresses. Both these arrangements – aisled hall or buttressed wall – have good German parallels. The gable end was bowed, presumably supporting a hipped roof, and was broken by a double door 7 ft 6 in. wide. From the evidence of the ancestral homelands, buildings like this should have been the normal dwellings of pagan Saxon farmers, but in England Linford stands on its own against a host of sunken-floored houses.*

Whatever their architectural or social status the sunken-floored dwellings certainly provide very abundant evidence of pagan Saxon material culture at a domestic level. The pottery from them consists principally of baggy vessels with flat or rounded bases [Fig. 27g]. Decoration is rare compared with the cinerary urns from the cemeteries, but includes simple furrows in the Anglo-Frisian style on early

---

*Since this was written, the fuller publication of West Stow has revealed three sizeable ground-level buildings associated with sunken-floored huts: West, S.E., 'The Anglo-Saxon Village of West Stow: An Interim Report of the Excavations 1965-8', Med. Arch. 13, 1969, pp. 1-20.

pots and some stamped ornament on later ones. Sutton Courtenay has an interesting form of cooking pot derived from a bronze bowl which had two triangular lugs or ears projecting above the rim to take a handle [Fig. 27h]. The pottery version probably had a thong or rope for handle, but it was found that this tended to burn when the pot was suspended over a fire, so cups of clay had to be fashioned to protect it. Conical vessels with their walls perforated with many small holes may have served as braziers. Rings of baked clay are also very common, and their occurrence with pairs of post-holes which are not part of the roofing structure of a dwelling shows that they were loom-weights for a vertical loom.[20]

Objects of bone and antler include double-edged composite combs similar in every way to those from British and Irish sites [Fig. 31a], and single-edged ones which are more distinctly Germanic. Spindles for wool-spinning, and the whorls which gave them momentum were also fashioned from bone [Fig. 21h], and so were handles for the ubiquitous iron knives. Weapons were altogether rare, but tools and implements like awls, chisels, keys, and bucket-fittings were relatively common. The presence of iron slag at Sutton Courtenay shows that ore was being smelted on the site. Bronze objects, apart from stray Roman brooches and coins, are rare and simple, and published examples of jewelry are confined to a worn and broken silver-gilt equal-armed brooch from Sutton Courtenay and a gilt-bronze disk from a sunken-floored dwelling at Portchester. This would seem to present a picture of impoverishment. But it is scarcely to be expected that settlements should be littered with jewelry in a good condition. A more balanced picture is obtained when, as at Mucking in Essex, graves are found in the neighbourhood of a settlement, for in this case the graves include early jewelry [Pls. 17, 18a], of spectacular quality.[21]

One class of artifact is conspicuously missing from the pagan Saxon settlements, namely agricultural implements. Iron shears were in fact discovered in a house at Mucking; and may well belong to the pagan Saxon village rather than to its Romano-British precursor. They would certainly accord with the leading role of sheep among the bones of domestic animals from such villages, though even here the warning must be given that no systematic study of such bones has yet been published. We have already noticed the scarcity of plough-parts on

Irish settlements, but in the pagan Saxon villages this scarcity becomes absolute. Even this could be explained away as an extreme instance of a general trend were it not for the absence of hand-mills as well. The only querns found in sunken-floored dwellings appear to be worn fragments derived from earlier Romano-British occupation of the site. In fact the only direct evidence for the growing and consumption of cereal appears to be some impressions of grain, principally barley, on a few pagan Saxon pots. The overall impression left by the sunken-floored dwellings is that they mark communities of small-time sheep-rearers and weavers of homespun. This is so much at variance both with continental evidence and with our soundly-based model of the Late Saxon peasant economy that we are forced back to the hypothesis mentioned at the start of this section (above, p. 302) that the villages recovered by excavation are not typical.

Is there any other evidence which might serve to check this hypothesis, by revealing the locations of the earliest settlements? Two lines of approach have been tried, through place-names, and through the cemeteries. Without accepting the proposition that all cremation cemeteries must be early, we can at least determine, on the basis of pottery- and brooch-typology, those which are likely to begin in the fifth century, and which therefore imply a settlement of that date. Second, there is a group of place-names containing the element -*ingas*, meaning 'people of' or 'followers of', which have philologically early characteristics, and which seem to imply a primitive social structure appropriate to the migration phase.[22] But it has long been noticed that the distribution of -*ingas* names and of early cemeteries does not coincide in detail. Were the two randomly intermixed, we could believe that the cemeteries were on the edge of the settlements implied by the names. But this will not do, because the distribution is frequently one of mutually exclusive blocks. It is now thought likely that the -*ingas* names really belong to a mature rather than a primitive phase of settlement. On the other hand, the markedly riverine distribution of cremation cemeteries in central and western Wessex has led to the suggestion that bodies were brought by water to a few cemeteries, in which case the cemeteries are not necessarily a guide to the location of the settlements themselves.

We have already seen the possibility that those villages of the migration phase which really flourished now lie beneath Late-Saxon-medieval-modern villages. Could the same process have concealed their cemeteries if they were in the vicinity of the village? A pagan cemetery might be christianized on the conversion of the English. Like the enclosed cemeteries of the Celtic lands, it might then become a focus for Christian worship, ultimately provided with a church. So a pagan cemetery might evolve into a Christian churchyard. In such circumstances, repeated turning over of the ground for successive interments throughout fifteen hundred years would have destroyed most traces of the pagan burials. The occasional recognition of pagan remains within churchyards proves that the hypothetical sequence we have suggested did in fact occur, even if we cannot estimate its frequency. The basic proposition remains: given the continuity of farming practice and the stability of rural settlement, it is inevitable that those migration-period villages which took root and flourished are now most inaccessible to us.

The conversion of the English

In AD 582 Maurice became Emperor ... in the 14th year of this ruler, and about 150 years after the coming of the Angles to Britain, Pope Gregory, moved by divine inspiration, sent Augustine, the servant of God ... to preach the gospel to the English people.

Thus Bede introduces the mission of St Augustine, which landed in Kent in 597. Kent was presumably chosen in preference to the major Roman centre of London because of its strong links with Christian Gaul, symbolized by the marriage of King Æthelberht to the Christian Bertha. This no doubt facilitated the work of Augustine, so that a monastery was founded and churches were built in Canterbury itself and also at Rochester. Moreover, Æthelberht's position as overlord of much of southern England made expansion possible, so that before Augustine's death in about 604 he had consecrated a bishop for London and Essex, while Æthelberht himself induced Rædwald of East Anglia to accept Christianity. But outside Kent these early conversions were precarious. Rædwald had altars both to Christ and to pagan gods. Essex lapsed in 617, and then remained pagan for about another thirty years. Even in Kent Christianity was probably largely confined to the court. A second wave of evangelization began in 625 when Paulinus went from Canterbury to the Northumbrian court of Edwin, whose wife Æthelburh, daughter of Æthelberht of Kent, was already a Christian. The conversion of Edwin in 627 was followed by vigorous missionary work both in Northumbria and Lindsey, but all this was brought to a halt by Edwin's death at the hands of Cadwallon and the pagan Penda of Mercia. When the Christian Oswald consolidated his power in Northumbria, it was not to the Roman mission at Canterbury that he turned for a bishop but to the Celtic church of Iona.

This bald summary of the first two phases in the conversion of the English provides us with a framework within which wider topics can be discussed. It is noticeable for a start that in Bede's narrative British clerics and British churches play no part in the conversion, and that when Augustine met the British bishops he had to travel to the far west of England to do so. On the other hand, Bede's statement that until Oswald set up a wooden cross on the eve of his victory at Denises-burna 'no sign of the Christian faith, no church, no altar had been set up in the whole nation of the Bernicians' is frankly incredible. There is also good reason to believe that Bede has suppressed the British contribution to the conversion of Edwin. In Kent, he tells us that Queen Bertha, before Augustine's mission, was worshipping in St Martin's church which had been built by the Romans; and that Æthelberht after his conversion gave Augustine 'permission to build or restore churches', *ecclesias fabricandi vel restaurandi licentiam*. There may indeed be Roman work in the oldest fabric of St Martin's, Canterbury, but none has been recognized elsewhere. Once again we find ourselves confronted with the ambiguous character of the Romano-British church, and its nebulous contribution to later Christianity. As for the churches of the Augustinian mission, they were simple affairs, with short broad naves, stilted apsidal chancels, and projecting side chapels or *porticus* intended primarily for the burials of royalty and clergy [Fig. 8c, d]. For more pretentious architecture in England we have to look to the second half of the seventh century.[23]

It is certain that Christianity had little effect on the life and practices of the people for some generations. We have seen that Rædwald had both Christian and pagan altars, and Bede makes it clear that the sons of a Christian king might themselves be pagans. Inevitably the conversion was only slowly reflected in the cemeteries, which remain a major source of evidence throughout much of the seventh century. Even the Sutton Hoo ship-burial may be a memorial to the half-Christian King Rædwald or to one of his Christian – or pagan – successors. Quite certainly some of the finest Kentish jewels – especially the composite disk brooches with cloisonné garnets and lapis-lazuli, bosses of white inlay, and filigree animals in Style II – were made and buried in the generation after the conversion of Æthelberht. Gradually, however, simpler ornaments came to be placed in graves, especially annular brooches and silver rings. This in itself is symptomatic of the fact that early Anglo-Saxon craftsmanship in metal had passed its climax. More relevant to the spread of Christianity is the occasional occurrence of pendants in the form either of cloisonné garnet crosses, or of gold disks with simple cross designs in filigree. But these, and the increasing number of graves with east-west bodies and no grave-goods, take us to the middle of the seventh century and beyond the limits of this book.

One of the historical advantages of the conversion was that it brought literacy to the Anglo-Saxons, and this in turn means that we have topographical references which are lacking in the pre-literate period. The most spectacular result of this has been the identification of what Bede calls the royal court at Yeavering – *villam regiam quae vocatur Adgefrin* – where Paulinus catechized and baptized Edwin's Northumbrian subjects for thirty-six days. First located from the air in 1949, Yeavering was excavated over the period 1953–8.[24] The sketchy reports which have appeared since then indicate that the principal feature of the *villa regia* was an aisled hall, of elaborate timber construction, rather under 100 ft in length and about half as wide. Beside this were lesser halls and other rectangular buildings, of which one is claimed as a pagan temple later converted into a church. The most unexpected feature was a timber grandstand, resembling one segment of a Roman theatre, which had probably served as a folk-moot. The court had suffered destruction by fire on at least two occasions, and underwent various modifications both in its overall plan and in its structural details. It has been suggested that it was founded under Æthelfrith, destroyed by Cadwallon after his slaughter of Edwin in 632, rebuilt by Oswald and destroyed by Penda in 651, rebuilt again and finally abandoned in the 680s. There may indeed be archaeological evidence for this extended sequence, but it is difficult to reconcile it with Bede's plain statement that Adgefrin was deserted in the time of Edwin's successors – *haec villa tempore sequentium regum deserta.*

Although the royal court at Yeavering was a Germanic – specifically, an Anglian – foundation, it had certain romanizing and British features about it. The Roman ancestry of the timber moot has already been mentioned, and it can be added that the Roman foot appears to have been the measure used in setting out the buildings. The court was apparently preceded by a timber fort of British ancestry, while some of the structural techniques used in the earliest halls find parallels in a British hall excavated at Dunbar. That native influences should be strong in the Anglian court of Bernicia is not perhaps surprising when we recall the extreme scarcity of pagan cemeteries in the region. In the large area north of the Tees not more than ten possible pagan cemeteries have been discovered, plus a handful of stray burials. The conclusion is inescapable that in Bernicia a very small, and largely aristocratic, Anglian element ruled over a predominantly British population.

Relations between Britons and English

This is a convenient introduction to a brief discussion of the relations of the Anglo-Saxon settlers with the native romanized Britons, the *wealas* or Welsh as the English called them. The evidence of recognizable pagan cemeteries and isolated burials should make it possible for a start to assess the Anglo-Saxon settlement in numerical terms. It immediately becomes apparent that the sparseness of detectable Anglians in Bernicia merely represents the extreme instance of a general phenomenon. The total number of pagan Saxon pots now available for study is estimated at around 4000, and though this figure probably doubled between 1930 and 1970, and we may look for similar large increases in the future, none the less it is true that all the pots known in England could be matched in numbers by two or three cemeteries in the continental homelands. On another basis, it has been reckoned that between twenty- and twenty-five thousand burials belonging to the three pagan centuries have been found and recorded. This estimate can be adjusted and manipulated to suggest that in the sixth century the Anglo-Saxon element in the population of Britain amounted to no more than fifty to a hundred thousand. This can be set against an estimate for the rural population of the lowland zone of Roman Britain – roughly the same area as that with recognizable Anglo-Saxon burials – as at least a million. This was at the end of the second century, and there can be no doubt that the population had declined markedly by the start of the fifth century. But it would require at least a ten-fold decline to bring the British figure down to the most optimistic estimate for the English.

It seems reasonable to claim that throughout much of the fifth century the numerical advantage would have lain even more heavily with the Britons. This in turn must affect our acceptance of a model of the English settlement which involves the wholesale extermination or expulsion of the Welsh. Leaving aside the preaching of Gildas and the account of the fifth century which Bede derived from it, the model is based partly on the *Anglo-Saxon Chronicle* and partly on the more reliable sections of Bede. The fifth-century entries of the *Chronicle*, and to a lesser extent those of the sixth, are full of the flight or slaughter of the Britons. We may suspect a large element of – literally – poetic exaggeration here (above, p. 44), while still accepting a kernel of historical truth. But the most telling statement is in Bede's account of Æthelfrith of Northumbria (above, p. 121), who devastated the British people more than any other English king, and added more territory to English rule, 'having killed off or vanquished the natives.' But two comments are necessary here. Bede elaborated Gildas's theme that the English were a divinely appointed scourge for the sinful Britons, and in particular cast Æthelfrith in this role, so that there is an element of hagiography in the account of his ravaging of the Britons. Secondly, Cadwallon's dealings with Northumbria (above, p. 140) make it plain that, given the fortunes of war, the Britons were as competent at genocide as the English. All our sources concur that internecine raiding and warfare were endemic among both nations.

One criterion which has been much used to assess how far the Britons escaped extermination or expulsion is that of place-names. Recognizably Celtic names are chiefly those of natural features – hills, woods, and rivers. River-names have been studied in detail, and it has proved possible to divide Britain into four zones ranging from the east, where only large and medium-sized rivers have Celtic names, through intermediate zones where smaller river- and even stream-names are Celtic, to the west where of course the British language was not displaced.[25] It has been supposed that these zones correspond with advancing waves of colonization from the fifth to the eighth century. But this is too simple a model of the settlement, and it is interesting to notice the cluster of Celtic names in an area of very early colonization in the middle and upper Thames.

When we turn from the names of natural features to those of towns and villages, we find that Celtic-derived names are very rare except for a small number of towns which have Roman origins. This has been held to prove that the villages of the Romano-Britons did not survive, even under new proprietors. But the far from unique case of Rochester (above, p. 194) has already warned us that a British name may become unrecognizable on English lips, unless we have a written version of it prior to the migrations. Since we do not know the names of most of the smaller Romano-British settlements, we have no hope of detecting cases where a transmogrified British name underlies the earliest recorded English version, itself some centuries later than the migration period. More helpful are those place-names which contain an Old English element meaning 'Briton' or 'Welshman', which demonstrate the existence of villages distinguished by their native population.[26] Unfortunately the identification of such names is not without difficulties, and a modern Walton may originally have been the *tun*, 'farmstead or village' by the forest – *weald*; with a wall – *weall*; or belonging to the British – *weala*. But the Old English word *wealh* (plural *weala*), is also significant for the social status of the Britons, for it came to mean 'serf' as well as 'Welshman'. In both senses it would seem appropriate to the Britons whom Æthelfrith subjugated. Yet this was not the only social position which a Briton might occupy. In the late seventh century the laws promulgated by King Ine of Wessex make it clear that Welshmen might be substantial landowners, at some legal disadvantage compared with Englishmen, but still far from servile in their status. In other words, when the laws of Ine were drawn up, Britons formed a definite and often substantial element in society. This may, of course, reflect their position in the newly conquered land of eastern Dumnonia rather than in the long-settled areas of mid Wessex.

It is unlikely, however, that these Welsh landowners represented a seventh-century reflux into Wessex, and altogether more probable that they were the direct descendants of the British peasant proprietors, yeomen farmers and even larger landowners of the time of the migrations. If this is so, then we are forced to think of the English colonists holding land and tilling the soil alongside the native Britons, with one nation numerically predominant in one area, the other predominant elsewhere. The small size of some pagan cemeteries hints at English communities which were no more than hamlets, perhaps even single farmsteads.[27] At this point we must reaffirm from the English point of view what has already been stated from the British (above, p. 193). Much forest clearance took place in later Saxon England, especially in the form of expanding the arable fields of established villages. But the first immigrants were emphatically not colonizing virgin forest. They were not even, like the colonists of New England and the Middle Atlantic states, bringing an advanced farming technology into an area only sparsely cultivated. It is even doubtful whether they had to clear much scrub or secondary forest from lands abandoned by the Britons. The point can perhaps never be proved, but it seems most probable that the English immigrants, used to a farming system comparable with that of the natives, fitted into the gaps in the fifth-century countryside, whether those gaps resulted from the late Roman decline in population or from the local expulsion or extermination of the Britons.

Eleven

Economy, Society and Warfare

The economy of the Britons and their enemies

The preceding chapters have dealt with the varied material cultures of the Britons and of their enemies, both Celtic and Germanic. One cultural trait was shared by all these essentially barbarian peoples: the pursuit of warfare as a major activity of society. This was as true of the Britons of the sixth century AD as of the Anglo-Saxons or the *Scotti*. In this, of course, there was a great contrast with Romano-British society, which even in the fourth century was largely organized for peaceful pursuits. It cannot be disputed that war was a central element in the Arthurian situation, and no account of Arthur's Britain could be considered complete without an analysis of the character of warfare in the period. As a preliminary to that analysis, the structure of the society and economy from which it drew its strength must be lightly sketched.

The basic economy of the various peoples active in Britain in our period was the same: mixed farming, supplemented with cottage industries and a little trade, but lacking currency. Some of the material evidence for this has already been mentioned in connection with the descriptions of both British (above, pp. 231-3) and Anglo-Saxon (above, pp. 304-6) sites. So far as the Britons are concerned, the evidence has been most fully worked out in Wales, where both verbal and material evidence have been used to revolutionize our picture of early Welsh – and by implication early British – economy and the social structure erected upon it.[1] The former view was that the early Welsh had been meat-eating, bread-scorning cow-herds, who roamed the Cambrian mountains without settled abodes or any fixed pattern of land-holding – in a phrase, 'footloose Celtic cowboys'.* This view

*The phrase is from Piggott, S., 'Native Economies', in Richmond, I. A. (ed.), *Roman and Native in North Britain*, Edinburgh, 1958, p. 25.

was maintained firstly by a biased selection from the observations made by early medieval writers, and secondly by ignoring the limitations of archaeological evidence for arable farming, and arguing then from the negative evidence. It is now certain that the Britons of our period were grinding corn, and it seems possible that at Pant-y-saer and at Gwithian we even have the fields in which they grew it. In this case archaeology can only supplement the clear proof provided by the Welsh Laws for the importance of both grain and bread in the economy. The importance of animal husbandry, and especially the raising of cattle, is equally undeniable, and it is now clear that we must think in terms of unspeccialized mixed farming.

A similar statement can now be made about the *Scotti*, on the basis both of archaeological finds from raths and crannogs, and of the actual siting of the raths themselves.[2] Where this has been studied in relation to the distribution of different qualities of soil, it appears that the rathbuilders favoured the best farming land. Since this must have put the raths at risk from latter-day agricultural activities, their survival in tens of thousands appears all the more remarkable. In excavated raths the best proof of arable farming is provided by occasional ploughshares or coulters of iron [Fig. 21a, b], which imply the use of a heavy plough. Such shares and coulters are indeed rare, and so are sickles which might have been used for reaping corn or cutting hay. But it has already been pointed out (above, p. 145) that broken objects of iron can be reforged so easily that no argument can be based on their scarcity. On the other hand the abundance of hand-mills makes it certain that corn was being ground, and occasionally the kilns in which it was dried have also been excavated. Alongside the evidence for cereal-growing must be set the enormous amounts of quantity bones recovered from both crannogs and raths. Clearly the raising of cattle, pigs and sheep (in that order of frequency) was a major activity of the farmer. But it is not possible, either in Britain or Ireland, to estimate the relative importance of arable and pasture.

When we turn to the Anglo-Saxons we find that no systematic analysis of their economy in the settlement period has yet been worked out. This is partly because so few domestic sites are known and because, as we have seen (above, p. 306), it is permissible to doubt whether an excavated village like Sutton Courtenay is truly representative.[3] The archaeological evidence for small-time sheep-rearers and weavers of homespun is impossible to reconcile with continental evidence for prosperous mixed farming among the ancestral English. At the same time it is impossible to doubt that the large-scale exploitation of the arable potential of lowland England, which was fully established by the eleventh century, had its beginnings in the seventh, sixth and fifth centuries, if not actually in Roman Britain. Certainly the literary evidence from Late Saxon England is in favour once again of mixed farming.

All these communities of farmers, British, Irish and English, supported craftsmen at two levels. The higher of these was represented by the jeweller and the armourer, the maker of fine swords and rare helmets. Such craftsmen are not likely to have been found at village level, or in the humbler raths. The literary evidence suggests that they were peripatetic, seeking the patronage of chiefs and princes. Indeed, the Welsh tale *Culhwch and Olwen* ranks 'a craftsman bearing his craft' along with the 'son of a rightful prince' in terms of the welcome he might expect at a royal court. Apart from lay patrons, of course, the bronze- or gold-smith might seek employment in a monastery, to make vessels for the service of the church as well as ornamented book-covers, reliquaries and other religious objects. Consistent with this, the sites which produce copious evidence for the manufacture of fine metalwork – crucibles, moulds, scrap bronze and glass, 'sketch-pads' and so on – are either monasteries like Nendrum, royal sites like Lagore or Garranes, or forts like Garryduff I, Mote of Mark and Dinas Powys where the total evidence argues for a high social status.

The lower level of craftsmanship is represented by cottage or village industries. It is reasonable to believe that these included the production of iron tools and implements for farming and other crafts, but no smithies have been found by excavation. The principal evidence is in fact for textile production. Both British and Irish sites have yielded highly polished stones which may have served as linen-smoothers. Whorls for spinning wool are common and bone and iron spindles also occur occasionally [Fig. 21h]. Anglo-Saxon villages, and even isolated houses like that at Bourton-on-the-Water [Fig. 25e], have produced evidence for upright looms in the form of clay loom-weights which are sometimes associated with the post-holes of the loom itself.

Iron awls [Fig. 21*f*] and heavy needles suggest that leather goods – vessels, clothes and shoes – were also made domestically. Potting was no doubt another home industry in those areas – Ulster, Cornwall and pagan England – where native as opposed to imported pottery was in use. It may however be questioned whether the more elaborate Anglo-Saxon cinerary urns were made in the home, rather than by specialized potters. Certainly in East Anglia in the later sixth century pots bearing similar designs and even identical stamped ornament were buried in several cemeteries [Fig. 27*f*]. The implication is that these vessels had all been made by the same potter, who was working not to meet immediate local needs but to sell to a market.

This is virtually the only evidence that we have for internal trade in our period, and it is important to determine its scale. About 90 per cent of the vessels made by the so-called 'Illington/Lackford' potter are found within a radius of eight miles – a day's walk to market and back. Within the framework of the farming economy this was probably the limit of trade, or indeed of movement at all, except for certain necessities with a naturally limited distribution like salt and iron. When we move from the level of the village and farm to that of court and monastery the range of trade widens at once. The raw materials required for fine jewelry are of restricted occurrence in nature – tin and gold extremely so, copper and silver (derived from lead) less restricted. So the very fact that these materials were used implies a trade in metals, and suggests also the existence of specialized communities engaged in extracting and refining the ores. But this last suggestion should not be given too much weight, for the Dinas Powys evidence demonstrates that some jewelry was made by melting down the trinkets of other peoples or earlier times. A trade in scrap metal remains indisputable of course, but a trade in finished products cannot be proved incontrovertibly. Even when closely similar jewels are found in different cemeteries, we may be dealing with the movement of people – craftsmen, brides, hostages, or even whole nations – rather than with commercial activity.

External trade, by contrast, ranged over quite surprising distances. In western Britain and Ireland this is best reflected by the imported pottery, of which Class D comes probably from western Gaul, Class A has its best parallels in Greece and farther east, while the only known kilns producing Class B are by the Black Sea [Map 5]. The millefiori glass used for ornamenting brooches and religious objects found at princely sites like Dinas Powys and Garranes probably originated in Alexandria. The extent of external trade among the Anglo-Saxons is no less remarkable. Even if we make an exception of the Byzantine silverware from the Sutton Hoo ship-burial, the range of imports extends to Africa and Asia for bronze bowls, ivory, lapis-lazuli and above all garnets. But however impressive these imports are in geographical terms, their real economic significance is far more questionable. We have already seen that the commerce between the Celtic West on the one hand and Gaul and the Mediterranean on the other was at best sporadic (above, p. 206). We have also surmised that the church played a large part in its organization, but we can scarcely even speculate about how the Anglo-Saxons arranged to import quantities of garnet or lapis. In the case of the less common exotic objects, it is probable that they came as bribes, loot, dowries, diplomatic gifts, or in other ways which had no commercial aspect.

It should be remembered here that trade, whether internal or external, was hampered by the lack of conventional means of exchange. From the mid-fourth to the late seventh century the economy of these islands was a natural one, and the use of currency was unknown. This at least is the archaeological evidence, for it is impossible to imagine that the Sutton Hoo coins had ever circulated in this country, and no others have been found. Commerce was therefore a matter of barter and personal negotiation – perhaps a dozen eggs for one of the Illington-Lackford potter's urns, or a cow with calf for the Pant-y-Saer silver penannular brooch. There is indeed a little evidence from Wales that cattle provided a standard of value. But the archaeological and numismatic evidence may not be the whole story here. In the very first English law code, the Laws of Æthelberht of Kent, promulgated early in the seventh century, the penalties are regularly quoted in shillings or in *sceattas*, the *sceat* being one twentieth of a shilling. Moreover, the very lukewarm account of trade given in the preceding paragraphs needs to be read in the light of Bede's description of seventh-century London as a 'market for many peoples coming thither by land and sea', *ipsa multorum emporium populorum terra marique venientium.*

Heroic society[4]

Among all the peoples of Arthur's Britain, the basic economy of mixed farming and cottage industry supported a social pyramid of which the apex was a warrior king. Wherever the evidence is available, the institution of kingship is seen to have deep ancestral roots. The pre-Roman Britons had certainly been ruled by kings – or occasionally queens – and though the institution was rapidly suppressed after the Roman Conquest, it is likely that a folk-memory of it persisted to inspire political developments in the fifth and later centuries. Classical writers, especially Caesar and Tacitus, make it clear that one function of British kings and queens was to lead their people on the battlefield. Tacitus is also our chief witness for political arrangements among the early Germans.[5] His epigrammatic style tends to obscure rather than elucidate the complexities of the institution, but it seems that the Germans of the first century AD recognized both kings chosen from a royal stock and war-leaders chosen for their valour and military skill. It seems probable that under the stress of folk-movement and land-seizure these two aspects of leadership coalesced. For the prehistoric Irish and Picts there is no comparable evidence, but kingship was certainly well developed among them when they appear on the historical scene. One curious exception to these generalizations must be noted among the Old- or continental Saxons, who even in Bede's day had no king, only a number of co-equal rulers from whom a temporary leader was chosen in time of war.

It may be that this last arrangement lies behind the title of *ealdorman* which the *Anglo-Saxon Chronicle* bestows on the two Saxon leaders Cerdic and Cynric. In other words, among their own people they may well have been co-rulers before they ventured forth to found the dynasty of Wessex. Only of these two is the term *ealdorman*, or any other constitutional expression used, and we are in fact generally ignorant of the personal status of the men who established dynasties in England. It is true that they normally trace their descent from the god Woden, and this may imply that they were members of various divinely recognized royal families, but it is also possible that the genealogies are post-conquest fabrications designed to put the seal of divinity on *de facto* rulers. In the west, however, Eochaid mac Artchorp of the Dési was of royal stock, for two of his brothers ruled in succession in Ireland. Eochaid was probably a cadet of the family, who went adventuring with his personal following and gained a kingdom in Dyfed through the invitation of the Romans. For the original status of men like Cunedda we have no early evidence, but we need not doubt that north of the Antonine Wall, and perhaps even south to Hadrian's Wall, the prehistoric roots of kingship had been strengthened by Roman cultivation.

But we cannot invoke such ancestral kingship to explain the emergence of British kings in the former civil zone of Roman Britain. Whatever construction we place on the events of AD 407–10 (above, pp. 98–9) we have still to explain the emergence of the *superbus tyrannus* of Gildas out of the framework of Roman civil administration. Our only clue to the constitutional processes involved is the word *tyrannus* itself. At its simplest it means merely 'ruler', then by extension, 'one who rules despotically'. This scarcely seems appropriate to the *superbus tyrannus*, who shared the decision to invite in the Anglo-Saxon with a council: *tum omnes consiliarii una cum superbo tyranno caecantur*, 'all the assessors together with the chief ruler were blinded', as Gildas puts it. The most likely meaning is in fact 'usurper', for the word is used in this sense by Greek writers of the fourth and fifth centuries AD, and Gildas himself uses it of Magnus Maximus. The probability is, then, that the *superbus tyrannus* of the mid-fifth century was following in the tradition of Maximus in the late fourth and of Marcus, Gratian and Constantine III in 406–7. If, as we have suggested (above, p. 103), Vortigern is someone other than the *superbus tyrannus*, he is none the less in the same constitutional position. Finally, the kings of Gildas's own day were *tyranni* in his eyes (above, p. 121), either because they were the creation of usurpers like Maximus and Vortigern, or because they had seized by force their small territories.

The adjective *superbus* may indicate that among the Britons, as was certainly the case among the English and the Irish, kingship was not the simple and absolute institution which it became in the Middle Ages. The *superbus tyrannus* was perhaps the 'high king' or 'supreme ruler', with the implication that there were also lesser kings. We have already seen that the dynasty of Gwynedd claimed a special position among British kings (above, pp. 136–7) and it may well be that when

Cadwaladr is said to be *regnante apud Brittones*, 'ruling among the Britons', or when his grandfather Cadfan is described as *opinatis[s]imus omnium regum*, 'most renowned of all kings' [Pl. 27*b*], they are being accorded the same kind of supremacy as the *superbus tyrannus* had enjoyed nearly two centuries earlier. On the other hand the rulers of Rheged or Strathclyde can scarcely be described as sub-kings. For men in that position we must look to the three British *cyninges*, Conmail, Condidan and Farinmail, slain at the battle of Dyrham in 577. It may be no more than a coincidence that their deaths led to the English capture of the three towns of Cirencester, Gloucester and Bath. But it is worth recalling that it was to the towns that Honorius remitted the responsibility for defence in 410, and that the archaeological evidence suggests the presence in the towns of military forces which might serve as the instruments for local seizures of power. The men in the best position to profit by this were the magistrates. A sixth-century inscription from Penmachno shows that the office was still in existence then [Pl. 28], and leaves the thought that the three men who appeared as *cyninges* to the Saxons might have been *magistratus* to their fellow Britons.

Whatever the case among the Britons, it is clear that the English used the term *cyning* to describe more than one grade in a constitutional hierarchy. When in 626 Edwin of Northumbria undertook an expedition against Wessex in retaliation for an attempt to assassinate him, he slew five 'kings' as well as many of the people. But Cwichelm, the king responsible for the assassination attempt, survived to be baptized in 636. It seems likely therefore that Edwin's victims were mere under-kings, the kind of men who are described as *sub-regulus* in Latin documents of the seventh century. Above them in the hierarchy come the rulers of the individual English kingdoms. They in turn frequently share their rule with a son or other member of the royal stock. Finally, at the head of the system stand those rare kings on whom, in the entry for 829, the *Anglo-Saxon Chronicle* bestowed the title *Bretwalda*, 'ruler of Britain'. The *Chronicle* list of these supreme rulers is based on Bede's account of the kings who had held *imperium* over the English. The first four of these – Ælle of Sussex, Ceawlin of Wessex, Æthelberht of Kent and Rædwald of East Anglia – exercised sway south of the Humber only, but they were then followed by three

Northumbrian rulers, Edwin, Oswald and Oswiu, who claimed supremacy over all the inhabitants of Britain, both Britons and English, excluding Kent. It will be recalled that Edwin's assertion of this suzerainty provoked the hostility of both Penda of Mercia and Cadwallon of Gwynedd, while Cadwallon's challenge to Northumbria was ultimately fatal to himself.

This reminds us that the claim to *imperium* was both asserted and denied by military might, and we must therefore examine the military role of kingship. But before we do, it is pertinent to ask how the institution and its activities, whether civil or military, were paid for. To a limited extent, of course, warfare was financed out of loot. The Laws of Hywel Dda show that a British king took a third share of spoil, and they set out elaborate arrangements for its division. To give a concrete example:

If a king's body-guard takes spoil, the chief of the body-guard receives the share of two men, and any animal which he shall choose from the third of the king.

But loot must always have been a precarious source of income, and it is clear that the main support of the king was an elaborate system of tributes, food-rents, and obligatory service. Again, it is worth quoting the Welsh Laws:

From the bondmen the king is to have packhorses in his hosting, and from every bond township he has a man and a horse with axes for constructing his strongholds, and they are to be at the king's expense.

Although such arrangements for the exaction of military service are most fully set out in the Welsh Laws they were obviously not confined to the Britons. A Dalriadan document, though obscure in general, makes it clear that among the *Scotti* households were organized into hosts or musters three hundred or seven hundred strong, with sea musters of 'twice seven benches to each twenty houses'.[6] Likewise when Bede, describing Edwin's conquest of Anglesey and Man, describes these islands in terms of 960 and more than 300 households respectively, he is referring to an assessment for the purpose of levying tribute.

The Laws of Hywel also list in great detail the food-gifts owed to the king by both bondmen and free, even to the extent of prescribing 'each loaf as broad as from the elbow to the wrist', or 'a tub of butter three hand-breadths across and three in depth', or 'a sow three fingers thick in her hams'. It is declared: 'The township is to bring all these [and many other items] to the king and to light a fire three days and three nights for him.' What is not clear here is whether the king and his court had come to the township in the first instance – in other words whether the court was static or peripatetic, that is to say moving from township to township eating up the food-rents of each in turn. This was certainly the later medieval pattern among both kings and nobles. Apart from winter and spring food-gifts, four were due in summer, and this may mean that the court visited each township six times during the year. It is at least certain that the bodyguard and some of the court officials were entitled to 'a circuit' or to be billeted on the bondmen, while others received specified food when travelling on the king's business. In early English society the *villae regiae* or *regales*, 'royal townships', probably functioned as centres for a peripatetic court to which tribute in kind would be brought. Bede mentions three in Edwin's reign alone, by the river Derwent, at Yeavering, and at *Campodonum* near Dewsbury.

Returning now to the military role of kingship, we find that it was customary, though not invariable, that the king should lead the muster or hostings whether it was to another kingdom or in defence of his own. As the Laws of Hywel Dda state:

Once every year the king is to have a hosting along with him from his country to a border country; always however when it may be necessary a host is to attend him in his own country.

And in the early years of the *Anglo-Saxon Chronicle* the most frequent class of entry runs: 'In this year Hengest and Æsc – or Ælle, or Cerdic and Cynric, or Ceawlin and Cutha – fought against the Britons.' We can be sure that this is not just an elliptical expression for 'the hosts of Hengist or Ælle or whoever' because of the frequency with which the kings of the period met their death on the battlefield. On the other hand, the account of the battle of *Degsastan* given in the northern recension of the *Chronicle* suggests that even when a ruler is mentioned in relation to a specific campaign or battle, he may not have taken part personally. The opening sentence for the year 603 is 'Aedan, king of the Scots, fought along with the people of Dal Riada against Æthelfrith, king of the Northumbrians . . .' But it seems certain that Æthelfrith was not himself involved in the battle, for the entry concludes 'Hering, son of Hussa, led the army.' Hering was of the royal stock, for his father is mentioned in the 'Northern British History' and appears as Æthelfrith's predecessor in the Northumbrian king-list. Moreover, Æthelfrith's brother Theodbald was killed with all his own force at the battle, so the royal family was well represented. If we find the absence of the king himself surprising, we should recall that the most renowned of British battles, the defeat of the men of Gododdin at *Catraeth*, was also fought without the personal leadership of the king who had instigated it, Mynyddog Mwynfawr of *Din Eidyn*, Edinburgh.

Some of the warriors celebrated in the Gododdin's elegiac stanzas were certainly of royal descent, and the terse *Chronicle* account of *Degsastan* demonstrates the military function of the royal family even more clearly. In the Laws of Hywel, 'the chief of the bodyguard is to be a son of the king or his nephew'. The bodyguard or personal warband, *comitatus*, attendants, in Latin, *heorð-geneatas*, hearth-companions in English and *teulu*, family, in Welsh, represents the layer immediately below the royal stock in a highly stratified society. It seems likely that among the Britons and their various enemies there was an aristocracy both of birth and of service to the king. The rates of *wergild*, blood-price (below, p. 326), laid down in the early English laws reveal that there were grades even within the aristocracy, and show us too that some but not all of the nobility were great landowners. These are the men whom we expect to find buried with sword, shield and spear and jewelled belt-fittings [Fig. 26a], while their wives have elaborate jewel suites, and symbols of matronhood like chatelaines and weaving-swords or beaters. In the north and west they are presumably the builders of small fortified homesteads, especially the raths of Ireland and some of the duns of western Scotland.

Beneath the nobility were various classes of freemen. Perhaps the clearest group is that of men who had some craft, skill or mystery, the *aes dána*, men of art, of Irish society. One of the triads of the Welsh Laws is significant here, because it both sets limits within the hierarchy and hints at the possibility of social advancement:

Three arts which a bondman cannot teach his son without the consent of his lord: clerkship and smithcraft and bardism; for if the lord be passive until the clerk be tonsured or the smith enter his smithy or a bard graduate, he can never enslave them after that.

Apart from these specialists, who must always have been few, it would be reasonable to expect that the largest class of freemen would have been that of yeoman farmers or peasant proprietors. But it is not easy to detect such men in Celtic society, where there is no evidence for common soldiery who were free but not noble. Among the Anglo-Saxons, this class is represented by the *ceorl*, no mean person as his *wergild* shows. Among the pagan graves the *ceorl* is presumably represented by a large class of burials which are accompanied only by an iron spear, or possibly a spear and simple shield. If this correlation is correct, then the *ceorl* was a warrior as well as a farmer. A clause in a late seventh-century Wessex law does indeed assign military duties to the *ceorl*, but this is difficult to reconcile with a story told by Bede in which a Northumbrian king's thegn, *minister regis*, escapes death on the battlefield by pretending to be *rusticus*, not *miles*, a yokel, not a warrior.

Just as British society seems to lack anyone corresponding to the *ceorl* in his military capacity, so too there appears to be no class of free farmers, and the British equivalent of the *ceorl* as tiller of the soil was in fact a bondman. The Welsh Laws give no systematic account of this class, but none the less they make it clear that the bondman, or settlement of bondmen, owed considerable services and food-gifts to the king as well as lodging the bodyguard and court officials. We have seen that the bondman could not learn a craft without his lord's permission, and he was in effect bound to his fields. A detailed study of bond townships in Gwynedd has shown that in compensation they occupied the best farming land. All the available evidence suggests that the tilling of the soil by nucleated settlements of bondmen was the main basis of the British economy and the real source of the king's wealth. Below the bondmen in the hierarchy were the slaves, probably not a large class in British society, but all too numerous among the Anglo-Saxons even after the conversion. Capture in war and failure to meet legal obligations were among the causes which could reduce even a king's thegn to slavery, and Bede makes it clear that the slave-trade was one aspect of commerce between England and the Continent.

One other social group, the religious, should be mentioned briefly. Whatever ritual functions the king performed in pagan society, whether Celtic or Germanic, there was certainly also a priesthood. Bede tells how Coifi, chief of the Northumbrian priests, violated his own temple at the time of the conversion, and simultaneously broke the taboos which forbade a priest to carry arms or to ride a stallion. After the conversion, it was necessary to fit the church into the framework of society. Both the English and Welsh Laws show how this was done without disturbing too much a pre-Christian system in which violence or sexual irregularity were not sins but offences demanding compensation. It was also necessary to provide for the church in the physical sense by grants of land and other endowments. Presumably it was by royal gift that a number of forts were converted into monastic enclosures: Reculver and Burgh Castle [Pl. 1a] in England, Caer Gybi in Wales, Nendrum in Ireland, are all instances of this. The church made repayment by praying for the king and his army. When Æthelfrith found the monks of Bangor-on-Dee praying for the Britons at the battle of Chester, he ordered that they should be slain first, on the grounds that 'although they do not bear arms they fight against us with their hostile prayers.'

It was not in fact the sanctions of the church which held together or controlled the barbarian societies of Arthur's Britain. The major controlling element was the duty of the kindred, on the one hand to protect and if necessary to avenge its members, on the other hand to make compensation to other kin-groups on behalf of its own delinquents. In primitive conditions the responsibility of the kin was given teeth by the blood-feud, which could be incurred even by slaying a man on the battlefield. In our period, the self-perpetuating feud was being replaced by a system of blood-payments such as *wergild* and *manbot* in English, *galanas* and *sarhad* in Welsh. Traces of the blood-feud linger in Bede, but the weight of the church's influence was obviously in favour of non-violent compensation for offences. Bede relates with great approval how, after Ælfwine, the younger brother of the Northumbrian king Ecgfrith, had been killed in battle with the Mercians, Archbishop Theodore arranged that no more human lives were given for the dead man, but that a money compensation was accepted instead; as a result, there was then a long period of peace between the two kingdoms.

The various nations of Arthur's Britain were barbarian in the technical sense that they lacked urban civilization. Their societies were also heroic in the technical sense that martial valour was the principal virtue of the leading social class, and that society, economy and both spiritual and material culture were all directed towards the maintenance of warfare as a major activity. But the warrior noble was distinguished by other characteristics as well as by valour. The king's thegn who tried to pass himself off as a yokel was ultimately betrayed 'by his countenance, his deportment and his conversation', *ex vultu et habitu et sermonibus eius.* The warriors of Gododdin, however fierce in battle, were liberal in gifts, civil to suppliants, gentle, even bashful, in the presence of maidens. If we were to seek the spirit of the age, we need not look further than the elegy of Gorthyn son of Urfai: 'a hundred men bore away his harsh warning from battle yet he provided song at the New Year Feast.'

Weapons, tactics and strategy

We turn now to the technical aspects of warfare in Arthur's Britain. Our sources of information are many, and of very varied worth. First of course we have the actual weapons and armour, which are abundant in pagan Saxon graves. Then from the late seventh century on we have pictures of warriors and occasionally battle scenes drawn in illuminated manuscripts or carved on stones or even on a whale-ivory casket. The value of these pictures is in fact highly suspect, for some are certainly based on Mediterranean book illustrations, and depict Roman or Byzantine methods of warfare. The verbal evidence includes battle poetry, at once stylized and elegiac; terse but often factual statements in annals and chronicles; and longer accounts from the pens of well-informed but cloistered writers like Bede. Field monuments, both forts and dykes, provide certain clues for the archaeologist. All these forms of evidence have to be examined in the light of a general interpretation of politico-military developments among the barbarian peoples in the post-Roman centuries. In turn they help to create and modify that general interpretation.

It is simplest to begin with the individual warrior and his equipment. The principal weapons of the period were the spear, the sword and

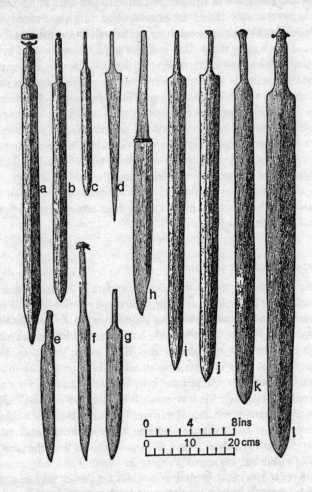

28. Anglo-Saxon and Irish swords: *a, b, c* Irish double-edged swords, Lagore crannog, Co. Meath; *d, g* single-edged swords, Lagore; *e seax*, Burwell, Cambridgeshire, grave 47; *f seax*, Shudy Camps, Cambridgeshire, grave 36 (see Fig. 26*b*); *h seax*, Northolt, Middlesex; *i, j* Saxon double-edged swords, Abingdon, Berkshire, graves 49 and 42; *k, l* Saxon swords, Croydon, Surrey.[7]

the shield, which are only rarely supplemented by the axe. In pagan Saxon graves swords are relatively uncommon and when they occur they are normally accompanied by other weapons and military gear, in short, by a rich grave assemblage. It is reasonable to conclude from this that the sword was confined to the nobility. This is very likely if we accept the calculation that, in terms of modern values, there was at least £100 worth of workmanship in a sword. The Saxon sword had a long, parallel-sided blade and sharply tapering point, no true hilt guard and only a light pommel.[8] Its length overall, around 3 ft, relates it to the long iron sword of the pre-Roman Celts. This had been wielded both by them and by Roman auxiliary troops as a cavalry weapon, but among the English the longsword was used entirely for fighting on foot. The Britons also used swords, but we have no evidence of their form. In *Y Gododdin* references to sword-strokes or blades are less frequent than those to spears, suggesting that for the British forces, as for the Saxon, the sword was not the common weapon. In Ireland again we find parallel-sided sword blades, but they are markedly smaller than the Saxon examples, ranging from about 14 in. to not more than 26 in. at the largest.[9]

Single-edged swords or military knives are also found in Saxon graves and Irish crannogs, and a passing reference in *Y Gododdin* suggests that the Britons used them too. *Seax*, the word for knife, is considered to have given the Saxons their tribal name, but despite this, knives suitable for battle are not often found in the graves. In the Arthurian period war-knives had a narrow blade from about 12 to 20 in. long, and it was only after AD 600 that the blade became first broader and then longer as well. The Irish examples have either long tapered blades or parallel-sided ones in a comparable range of sizes. Occasionally both the longsword and the knife are found in graves in positions showing that they were slung at the hip [Fig. 26].

The spear was by far the commonest weapon among the barbarians – indeed, a single spear is the minimum equipment of a warrior-grave. We are really dealing here with three separate weapons, which cannot always be distinguished one from another on the basis of the metal parts which the archaeologist finds. The javelin is for throwing, and it is sometimes thought that small spear-heads, around six inches long or less, are from javelins. They are found occasionally among both the

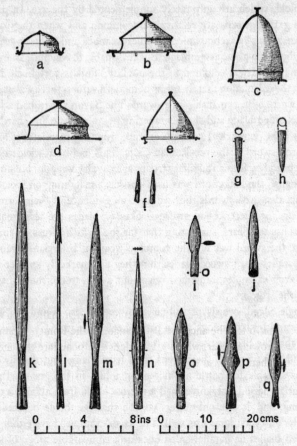

29. Anglo-Saxon, British and Irish weapons: *a* Irish shield-boss, Lagore;
b, *d* Saxon shield-bosses, Petersfinger, graves 20 (see Fig. 26*a*) and 7;
c Saxon 'sugar-loaf' boss, Lowbury Hill, Berkshire; *e* Saxon boss, Alton,
Hampshire; *f* arrow-heads, Buston crannog, Ayrshire; *g, m* Saxon spear-
head and ferrule, Petersfinger, grave 20; *h* Irish spear-ferrule, Lagore;
i Irish spear-head, Garryduff, Co. Cork; *j* British, Irish or Pictish spear-head,
Dunadd, Argyll; *k* Saxon spear-head, Snell's Corner, Hampshire, grave
S 14; *l* angon, Abingdon, Berkshire, grave 69; *n* Irish ribbed spear-head,
Ballinderry crannog no. 2, Co. Offaly; *o* British spear-head, Buston; *p, q*
Saxon spear-heads, Petersfinger, graves 27 and 6.[10]

English and the Irish, and there are also British references to throwing-spears. A hand-held spear, used with a thrusting motion, is either a cavalry lance or an infantry pike. In pagan graves we find angular, leaf-shaped or long tapered blades, exceptionally up to 16 in. long. The shaft has normally decayed, but sometimes a soil-stain, or the presence of an iron ferrule in line with the head, shows that the overall length of a pike may have been 7 ft [Fig. 26a]. In pre-Viking Ireland there are also leaf-shaped or long tapered pike blades which occasionally exceed 12 in. A British spear-head, with a heavy leaf-shaped blade 8½ in. long is known from Buston, but it is impossible to know whether this is from a lance, a javelin, or even a pike. Two further comments are needed on the ubiquity of spears. First, many though by no means all the spears in pagan graves are wrought very simply, so they cannot have been costly weapons. Second, the spear is a hunting weapon as well as a martial one, and a necessary defence for swineherd and cow-herd in lands where bears, wolves and boars roamed wild.

Certain highly specialized weapons occur only rarely in pagan graves. The angon has a short head which may be barbed, a long slender iron shaft, and a short socket, all in one piece, with an overall length of about 2 ft. Married to the socket is a wooden shaft which may add a further 6 ft. The ancestor of the angon is the Roman legionary *pilum* or throwing-spear, which was designed to penetrate the enemy shield and then bend, so that its weight bore the shield down imme-diately before the legion charged. Angons occur in the Nydam and Thorsbjerg bog deposits, and also in Germanic warrior-graves of the fifth and later centuries. A few have been found in England, and their presence in royal graves at Sutton Hoo and Taplow suggests that they were prestige weapons. Also rare in this country is the *francisca* or throwing axe, which is considered characteristic of the Franks on the Continent. The distribution of *francisca*s in this country may also denote a Frankish element, for they are relatively common in Kent. They are, however, also known from Saxon areas including Essex, Sussex and Wiltshire. The hand-held axe is even more rare, though its occasional presence with a sword or other military gear shows that a simple woodman's axe might also rank as a prestige weapon.

Another potential weapon, the bow and arrow, seems not to have been used for military purposes. It was certainly known to the Germanic peoples, for arrows occur in large numbers in the Thorsbjerg and Nydam bog deposits, accompanied by bows 5 ft long – true longbows, in fact. Arrow-heads are certainly found in graves of the fourth and later centuries on the Continent, especially in the Frankish area. In England, however, only six occurrences are known, mostly in cemeteries in Kent and the Isle of Wight which display other Frankish influences. The probability that the bow and arrow was in fact widely known is shown by an incident in the Whitby *Life of Saint Gregory*; which tells how Paulinus, after preaching to Edwin of Northumbria, was mocked by a crow, which was promptly shot by one of Paulinus' servants. In other words, bows were certainly ready to hand but perhaps only as hunting weapons. This would be consistent with the absence of bows and arrows from both warrior-graves and battle poems. On the other hand, Buston crannog yielded two arrows with heavy pyramidal heads which appear to be cross-bow bolts of seventh-century (rather than medieval) date.

Against this array of offensive weapons the principal defence was the shield. This is common even in the simplest warrior-graves which otherwise contain only a spear. The principal traces left by the shield are its iron fittings: a hand-grip and a circular, domed or conical boss. In our period the boss of the English shield is commonly 5 to 6 in. in diameter and stands 3 to 6 in. high. This reminds us that among the Germans, at least from the first century AD, the shield with its protruding boss was an offensive as well as defensive weapon, one which could be thrust with devastating effect into the face of an enemy. Other parts of the Saxon shield are not well preserved, but from stains in the ground, and odd residues of wood and leather it can be inferred that the main part, the orb, was circular and either flat or concave. It might be up to 2 ft 9 in. in diameter, and a quarter of an inch thick, made up of leather-covered plywood. Copious references in the poetry make it clear that the Britons also used shields, but no remains have been discovered. From Ireland come rare shield bosses, scarcely more than 4 in. in diameter and 2 in. high. This is consistent with the undeveloped form of Irish swords, and it reminds us of the small circular targes depicted in the Book of Kells.

The question of body armour is exceptionally difficult. The manufacture of chain mail was known to both the Celts and the Germans independently of Roman influences. Cuirasses of chain mail were present in Britain in the Roman army, they were included among the loot or bribes in the Danish bog deposits, and they may well have passed to the Picts, the Scots and the Britons in the same way. Fragments of mail are known from the royal or princely Anglian burials at Sutton Hoo and Benty Grange, but not from other graves, so it is reasonable to conclude that mail armour was worn only by the very highest rank in the Anglo-Saxon armies. In contrast, the impression has been created that British warriors regularly wore armour, including coats of mail. This hypothesis is based on two words which we find used in *Y Gododdin*. The first is *seirch*, which has been translated 'armour' or 'harness'. It is probably derived from the Latin *sarcia*, 'rigging' of a ship, and if this is so then it refers to the leather straps of horse- or sword-harness. The more important word, regularly translated as 'mail-coat', is *lluric*, which certainly comes from Latin *lorica*. Now *lorica* is used for any form of protective device, including the breastwork of a fortification, but more particularly it means a leather cuirass. It also occurs in combinations like *lorica squamata*, 'cuirass of scale armour', or *lorica hamata*, 'cuirass of chain-mail', but without the qualifying adjective it means simply a protective leather jerkin. *Lluric* should mean the same, and if it does then the Gododdin warriors wore simple cuirasses of leather. The Anglo-Saxon analogy would suggest nevertheless that their principal commanders may have worn chain-mail.

The helmet was as rare as mail-armour. In fact, the only graves in which helmets have been found are the two already mentioned for their mail, the seventh-century royal burials of Sutton Hoo and Benty Grange. The remains of the Benty Grange helmet consist merely of a framework of iron bands which, according to the excavator, bore traces of plates of horn. The crown of the helmet was surmounted by a wrought-iron boar. The Sutton Hoo helmet was of iron, ornamented with silver inlays, cloisonné garnets, and tinned bronze panels with designs of gods and heroes. It had a visor, a neck-guard and hinged cheek-pieces, and its dimensions showed that it must have been heavily padded to fit the warrior's head. Its elaboration argues that it was intended as a parade piece rather than for use in combat. There is indeed no evidence that either the Anglo-Saxons or the Britons wore helmets on the field of battle.

It has already been pointed out that some iron spear-heads might come from either infantry pikes or cavalry lances. Any discussion of the weapons and equipment of the individual warrior must therefore involve the question of whether or not he was mounted. It is notorious that some of the Germanic barbarians were cavalrymen, and much – perhaps too much – has been made of the defeat of the infantry legions by Gothic cavalry at Adrianople in AD 378. But there is no evidence that the Germanic peoples who assaulted Britain – Angles, Saxons, Jutes, Franks, Frisians or others – were horsemen. Consistent with this is the almost complete absence of horse-harness from pagan burials. On the other hand, *Y Gododdin* has enough references to horses to make it clear that the British warriors did use them, and the question arises, how? Did they ride to the field of battle and then fight dismounted as the Late Saxons and their Viking opponents certainly did? Or did they actually fight from horseback, either as a disciplined body sweeping the Saxon infantry away with a massed charge, or in some more irregular manner? It is not easy to see any clear or convincing tactical picture in the Gododdin elegies (below, p. 344), but for what they are worth they suggest that the last of these alternatives is correct. Thus we hear of Bleiddig, son of Eli, that 'on the day of combat he would do feats of arms, riding his white steed.' Even more telling is the verse in praise of Marchlew: 'he showered spears in fight from his bounding, wide-coursing [horse].'

The picture which emerges from this and other references to horses in *Y Gododdin* is certainly not one of disciplined cavalry charges. It has even been doubted whether the horsemen of the time, lacking stirrups, could withstand the shock of riding a footsoldier down with a lance.[11] Too much weight should not be given to this suggestion, for a long series of Greek and Roman funerary monuments going back to around 400 BC depict a stirrup-less lancer riding down an infantryman. None the less, our clearest reference in *Y Gododdin*, the Marchlew verse, shows the spear as a missile, not a lance. The thrown spear, together with the sword wielded from horseback, would have suited the spirit of heroic warfare, with its emphasis on individual feats of arms rather than on disciplined common action. It may also be suggested that such weapon-play harks back to the ancestral Celtic cavalry of pre-Roman Britain and Gaul, rather than to military models derived from the Romans.

Having equipped the warrior, we may now inquire into the size and organization of the army of which he was a member. To judge from the casualty figures which the *Anglo-Saxon Chronicle* gives the armies of the Britons were numbered in thousands: 4,000 Britons (or 'four troops' in some versions) were slain at *Creacanford* in 456; 5,000 were killed with their king Natanleod in 508; and in 614 Cynegils and Cwichelm slew over 2,000 Britons at *Beandun*. These figures are almost certainly quite misleading.[12] It is notorious that even in modern warfare claims about enemy slain or aircraft shot down may add up to more than the entire hostile force. In medieval battle accounts too it is well known that when chroniclers' figures for combatants can be tested against actual payments to troops, they may be found to exaggerate by a factor of ten or even fifty. Fortunately we have some very specific figures to control our ideas on the armies of Arthur's Britain. The Laws of Ine of Wessex in the late seventh century defined three grades of raiding party or robber band: up to seven men were thieves, from seven to thirty-five constituted a band, but above three dozen was an army, *here* in Old English. Obviously this was a minimum figure. But when in 786 Cyneheard, brother of the dispossessed Wessex ruler Sigeberht, tried in turn to overthrow king Cynewulf, his following amounted to eighty-five men, and this was almost enough to capture the kingdom.

Figures like these make the *Chronicle* accounts of the actual immigrant bands seem entirely reasonable. Hengist and Horsa in 449, Ælle and his three sons in 477, and the West Saxons in 514, are all said to have come in three ships. It might be thought that 'three' was a conventional poetic number but for the fact that Cerdic and Cynric in 495 are said to have had five ships, and Port, Bieda and Maegla in 501 two only. But even if we are dealing with conventionalized, even partly fictional accounts, we can at least be sure that we have here the right order of magnitude: two to five ship's companies, perhaps one hundred to two hundred and fifty men. 'Three times fifty men passed over in the fleet with the sons of Erc,' says a mid eighth-century survey of Dalriada. This same document attributes to the three principal districts of Dalriada an armed muster of twelve (or possibly fifteen – the figures are corrupt) hundred men, and a sea muster of about one thousand 'rowing benches'. If their armed forces were on this scale, it becomes possible to understand how the Scots were able to accept losses of three hundred and three in a victorious battle against the Pictish *Miathi*. The figure itself has a poetic ring, but since our source, Adomnan, is sympathetic to Dalriada there is no reason to suspect that he has exaggerated the losses.

It is in the light of all these examples that we must consider the size of the army which set out from Edinburgh, *Din Eidyn* [Pl. 2], to attack the kingdom of Deira at the battle of *Catraeth*, Catterick: the army of the Gododdin. In the poem this force is repeatedly said to have numbered three hundred, though there is also a variation which puts it at three hundred and sixty three. These figures are clearly poetic conventions, the latter being three hundreds and three score and three. We therefore cannot know the exact size of the army, but assuming that *Y Gododdin* is narrating an historical event we can at least ask whether this is the right order of size. On the basis of the Dalriadan evidence we might think not, for a force that was no more numerous than the Dalriadan casualties in a single battle could scarcely have hoped to achieve anything against an established Anglian kingdom. But when we consider how close Cyneheard came to winning the throne of Wessex with a force of less than a hundred, it seems not at all impossible that the Guotodin warriors, given three times that number, might have overthrown the Deiran dynasty if they had enjoyed the luck of battle. Attempts to expand the numbers of the British force by any significant factor depend on the assumption that the mounted nobility was accompanied by a much larger body of footsoldiers who were ignoble and therefore unsung. But it is difficult to see in the social structure of the Britons any large class of ignoble but free-born men who had the right and the responsibility to bear arms. There is one other strict control over our estimates for the size of British and Anglo-Saxon armies. The best calculation for the field army of Roman Britain in about AD 400 puts it at not more than 6,000 troops. In the face of this it is impossible to believe that any of the dozen or so successor-kingdoms could have raised a force of a thousand men.

The organization of these small armies was on a highly personal basis. Its nucleus was the war-band or bodyguard of the king or of a great lord. At the battle of *Degsastan* the king's brother Theodbald was slain 'with all his troop'. There is an echo here of the irregular units of the Roman army, recruited from the barbarians and serving under their own tribal chiefs – the *numerus Hnaudifridi*, for instance. But there is an even stronger echo of the *comitatus*, 'band of companions', which Tacitus described in his account of the Germans of the first century AD. Essentially this was a group of warriors, not necessarily all from the same tribe, who attached themselves voluntarily to a leader of repute in return for arms, food, a share of the booty, and perhaps a permanent grant of land. This institution was of course Celtic as well as Germanic, British as well as Anglo-Saxon. *Y Gododdin* says of Gorthyn, son of Urfai, that 'his gifts and his fame brought visiting throngs', and it is implicit that the 'throngs' were of young warriors who wished to fight under Gorthyn's leadership. In fact the Gododdin army was the *comitatus* of Mynyddog of *Din Eidyn*. It is interesting to notice that Gorthyn had come to Edinburgh from Gwynedd along with other Venedotian soldiers, and that there were also warriors from Elmet and from Pictland in Mynyddog's army. These men should not be thought of as mercenaries, but rather as adventurous young men who offered their military skill to any prince who would reward them with fine weapons, gold rings, mead, feasting and the praise of bards.

But though part of the *comitatus* might be recruited from outside a kingdom in this way, there is no doubt that in our period its kernel was the royal family itself. It was not only his gifts and his fame that brought visiting throngs to Gorthyn, but the fact that 'he was son of a rightful king'. In the Laws of Hywel Dda 'the chief of the bodyguard is to be a son of the king or his nephew'. We have already seen one of Æthelfrith's brothers, Theodbald, killed with his troop at *Degsastan*, and the Northumbrian army was led to battle by another member of the royal family, Hering, son of Æthelfrith's predecessor Hussa. This is not to say that the royal kin would or could have provided the whole of the war-band, even when kinship was reckoned to six or seven degrees. Part at least must have been recruited from the nobility, whether of birth or of service, within or without the kingdom or the tribal territory. But however they were recruited, they were bound to their lord to the death, as numerous contemporary witnesses reveal. The Gododdin band provides one example, Theodbald's troop another. All save one of Cynewulf's companions were slain in 786, and on the following day there was only a single survivor from the *comitatus* of the pretender Cyneheard.

Our next concern must be the kind of military activity in which these armies engaged. We should look at this first from a geographical point of view – where were battles fought, what strategic ideas can be discerned, and so on. No very clear picture emerges before about AD 600, because many of the early battle sites in the *Anglo-Saxon Chronicle* cannot be identified and because the kingdoms themselves were still undefined. The only reasonable generalization is that battles were fought at relatively short range, and mostly within the area that was to crystallize out as a kingdom. The clearest example of this is provided by Wessex in the 570s, when the places captured ranged from Limbury in the east in 571 to Bath in the west in 577, a total crow-distance of ninety miles. The seventh century immediately presents us with a markedly increased range of military operations but this is a reflection of the greater detail of our sources rather than of any revolution in the mobility of armies. We can therefore reasonably infer that a sixth-century army would have been capable of similar movements.

Some concrete examples may be calculated on the assumption that the attacking army set out from the capital or principal stronghold of its own kingdom, though in fact we are never told this in the sources. The century opens, then, with Aedan mac Gabran's army moving from the Dalriadic fortress of Dunadd to a defeat at Dawston (*Degsastan*) in Liddesdale: 120 crow-miles, but a considerably longer journey if it was done overland all the way. In 616 Æthelfrith, victor of Dawston, led an army 175 crow-miles from his capital of Bamburgh to Chester to defeat Selim, son of Cynan Garwyn on the borders of Powys. In 633 Edwin was slain at Hatfield Chase only thirty miles from his own capital at York, but sixty-five from Penda's chief centre at Tamworth, and 145 from Cadwallon's principal seat at Aberffraw. Within two years, Cadwallon himself had been killed even further from home, at Denisesburna in the heart of Northumbria. But the most remarkable campaign is that recorded in the 'Northern British History', in which the kings of the Britons went on an expedition with Penda of Mercia against Oswy of

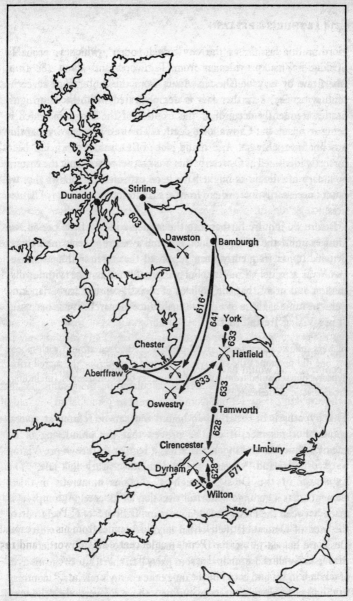

Map 10. Some historically documented campaigns of the late 6th and 7th centuries.

Northumbria 'as far as the city called Iudeu', which is probably Stirling.[13] This is 250 miles from Tamworth and about 280 from Aberffraw by way of Chester. Apart from the mobility of seventh-century armies, a further fact is demonstrated by these campaigns. Battles frequently occur near the frontier of the kingdom which is being attacked, but Cadwallon's death at Denisesburna shows that this was not invariably so. And if the place of Oswald's death has been correctly identified as Oswestry, this was on the western, not the eastern boundary of Mercia as might have been expected. It follows that we cannot necessarily infer where frontiers lay from the evidence of battle-sites.

Before we inquire further into the strategic ideas of the period, we must examine the motives which inspired a resort to arms in Arthur's Britain. It has frequently been supposed that territorial aggrandize-ment was a principal motive, but we should not assume without dis-cussion and proof that the policies of a sixth-century barbarian king were the same as those of a post-Renaissance monarch. It has been said of pre-Viking Ireland that

all wars followed a curiously ritual pattern ... hedged around with taboos ... one did not annex the enemy's territory [nor] dethrone the sacred tribal dynasty; one refrained from attacking a number of 'neutral zones' [including] the monastic settlements.[14]

This hypothesis of ritual, taboo-bound war can be refuted at several points. For instance, it can be proved that the plundering of an enemy's churches and monasteries was a regular feature of pre-Viking warfare in Ireland.[15] Again, the mid-eighth-century folk-tale, 'The Expulsion of the Dessi', though it contains numerous mythical elements, has a genuine historical situation as its core. A compact is made between the Dessi and Oengus mac Nadfraich of Cashel to drive the men of Ossory off their tribal land; after a series of defeats the Dessi are helped to victory by the magic of their druids; 'thereupon the Dessi divide those lands into four parts'. In short, one of the motives of warfare in Ireland could be to 'annex the enemy's territory', contrary to the hypothesis of ritual war outlined above. Nevertheless the very fact that the hypothesis has been put forward demonstrates that we must produce evidence for the causes of war in our period and not simply assume that they are ones familiar to us in the field of post-Machiavellian power politics.

For a start, we should make an analytical distinction between personal reasons and reasons of state, with the caution that in a heroic society this may well be a distinction without a difference. The personal motives of the individual warrior are well set out in *Y Gododdin*:

> When my comrade was struck, he struck others, there was no insult he would put up with. Steady in guarding the ford, he was glad when he bore off the honoured portion in the palace [i.e. a picked portion of meat as a recognized reward at the feast after battle].

and again: 'he slew a great host to win reputation, the son of Nwython slew a hundred princes wearing gold torques so that he might be celebrated.' Ambitions such as these are the driving force of heroic society, and granted the personal nature of kingship, they would have appealed as readily to the king as to any of his lords. And in the realm of ideas, the king would have the further inspiring goal of overlordship over neighbouring rulers.

Apart from these ideal motives, there were of course solid material gains from war. The first of these was loot, expressed most simply in terms of cattle driven in from border countries. Cattle-raiding was endemic in later centuries in Ireland, and there is every reason to project it back into our period and earlier.[16] The Laws of Hywel Dda made provision for the king to take a hosting every year to a border country, and regulated in detail the division of the spoil, which was thought of entirely in terms of cattle. It has been suggested that cattle-raiding was an exciting sport for the young men which did not necessarily breed internecine strife. But there are reasonable analogies here with the better documented sports of horse-raiding among the Blackfoot Indians, or camel-raiding among the Bedu.[17] The purpose in all cases is to take animals, not lives; but if a raiding party is opposed, homicide may result, with all that it entails in blood-feud and vengeance. As it happens, cattle-raiding was more socially acceptable among the Irish, and probably the Britons too, than horse-raiding among the Blackfoot. An extension of the policy of raiding for cattle and other spoil was that of ravaging alien territory in order to exact tribute or, more crudely expressed, to extort bribes [Pl. 14b]. This policy had been well tried against the Roman empire, and it was continued between the various peoples and kingdoms of these islands in the fifth and later centuries. Gildas's description of the Saxon revolt suggests that it had been actuated by motives like these, rather than by any intention of land-taking.

It is nevertheless clear that another objective in warfare might be the extermination, expulsion or subjugation of a native people in order to occupy their territory. The case of the Dessi and the men of Ossory has already been cited. Similarly Cunedda and his sons – a short-hand statement for his war-band – expelled the *Scotti* from Gwynedd and then took over that territory. It should be observed however that there is no reason to think that this particular operation involved either a folk-movement from Manau to Gwynedd, or the extermination and expulsion of the peasant masses. The bondmen merely exchanged one set of masters for another. Likewise, when the *British Historical Miscellany* tells us that Edwin of Northumbria took possession of Elmet and drove out Ceretic the king of that district, there is no reason to think that anyone was affected beyond the king and his war-band. It is not in fact easy to assess the evidence for Anglo-Saxon action against the Britons. For centuries the *Anglo-Saxon Chronicle* is full of items about the Britons being slaughtered or put to flight, in terms which seem significantly different from the accounts of battles between one English king and another in the same source. It is almost as though there is an element of literary convention about the record of battles against the Britons. And when we find Bede praising Æthelfrith because of the lands which he had brought under English control, 'having killed off or subjugated the natives', we should also remember that he compared Æthelfrith to Saul and regarded him as an agent of divine retribution on the faithless or heretic Britons. Given the nature of our sources, it is impossible to arrive at an objective assessment of the extent to which the Britons were removed, by slaughter or expulsion, from the lands which fell to the English kingdoms.

Land-taking is, of course, an understandable motive of state. But it seems necessary to conclude this survey of the occasions of war in Arthur's Britain with some more examples of the personal character of politics. In 626 there was war between Northumbria and Wessex because of Cwichelm's attempt to have Edwin assassinated. We are not told the reasons for the attempt, but it may be permissible to recall the assassination of Urien of Rheged, which was arranged by his fellow-Briton Morcant out of jealousy. Was it likewise personal jealousy of the success of Æthelfrith of Northumbria, or was it reasons of state, justifiable fear of an expanding neighbour, which caused Aedan mac Gabran to send an army against him? Again we may ask whether it was a clash of personalities or a matter of politics that led Æthelfrith to threaten war against Rædwald of East Anglia for harbouring the refugee Edwin. Whatever the motive, the outcome was in fact that Æthelfrith lost his life and Edwin was set on the Northumbrian throne by Rædwald. A clear-cut case is noted in the middle of the seventh century, when Cenwealh was driven from the throne of Wessex by Penda of Mercia because he had repudiated his wife who was Penda's sister. Surveying the records as a whole, and remembering that they are necessarily incomplete, we cannot escape the impression that war between kings, of whatever nation, was a normal state of affairs; that war was what kingship and nobility were about; and that no further reason of state was required: 'Once every year the king is to have a hosting to a border country.'

If this is so, it is perhaps unreasonable to look for any clear-cut strategic ideas in the warfare of the time. Rædwald's defeat of Æthelfrith is a classic example of a pre-emptive strike. Having been threatened by Æthelfrith, Rædwald raised a large force and overthrew him before he had had time to muster his whole army. The battles of Dyrham in 577 and Chester in 616 have both been seen as strategic moves, respectively by Wessex and Northumbria, to divide the British kingdoms which opposed them. Given our total ignorance of affairs west of the Pennines there is no evidence to support this interpretation of the battle of Chester, and despite Æthelfrith's success there, it appears to have been a hazardous move to operate so far from his main centre of power. Dyrham should be seen simply as a westward expansion from the Wessex heartland, comparable with the eastern expansion along the Chilterns in 571, rather than as part of a strategic plan. On the whole, politics and strategy in the sixth and seventh centuries might be summed up in these terms: every other kingdom, Christian or heathen, English, British, Pictish or Scottish, might be a potential ally, but was certainly an enemy, to be hit whenever the opportunity offered.

It is not easy to say much of contemporary tactics. The chronicles and annals are normally too terse, while Bede is obsessed with the triumph of the small armies of righteousness against the legions of evil. We are left with the colourful details of the battle poetry, but there is good reason to suspect the evidence offered by that genre. The heroic poetry of the *Iliad* appears to offer circumstantial accounts of personal combat, but a detailed study has shown that these by no means exhaust the possible combinations of events in man-to-man encounters.[18] The inference is that battle poetry, far from providing accurate and comprehensive descriptions of the incidents of battle, is a highly stylized medium, bound by set formulas, and to that extent it is a very limited witness. In British battle poems, the emphasis is mostly on personal feats of arms, and on the prowess with spear or sword of the individual warrior. The battle of *Catraeth* has an incoherent, untidy look, which is no doubt realistic enough for close-locked combat, but which blurs any tactical plan or scheme of cooperative action. *Y Gododdin* has, it is true, many apparent references to tactical matters: to vans and wings, to arrays and battle-pens, to plans and designs. But these cannot be used as a basis for writing a sensible account of British weapon-handling and tactics. They fail because they are too stylized, or too vague, or even, in some critical cases, because scholars of equal competence cannot agree on a translation.[19]

Two tactical moves can be discerned more clearly. The first is the dawn attack, which is mentioned repeatedly in *Y Gododdin*, and also in an interpolated verse which tells not of *Catraeth*, but of the battle at Strathcarron, near Falkirk, in 642. Similarly, at the battle of *Denisesburna* Oswald advanced against Cadwallon *incipiente diluculo*, 'as dawn was breaking'. It is not known whether these dawn actions were preceded by night marches of any length, and it is unlikely that they were, given the difficulty of such a manoeuvre. The second tactic is the defence of river-lines, with the consequence that battles frequently take place at fords. One of the Gododdin warriors is praised because he was 'steady in guarding the ford'. Out of the handful of poems reliably attributed to the sixth-century poet Taliesin, one describes a hard-fought battle at a river-crossing in the unidentified Gwen Ystrat. We have already seen (above, p. 57) that out of the dozen battles attributed to Arthur in the *Historia Brittonum*, no less than seven were fought at rivers. Whether or not the *Historia Brittonum* is a reliable source here for the historical Arthur, the fact remains that its compiler, or the bard whose battle poem lies behind it, regarded river-lines as the most obvious place for battles to take place. It has been claimed that at fords even a small force of British horsemen would enjoy a great advantage over Anglo-Saxon infantry. This is to ignore the fact that many of the earliest English victories, as reported in the *Anglo-Saxon Chronicle*, were also won at river-crossings.

The emphasis on river battles has as its corollary that warfare was open and mobile, and that strongholds or prepared positions played no great part in it. This makes the rare attacks on fortified places all the more interesting. We have already dismissed the suggestion that Badon was fought at a hill-fort, for this has no support in the earliest accounts of the battle. But the pre-Roman hill-forts of Old Sarum, *Searoburh* in English, and Barbury Castle, *Beranbyrig*, were the scenes of battle between the Britons on the one hand and Cynric and Ceawlin of Wessex on the other in the 550s. The cryptic entries of the *Chronicle* conceal whether or not the engagements took place near the hill-forts, or actually in them, and if the latter, whether the Britons or Saxons were the defenders. Nor is there archaeological evidence to show whether either place had been comprehensively refortified like Cadbury-Camelot (above, p. 223), or reoccupied with a minimum of refurbishing like Castle Dore (above, p. 212). Altogether more remarkable are the *Chronicle* entries of AD 491 and 530:

491. Ælle and Cissa besieged Andredes ceaster and slew all who were in there. Not one Briton was left alive.
530. Cerdic and Cynric seized the Isle of Wight and slew a few men in Wihtgaræsbyrg.

Andredes ceaster is certainly the Saxon Shore fort of Anderida or Pevensey [Pl. 1*b*], while *Wihtgaræsbyrg* is almost certainly the Saxon Shore fort which has been detected beneath Carisbrooke Castle.[20] We have no idea whether the Britons who were slain were regular garrisons, or mere civilian refugees seeking the protection of long-abandoned walls. The fact remains that the main defences at both Pevensey and Carisbrooke would have been substantially intact at the time, and Pevensey would be a formidable obstacle to infantry assault even today.

Another example of an English force besieging a British army within a Roman fortification is provided by Osric king of Deira who, as Bede says, rashly besieged Cadwallon in an unlocated fortified town (above, p. 140). British sieges and attacks on strongholds are also known. According to the 'Northern British History', Urien of Rheged shut up Theodric of Northumbria for three days and nights on the island of Metcaud, Lindisfarne. Here there is no suggestion of a fortified position, and indeed there is little evidence that the Anglo-Saxons made use of prepared strongholds. But if *Catraeth* is correctly identified with Catterick Bridge, *Cataractonium*, then this was a Roman town which had grown up on the site of an original fort. If this is the place referred to when Gwawrddur 'glutted black ravens on the wall of the fort', then that wall was stone-built, $7\frac{1}{2}$ ft thick, and enclosed eighteen acres. There is no reason to suppose that it was in ruins by AD 600. One other stronghold can certainly be attributed to the English of Northumbria: Bamburgh. The northern recension of the *Anglo-Saxon Chronicle* attributes the building of this to Ida, who founded the Anglian dynasty of Bernicia in 547, and states: 'It was enclosed with a hedge and later with a wall.' But the *British Historical Miscellany* says that Æthelfrith gave *Dinguoaroy* to his wife Bebba, and from her it took its name, that is *Bebbanburh*, Bamburgh. The question immediately arises, if Ida was responsible for building Bamburgh, why it had a British name, which is what *Dinguoaroy* clearly is. There seems to be a strong possibility that Ida took over a pre-existing British promontory fort, and used it first as a beach-head and subsequently as the citadel of his kingdom.

Whether this was so or not, Bamburgh is the only certain instance of a fortified place used by the early English. But among the Celtic peoples such strongholds were normal, and we must now examine their role in warfare. In Ireland they played an important part as is demonstrated by the frequent references to battles, sieges and burnings at *dun*s, that is, at ring-forts, in the contemporary annals. These are supplemented by St Columba's prophecy of a battle in Dun Cethirn, on Sconce Hill near Coleraine: '*in hac vicina munitione Cethirni belli-gerantes committent bellum*'. In the British sources, by contrast, notices of attacks on strongholds are rare. Except for the rampart of the Roman town of *Cataractonium*, *Catraeth*, there are none in the battle poetry. In the list of Arthur's battles, the ninth was '*in urbe Legionis*', the Roman fortress of Chester or Caerleon; the eighth was '*in castello Guinnion*', an unidentified site which sounds like a Roman auxiliary fort; and the eleventh, if we accept one group of manuscripts and one interpretation of these, may have been at the auxiliary fort of High Rochester (above, pp. 63-4). Two points emerge quite clearly. First, the dearth of references to strongholds helps to reinforce the view that warfare was essentially open, and that its major incidents were not sieges and assaults on fortifications but battles at river-crossings. Second, none of the strongholds listed above is known to have been a British fort, whereas those which can be identified for certain are Roman fortifications, whether urban or military.

There is an obvious causal connection between the absence of attacks on British fortifications and the relative weakness of the known defensive works. These as we have seen (above, pp. 212-15) often consist of a feeble wall, set, however, in a position of natural strength. There is also a clear relationship between the social structure of the time and the small area of most of these forts. Sites like Castle Dore, Chun, Dinas Powys and Dunadd are essentially defended homesteads, suitable for a prince and his war-band, together with his personal retainers, servants and craftsmen. They contrast with the medium and large hill-forts, enclosing more than three acres, which comprise nearly a half of the pre-Roman forts of southern Britain. These presumably protected social units at the level of the clan or tribe. The contrast is starkest in the case of Garn Boduan, where the post-Roman work, less than half an acre in size, was set within the decayed ramparts of an Iron-Age fort twenty-eight acres in extent. Sometime between the first and the sixth centuries AD there was a social revolution marked by the change in the unit of defence from the tribe as a whole to the chief and his warrior-band. It may be that the abandonment of the thirty-acre tribal capital of Traprain Law in the early fifth century (above, p. 181) marks the precise moment of that change. If these generalizations are sound, they emphasize the unusual character of Cadbury-

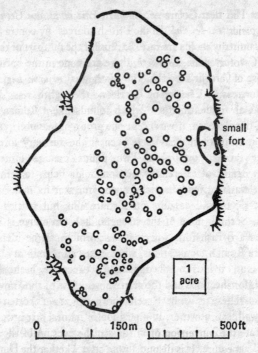

small
fort

1
acre

0   150m   0   500ft

30. Garn Boduan, Caernarvonshire, general plan, showing post-Roman small fort set within the defences of the pre-Roman hill-fort. (See also Fig. 17.)

Camelot among British strongholds, in terms both of the strength of its post-Roman refortification and of its large extent (above, p. 224) [Pl. 5]. It seems unlikely that this eighteen-acre fort was intended as a prince's defended homestead, and it is unthinkable that it was a tribal centre on the pre-Roman model. It seems most likely to have served as the base for an army that was large by the standards of the time. This might have been recruited widely like the Gododdin host, or might have combined the war-bands of several kingdoms for the defence of southern and western Britain against Saxons on the south coast and in the Thames valley. Within our present framework of knowledge, it seems plain enough that Cadbury-Camelot played some special part in the warfare of southern Britain in the late fifth and sixth centuries.

We turn finally to the most difficult of all problems in the military archaeology of the Late Roman and post-Roman centuries: that of the 'dykes'. It is known that in the fourth century an imperial estate in north Dorset was defended by Bokerly Dyke, a rock-cut ditch and upcast bank.[21] There were three structural phases, of which the second was a response to the great barbarian raid of 367, while the last is dated to the early fifth century. In Cambridgeshire there are several similar dykes which may also have been built in the late fourth century, though it is fair to stress that over the last fifty years their supposed date has fluctuated from the pre-Roman Iron Age to the mid seventh century A D.[22] If, however, we accept a late Roman date for them, then the crossings through the Cambridgeshire dykes may have been manned by troops from the Saxon Shore forts as ambuscades against raiding parties. The greatest of all the dykes attributed to our period is *Wodnesdic*, Wansdyke [Pl. 13], which ran from near Savernake Forest in Wiltshire to Maes Knoll in Somerset, with a fifteen-mile gap in the middle.[23] Excavation has shown that the dyke is late Roman or later, while its very name, 'Woden's Dyke', shows that it was in existence before the conversion of Wessex in the 630s. All else about its history is conjecture. It is disputed for a start whether the two separate halves, East and West Wansdyke, are part of the same scheme. East Wansdyke may have been a defensive frontier for the Britons of Salisbury Plain against early Saxon settlers in the Thames valley; or it may be a creation of the Saxons themselves in the course of some internal struggle. West Wansdyke may likewise be interpreted in terms of Wessex politics, or it may be a British defence thrown up after the battle of Dyrham in 577. In that case, it would be part of that same scheme of British response to Dyrham as we have already seen in the second phase of the sixth-century gate at Cadbury-Camelot.

There is at present no evidence to help us decide between these hypotheses, but even if there were we would still be left with the tactical problem: how were the dykes used? We have already noticed the possibility that the Cambridgeshire dykes were used to ambush raiding parties. This seems reasonable granted first that the raiders were encumbered by loot, cattle and captives and were thereby compelled to use the crossings through the dykes; and second, that the posse of the defenders was highly mobile. But these conditions would not apply if the Wansdyke were intended as a defence against military operations other than raiding parties. It is difficult to believe that the infantry of Wessex, whether attacking Britons or fellow-Saxons, would have found the ditch and bank an insuperable obstacle. They would not, therefore, have been constrained to use the gaps through the dyke, where they might be ambushed. At the same time it is impossible that the ten miles of East Wansdyke and the thirteen miles of West Wansdyke could have been manned continuously either in time or space. It is pertinent here to recall that the Roman walls of northern Britain, which presumably provided the inspiration for these unsophisticated copies, were dependent for their success on a permanently manned barrier, supplemented by garrisoned forts to front and rear. There were no such permanent garrisons along Wansdyke. It is of course typical of our period that one of its major archaeological monuments should defy attempts to date it, to set it in its political context, or to understand its tactical function.

Twelve

Arthur and Britain

Throughout the preceding chapters, the ambiguities and inconsistencies of the evidence have been left largely unresolved. This may well have created confusion in the mind of the reader; but it was done deliberately, so that he should not be deceived about the character of the evidence. It may however reasonably be asked of a historian who has spent some time in direct contact with the evidence, both verbal and material, that he should be prepared, eventually, to commit himself one way or another. He can rightly be asked to state, without further hedging, what seem to him the most likely interpretations and the most coherent historical pattern. This final chapter attempts to do just that.

It is useful first of all to stress that within the period of this book – roughly the late fourth to the early seventh centuries AD – the British Isles are a microcosm of Europe as a whole. In both, an inner area with a culture that was romanized and urban was under attack from outer areas that were, in the technical sense, barbarian.[1] The attacks ranged in degree from raids of varied intensity to full-scale folk-movement and land-settlement. Their causes were equally varied. The Roman empire as a whole was undergoing a social and economic decline, accompanied by depopulation, which created a vacuum to draw in the barbarians. At the same time its material wealth was still real enough to serve as a magnet to nations who were paupers by comparison. They might hope to share that wealth, either as diplomatic bribes, payments to mercenaries, grants of land, and the like, or as simple loot. The most negotiable items of Roman wealth – gold and silver– were welcomed as raw material for the production of barbaric jewelry. Apart from these attractions from the inner area, the barbarian nations were themselves subjected to external pressures, ranging from the westward flood of the Huns, through localized land-hunger in Ireland or northern Germany, right down to the endemic blood-feuds which drove war-leaders into exile to seek their fortunes in foreign lands.

Under these attacks, the politico-military structure of the western empire collapsed, and the eastern, or Byzantine, empire, despite valiant attempts, was never able to restore it. And with the western empire went the diocese of Britain. However 'fertile in tyrants' Britain may have been, the history of the third and fourth centuries shows that, even after the events of 407–10, the island would have been recovered for Rome had the military means been available in Gaul. The most typical event of the fifth century was the failure of Aëtius, commander in Gaul, '*magister militum per Gallias*', to respond to the appeal of the Britons for help against the Picts because, says Bede, 'he was engaged at that time in most serious warfare with Blaedla and Attila, kings of the Huns'. As a result, what had been a Roman diocese surrounded by both friendly and hostile barbarian kingdoms was converted into a number of mutually hostile successor states, both Celtic and Teutonic.

Still viewing developments at imperial rather than diocesan level, we must consider one other feature of the relationships between the barbarians and Rome. Looters of Roman lands and treasure though they were, the barbarians none the less had considerable respect for *romanitas* and even for the institutions of the empire. This can be illustrated in various ways. We have already noticed (above, pp. 284–6) that Germanic metalwork was essentially a barbarian interpretation of Roman art forms. Much of the political history of the west in the fifth and sixth centuries is concerned with attempts by German kings to prop up the imperial throne.[2] It has, moreover, been noted that 'the administrative shape of Frankish Gaul is for the most part sub-Roman'. A similar statement could be made about the Vandal kingdom in North Africa. And it is not insignificant that throughout the western empire the future lay with the Romance languages, not the Germanic.

It may be argued that however true these comments are in Europe, they are irrelevant to Britain, as the linguistic change shows so decisively. A partial reason for the difference may be that a majority of the Germanic inheritors of Gaul, Spain and Italy had been in close contact with Rome for generations before they crossed the frontier, whereas the Angles, Saxons and Jutes had always been more remote.

But even the Angles were not wholly insensible to the prestige of Rome. Edwin's sovereignty or '*imperium*', as described by Bede, was a recreation of the diocese of Britannia, and Edwin himself used to have carried before him 'that kind of standard which the Romans call a *tufa* and the English a *thuf*'.[3]

From these wide concepts we turn to the details of insular developments. For a start we may summarize the raiding and migrations which

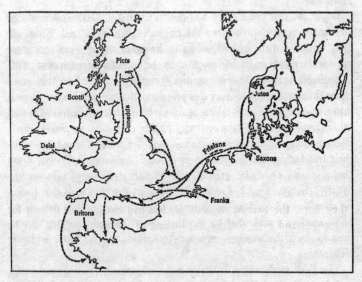

Map 11. Folk-movements affecting the British Isles in the 5th and 6th centuries.

affected the islands. The west coasts of Britain were subjected to Irish raiding, while Patrick's letter to Coroticus (above, p. 11) demonstrates that at times this was a two-way process. Ogham-inscribed stones, and Goidelic personal- and place-names, demonstrate that all along the coast raiding passed into settlement of greater or lesser intensity. Particularly important was the establishment of Irish dynasties in Dyfed, Brycheiniog and above all Dalriada. In all cases, it is probable that these were not wholesale folk-movements but the migrations of warrior-chiefs and their war-bands. The rounded number of one hundred and fifty for the sons of Erc and their following sounds very reasonable. In the north, there was considerable Pictish pressure throughout the fourth century and the first half of the fifth, but this seems to have been confined to raiding. There is no evidence of serious Pictish settlement south of the Antonine Wall. On the other hand, the migration of Cunedda and his following to Gwynedd, whatever its precise date and motive, forged links between north-west Wales and Pictland.

Down the east coast there was both Pictish and Germanic raiding, and Saxon piracy spread into the English Channel as well. From an early date German soldiers, often in irregular units, were recruited against the northern barbarians, and by the end of the fourth century it is probable that whole communities were being settled on the land. Some time in the fifth century this process of licensed settlement passed into free-enterprise land-taking again involving the entire folk. On the other hand the establishment of English dynasties in Sussex and Wessex, and possibly in Bernicia too, was the work of chieftains with their war-bands, like the setting up of Irish dynasties in Dyfed, Brycheiniog and Dalriada, and of the Pictish dynasty of Gwynedd. Finally, though it has not seemed relevant to the theme of this book, we should not forget the movements out of Britain itself to Armorica, on so massive a scale that by 469 they could allegedly muster 12,000 men to assist the western emperor Anthemius against Euric and the Visigoths.

The Irish settlements in Wales were important on a regional basis and the settlement of Dalriada was pregnant for the future of Scotland. Without any doubt, however, the most decisive among all these migrations were those which brought the early English to Britain. It is necessary to stress here that, contrary to Bede's view, the coming of the English, *adventus Saxonum*, was not one single event, but a whole series. For many of the English migrations there is no historical record, though they may be detected in the archaeological remains. They go well back into the Roman period, they continue as acts of Roman or romanizing policy to the middle of the fifth century, and they were intended as bulwarks against the northern barbarians. Sometime around 450, however, the British government began to lose control, the scale and character of the English settlement altered decisively,

and over the next two centuries the more romanized parts of Britannia
became the English Heptarchy. This is acceptable fact, but the scale,
and above all the supposed destructiveness of the Anglo-Saxon settlement may both be questioned. We have seen that the size of the pagan
cemeteries suggests that the number of settlers was not large (above,
pp. 310–11). We have suggested that the alleged evidence for massacres at Roman villas may bear quite a different interpretation (above,
p. 191). We have noticed the absence of layers of burning and destruction from the stratification of Roman towns (above, p. 186). This last
point is decisive: the conventional picture of the English settlement,
with the reek of blood and burning towns, is based entirely on a
chapter of Gildas. Until burning layers have been found in a number
of Romano-British towns, we must remove this chapter from the
documents of history and regard it as a figment of Gildas's apocalyptic
imagination.

It is interesting at this point to compare the material culture of the
ancestral and early English with that of the Roman and sub-Roman
Britons. If we take for a start the Romans of the civil zone in the fourth
century, the contrast is very great. A sizeable proportion of them lived
in towns, which were unknown to the ancestral English on the Continent. Others, in the countryside, had the advantages of heated rooms
and mosaic floors, even if the superstructure of a villa was no more
solid than that of a German long-house. The Britons lived within a
sophisticated legal, social and economic system: the Germans did not.
But when we look to the lower classes of peasant in the civil zone, to
the inhabitants of the military zone or to the Britons beyond Hadrian's
Wall, the contrast with the ancestral English is markedly diminished.
The German yeoman enjoyed a higher architectural standard than
Romano-British farmers in the west and north. He lacked a money
economy and wheel-thrown pottery, but his tools and implements and
trinkets of bronze were certainly as good. In fact, the standard of living
in a Frisian village was higher than that in Traprain Law, one of the
principal centres of the northern Britons.

It is equally clear that during the course of the fifth century the
cultural superiority of the former Roman civil zone largely disappeared.
Indeed, if we were to judge merely by the material relics preserved in
museums, we should reckon the culture of the sub-Roman Britons as

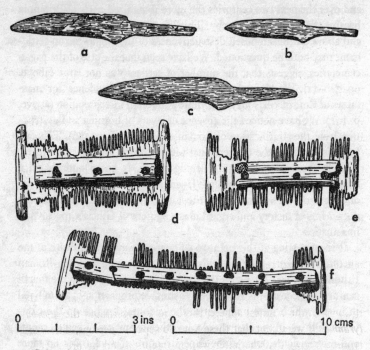

31. Cultural homogeneity reflected by iron knives and bone combs from British, Anglo-Saxon and Irish sites: *a* Winnall, Hampshire, cemetery II, grave 24; *b, d* Dinas Powys, Glamorgan; *c, e* Carraig Aille, Co. Limerick; *f* Sutton Courtenay, Berkshire.[4]

negligible compared with that of the pagan Saxons. To some extent this would be a false judgement, biased by the fact that the Saxons buried grave-goods and the Britons did not. But with the arguable exceptions of hanging bowls and some penannular brooches, it is difficult to point to anything produced by British hands outside the old military zones of the west and the north. Romanization too had largely evaporated. This is most obvious in the economic sphere, where the disappearance of coinage and of industrially made pottery are key symptoms. The towns lost their social and commercial functions, and though they probably retained a military, or at least defensive, role for some decades, only a shadowy form of urbanized life remained. But if the romanization of material culture had gone, more remained in spiritual and conceptual terms. The Britons were nominally Christian. The church at least preserved some Latin learning, and also the Latin language in so correct a form as to suggest that it was not a living tongue. Moreover the Britons still used Latin terms like *medicus*, doctor or medical officer, and *magistratus* as we see from inscribed stones. And from the same source, as well as from Gildas and the 'Northern British History', we know they still regarded themselves as *cives* (Roman) citizens. But by AD 500 it would not have been easy to distinguish between *cives* and *hostes*, the enemy, in technological or sociological terms. Picts, *Scotti*, *Anglorum sive Saxonum gens* and Britons were all at the technological level known as barbarism, and organized in the kind of society known as heroic. For all but the Britons of the Roman civil zone, this was their ancestral condition, while for them it represented a reversion to ancestral patterns after the veneer of romanization had peeled away during the course of the fifth century.

While the historical details of that century are completely obscure, three or four leading figures may be dimly discerned among the Britons. In the political sphere, there are Vortigern and the *superbus tyrannus*, if we accept that these are two separate persons. The word *tyrannus* shows that the latter was, in intention and by precedent, a usurper in the hallowed Romano-British tradition. The qualifying *superbus* implies that he held sovereignty over several minor *tyranni*. He was not, in modern terms, an unconstitutional despot, for he ruled with a group of *consiliarii* like a Roman – or for that matter a Visigothic – provincial governor. His one recorded act, the settlement of Hengist and his three ship-loads of followers in Kent with a commission to fight the northern barbarians, continued a Roman policy. What we know of Vortigern shows that he was cast in the same Roman-provincial mould. His British name should not mislead us, for civilian tombstones demonstrate that Celtic personal names had persisted even in romanized circles in the third and fourth centuries. Himself the son-in-law of the usurper Magnus Maximus, Vortigern continued the line of British *tyranni* in the 420s and 430s, and continued likewise the Roman policy of settling Germans as *laeti* or *foederati* for the defence of Britain. Historians whose vision is obscured by an excess of hindsight may see Vortigern and the *superbus tyrannus* as Celtic warlords; but their contemporaries would have regarded them as purely Roman phenomena.

This, then, is the political framework within which two great soldiers acted: Ambrosius and Arthur. They both bore Roman names, but the clash of Ambrosius with the equally Roman-sounding Vitolinus at *Cat Guoloph* warns us that we should not therefore think of Ambrosius and Arthur as representing a pro-Roman, anti-Celtic element in British politics. The plain statement of the *Historia Brittonum* that 'Arthur fought along with the kings of the Britons, but he himself was battle-leader', shows him as commander of a combined force drawn from several petty kingdoms; in other words, as the agent of a *superbus tyrannus* leading the armies of subordinate *tyranni*. Much has been made in the past of *dux bellorum* as a formal title, akin to *dux Britanniarum*, duke of the Britains, but there is no substance in this if the Arthurian section of the *Historia Brittonum* translates and summarizes a Welsh battle-listing poem. This is not to say that it would be wrong to think of Arthur bearing a Roman rank or title, for we have seen that the use of such titles did survive. If we had to invent one for him, the most likely, on the analogy of Gaul, would be *magister militum per Britannias*, which we might translate as 'General Officer Commanding British Land Forces'. So far as Gildas's phraseology allows us to infer anything about Ambrosius, we may cast him in a similar role, as supreme commander of the Britons under the *superbus tyrannus*. But Gildas adds about Ambrosius that his parents 'had been no doubt decked with the purple', '*purpura nimirum indutis*'. It is quite impossible to believe that Ambrosius was the son of anyone whom Gildas would have recognized as a legitimate emperor, and the phrase must mean 'of senatorial or magisterial rank'.

It is worth pausing here to examine the historical credibility of these three British figures, Vortigern, Ambrosius and Arthur. Much of the widespread scepticism about the historicity of Arthur stems from the undoubted fact that his name became attached to unhistorical tales, to fabulous wonders, and to places which can never have been connected with him. But just the same thing happened in the cases of both Vortigern and Ambrosius, whose historicity has never been called in question. In terms of place-names, it is difficult to believe that the one had any personal connection with Craig Gwrtheyrn in Carmarthenshire or the other with Dinas Emrys in Caernarvonshire. By the ninth century, as the *Historia Brittonum* shows, Arthur's son and Arthur's horse were featured in two of the 'Wonders of Britain'. At the same time Vortigern was already the villain of a developed cycle of fabulous tales, in which Ambrosius also figured as the boy without a father who confuted Vortigern's magicians. It is clear that these unhistorical accretions are irrelevant to the genuineness of our three figures. Their claim to historicity is based on contemporary or near-contemporary notices: of Ambrosius by Gildas, of Vortigern in the *calculi* at the head of the British Easter Table compiled in 455, and of Arthur in the British Easter Annals. The fact that fables gathered around the name of Ambrosius is, however, relevant to the question whether he or Arthur was the victor of Badon (above, p. 29). If Ambrosius had indeed won Badon, as well as the first 'God-given' victory against the Anglo-Saxons, this would surely have been remembered and magnified. There would have been no occasion for later ages to attribute the victory to Arthur, still less to invent Arthur for the purpose. In this sense, Ambrosius is the touchstone to prove the genuineness of Arthur.

So we come to Arthur himself. He was not a king, and unlike the warlords of the Germanic and Celtic heroic societies, he founded no dynasty. He was instead the leader of the combined forces of the small kingdoms into which sub-Roman Britain had dissolved. It is impossible to see how these forces were raised. We can only speculate whether they were mercenary bands recruited by those city administrations to which Honorius had remitted authority, or whether they were already personal war-bands. Any estimate of the size of the combined force can be no more than a guess, but bearing in mind that the Roman army in Britain at the end of the fourth century numbered about six thousand, a figure of one thousand for Arthur would be of the right order. His major victory, the siege of Mount Badon, was fought against the English about 490, most probably on a hill outside Bath. Its significance we will consider shortly. His other battles were widespread and against uncertain enemies. One, Cat Coit Celidon, was in Scotland; that at the City of the Legion was in the west, either at Caerleon or Chester; others, on the *Glein* and *Dubglas* rivers, were very probably fought in eastern England with the intention of carrying war into the heart of long-established English settlements. He died about 510 in the battle of Camlann, on which we have no firm information. Tradition suggests, however, that it resulted from the break-up of the combined force, and was an internecine struggle of the kind we have already noticed at Cat Guoloph.

The tactical pattern of Arthur's battles is one of open warfare, in which fortified places played little part, and river-crossings were all-important. Most if not all of his troops would have been mounted, and would have fought from horseback with sword, lance and javelin, approaching the enemy in a series of rushes rather than in a coordinated cavalry charge. We have no archaeological evidence for the details of weapons and equipment, and it is wholly uncertain how far we can extrapolate back from *Y Gododdin* or forward from the Late Roman army into the Arthurian age. It seems probable that most warriors were armed with spears, carried shields, and had their bodies protected by tough leather cuirasses. Fewer fought with swords, probably long cavalry swords of the type borrowed by Roman cavalry units from the earlier Celts. High-ranking officers wore chainmail, and possibly helmets as well. Arthur himself when on parade, though not necessarily on the battle-field, would have worn a uniform based on that of a Roman emperor or high-ranking general: a fine, knee-length tunic and breeches, a leather jerkin with metal-studded fringe to protect the abdomen, and a cloak pinned at the shoulder with a penannular brooch. An essentially similar uniform has been reconstructed for the warrior-kings of East Anglia from the evidence of the jewelled fittings discovered at Sutton Hoo, and there is no doubt that both Germanic and Celtic warriors aped Roman parade dress in this way.

We must now ask what was the long-term significance of the campaigns which Ambrosius initiated and which Arthur brought to a climax at Badon. In terms of political history the answer must be very little. It is possible that the deep penetration of Anglo-Saxon settlers into the upper Thames valley was pushed back as a result of Badon; this at least has been suggested on the basis of a break in the sequence of pagan Saxon pottery in the area. But no comparable disruption has been noticed in other areas of early settlement. In the years after Badon, Saxon adventurers were able to establish a beach-head on the south coast, to capture the Isle of Wight, and to push some way

32. Reconstruction of a British officer's dress, from verbal and archaeological evidence.[5] Original drawing by D. Lloyd Owen.

33. The East Anglian king in a chieftain's parade armour of Roman type. A reconstruction of the Sutton Hoo find after O. Gamber.[6]

inland. Indeed it has been claimed on archaeological grounds that Saxons were settled around Salisbury long before 552, and that the battle at Old Sarum which the *Anglo-Saxon Chronicle* places in tha year marks not a new Saxon advance, but the defence of a generation-old settlement against a British counter-attack.[7] In other areas, un-illumined by the fitful light of the *Chronicle*, further English advances may have been achieved in the early sixth century. This hypothesis may seem difficult to reconcile with Gildas's emphasis on the cessation of foreign wars during his life-time. But his own viewpoint was very circumscribed, if we may judge from the fact that the five kings whom he castigates ruled in a tight arc from Cornwall to Anglesey. It is a reasonable assumption that his knowledge of British affairs was res-tricted to this area, and that he was altogether ignorant of events further east and north. Throughout eastern Britain from the Channel to the Tees we can be sure that the decades after Badon saw the con-solidation, if not the expansion, of English settlements.

In the long run, the disintegration of Arthur's combined force, which was reflected in '*gueith Camlann*', 'the strife of Camlann', must have greatly facilitated the Anglo-Saxon advance. Whatever political history lies concealed here, the result must have been the fragmentation of a *Britannia* united under the sovereignty of a *superbus tyrannus* into a number of small British kingdoms. Most of these disap-peared in the course of the next century without leaving the least trace, but the kingdom of Elmet shows what they may have been like, and the fate of Ceretic of Elmet at the hands of Edwin of Northumbria demonstrates how vulnerable they were. But after Badon itself we hear nothing in British sources about resistance to the Anglo-Saxons until the later sixth century. Then, first Outigirn and later Urien of Rheged, Riderch Hen of Strathclyde, Guallauc and Morcant are all known to have fought against Northumbria. It is because of this, of course, that these British kings figure in the 'Northern British His-tory', and that some brief record of their deeds has come down to us. Elsewhere, we can infer fragmented and ineffectual British resistance from the English victories recorded in the *Anglo-Saxon Chronicle*, but no coherent account of the replacement of British by English kingdoms can be written on the basis of the available evidence. It would seem, however, that after Arthur's death there was no British counter-attack on the grand scale until Cadwallon's overthrow of Edwin at Hatfield and his subsequent ravaging of Northumbria. Even that was only achieved in alliance with Penda of Mercia.

Badon, then, had no long-term effect in preventing the creation of England and Wales out of the diocese of *Britannia*. Any short-term results, in the way of disrupting settlements or checking advances, were purely localized. There is no reason to believe that the character of the English settlement was changed in any way by Arthur's victory. Apt symbol though he is for the period between the break with Rome in 407–10 and the emergence of the Heptarchy in the seventh century, in terms of *realpolitik* his achievement is negligible.

As a person, his significance comes later, in the realms of literature and romance. It may reasonably be asked here how the Arthur of romance could evolve at all from a figure whose political significance was so slight. It is not the purpose of this book to trace the evolution of the legend of Arthur, but some hints may be given about the circumstances which gave it birth. To begin with, Arthur was far from insignificant in military terms. His victories were real enough at the time, they were widespread, and they were celebrated. Moreover, the very scarcity of written records, and the expansive character of oral transmission, must have swollen the report of each battle. Even today it is possible to see a man become a legend in his own lifetime by performing deeds of valour in a context where they are reported by word of mouth.[8] Finally, a defeated people cherished tales true or false, sober or exaggerated, of a period when they were the victors, as some relief from the bitter elegies of *Y Gododdin*, or the laments of Llywarch Hen.

Bibliography and References

Certain cautions are necessary about the character and function of the references given here. They are not intended as a list of authorities for statements made in the text. In so far as we can think of 'authorities' in the period, they are pot-sherds and brooches, inscribed stones and ancient manuscripts. Nor does the bibliography aim at being comprehensive. This would be out of place, not to say impossible, in a short survey of this kind. The reader who needs a full bibliography should refer to Bonser, W., *An Anglo-Saxon and Celtic Bibliography (450–1087)*, Oxford, 1957, and *A Romano-British Bibliography (55 BC–AD 449)*, Oxford, 1964. In the case of long-continued discussions and controversies I have usually contented myself with listing only recent articles, especially where they have copious references to earlier phases of the discussions. For the sake of the non-specialist reader I have concentrated on the more accessible general surveys. Finally, I have considered it a special duty to refer to those articles which argue the case for hypotheses drastically different from those which I have propounded myself.

New discoveries and interpretations in the field of Arthurian Britain are recorded in such periodicals as the *Bibliographical Bulletin of the International Arthurian Society*, *Antiquaries Journal*, *Antiquity*, *Archaeologia*, *Archaeological Journal*, *Britannia*, *English Historical Review*, *Journal of the British Archaeological Association*, *Journal of Roman Studies*, *Medieval Archaeology*, and *Speculum*, as well as in regional archaeological and historical journals and reviews.

General Surveys

BLAIR, P. H. *Introduction to Anglo-Saxon England*, Cambridge, 1956.
BLAIR, P. H. *Roman Britain and Early England, 55 BC–AD 871*, Edinburgh, 1963.

CHADWICK, H. M. *Early Scotland*, Cambridge, 1949.

CHADWICK, N. K., ed., *Studies in Early British History*, Cambridge, 1954.

CHADWICK, N. K., ed., *Studies in the Early British Church*, Cambridge, 1958.

CHADWICK, N. K., ed., *Celt and Saxon*, Cambridge, 1963.

COLLINGWOOD, R. G. and MYRES, J.N.L. *Roman Britain and the English Settlements*, Oxford History, vol. I, 2nd edn 1937.

DEANESLY, M. A. *A History of Early Medieval Europe, 476–911*, 1956.

DILLON, M. and CHADWICK, N. K. *The Celtic Realms*, 1967.

FRERE, S. *Britannia, a History of Roman Britain*, 1967.

HODGKIN, R. H. *History of the Anglo-Saxons*, 3rd edn, Oxford, 1952.

JONES, A. H. M. *The Later Roman Empire 284–602: A Social, Economic and Administrative Survey*, Oxford, 1964.

JONES, A. H. M. *The Decline of the Ancient World*, 1966.

KIRBY, D. P. *The Making of Early England*, 1967.

LLOYD, J. E. *History of Wales from Earliest Times to the Edwardian Conquest*, 1911; 3rd edn 1939.

LOYN, H. R. *Anglo-Saxon England and the Norman Conquest*, 1962.

MCEVEDY, C. *The Penguin Atlas of Medieval History*, 1961.

ORDNANCE SURVEY, *Map of Roman Britain*, 3rd edn, Chessington, 1956.

ORDNANCE SURVEY, *Map of Britain in the Dark Ages*, 2nd edn, Chessington, 1966.

STENTON, F. *Anglo-Saxon England*, Oxford History, vol. II, 1943.

WALLACE-HADRILL, J. M. *The Barbarian West, 400–1000*, 1957.

WHITELOCK, D. *The Beginnings of English Society*, Pelican Histories, vol. II, 1952.

Principal Texts and Translations

Only those texts which are quoted frequently are listed here. References to others will be found in the notes to chapters below.

Whitelock, D., ed. and trans., *English Historical Documents, vol. I, c. 500–1042*, 1955, is the basic compendium of translations, accompanied by historical introduction, full comments on the texts, and copious bibliography. It is weighted inevitably towards strictly English affairs, and needs to be supplemented from the British point of view. There is no similar British collection.

The principal British texts are Gildas, *De excidio et conquestu Britanniae* and Nennius, *Historia Brittonum*. The standard edition of *De excidio* is Mommsen, T., *Monumenta Germaniae historica chronica minora saec. IV.V.VI.VII.*, vol. 3, Berlin, 1898; reprint 1961, pp. 1–85. This edition is reprinted and translated by Williams, H., *Cymmrodorion Record Series No. 3*, 1899. The standard edition of *Historia Brittonum* is in the same volume of *Chronica minora*, pp. 111–222. Another text, with valuable commentary, is in Lot, F., *Nennius et l'Historia Brittonum*, Paris, 1934. A translation of Nennius, together with the 'historical' chapters of Gildas, is given in Wade-Evans, A. W., *Nennius's 'History of the Britons'*, 1938.

The text of six variant manuscripts of the *Anglo-Saxon Chronicle* is in Thorpe, B., ed. and trans., *The Anglo-Saxon Chronicle According to the Several Original Authorities*, Rolls Series, 2 vols., 1861. Altogether more valuable for its notes and commentary is Earle, J. and Plummer, C., *Two of the Saxon Chronicles Parallel*, 2 vols., Oxford, 1892, 1899. Two translations have important introductions: Garmonsway, G. N., *The Anglo-Saxon Chronicle*, 1953 and Whitelock, D. with Douglas, D. C. and Tucker, S. I., *The Anglo-Saxon Chronicle, a Revised Translation*, 1961.

The latest edition and translation of Bede's *Historia ecclesiastica gentis Anglorum* is by Colgrave, B. and Mynors, R. A. B., Oxford, 1969. The introduction and notes to this do not wholly supersede Plummer, C., *Venerabilis Baedae opera historica*, 2 vols., Oxford, 1896.

Anderson, A. O. and Anderson, M. O., eds. and trans., *Adomnan's Life of Columba*, 1961, provides, in addition to an important text, an invaluable discussion of early Scottish history.

Within the scope of this book, English legal texts are covered very adequately in Whitelock's *English Historical Documents* with discussion and references. For English readers, the Welsh laws are readily accessible in Richards, M., trans., *The Laws of Hywel Dda*, Liverpool, 1954.

For early Welsh poetry the standard texts are Williams, I., *Canu Aneirin*, Cardiff, 1938; and *Canu Taliesin*, Cardiff, 1960, English version by Williams, J. E. C., Dublin, 1968. Neither of these have English translations, which must be found in Jackson, K. H., *The Gododdin*, Edinburgh, 1969 and Morris-Jones, J., *Taliesin* (=*Y Cymmrodor* XXVIII, 1918; this needs to be modified in the light of *Canu Taliesin*).

The standard text of *Beowulf* is Klaeber, F., *Beowulf and the Fight at Finnsburg*, 3rd edn with supplements, etc., Boston, 1951. A translation with useful ancillary material is Garmonsway, G. N., Simpson, J. and Davidson, H. E., *Beowulf and its Analogues*, 1968.

The inscribed stones which form the primary documents for the Celtic West are collected in Macalister, R. A. S., *Corpus inscriptionum insularum celticarum vol. I*, Dublin, 1945, abbreviated CIIC.

Monuments within Wales are more accurately recorded in Nash-Williams, V. E., *Early Christian Monuments of Wales*, Cardiff, 1950, abbreviated ECMW.

Handy translations in the Penguin Classics series are Wright, D., *Beowulf*, 1957; Alexander, M., *The Earliest English Poems*, 1966; and Webb, J. F., *Lives of the Saints*, 1965.

Abbreviations used in the notes

Ant. J.	*The Antiquaries Journal*, London.
Arch. Camb.	*Archaeologia Cambrensis*, Cardiff.
Arch. J.	*The Archaeological Journal*, London.
CB	Barley, M. W. and Hanson, R. P. C., eds., *Christianity in Britain 300–700*, Leicester, 1968.
DAB	Harden, D. B., ed., *Dark-Age Britain*, 1956.
JBAA	*Journal of the British Archaeological Association*, 3rd series, London.
Med. Arch.	*Medieval Archaeology*, London.
PRIA	*Proceedings of the Royal Irish Academy*, Section C, Dublin.
PSAS	*Proceedings of the Society of Antiquaries of Scotland*, Edinburgh.
UJA	*Ulster Journal of Archaeology*, 3rd series, Belfast.
WHR	*Welsh History Review*, Cardiff.

Notes to Chapters

CHAPTER ONE

1. No general account of the evidence for this period and the technical problems which it poses is available to the student of history. He must be content to learn by example from discussions of individual manuscripts and sources.

2. Much that is relevant to the manuscripts of our period can be learned from discussions of the transmission of the texts of Greek and Latin writers. See, for instance, Dain, A., *Les Manuscrits*, 1949; Reynolds, L. D. and Wilson, N. G., *Scribes and scholars*, Oxford, 1968; also Chaytor, H. J., *From script to print*, Cambridge, 1945.

3. This discussion of Easter annals, and the use which I make of them throughout, rely heavily on Poole, R. L., *Chronicles and Annals*, Oxford, 1926 and especially on Jones, C. W., ed., *Bedae opera de temporibus*, Cambridge, Mass., 1943, and Jones, *Saints' Lives and Chronicles in Early England*, Cornell, 1947; reprint 1968.

4. Warren, F. E., *The Leofric Missal*, Oxford, 1883, p. 50.

5. Few Lives of Celtic saints are early, and fewer still have been edited to modern rigorous standards. For some of the problems, see Morris, J., 'The Dates of the Celtic Saints', *Journal of Theological Studies*, n.s. 17, 1966, pp. 342–91.

6. The critical standards established by Sisam, K., 'Anglo-Saxon Royal Genealogies', *Proceedings, British Academy*, 39, 1953, pp. 287–348, have yet to be applied in the British field.

7. Hanson, R. P. C., *Saint Patrick*, Oxford, 1968.

8. Richardson, H. G. and Sayles, G. O., *Law and Legislation from Æthelberht to Magna Carta*, Edinburgh, 1966, pp. 1–30 and 157–69.

9. Jenkins, D., 'Legal and Comparative Aspects of the Welsh laws', *Welsh History Review, Special Number 1963: the Welsh Laws*, pp. 51–9. Rees, W., 'Survivals of Ancient Celtic Custom in Medieval England' in *Angles and Britons; O'Donnell lectures*, Cardiff, 1963, pp. 149–68.

10. In addition to the texts and translations given in Section B above, see Jarman, A. O. H., 'The Heroic Ideal in Early Welsh poetry' in Meid, W., ed., *Beiträge zur Indogermanistik und Keltologie, Pokorny Festschrift (Innsbrucker Beiträge zur Kulturwissenschaft 13)*, 1967, pp. 193–211. Also Cramp, R. J., '*Beowulf* and Archaeology', *Med. Arch.* 1, 1957, pp. 57–77.

11. Translation by I. Ll. Foster, in Foster and Daniel, G., *Prehistoric and Early Wales*, 1965, pp. 229–30.

12. Translation by Williams, G., *The burning Tree, Poems from the First Thousand Years of Welsh Verse*, 1956, pp. 42–5.
13. Translation by Alexander, M., *The Earliest English Poems*, 1966, pp. 38–42.
14. These matters are expounded in Cheney, C. R., ed., *Handbook of Dates for Students of English History*, Royal Historical Society Guides and Handbooks No. 4, 1945.
15. Blair, P. H., 'The *Moore Memoranda* on Northumbrian History' in Fox, C. and Dickins, B., eds., *The Early Cultures of North-West Europe*, Cambridge, 1950, pp. 245–57.

CHAPTER TWO

1. The major controversies about the *De excidio* are covered by: Stevens, C. E., 'Gildas Sapiens', *English Historical Review* 56, 1941, pp. 353–73; Deanesly, M., 'The Implications of the Term *Sapiens* as Applied To Gildas' in Gordon, D. J., ed., *Fritz Saxl 1890–1948*, 1957, pp. 53–76; Grosjean, P., 'Notes d'hagiographie celtique', *Analecta Bollandiana* 75, 1957, pp. 158–226; Davies, W. H., 'The Church in Wales' in *CB*, pp. 131–50, especially pp. 137–42; Kerlouégan, F., 'Le Latin du *De excidio Britanniae* de Gildas' in *CB*, pp. 151–76.
2. Jackson, K. H. in Loomis, R. S., ed., *Arthurian Literature in the Middle Ages*, Oxford, 1959, p. 3.
3. No complete text of the *British Historical Miscellany* has been printed, and I have worked principally from a photo-copy of the relevant folios of Harley 3859. There is, however, a translation with some commentary in Wade-Evans, A. W., *Nennius's 'History of the Britons'*, 1938.
4. Chadwick, N. K., 'Early Culture and Learning in North Wales' in *Studies in the Early British Church*, Cambridge, 1958, pp. 29–120.
5. Jackson, K. H., 'On the Northern British Section in Nennius' in Chadwick, N. K., ed., *Celt and Saxon, Studies in the Early British Border*, Cambridge, 1963, pp. 20–62.
6. Good text and commentary in Phillimore, E., 'The *Annales Cambriae* and Old-Welsh Genealogies from *Harleian Ms 3859*', *Y Cymmrodor* 9, 1888, pp. 141–83.
7. For texts and commentaries, see Section B above.

CHAPTER THREE

1. The fundamental discussion remains that of Chambers, E. K., *Arthur of Britain*, 1927; reprint with supplementary bibliography by Roberts,

B. F., Cambridge, 1964. Armed with this and the annual *Bibliographical Bulletin* of the International Arthurian Society the reader could hope to keep abreast of developments in the fields of Arthurian fact and fancy. In addition, the basic texts are printed by Faral, E., *La Légende Arthurienne, études et documents: première partie, les plus anciens textes*, 3 vols., 1929; there is a short but pointed discussion by Jackson, K. H., 'The Arthur of history' in Loomis, *Arthurian Literature in the Middle Ages*, pp. 1–11; and Jones, T., 'The Early Evolution of the Legend of Arthur', *Nottingham Medieval Studies* 8, 1964, pp. 3–21, has been seminal for all my thinking.

2. Wade-Evans, A. W., *Vitae sanctorum Britanniae et genealogiae*, Cardiff, 1944, pp. 26–8 and 68–70 for Cadog; 260 for Padarn. See also Loomis, C. G., 'King Arthur and the Saints', *Speculum* 8, 1933, pp. 478–82.

3. Jackson, K. H., *Language and History in Early Britain*, Edinburgh, 1953.

4. The authoritative statement here is by Jackson, 'Once Again Arthur's Battles', *Modern Philology* 43, 1945, pp. 44–57, supplemented by the same author's 'Arthur's Battle of Breguoin', *Antiquity* 23, 1949, pp. 48–9 and 'The Site of Mount Badon', *Journal of Celtic Studies* 2, 1953, pp. 152–5.

5. The sceptical view is ably set out by Treharne, R. F., *The Glastonbury Legends, Joseph of Arimathea, the Holy Grail and King Arthur*, 1967. The archaeological evidence is most conveniently presented by Radford, C. A. R., 'Glastonbury Abbey' in Ashe, G., ed., *The Quest for Arthur's Britain*, 1968, pp. 119–38.

6. The case for the northern Arthur is argued by Bromwich, R., 'Scotland and the Earliest Arthurian Tradition', *Bibliog. Bull. Int. Arthurian Soc.* 15, 1963, pp. 85–95.

7. Eadie, J. W., 'The Development of Roman Mailed Cavalry', *Journal of Roman Studies* 57, 1967, pp. 161–73.

CHAPTER FOUR

1. The substance of this and Chapter 5 is covered by the general historical surveys listed in the section above covering general surveys. Where the account given here differs from that in the text-books, it is because my analysis of the sources leads me to weight the evidence differently.

2. The pioneer of a new approach has been Myres, J. N. L., with such articles as 'Some English Parallels to the Anglo-Saxon Pottery of Holland and Belgium in the Migration Period', *L'antiquité classique* 17, 1948, pp. 453–72, and 'The adventus Saxonum' in Grimes, W. F., ed., *Aspects of Archaeology in Britain and Beyond*, 1951, pp. 221–41.

3. Collingwood, R. G. and Wright, R. P., *The Roman Inscriptions of Britain, I, Inscriptions on Stone*, Oxford, 1965; *numerus Hnaudifridi*, no. 1576; *cuneus Frisorum*, no. 1594 from Housesteads, nos. 882, 883 from Papcastle.

4. Map 3 is based on the following sources: signal stations and Saxon Shore forts from O.S. *Map of Roman Britain*; northern forts from Birley, M. I., 'The Distribution of Crambeck Ware', *Ant. J.* 17, 1937, pp. 412–13; Welsh forts from Nash-Williams, V. E., *The Roman Frontier in Wales*, 2nd edition, ed. by Jarrett, M. G., Cardiff, 1969; sites with 'Germanic' buckles from Hawkes, S. C. and Dunning, G. C., 'Soldiers and Settlers in Britain, Fourth to Fifth Century', *Med. Arch.* 5, 1961, pp. 1–70; towns with artillery arrangements from Corder, P., 'The Reorganization of the Defences of Romano-British Towns in the Fourth Century', *Arch. J.* 112, 1955, pp. 20–42; sites with early Germanic pottery based on Myres, J. N. L., *Anglo-Saxon Pottery and the Settlement of England*, Oxford, 1969.

5. For a very full analysis of the sources used here, which reaches quite different conclusions, Morris, J., 'Dark Age Dates' in Jarrett, M. G. and Dobson, B., eds., *Britain and Rome*, Kendal, 1965, pp. 145–85.

6. Myres, J. N. L., 'Pelagius and the End of Roman Rule in Britain', *Journ. Roman Studies* 50, 1960, pp. 21–36.

7. The most recent analysis is Kirby, D. P., 'Vortigern', *Bulletin, Board of Celtic Studies* 23, 1968–70, pp. 37–59.

8. Mommsen, T., *Monumenta germaniae historica, chronica minora saec. IV.V.VI.VII* vol. 1, Berlin, 1892; reprint 1961, pp. 617–66.

CHAPTER FIVE

1. Copley, G. J., *The Conquest of Wessex in the Sixth Century*, 1954.

2. Blair, P. H., 'The Origins of Northumbria', *Archaeologia Aeliana* 4th series 25, 1947, pp. 1–51.

3. Meyer, K., 'Early Relations between Gael and Brython', *Transactions, Honourable Society of Cymmrodorion*, 1895–6, pp. 55–86; 'The Expulsion of the Dessi', *Y Cymmrodor* 14, 1900, pp. 101–35.

4. Jackson, K. H., 'The Britons in Southern Scotland', *Antiquity* 29, 1955, pp. 77–88 has a critical discussion.

5. Toynbee, J. M. C., 'Christianity in Roman Britain', *JBAA* 16, 1953, pp. 1–24 was a pioneering study. Barley, M. W. and Hanson, R. P. C., eds., *Christianity in Britain 300–700*, Leicester, 1968, is an important collection of essays. See also Wilson, P. A., 'Romano-British and Welsh

Christianity: Continuity or Discontinuity?', *WHR* 3, 1966–7, pp. 5–22 and 103–20.

CHAPTER SIX

1. Numerous books are available in this field. Particularly relevant to the present study is Wainwright, F. T., *Archaeology and Place-Names and History*, 1962. Accessible in Penguin editions are Woolley, L., *Digging Up the Past* – still the best account of the imaginative use of archaeological material as historical evidence; Wheeler, R. E. M., *Archaeology from the Earth*; Piggott, S., *Approach to Archaeology*. A continental point of view, important for the problems of correlating the cultures of the archaeologist with the nations and tribes of the historian is de Laet, S. J., *Archaeology and its Problems*, 1957. The distinctive, 'anthropologically oriented' American approach is well displayed by Deetz, J., *Invitation to Archaeology*, New York, 1967. Detailed statements made in the present chapter will be documented as appropriate in Chapters 7–10.
2. Barker, P., 'Some Aspects of the Excavation of Timber Buildings', *World Archaeology* 1, 1969–70, pp. 220–35.
3. CIIC 470.

CHAPTER SEVEN

1. General surveys and handbooks are: Rivet, A. L. F., *Town and Country in Roman Britain*, 1958; Collingwood, R. G. and Richmond, I. A., *The Archaeology of Roman Britain*, 1969; Wacher, J. S., ed., *The Civitas Capitals of Roman Britain*, Leicester, 1966; Rivet, A. L. F., ed., *The Roman Villa in Britain*, 1969.
2. Hogg, A. H. A., 'Some Unfortified Hut-Groups in Wales', *Celticum* 6, 1963, pp. 245–56.
3. Bonney, D. J., 'Iron-Age and Romano-British Settlement Sites in Wiltshire', *Wilts. Archaeological & Natural History Magazine* 63, 1968, pp. 27–38.
4. Frend, W. H. C., 'Religion in Roman Britain in the Fourth Century AD', *JBAA* 18, 1955, pp. 1–18; Wheeler, R. E. M. and Wheeler, T. V., *Report on the Excavation of the Prehistoric, Roman and Post-Roman Site in Lydney Park, Gloucestershire*, 1932; Lewis, M. J. T., *Temples in Roman Britain*, Cambridge, 1966.
5. Silchester after Collingwood-Richmond, *Archaeology of R. Britain*, Fig. 54; Caerwent after Nash-Williams, V. E., *Bulletin, Board of Celtic Studies* 15, 1952–4, pp. 165–7; Canterbury, SS Peter and Paul after

Taylor, H. M. and Taylor, J., *Anglo-Saxon Architecture* 2 vols., Cambridge, 1965, Fig. 62; Lyminge, St Mary after Taylor & Taylor, Fig. 187.

6. These points are largely covered in *C B*.

7. Myres, J. N. L., *Anglo-Saxon Pottery and the Settlement of England*, Oxford, 1969; Hawkes, S. C. and Dunning, G. C., 'Soldiers and Settlers in Britain, Fourth to Fifth Century', *Med. Arch.* 5, 1961, pp. 1–70.

8. Dinorben: Gardner, W. and Savory, H. N., *Dinorben, a Hill-Fort Occupied in Early Iron Age and Roman Times*, Cardiff, 1964,; Castell Degannwy: Alcock, L., 'Excavations at Degannwy castle, Caernarvonshire, 1961–6'. *Arch. J.* 124, 1967, pp. 190–201; Dinas Emrys: Savory, H. N., 'Excavations at Dinas Emrys, Beddgelert (Caern.), 1954–56', *Arch. Camb.* 109, 1960, pp. 13–77; Coygan: Wainwright, G. J., *Coygan Camp, a Prehistoric, Romano-British and Dark-Age Settlement in Carmarthenshire*, Cardiff, 1967.

9. Feachem, R. W., 'The Fortifications on Traprain Law', *PSAS* 89, 1955–6, pp. 284–9; my Fig. 9 is redrawn from this. Burley, E., 'A Catalogue and Survey of the Metalwork from Traprain Law', *PSAS* 89, 1955–6, pp. 118–226.

10. My Fig. 10 attempts to reconstruct the main components of a pit-group which has never been illustrated as a group before. The pit is Pit 1, Temples Site, Richborough. In addition to the illustrated pieces it contains a Samian bowl, Drag. 31; a rouletted beaker; bowls and mortaria in the same broad class as 99 and 102; and other flanged bowls comparable with 109 and 112. There was also a barbarous coin of Constantinopolis type. The pit was cut through the ruins of a temple. Other adjacent pits had similar pottery and coins of the houses of Valentinian and Theodosius. Bushe-Fox, J. P., *Third Report on the Excavations of the Roman Fort at Richborough, Kent*, 1932.

11. Cunliffe, B., 'The Saxon Culture-Sequence at Portchester Castle', *Ant. J.* 50, 1970, pp. 67–85.

12. For a different exposition, with full references, see Frere, S. S., 'The End of Towns in Roman Britain' in Wacher, *Civitas capitals*, pp. 87–100.

13. Discussion by Webster, G., 'The Future of Villa Studies', in Rivet, *The Roman Villa in Britain*, 1969, pp. 217–49.

14. Brodribb, A. C. C., Hands, A. R. and Walker, D. R., *Excavations at Shakenoak Farm near Wilcote, Oxfordshire*, Oxford, Part 1 1968; Part 2 1971.

15. Finberg, H. P. R., *Lucerna*, 1964, pp. 21–65. The theme of much of *Lucerna*, though undoubtedly overstated, is highly relevant to the present work.

16. Sylvester, D., *The Rural Landscape of the Welsh Borderland*, 1969, especially pp. 87–8.
17. For useful introductions to the wide topic of place-names: Reaney, P. H., *The Origin of English Place-Names*, 1961; Cameron, K., *English Place-Names*, 1961. Ekwall, E., *The Concise Oxford Dictinary of English Place-Names*, Oxford, 1936; 3rd edn 1947, etc., is the fundamental work of reference. Jackson, K. H., *Language and History in Early Britain*, Edinburgh, 1953, examines the linguistic processes.
18. Another exposition of many of the topics discussed in this last section is Alcock, L., 'Roman Britons and Pagan Saxons: An Archaeological Appraisal', *WHR* 3, 1966–8, pp. 229–50.

CHAPTER EIGHT

1. There is no general survey of the subject of this chapter, but a preliminary sketch was attempted by Alcock, L., *Dinas Powys*, Cardiff, 1963, especially pp. 34–72.
2. Kent, J. P. C., 'From Roman Britain to Saxon England' in Dolley, R. H. M., ed., *Anglo-Saxon Coins*, 1961, pp. 1–22.
3. Alcock, L., 'Pottery and Settlements in Wales and the March, AD 400–700' in Foster, I. Ll. and Alcock, eds., *Culture and Environment*, 1963, pp. 281–302. The claim is too sweepingly rejected by Gelling, P. S. and Stanford, S. C., 'Dark-Age Pottery or Iron-Age Ovens?', *Transactions, Birmingham Archaeological Society* 82, 1967, pp. 77–91.
4. Thomas, C., 'Grass-Marked Pottery in Cornwall' in Coles, J. M. and Simpson, D. D. A., eds., *Studies in Ancient Europe*, Leicester, 1968, pp. 311–31.
5. The seminal article was Radford, C. A. R., 'Imported Pottery Found at Tintagel, Cornwall' in *DAB*, pp. 59–70. The classification was developed further by Thomas, C., 'Imported Pottery in Dark-Age Western Britain', *Med. Arch.* 3, 1959, pp. 89–111. I am most grateful to Professor Thomas and Mr J. W. Hayes for making the unpublished results of their researches available to me.
6. Irimia, M., 'Cuptoarele Romano-Bizantine de ars ceramică de la Oltina Jud. Constanța)' in *Pontice, studii și materiale de istorie, arheologie și muzeografie*, Muzeul de Arheologie Constanța, 1968, pp. 379–407; French summary, p. 408.
7. Rigoir, J., 'Les sigillées paléochrétiennes grises et orangées', *Gallia* 26, 1968, pp. 177–244.
8. Peacock, D. and Thomas, C., 'Class E Imported Post-Roman Pottery: A Suggested Origin', *Cornish Archaeology* 6, 1967, pp. 35–46.

9. This map is based essentially on the research, both published and unpublished, of Professor Charles Thomas. I am most grateful to Professor Thomas for checking it as a factual statement, though he would probably reject the conclusions which I attempt to draw from it.

10. Leeds, E. T., 'Excavations at Chun Castle in Penwith, Cornwall', *Archaeologia* 76, 1926–7, pp. 205–40; 81, 1931, pp. 33–42.

11. Radford, C. A. R., 'Report on the Excavations at Castle Dore', *Journal, Royal Institution of Cornwall*, new series 1, appendix, 1951.

12. Alcock, L., *Dinas Powys*.

13. For Castell Degannwy, Dinas Emrys, Dinorben and Coygan, see Note 8 to Chapter 7.

14. Phillips, C. W., 'The Excavation of a Hut-Group at Pant-y-saer ... in Anglesey', *Arch. Camb.* 89, 1934, pp. 1–36.

15. Hogg, A. H. A., 'A Fortified Round Hut at Carreg-y-llam near Nevin', *Arch. Camb.* 106, 1957, pp. 46–55.

16. Hogg, A. H. A., 'Garn Boduan and Tre'r Ceiri', *Arch. J.* 117, 1960, pp. 1–39.

17. MacIvor, I., *Dumbarton Castle, Ministry of Works Official Guide-book*, Edinburgh, 1958.

18. Curle, A. O., 'Report on the Excavation ... of a Vitrified Fort ... Known as the Mote of Mark', *PSAS* 48, 1913–14, pp. 125–68.

19. The striking results of the first season are fully and promptly reported in Fowler, P. J., Gardner, K. S. and Rahtz, P. A., *Cadbury Congresbury, Somerset*, 1968, Bristol, 1970. Season-by-season accounts are in *Current Archaeology*.

20. Season-by-season accounts in *Ant. J.*, 1967–71, and in *Antiquity*, 1967–70. Fully illustrated summary by Alcock, L., *Cadbury-Camelot: Excavations at Cadbury Castle 1966–70*, in the series *New Aspects of Antiquity*, 1972.

21. Munro, R., *Ancient Scottish Lake-Dwellings or Crannogs*, Edinburgh, 1882, pp. 190–239.

22. Thomas, C., *Gwithian, Ten Years' Work (1949–1958)*, Gwithian, 1958.

23. Axe, spoon-bit, padlock-spring and awl from Buston, Note 21 above; axe from Cadbury-Camelot, unpublished; axe from Petersfinger, Note 9 to Chapter 10; coulter from White Fort, Waterman, D. W., 'The Excavation of a House and Souterrain at White Fort, Drumaroad, Co. Down', *UJA* 19, 1956, pp. 73–86; ploughshare from Dundrum Castle, Co. Down, *Archaeological Survey of County Down*, H.M.S.O., Belfast, 1966, p. 138, Fig. 79.1; spindle from Sutton Courtenay, Note 16 to Chapter 10, *3rd Report*, pl. xxii.

24. Fowler, P. J. and Thomas, A. C., 'Arable Fields of the Pre-Norman Period at Gwithian', *Cornish Archaeology* 1, 1962, pp. 61–84.

25. Fowler, E., 'Hanging Bowls' in Coles and Simpson, *Studies in Ancient Europe*, pp. 287–310, gives references to the extensive and inconclusive literature on the subject.

26. Henry, F., 'Irish Enamels of the Dark Ages and their Relation to the Cloisonné Techniques' in *DAB*, pp. 71–88, especially pp. 81–2.

27. Kilbride-Jones, H. E., 'The Evolution of Penannular Brooches with Zoomorphic Terminals in Great Britain and Ireland', *PRIA* 43, 1937, pp. 379–455, is the classic statement, well illustrated; its dating is rejected here in the light of more recent evidence. The present position is given by Fowler, E., 'Celtic Metalwork of the Fifth and Sixth Centuries AD', *Arch. J.* 120, 1963, pp. 98–160.

28. Cameron, K., '*Eccles* in English Place-Names' in *CB*, pp. 87–92.

29. Collected in Macalister, CIIC and Nash-Williams, ECMW. General surveys, making use of the evidence of the stones, include: Bu'lock, J. D., 'Early Christian Memorial Formulae', *Arch. Camb.* 105, 1956, pp. 133–41; Foster, I. Ll., 'The Emergence of Wales' in Foster and Daniel, G., eds., *Prehistoric and Early Wales*, 1965, pp. 213–35; Thomas, A. C., 'The Evidence from North Britain' in *CB*, pp. 93–122.

30. ECMW no. 294.

31. ECMW no. 142.

32. CIIC no. 520. For a more likely reading and translation, Radford, C. A. R. and Donaldson, G., *Whithorn and Kirkmadrine, Wigtownshire, Ministry of Works Official Guide*, Edinburgh, 1953.

33. Nordenfalk, C., 'Before the Book of Durrow', *Acta Archaeologica* 18, 1947, pp. 141–74.

34. ECMW no. 104.

35. ECMW no. 138.

36. ECMW no. 13.

37. ECMW no. 319.

38. Fox, C., 'The Re-erection of Maen Madoc, Ystradfellte, Breconshire', *Arch. Camb.* 95, 1940, pp. 210–16.

39. CIIC no. 516; preferred reading, Radford and Donaldson, *Whithorn and Kirkmadrine ... Guide*.

40. ECMW no. 78.

41. Rahtz, P. A., 'Sub-Roman Cemeteries in Somerset' in *CB*, pp. 193–5.

42. Thomas, C., 'An Early Christian Cemetery and Chapel on Ardwall Island, Kirkcudbright', *Med. Arch.* 11, 1967, pp. 127–88. For the back-

ground, Radford, C. A. R., 'The Early Church in Strathclyde and Galloway', *Med. Arch.* 11, 1967, pp. 105–26.

43. Radford, C. A. R., 'The Celtic Monastery in Britain', *Arch. Camb.* 111, 1962, pp. 1–24; *Tintagel Castle, Ministry of Works Official Guide*, 1935; 2nd edn 1939, etc.

44. Radford, C. A. R., 'The Church in Somerset down to 1100', *Proceedings, Somerset Archaeological & Natural History Society* 106, 1962, pp. 28–45.

45. Rahtz, P. A., 'Glastonbury Tor' in Ashe, G., ed., *The Quest for Arthur's Britain*, 1968, pp. 139–53.

CHAPTER NINE

1. Some general surveys are: Bieler, L., *Ireland: Harbinger of the Middle Ages*, 1963; De Paor, M. and De Paor, L., *Early Christian Ireland*, 1958; Henry, F., *Irish Art in the Early Christian Period to 800 AD*, 1965; Norman, E. R. and St Joseph, J. K. S., *The Early Development of Irish Society*, Cambridge, 1969; Ó Ríordáin, S. P., *Antiquities of the Irish Countryside*, 1942; 3rd edn 1953.

2. Ó Ríordáin, S. P., 'Roman Material in Ireland', *PRIA* 51, 1947, pp. 35–82, is the basic survey, but includes pottery which is now accepted as post-Roman (especially of Class E) rather than earlier. Mattingly, H. and Pearce, J. W. E., 'The Coleraine Hoard', *Antiquity* 11, 1937, pp. 39–45.

3. Painter, K. S., 'A Roman Silver Treasure from Canterbury', *JBAA* 28, 1965, pp. 1–15.

4. O'Kelly, M. J., 'Problems of Irish Ring-Forts' in Moore, D., ed., *The Irish Sea Province in Archaeology and History*, Cardiff, 1970, pp. 50–54, is a recent introductory survey.

5. Ó Ríordáin, S. P., 'A Large Earthen Ring-Fort at Garranes, Co. Cork', *PRIA* 47, 1942, pp. 77–150.

6. Raftery, B., 'Freestone Hill, Co. Kilkenny: An Iron Age Hill-Fort and Bronze Age Cairn', *PRIA* 68, 1969, pp. 1–108.

7. Proudfoot, V. B. and Wilson, B. C. S., 'Further Excavations at Larrybane Promontory fort, Co. Antrim', *UJA* 24–5, 1961–2, pp. 91–115.

8. Hencken, H. O'N., 'Ballinderry Crannog No. 2', *PRIA* 47, 1942, pp. 1–76, is an example with two periods of occupation separated by a flood deposit.

9. Hencken, H. O'N., 'Lagore Crannog: An Irish Royal Residence of the 7th to 10th Centuries AD', *PRIA* 53, 1950, pp. 1–247.

10. Collins, A. E. P., 'Excavations in Lough Faughan Crannog, Co. Down, 1951-52', *UJA* 18, 1955, pp. 45-82.

11. *Archaeological Survey of County Down*, Belfast, 1966, pp. 133-5.

12. For a further account of the north-east, Collins, A. E. P., 'Settlement in Ulster, 0-1100 AD', *UJA* 31, 1968, pp. 53-8.

13. O'Kelly, M. J., 'Two Ring-Forts at Garryduff, Co. Cork', *PRIA* 63, 1962, pp. 17-125.

14. The escutcheon from the river Bann, item 8 of the list on p. 80 of Henry, F., 'Irish Enamels . . .' in *DAB*, pp. 71-88. Mlle Henry's argument is the opposite of that advanced here.

15. Leeds, E. T., *Celtic Ornament in the British Isles down to AD 700*, Oxford, 1933, gives one view of these developments.

16. CIIC no. 145.

17. General survey, Hughes, K., *The Church in Early Irish Society*, 1966.

18. Leask, H. G., *Irish Churches and Monastic Buildings. I. The first Phases and the Romanesque*, Dundalk, 1955.

19. Lawlor, H. C., *The Monastery of St Mochaoi of Nendrum*, Belfast, 1925.

20. O'Kelly, M. J., 'Church Island near Valencia, Co. Kerry', *PRIA* 59, 1958, pp. 57-136.

21. Lethbridge, T. C., *Herdsmen and Hermits*, Cambridge, 1950, for a lively and knowledgeable discussion. Johnstone, P., 'The Bantry Boat', *Antiquity* 38, 1964, pp. 277-84; Evans, A., 'On a Votive Deposit of Gold Objects from the North-West Coast of Ireland', *Archaeologia* 55, 1894-7, pp. 391-408 for the Broighter boat.

22. Feachem, R. W., *A Guide to Prehistoric Scotland*, 1963, epecially pp. 175-86.

23. Christison, D. and Anderson, J., 'Excavations of Forts on the Poltalloch Estate, Argyll, in 1904-5', *PSAS* 39, 1904-5, pp. 292-322; Craw, J. H., 'Excavations at Dunadd. . . .', *PSAS* 64, 1929-30, pp. 111-27. For discussions, Stevenson, R. B. K., 'The Nuclear Fort of Dalmahoy, Midlothian, and Other Dark Age Capitals', *PSAS* 83, 1948-9, pp. 186-98; Feachem, R. W., 'The Hill-Forts of Northern Britain' in Rivet, A. L. F., ed., *The Iron Age in Northern Britain*, Edinburgh, 1966, pp. 59-87, especially p. 85.

24. Richards, M., 'The Irish Settlements in South-West Wales', *Journ. Royal Society of Antiquaries of Ireland* 90, 1960, pp. 133-62, covers a wider area than the title suggests.

25. Wright, R. P. and Jackson, K. H., 'A Late Inscription from Wroxeter' *Ant. J.* 48, 1968, pp. 296-300.

26. Alcock, L., 'The Irish Sea Zone in the Pre-Roman Iron Age' in Thomas, C., ed., *The Iron Age in Western Britain and Ireland*, forthcoming.

27. Thomas, C., 'People and Pottery in Dark-Age Cornwall', *Old Cornwall* 5, 1960, pp. 1–9.

28. Greene, D., 'Some Linguistic Evidence Relating to the British Church' in *CB* pp. 75–86.

29. Alcock, L., 'Was There an Irish Sea Culture-Province in the Dark Ages?' in Moore, D., ed., *The Irish Sea Province in Archaeology and History*, Cardiff 1970 pp. 55–65. The thesis advanced there, and in the present chapter, should be considered in the light of the discovery of 'grass-marked' pottery, presumably derived from the souterrain ware of Ulster, in the earliest structural phases of the Columban monastery of Iona. This serves to emphasize the absence of such pottery from mainland Scotland; Megaw, J. V. S., 'Iona and Celtic Britain, with an Interim Account of the Russell Trust Excavations, 1958–63', *Journal of Religious History* 3, no. 3, Sydney, 1965, pp. 212–37.

30. Wainwright, F. T., ed., *The Problem of the Picts*, Edinburgh, 1955, is the fundamental study, now supplemented by Henderson, I., *The Picts*, 1967. Feachem, R. W., *A Guide to Prehistoric Scotland*, 1963, is an accessible source for many of the relevant monuments.

31. Earlier accounts are now wholly superseded by Mackie, E. W., 'The Origin and Development of the Broch and Wheelhouse Building cultures of the Scottish Iron Age', *Proceedings, Prehistoric Society* 31, 1965, pp. 93–146 and 'Radio-Carbon Dates and the Scottish Iron Age', *Antiquity* 43, 1969, pp. 15–26.

32. Hamilton, J. R. C., *Excavations at Clickhimin, Shetland*, Edinburgh, 1968.

33. Young, H. W., 'Notes on the Ramparts of Burghead Revealed by Recent Excavations' *PSAS* 25, 1890–91, pp. 435–47, is the original account of the structure; Small, A., 'Burghead', *Scottish Archaeological Forum* 1969, pp. 61–8 discusses the C 14 dating.

34. I am grateful to Dr Anna Ritchie for information about this site in advance of publication.

35. Wainwright, F. T., *The Souterrains of Southern Pictland*, 1963.

36. Allen, J. R. and Anderson, J., *The Early Christian Monuments of Scotland*, Edinburgh, 1903, is the essential corpus. In addition to the commentaries in Wainwright, *Problem*, and Henderson, *Picts*, see Thomas, C., 'The Animal Art of the Scottish Iron Age and its Origins', *Arch. J.* 118, 1961, pp. 14–64, and 'The Interpretation of the Pictish Symbols', *Arch. J.* 120, 1963, pp. 31–97.

CHAPTER TEN

1. Two classic studies which are still invaluable are: Brown, G. B., *The Arts in Early England*, especially vols 3 and 4, *Saxon Art and Industry in the Pagan Period*, 1915; Hodgkin, R. H., *A History of the Anglo-Saxons* 2 vols, Oxford, 1935: 3rd edn 1953.

2. Recent studies of English material with particular reference to continental connections are: Hawkes, C. F. C., 'The Jutes of Kent' in *DAB*, pp. 91–111; Chadwick, S. E., 'The Anglo-Saxon Cemetery at Finglesham, Kent: A Reconsideration', *Med. Arch.* 2, 1958, pp. 1–71; Hawkes, S. C., 'The Jutish Style A: A Study of Germanic Animal Art in Southern England in the Fifth Century AD', *Archaeologia* 98, 1961, pp. 29–74; Evison, V. I., *The Fifth-century Invasions South of the Thames*, 1965; Myres, J. N. L., *Anglo-Saxon Pottery and the Settlement of England*, Oxford, 1969.

3. Tischler, F., 'Der Stand der Sachsenforschung, archäologisch gesehen', *Bericht der Römisch-Germanischen Kommission* 35, 1954, pp. 21–215; 'Saxons and Germans', *Antiquity* 29, 1955, pp. 17–20.

4. Accessible English accounts are: Jankuhn, H., 'The Continental Home of the English', *Antiquity* 26, 1952, pp. 14–24; Wheeler, Sir M., *Rome Beyond the Imperial Frontiers*, 1954, Chapter 4.

5. English accounts with references to the continental literature are: Klindt-Jensen, O., Tr. E. and D. Wilson, *Denmark Before the Vikings*, 1957; Radford, C. A. R., 'The Saxon House: A Review and Some Parallels', *Med. Arch.* 1, 1957, 27–38; Parker, H., 'Feddersen Wierde and Vallhagar: A Contrast in Settlements', *Med. Arch.* 9, 1965, pp. 1–10. The sources of the German houses in Fig. 25 are: Ostermoor bei Brunsbüttelkoog, Bantelmann, A., 'Zur Besiedlungsgeschichte der Marschen Schleswig-Holsteins' in Krämer, W., ed., *Neue Ausgrabungen in Deutschland*, 1958, pp. 229–42; Winkelmann, W., 'Eine westfälische Siedlung des 8. Jahrhunderts bei Warendorf, Kr. Warendorf', *Germania* 32, 1954, pp. 189–213.

6. Holmqvist, W., *Germanic Art During the First Millenium AD*, Stockholm, 1955, is an excellent introduction; Salin, B., *Die altgermanische Thierornamentik*, Stockholm, 1935, remains the basic manual. There are good illustrations of metalwork in Rice, D. T., ed., *The Dark Ages*, 1965.

7. Classical studies on these lines are: Leeds, E. T., '*The Archaeology of the Anglo-Saxon Settlements*, Oxford, 1913; Åberg, N., *The Anglo-Saxons in England during the Early Centuries after the Invasion*, Uppsala, 1926; Leeds, E. T., *Early Anglo-Saxon Art and Archaeology*, Oxford, 1936; Kendrick, T. D., *Anglo-Saxon Art to AD 900*, 1938.

8. It is not feasible here to list even a small number of classic cemeteries, but a fully documented survey is Meaney, A., *A Gazetteer of Early Anglo-Saxon Burial Sites*, 1964.

9. Burwell and Holywell Row: Lethbridge, T. C., 'Recent Excavations in Anglo-Saxon Cemeteries in Cambridgeshire and Suffolk', *Cambridge Antiquarian Society, Quarto Publications*, n.s. 3, 1931. Shudy Camps: Lethbridge, 'A Cemetery at Shudy Camps, Cambridgeshire', *Cambs. Antiq. Soc., Q.P.*, n.s. 5, 1936. Petersfinger: Leeds, E. T. and Shortt, H. de S., *An Anglo-Saxon Cemetery at Petersfinger, near Salisbury, Wilts.*, Salisbury, 1953.

10. Ucko, P. J., 'Ethnography and Archaeological Interpretation of Funerary Remains', *World Archaeology* 1, 1969–70, pp. 262–80.

11. Leeds, E. T., 'The Distribution of the Angles and Saxons Archaeologically Considered', *Archaeologia* 91, 1945, pp. 1–106 is an important exposition of the method.

12. For a critical view, endorsed here, Wilson, D. M., *The Anglo-Saxons*, 1960, especially pp. 13–22; 'Almgren and Chronology: A Summary and Some Comments', *Med. Arch.* 3, 1959, pp. 112–19.

13. Figures 27*a* and *f* are after Dunning, G. C., Hurst, J. G., Myres, J. N. L. and Tischler, F., 'Anglo-Saxon Pottery: A Symposium', *Med. Arch.* 3, 1959, pl. ii; *b* is after Hodgkin, *Hist. Anglo-Saxons*, Fig. 25; *c* is after Myres, *Ant. J.* 34, 1954, pl. xxi *b* (mistakenly attributed to Icknell Bury); *d* is after Leeds, E. T., 'An Anglo-Saxon Cemetery at Wallingford, Berkshire', *Berks. Archaeological Journal* 42, 1938, pp. 93–101; *e* is after Petersfinger, Note 9 above; *g* and *h* are after Sutton Courtenay 3rd Report, Note 16 below.

14. Harden, D. B., 'Glass Vessels in Britain and Ireland, AD 400–1000' in *DAB*, pp. 132–67.

15. The literature is vast. Bruce-Mitford, R. L. S., *The Sutton Hoo Ship Burial: A Handbook*, 1968, summarizes the views of the British Museum pending the full publication of the find; Green, C., *Sutton Hoo: The Excavation of a Royal Ship-burial*, 1963, is an independent appraisal.

16. Leeds, E. T., 'A Saxon Village near Sutton Courtenay, Berkshire', 1st report, *Archaeologia* 73, 1922–3, pp. 147–92; 2nd Report, 76, 1926–7, pp. 59–79; 3rd report, 92, 1947, pp. 79–94.

17. Barton, K. J., 'Settlements of the Iron-Age and Pagan Saxon Periods at Linford, Essex', *Transactions, Essex Archaeological Society* 1, 1962, pp. 57–104.

18. Note in *Med. Arch.* 11, 1967, p. 269.

19. Addyman, P. V., 'A Dark-Age Settlement at Maxey, Northants.', *Med. Arch.* 8, 1964, pp. 20–73.

20. Dunning, G. C., 'Bronze-Age Settlements and a Saxon Hut near Bourton-on-the-Water, Gloucestershire', *Ant. J.* 12, 1932, pp. 279–93.

21. Jones, M. U., Evison, V. I. and Myres, J. N. L., 'Crop-mark Sites at Mucking, Essex', *Ant. J.* 48, 1968, pp. 210–30. The superb chip-carved buckle from Mucking grave 117 is in Evison, 'Quoit brooch style buckles', *Ant. J.* 48, 1968, pp. 231–49.

22. Latest discussion, with full references: Dodgson, J. McN., 'The Significance of the Distribution of the English Place-Name in -ingas, -inga- in South-East England', *Med. Arch.* 10, 1966, pp. 1–29.

23. Comprehensive account in Taylor, H. M. and Taylor, J., *Anglo-Saxon Architecture*, 2 vols, Cambridge, 1965. In the course of time this will doubtless be modified and amplified in detail by papers in, for instance *JBAA* and *Med. Arch.* See already Jenkins, F., 'St Martin's Church at Canterbury: A survey of the Earliest Structural Features', *Med. Arch.* 9, 1965, pp. 11–15; Fletcher, E., 'Early Kentish Churches', *Med. Arch.* 9, 1965, pp. 16–31; Jackson, E. D. C. and Fletcher, E., 'Excavations at the Lydd Basilica 1966', *JBAA* 31, 1968, pp. 19–26.

24. Plan in Colvin, H. M., ed., *The History of the King's Works, I: The Middle Ages*, 1963, pp. 2–4. Note in *Med. Arch.* 1 1957, pp. 148–9.

25. Jackson, K. H., *Language and History in Early Britain*, Edinburgh, 1953.

26. Jones, G., 'Early Territorial Organization in England and Wales', *Geografiska Annaler* 43, 1961, pp. 174–81, with map on p. 179, probably overstates the case.

27. A good idea of the range of cemetery-size can be obtained from the tables in Kirk, J. R., 'Anglo-Saxon Cremation and Inhumation in the Upper Thames Valley in Pagan Times' in *DAB*, pp. 123–31.

CHAPTER ELEVEN

1. In examining social structure, the pioneer has been Jones, G. R. J., in numerous papers including 'Settlement Patterns in Anglo-Saxon England', *Antiquity* 35, 1961, pp. 221–32 (followed by a debate between Alcock and Jones, *Antiquity* 36, 1962, pp. 51–5); 'The Distribution of Bond Settlements in North-West Wales', *WHR* 2, 1964–6, pp. 19–36. The archaeological evidence for economy and social structure is sketched in Alcock, L., 'Some Reflections on Early Welsh Society and Economy', *WHR* 2, 1964–6, pp. 1–7, and more fully in Alcock, *Dinas Powys.*

2. Proudfoot, V. B., 'The Economy of the Irish Rath', *Med. Arch.* 5, 1961, pp. 94–122, sets the pattern for such studies in other areas.

3. In default of any comprehensive survey of the archaeological evidence, Loyn, H. R., *Anglo-Saxon England and the Norman Conquest*, 1962, provides by far the best account.

4. In addition to works mentioned in Section A above: Chadwick, H. M., *The Heroic Age*, Cambridge, 1912; and an invaluable pamphlet, Dillon, M., ed., *Early Irish Society*, Dublin, 1954.

5. For some commentary on this, and for the social structure of the ancestral English, Thompson, E. A., *The Early Germans*, Oxford, 1965.

6. Skene, W. F., ed. and trans., *Chronicles of the Picts, Chronicles of the Scots, and Other Early Memorials of Scottish History*, Edinburgh, 1867, pp. 308–17, 'Tract on the Scots of Dalriada'.

7. The sources for Fig. 28 are: Abingdon: Leeds, E. T. and Harden, D. B., *The Anglo-Saxon Cemetery at Abingdon, Berkshire*, Oxford, 1936; Burwell: Note 9 to Chapter 10; Croydon: Brown, *Arts*, vol. 3, pls. xxv and xxvii; Lagore: Note 9 to Chapter 9; Northolt: Evison, V. I., in Hurst, J. G., 'The Kitchen Area of Northolt Manor, Middlesex', *Med. Arch.* 5, 1961, pp. 226–30; Shudy Camps: Note 9 to Chapter 10.

8. Davidson, H. R. E., *The Sword in Anglo-Saxon England*, Oxford, 1962.

9. Rynne, E., 'The Impact of the Vikings on Irish Weapons', *Proceedings, 6th International Congress of Pre- and Protohistoric Sciences*, 1966, pp. 181–5.

10. The sources for fig. 29 are: Abingdon: Note 7 above; Alton, and Lowbury Hill: Evison, V. I., 'Sugar-Loaf Shield Bosses', *Ant. J.* 43, 1963, pp. 38–96; Ballinderry crannog no. 2: Note 8 to Chapter 9; Buston: Note 21 to Chapter 8; Dunadd 1904–5: Note 23 to Chapter 9; Garryduff: Note 13 to Chapter 9; Lagore: Note 9 to Chapter 9; Petersfinger: Note 9 to Chapter 10; Snell's Corner: Knocker, G. M., 'Early Burials and an Anglo-Saxon Cemetery at Snell's Corner, near Horndean, Hampshire', *Proceedings, Hampshire Field Club* 19, 1958, pp. 117–70.

11. The technical point and its broad social implications are discussed by White, L., *Medieval Technology and Social Change*, Oxford, 1962.

12. Sawyer, P. H., *The Age of the Vikings*, 1962, pp. 121–2 has a parallel discussion of the size of Viking armies.

13. Crucial discussion of the identification *Iudeu* = Stirling, and of the significance of the campaign, by Jackson, K. H. in Chadwick, N. K., ed., *Celt and Saxon*, Cambridge, 1963, pp. 35–8.

14. Binchy, D. A., 'The Passing of the Old Order', *Proceedings, International Congress of Celtic Studies, Dublin 1959*, Dublin, 1962, pp. 119–32.

15. Lucas, A. T., 'The Plundering and Burning of Churches in Ireland, 7th to 16th Century' in Rynne, E., ed., *North Munster Studies*, Limerick, 1967, pp. 172–229.

16. Lucas, A. T., 'Cattle in Ancient and Medieval Irish Society', paper to the Dublin meeting of the British Association for the Advancement of Science, 1957.

17. Blackfoot Indians: Ewers, J. C., *The Blackfeet*, Oklahoma, 1958, accessible in Bohannan, P., ed., *Law and Warfare, Studies in the Anthropology of Conflict*, New York, 1967. Bedu: first-hand accounts in Thesiger, W., *Arabian Sands*, 1959.

18. Fenik, B., *Typical Battle Scenes in the Iliad*, Wiesbaden, 1968 = *Hermes Einzelschriften* 21.

19. Throughout this section, all references to the evidence of *Y Gododdin* should be read in the light of the very different conclusions of Jackson, K. H., *The Gododdin*, Edinburgh, 1969.

20. Rigold, S., 'Recent Investigations into the Earliest Defences of Carisbrooke Castle, Isle of Wight' in Taylor, A. J., ed., *Château-Gaillard 3, Conference at Battle, Sussex*, Chichester, 1969, pp. 128–38.

21. Rahtz, P. A., 'An Excavation on Bokerly Dyke, 1958', *Arch. J.* 118, 1961, pp. 65–99, summarizes and modifies earlier work.

22. Lethbridge, T. C., 'The Riddle of the Dykes', *Proceedings, Cambridge Antiquarian Society* 51, 1958, pp. 1–5 gives the evidence but fails to solve the riddle.

23. Latest discussion of evidence and hypotheses, Myres, J. N. L., 'Wansdyke and the Origin of Wessex' in Trevor-Roper, H. R., ed., *Essays in British History Presented to Sir Keith Feiling*, 1964, pp. 1–27.

CHAPTER TWELVE

1. Bury, J. B., *The Invasion of Europe by the Barbarians*, 1928.

2. Wallace-Hadrill, J. M., *The Barbarian West, 400–1000*, 1952; *The Long-haired Kings and Other Studies in Frankish History*, 1962.

3. Deanesly, M., 'Roman Traditional Influence among the Anglo-Saxons', *English Historical Review* 58, 1943, pp. 129–46.

4. The sources for Fig. 31 are: Carraig Aille: Ó Ríordáin, S. P., 'Lough Gur Excavations: Carraig Aille and the "Spectacles"', *PRIA*. 52, 1949, pp. 39–111; Dinas Powys: Note 1 to Chapter 8; Sutton Courtenay: Note 16 to Chapter 10; Winnall: Meaney, A. L. and Hawkes, S. C., *Two Anglo-Saxon Cemeteries at Winnall, Winchester, Hampshire*, 1970.

5. I am most grateful to Mr D. Morgan Evans for providing the material on

which this drawing is based, and for many helpful discussions of the topics of this and the preceding chapter.

6. Gamber, O., 'The Sutton Hoo Military Equipment – an Attempted Reconstruction', *Journal, Arms and Armour Society* 5, 1966, pp. 265–89.

7. Musty, J. and Stratton, J. E. D., 'A Saxon Cemetery at Winterbourne Gunner, near Salisbury', *Wiltshire Archaeological and Natural History Magazine* 59, 1964, pp. 86–109. At this point it is relevant to recall the remarks on the accuracy of archaeological dating made in Chapter 10, pp. 294–5.

8. I have in mind here the reputation of the rock-climber, Joe Brown, in the early 1950s.

Supplementary Bibliography, 1987

Introduction

As was briefly explained in the Revised preface, p. xvii, the years since the original publication of *Arthur's Britain* have seen an explosive growth, both in evidence relevant to the Arthurian period, and in discussions and interpretations of it. One index of that growth is the appearance of new journals devoted largely to the Dark Ages, or, as the period is now widely known, the early medieval period. Although these are principally concerned with the written evidence, they do also contain some archaeological material. Three of them normally appear once or twice a year: *Anglo-Saxon England* (abbreviated *ASE*) from 1972; *Cambridge Medieval Celtic Studies* (*CMCS*) from 1981; and *Peritia* from 1982. More sporadic are *Anglo-Saxon Studies in Archaeology and History* (*ASSAH*) from 1979; and *Studies in Celtic History* (*SCH*), likewise from 1979. Also from 1979 on, *Landscape History* (*LH*) often contains studies of Roman and early medieval settlement patterns. Finally, much important material, both archaeological and historical, including conference papers and monographs on both artefacts and monuments, appears with commendable promptitude in the invaluable *British Archaeological Reports* (*BAR*).

It is not easy, even for the professional archaeologist or historian, to keep track of new discoveries and ideas. The indispensable guide is the Council for British Archaeology's *British Archaeological Abstracts*, now (1987) at volume 20. The coverage is not confined to British archaeology, but includes a generous sample of Continental material as well as relevant historical papers. The present supplementary bibliography does not attempt to compete with *Abstracts*, but offers a sample of new work which appears both important in itself and relevant to the theme and content of *Arthur's Britain*.

The pattern of the Supplementary Bibliography is as follows. Three major writers on the question of the historical Arthur are first briefly mentioned. Recent critical approaches to the written sources are then considered. The bulk of the bibliography is devoted to new archaeological and historical evidence and syntheses, beginning with late Roman Britain, and proceeding thence to Celtic Britain in general, and thence to the Picts, the Scots and the North Britons; Ireland, secular and Christian; the Anglo-Saxons; and early Christian archaeology. Finally, a brief Conclusion sets out the author's present position on the Arthur of history.

It is also appropriate to mention two important reviews of *Arthur's Britain*, by T. Jones, *Studia Celtica* 7, 1972, pp. 184–6, and K. H. Jackson, *Antiquity* 47, 1973, pp. 80–81.

The Historical Arthur (Chapters 3 and 12)

The major statement on the possibility of detecting the historical Arthur is now that of the late J. Morris, *The Age of Arthur: A History of the British Isles from 350 to 650*, 1973 (and also 3 vols. paperback). Morris saw Arthur as an undoubtedly historical person, the last Roman emperor of Britain, whose Camelot was at Camulodunum, that is, Colchester, Essex. He argued this interpretation from a massive knowledge of both the archaeological evidence and the written sources, often of considerable obscurity. Unfortunately, it is generally considered that he lacked critical judgement of the value, or otherwise, of those sources; and consequently, most scholars have found it impossible to recommend *The Age of Arthur* to students, let alone to the general reader with Arthurian interests. For instance, D. P. Kirby and J. E. Caerwyn Williams, in their review in *Studia Celtica* 10–11, 1975–76, pp. 454–86, having described the book as 'an outwardly impressive piece of scholarship', go on to say that it 'crumbles upon inspection into a tangled tissue of fact and fantasy which is both misleading and misguided'. Even a more sympathetic review by J. Campbell in his *Essays in Anglo-Saxon History*, 1986, pp. 121–30, makes it clear that the work is seriously flawed in detail.

(It should here be mentioned that Campbell's review includes a brief but outstandingly sensible interpretation of events in fifth-century Britain.)

A quite different approach is that of R. Barber, who through a series of books, and most recently (1986) in *King Arthur: Hero and Legend*, has traced the development of medieval stories about Arthur from their origins in brief references to a heroic figure of the fifth or sixth century. Barber rejects the entries in the Welsh Annals as unhistorical, and claims that the oldest truly historical reference to an Arthur is that to Arthur son of Aedan mac Gabran, king of Dalriada (i.e. Argyll). A quite different appreciation of the significance of the Dalriadan Arthur will be found on p. 73 above.

Thirdly, from the quasi-mystical approach of his earliest books, such as *King Arthur's Avalon: The Story of Glastonbury*, 1957, G. Ashe has developed a greater knowledge of the historical and legendary sources. Most recently, in *The Discovery of King Arthur*, 1985, he has drawn attention to a British war leader, one Riothamus, as the model or prototype of the Arthur of the developed romances. Riothamus is indeed a well-attested historical figure, who is recorded as having taken a large war-band to Gaul at the invitation of Anthemius, Augustus in the West, to assist him against the Visigoths. Whatever role Riothamus may have played in Gaul, he is not recorded in British sources. In any case, the later decades of fifth-century Britain have plenty of room for an Arthur independent of both Riothamus and Ambrosius.

The Written Evidence (Chapters 1, 2 and 3)

To the list of principal texts and translations given above, pp. 366–8, two new editions should now be added. M. Winterbottom edits and translates *Gildas: The Ruin of Britain and Other Works*, 1978, in a series, *History from the Sources*, begun by J. Morris to provide supporting documentation for his *The Age of Arthur*. In the same series, Morris himself edited and translated *Nennius: British History and the Welsh Annals*, 1980. This remains the most accessible text and translation, especially of the Annals; but for the *Historia Brittonum*, it will eventually be superseded by D. N. Dumville's new edition of all the available texts, with commentaries, but apparently without translations. Part 3, *The 'Vatican' Recension*, appeared in 1985, but the promised reconstruction of the archetypal version, together with commentaries, is no doubt well into the future.

In chapter 2 of *Arthur's Britain*, I looked at what I called 'three key texts . . . which together provided the bulk of the [written] evidence for Arthurian Britain'. It will be convenient here to take each of these in turn and see how recent critical studies have dealt with them.

P. Sims-Williams, 'Gildas and the Anglo-Saxons', *CMCS* 6, 1983, pp. 1–30, deals sympathetically with that 'enigmatic figure'; but also critically with the historical value of chapters 3–26 of the *De excidio Britanniae*: as an account, 'it stands alone'. A much fuller discussion is edited by M. Lapidge and D. N. Dumville, *Gildas: New Approaches*, *SCH* 5, 1984. This ranges widely over Gildas's education and Latin style, and attempts to set the romanized culture of sub-Roman Britain against its Continental background. The chronology and geography of Gildas's background are considered to 'remain perhaps the most elusive problems' (p. x), and many aspects of research are still in their infancy. Despite much of great interest, and some positive conclusions as well as some decisively negative ones, the book as a whole is a monument to the reductionism of the current Cambridge school of early medieval scholars.

Turning now to what I called the *British Historical Miscellany*, that is, the text of the *Historia Brittonum*, the Welsh Annals, and other historical or quasi-historical material collected together in the British Museum manuscript Harley 3859, both the term itself and my attempt to treat these diverse texts in some unitary sense have not won acceptance. The most sustained criticism is that by D. N. Dumville, 'Sub-Roman Britain: history and legend', *History* 62, 1977, pp. 173–92. It is therefore necessary to consider the History and the Annals separately.

In part, Dumville is sniping from behind the battlements of his own, largely unpublished, new editions of the texts; but, for the most part, he is applying totally valid canons of source criticism. Indeed, in view of his criticisms of *Arthur's Britain*, it is fair to repeat here what I wrote in 1971 about the *Historia Brittonum*: 'The work of distinguishing earlier [elements] from later, genuine from bogus, is itself only in its early stages' (p. 41). The stage now reached by the severest critic is well represented by D. N. Dumville, 'The historical value of the *Historia Brittonum*', in R. Barber (ed.), *Arthurian Literature* 6, 1986, pp. 1–26. Dumville's considered verdict is that 'if [the *Historia*] does not serve to lighten the darkness of the fifth to seventh centuries, it nonetheless offers many unexplored possibilities when we come to consider the history and culture of the eighth and ninth centuries' (p. 26).

Turning now to the annals, the foundations for the modern study of annals in Celtic Britain and Ireland were laid as recently as 1972; for in that year there appeared A. P. Smyth's 'The earliest Irish annals: their first contemporary entries', *PRIA* 72, pp. 1–48; and also the late K. Hughes's *Early Christian Ireland: Introduction to the Sources*, with a long chapter on the annals. Smyth's view is that contemporary entries in the Irish annals begin about AD 550 (p. 10). Hughes, on the other hand, considers that 'there were probably no contemporary annals until late in the seventh century' (p. 145). At the same time, she concedes that, from at least 585, there was reliable earlier material to draw on, which might be entered retrospectively when chronicles including contemporary annals came to be compiled. A new turn to the discussion has now been given by D. Ó. Cróinín, 'Early Irish annals from Easter tables: a case restated', *Peritia* 2, 1983, pp. 74–86; he argues, *contra* recent views, that from early in the sixth century (though not demonstrably so in Ireland or Britain), historical events were entered on the margins of Easter Tables.

The relevance of this discussion to the Arthur entries in the Welsh Annals is immediately apparent. For an examination of those Annals themselves, we turn to K. Hughes, 'The Welsh Latin Chronicles: *Annales Cambriae* and related texts', originally published in *Proceedings of the British Academy* 59, 1973, pp. 233–58, and subsequently reprinted in *Celtic Britain in the Early Middle Ages*, SCH 2, 1980, pp. 67–85; and also 'The A-text of *Annales Cambriae*', SCH 2, pp. 86–100. A major theme of these papers is the dependence of the earliest entries in the Welsh Annals on the Irish Annals.

Concerning the Arthur entries, Hughes points out that they belong to the early section, dependent on the Irish Annals, from which they are absent. She continues: 'It should now be clear that there is no ground for Leslie Alcock's assurance that they go back to a contemporary source' (1980, p. 73). In fact, there is no compelling logic here: that the overwhelming majority of the early Welsh entries derive from an Irish chronicle does not preclude the possibility that some may derive from another source.

In fact, Hughes softens her position in a footnote which deserves quoting in full: 'Alcock (*Arthur's Britain*, pp. 3, 45-9) believes that the fifth- and sixth-century entries were made in contemporary Easter Tables. This is not impossible, but it is much more likely that they are based on the calculations of an eighth- (or perhaps seventh-) century scholar' (1980, p. 73, n. 41).

D. N. Dumville's version of this (*History* 62, 1977, p. 176) is: 'There is no question, as Dr Hughes has made clear, of the fifth- and earlier-sixth-century entries deriving from a contemporary source, and certainly not from marginal entries in paschal tables of the fifth century onwards, as Alcock would have us believe.' The modern historian may well consider that source criticism needs applying to the writings of Dr Dumville as much as to *Annales Cambriae* and the *Historia Brittonum*.

The third of my three key texts was the *Anglo-Saxon Chronicle*. The doubts which I cast upon the chronology of the early entries in the *Chronicle* (pp. 43-4 above) have been very powerfully reinforced by P. Sims-Williams, 'The settlement of England in Bede and the *Chronicle*', *ASE* 12, 1983, pp. 1-41. In his Conclusion, Sims-Williams puts forward some positive approaches to the written sources for fifth- and early-sixth-century history; but he ends by echoing the words of the pioneering scholar of the period, J. M. Kemble, in 1849: 'the genuine details of the German conquests in England [are] irrevocably lost to us'.

Finally, recent work in less central areas should be mentioned. Firstly, early Welsh poetry, with special relevance to *Y Gododdin*. R. Bromwich edited a series of pioneering essays by Ifor Williams, which had laid the foundations of the study, in *The Beginnings of Welsh Poetry*, 1972. What has been built on the foundation may be seen in R. Bromwich and R. B. Jones (eds.), *Astudiaethau ar yr Hengerdd*, 1978, which, despite its Welsh title, contains a major paper in English on 'The authenticity of the *Gododdin*: an historian's view' by T. M. Charles-Edwards; moreover, there is an English synopsis of all the papers.

Secondly, genealogies have, in the past, loomed large in attempts to write early British and Anglo-Saxon history. Modern critical approaches owe much to research in Africa, where European written records provide a check on tribal, oral memories. A good example of both principle and practice is D. P. Henige, *The Chronology of Oral Tradition*, which is significantly sub-titled *Quest for a Chimera*. Although concentrating on Africa, Henige includes a brief but pointed analysis of the royal genealogies of Scotland.

In Britain, the most important research is that of the late M. Miller, well summarized in 'Royal pedigrees of the insular Dark Ages: a progress report', published, significantly, in *History in Africa* 7, 1980, pp. 201–24. Miller's writings are both dense and detailed. Two may be cited to give the flavour: 'Historicity and the pedigrees of the Northcountrymen', *Bulletin, Board of Celtic Studies* 26.3, 1974–6, pp. 255–80; and 'Date-guessing and pedigrees', *Studia Celtica* 10–11, 1975–6, pp. 96–109. It should be stressed that Miller's critique of the historicity of early genealogies goes far beyond the tentative comments on pp. 10–11 above.

Thirdly, very difficult technical problems of chronology are discussed in detail by K. Harrison, *The Framework of Anglo-Saxon History to AD 900*, 1976. Again, this goes far beyond any of the chronological discussions in *Arthur's Britain*, especially on pp. 17–20 above.

New archaeological and historical evidence and syntheses

Later Roman Britain (Chapters 4 and 7)

The major authoritative study is P. Salway, *Roman Britain*, 1981, Parts IV and V. This, the new Volume I of the *Oxford History of England*, takes a far sounder view of the Arthurian problem than did R. G. Collingwood in the original volume. A wide-ranging survey of the problems of *The end of Roman Britain* is presented in the proceedings of a conference under that title edited by P. J. Casey as *BAR* 71, 1979. Several papers by E. A. Thompson appear to me to be highly credulous in their use of written sources: they are well represented by 'Saint Germanus of Auxerre and the End of Roman Britain', *SCH* 6, 1984.

A major contribution to the military archaeology is S. Johnson, *The Roman Forts of the Saxon Shore*, 1976, 1979; but the same author's *Later Roman Britain*, 1980, is frequently misleading when he moves into barbarian areas and into the fifth century. A controversial view of the role of the Saxons, especially as enemies of Roman Britain, is taken by P. Bartholomew, 'Fourth-century Saxons', *Britannia* 15, 1984, pp. 169–85.

The evidence for the fate of the towns is brought together in J. Wacher, *The Towns of Roman Britain*, 1974; but the interpretation of the evidence is open to much debate. A challenging paper by R. Reece, 'Town and country: the end of Roman Britain', *World Archaeology* 12, 1980, pp. 77–92, argues that by AD 350 the towns had gone, replaced by mere administrative villages, and that by the fifth century the Anglo-Saxon settlers would have encountered little remaining *romanitas*. A surprising but highly relevant discovery has been P. A. Barker's excavation, as the centre-piece of fifth-century Wroxeter, of a major building, classical in form but built of timber, not stone: *Wroxeter Roman City Excavations 1966–80*, Dept of Environment, 1981. A special problem, relevant both to the fate of the towns and to the credibility of Gildas, is that of the effects of plague. Here, M. Todd, '*Famosa Pestis* and fifth-century Britain', *Britannia* 8, 1977, pp. 319–25, should be read in the light of the wider studies of W. H. McNeill, *Plagues and Peoples*, 1976.

The other major element in the romanization of Britain was the villa. There appears to be no recent discussion of the fate of villas in general terms; but two case studies of a villa being succeeded by an Anglo-Saxon settlement are of considerable interest: D. F. Mackreth, 'Orton Hall Farm, Peterborough: a Roman and Saxon settlement' in M. Todd (ed.), *Studies in the Romano-British Villa*, 1978, pp. 209–23; and W. J. Rodwell and K. A. Rodwell, *Rivenhall: Investigations of a Villa, Church, and Village, 1950–1977*, CBA Research Report 55. At Rivenhall, the villa site continued in occupation, but with some changes in the form of the buildings, into the fifth and sixth centuries.

Post-Roman Britain: General

Before regional studies are considered, some more general references may be mentioned. There are broad historical surveys in H. P. R. Finberg, *The Formation of England 550–1042*, 1974, and P. H. Sawyer, *From Roman Britain to Norman England*, 1978. L. M. Smith (ed.), *The Making of Britain: The Dark Ages*, 1984, originated in a television series, but the contributors are all eminent scholars in the field. In a classic example of ultimate reductionism, 'the Arthur story' is simply dismissed as 'pure fiction'. For a good example of scholars talking to one another, D. A. Hinton (ed.), *25 Years of Medieval Archaeology*, 1983, covers modern theoretical approaches, as well as both archaeologists' and historians' views on a quarter-century's research in Anglo-Saxon England and Celtic Britain.

Celtic Britain (Chapters 7 and 8)

For the archaeology, Ll. Laing, *The Archaeology of Late Celtic Britain and Ireland c. 400–1200 AD*, 1975, aims to be comprehensive on both sites and artefacts, but it is careless or erroneous in detail (including in its bibliographical references) and its illustrations are also poor. Slighter, but altogether sounder, is C. Thomas, *Britain and Ireland in Early Christian Times AD 400–800*, 1971. The same author's *Celtic Britain*, 1986, adds some new material, but suffers from a heavy overlay of neo-Celtic nationalism.

For south-western England, the latest survey of the archaeology is M. Todd, *The South West to AD 1000*. For Wales, W. Davies, *Wales in the Early Middle Ages*, 1982, is an excellent introduction to the written sources, and makes some use of archaeology as well. For Wales and Dumnonia, Alcock, 1987, brings together a number of interlinked essays, some new, some republished with revisions, on the theme of *Economy, Society and Warfare among the Britons & Saxons* (abbreviated *ESW*). These include a shortened and up-dated version of the excavation report on the Welsh princely stronghold of Dinas Powys; and the most recently published thoughts on Cadbury-Camelot. In contrast to the interpretation advanced above and in Alcock, *'By South Cadbury is that Camelot . . .'*, 1972, that the function of the hill-fort around AD 500 was as a campaign base for the defence of Dumnonia and the Arthurian campaigns, leading up to the victory of Mount Badon, Cadbury is now seen as a permanently occupied political and administrative centre, taking over in the later fifth century the role of the Roman *civitas* capital at Ilchester.

A major advance in our ability to identify secular sites of high rank in Celtic Britain has been brought about by C. Thomas's dedicated research on imported pottery, now incorporated in his *Provisional List of Imported Pottery in Post-Roman Western Britain and Ireland*, 1981. This has made it possible to identify more closely the various Mediterranean and North African sources of the imports, and consequently to date their occurrence in Celtic Britain more precisely. Indeed, the pottery remains our best chronological indicator for early medieval sites; certainly more precise than radiocarbon dating.

Our greater understanding of the chronological evidence for the period – not just the imported pottery, but metalwork and metalworking debris, characteristic bone and antler combs and pins, the radiocarbon dates, and reliable historical references – has made it possible to double the list of sites on Map 6, p. 210 above. A map and documented gazetteer by E. A. Alcock appears as an appendix to L. Alcock, 'The activities of potentates in Celtic Britain, AD 500–800: a positivist approach', in S. T. Driscoll and M. R. Nieke (eds.), *Power and Politics in Early Medieval Britain and Ireland*, 1988. Although this paper deals with 'enclosed places', in many cases standard hill-forts, some of which can be shown to have been involved in the warfare of kings, its major aim is to demonstrate that such a military role was not their only function; they were also, as can be seen at Dinas Powys, economic, industrial and socio-political centres.

A broadly similar conclusion is presented in I. C. G. Burrow's regional study of *Hill-forts and Hill-top Settlement in Somerset in the First to Eighth Centuries AD*, *BAR* 91, 1981, which also provides the most recent (1981!) account of the important site of Cadbury-Congresbury. P. A. Rahtz, 'Celtic society in Somerset AD 400–700', *Bulletin. Board of Celtic Studies* 30, 1982, pp. 176–200, uses 'catastrophe theory' to model the historical processes which followed on the collapse of Roman rule; his account owes more to anthropological theory than to the available historical and archaeological evidence, and therefore tells us little about the actual course of events in Dumnonia.

For Cornwall, N. Johnson and P. Rose provide a copiously illustrated discussion of 'Defended settlement in Cornwall' from *c*. 600 BC to post-400 AD in D. Miles (ed.), *The Romano-British Countryside: Studies in Rural Settlement and Economy*, *BAR* 103, 1982, pp. 151–207. The major Cornish site, Tintagel, has undergone a radical reappraisal, from monastery (see pp. 249–51 above) to princely, or perhaps even royal, stronghold, in a series of papers: C. Thomas, 'East and west: Tintagel, Mediterranean imports and the early insular Church' in S. M. Pearce, *The Early Church in Western Britain and Ireland*, *BAR* 102, 1982, pp. 17–24; K. R. Dark, 'The plan and interpretation of Tintagel', *CMCS* 9, 1985, pp. 1–17; A. C. Thomas and P. J. Fowler, 'Tintagel: a new survey of the "Island"', Royal Commission on the Historical Monuments of England, *Annual Review 1984–85*, pp. 16–22.

Among leading classes of artefacts, H. E. Kilbride-Jones deals in general with *Celtic Craftsmanship in Bronze*, 1980; and more specifically with *Zoomorphic Penannular Brooches*, 1980; both are well illustrated, but the chronological scheme which they advance is highly questionable. A. MacGregor studies objects of *Bone, Antler, Ivory and Horn*, 1985, many of them characteristic of post-Roman Celtic Britain.

The Picts, the Scots and the North Britons (Chapters 8 and 9)

Two major historical studies, extending from the Roman period into the Middle Ages, which make use of archaeological evidence are A. A. M. Duncan, *Scotland: the Making of the Kingdom*, 1975, and A. P. Smyth, *Warlords and Holy Men: Scotland AD 80–1000*, 1984. The archaeology is covered in chapters 6–8 of G. and A. Ritchie, *Scotland: Archaeology and Early History*, 1981.

The conflicts between Roman military forces and northern barbarians, which were a major factor in the collapse of ordered government and the calling in of Germanic mercenaries, are sympathetically considered by D. J. Breeze, *The Northern Frontiers of Roman Britain*, 1982.

For the immediate post-Roman centuries, no general synthesis is currently available. L. Alcock analyses historical and archaeological evidence for fortifications in G. Guilbert (ed.), *Hill-fort studies*, 1981, pp. 150–80; but otherwise, new material is to be found in studies of particular areas or peoples. The history of the *Scotti* is dealt with in J. Bannerman, *Studies in the History of Dalriada*, 1974, and Marjorie O. Anderson, *Kings and Kingship in Early Scotland*, 1973, revised 1980. The field archaeology is reported in the Argyll *Inventories* of the Royal Commission on the Ancient & Historical Monuments of Scotland, 6 vols., 1971–88; but advances in the archaeology of the *Scotti* await the publication of A. Lane's excavations at Dunadd and Alcock's at Dunollie.

The Picts, however, have received much attention. The classic statements on Pictish history and archaeology were those in F. T. Wainwright (ed.), *The Problem of the Picts*, 1955, reprinted 1980, and I. Henderson, *The Picts*, 1967. Our knowledge has been radically revised in conferences in Glasgow and Dundee, published respectively by J. G. P. Friell and W. G. Watson (eds.), *Pictish Studies: Settlement, Burial and Art in Dark Age Northern Britain*, *BAR* 125, 1984 (Glasgow); and A. Small (ed.), *The Picts: A New Look at Old Problems*, 1987 (Dundee).

The historical evidence is surveyed in the Dundee volume by Marjorie O. Anderson in 'Picts – the name and the people'. Settlement archaeology among both the heartland Picts and the peripheral Picts of the Isles is widely examined by Alcock in the Glasgow volume. This paper, 'A survey of Pictish settlement archaeology', also includes the first account of securely dated Pictish fortifications. Other important forts are discussed in the Dundee volume by I. Ralston (Portknockie and other promontory forts) and J. Close-Brooks (Clatchard Craig). Our views on the density of settlement among the southern Picts has now been revolutionzed by the air survey evidence deployed by G. S. Maxwell in the same volume.

A major topic of the Glasgow conference was the burials of the Picts, which previously had been virtually unrecognized. J. Close-Brooks provides an overview, while details of characteristic burials, typically in cemeteries with both round and square cairns or barrows, are provided by G. F. Bigelow (Shetland), R. Gourlay (Caithness),

C. D. Morris (Orkney) and J. B. Stevenson and others (Inverness-shire).

The most stimulating paper at Glasgow was read by T. Watkins, who, under the question 'Where were the Picts?', and armed with evidence from his own excavations of Pictish and Proto-Pictish souterrains, pioneered a social archaeology of southern Pictland. His lead was followed at Dundee by Alcock, whose avowed intention was to demythologize the Picts and to reveal them as a typical north-west European barbarian society. A leading theme of these papers, and of others not listed here but published either in the Conference volumes or elsewhere, is that the Picts were not merely formidable warriors as the Romans and Northumbrians saw them, but also prosperous farmers.

Finally, the archaeology of the North Britons is summarized by Alcock in *ESW*, chapter 16, 'Warfare and poetry among the northern Britons'.

Ireland, Secular and Christian (Chapter 9)

Without suggesting that research into Late Iron Age and Early Christian Ireland has been dormant, there is relatively little new to report that is relevant to the theme or character of this book.

The salvage excavation of raths (ring-forts) continues apace; current opinion favours a date after AD 400 for their main period of building and occupation, but no extensive synthesis is available. The latest revision of S. P. O. Riordain's *Antiquities of the Irish countryside*, by R. de Valera, 1979, provides the best summary of relevant sites. B. Wailes's examination of 'The Irish "royal sites" in history and archaeology', *CMCS* 3, 1982, pp. 1–29, demonstrates how long-abandoned monuments such as Tara may be taken over by later legends.

Important surveys of early Irish society and economy, of wide relevance to other barbarian societies, and hence to chapter 11 above, appear in F. Mitchell, *The Irish landscape*, 1976, especially chapter 5, and in D. Ó Corráin, *Ireland before the Normans*, 1972, chapter 2. More detailed studies include C. Doherty on 'Exchange and trade...', *J. Royal Soc Antiq Ireland* 110, 1980, pp. 67–89, and on 'Hagiography as a source for economic activity', *Peritia* 1, 1982, pp. 300–328; M. Gerriets, 'Economy and society: clientship according to the Irish laws', *CMCS* 6, 1983, pp. 43–61; and E. James, 'Ireland and western Gaul . . .', in D. Whitelock *et al.* (eds.), *Ireland in Early Medieval Europe*, 1982, pp. 362–86. Of papers in T. Reeves-Smyth & F. Hamond (eds.), *Landscape Archaeology in Ireland*, *BAR* 116, 1983, special mention must be made of F. McCormick, 'Dairying and beef production . . . the faunal evidence', pp. 253–67.

The most interesting recent work concerns the Church: the indispensable guide here is K. Hughes and A. Hamlin, *The Modern Traveller to the Early Irish Church*, 1977. Major conference proceedings, edited by S. Pearce as *The Early Church in Western Britain and Ireland*, *BAR* 102, 1982, have done much to modify, if not sweep away entirely, the idea that remote oratories like Gallarus were at all typical. In particular, V. Hurley argued, in 'The early church in the south-west of Ireland: settlement and organization', that ecclesiastical enclosures had a distribution very similar to that of secular ring-forts. This idea is further elaborated in Reeves-Smyth & Hamond, pp. 269–94, by L. Swan on 'Enclosed ecclesiastical sites . . .'. Moreover, C. A. R. Radford, surveying 'The earliest Irish churches', *UJA* 40, 1977, pp. 1–11, has postulated timber churches of considerable size and grandeur on the basis of documentary evidence.

Finally, the combined significance of Ireland and of the church in early artistic developments is well demonstrated in M. Ryan (ed.), *Ireland and Insular Art AD 500–1200*.

The Anglo-Saxons (Chapter 10)

An excellent, brief but well-illustrated account of the Continental background to the Anglo-Saxons is P. Dixon, *Barbarian Europe*, 1976. Despite its 'coffee-table' format, D. M. Wilson (ed.), *The Northern World* is authoritative. M. Todd, *The Barbarians: Goths, Franks and Vandals*, 1972, 1980; and *The Northern Barbarians 100 BC–AD 300*, 1975, 1987, should also be mentioned. A recent brief but wide-ranging historical survey is H. G. Koenigsberger, *Medieval*

Europe 400–1500, 1987. More flamboyant in its approach is J. D. Randers-Pehrson, *Barbarians and Romans: The Birth Struggle of Europe, AD 400–700*, 1983.

Outstandingly the best account of Anglo-Saxon England, for its range, its illustrations, and above all its balanced judgement, is J. Campbell (ed.), *The Anglo-Saxons*, 1982. Altogether slighter, but still useful, is D. Brown, *Anglo-Saxon England*, 1978. Two other general surveys provide an interesting contrast. *The English Settlements*, 1986, by J. N. L. Myres, doyen of Pagan Saxon studies, replaces his original chapters in vol. I of the Oxford History of England, but still represents an essentially conservative approach. C. J. Arnold, *Roman Britain to Saxon England*, 1984, attempts a radical reinterpretation, in which written evidence is largely rejected – misguidedly in my opinion – in order to create a 'pure', text-free archaeology; even his account of the archaeological evidence had been much criticized by some reviewers: for instance, P. Dixon, 'Catastrophe and fallacy: the end of Roman Britain', *LH* 6, 1984, pp. 21–5. A useful corrective is the meticulous detail of C. Hills, 'The archaeology of Anglo-Saxon England in the pagan period: a review', *ASE* 8, 1979, pp. 297–329.

In a period which has tended to be dominated by typology and art history, D. M. Wilson (ed.), *The Archaeology of Anglo-Saxon England*, 1976, opens up new fields of settlement and economic studies. The theme of settlement is further pursued in T. Rowley (ed.), *Anglo-Saxon Settlement and the Landscape*, *BAR* 6, 1974. P. J. Fowler gives an archaeologist's review of 'Farming in the A-S landscape' in *ASE* 9, 1981, pp. 263–80; but for a larger survey, modified in detail by Fowler's paper, it is necessary to turn to H. P. R. Finberg (ed.), *The Agrarian History of England and Wales* vol. I, ii, AD 43–1042, 1972. More recently, M. G. Welch has considered 'Rural settlement patterns in the Early and Middle Anglo-Saxon periods', *LH* 7, 1985, pp. 13–25. Some of the technical problems of establishing settlement continuity are examined by R. Reece, 'Continuity on the Cotswolds: some problems of ownership, settlement and hedge survey between Roman Britain and the Middle Ages', *LH* 5, 1983, pp. 11–19; and M. L. Faull, 'Roman and Anglo-Saxon settlement patterns in Yorkshire: a computer-generated analysis', *LH* 5, 1983, pp. 21–40.

'The Anglo-Saxon house' is the subject of a paper by P. V. Addyman in *ASE* 1, 1972, pp. 273–307; but see also P. Dixon, 'How Saxon is the Saxon house?' and other critical papers in P. J. Drury (ed.), *Structural Reconstruction*, *BAR* 110, 1982. The royal halls and lesser buildings of the Northumbrian royal township of Yeavering (above, pp. 309–10), have now been fully published by the excavator, B. Hope-Taylor, *Yeavering: An Anglo-British Centre of Earthly Northumbria*, 1977; but their interpretation still awaits critical evaluation. That must take account of the meticulous excavation of other large timber buildings; for instance, M. Millett and S. James, 'Excavations at Cowdery's Down . . .', *Arch. J.* 140, 1983, pp. 151–279. The reassessment has already been begun by S. James, A. Marshall and M. Millett, 'An early medieval building tradition', *Arch. J.* 141, 1984, pp. 182–215; they argue that the tradition represents a hybrid of both Germania and Romano-British elements.

Burials have in the past provided most of the artefactual evidence for the study of the pagan Saxons; but little account has been taken of their importance for wider studies of early English society. A major step towards remedying this was taken at a symposium in 1979, published by P. Rahtz, T. Dickinson and L. Watts, *Anglo-Saxon Cemeteries 1979*, *BAR* 82, 1980. In particular, this introduced new theoretical approaches derived from social anthropology. Inevitably, an important element in the symposium was devoted to the major burial at Sutton Hoo (above, pp. 298–301). The 1939 excavations have now been published in a sumptuous and grossly extravagant format: R. Bruce-Mitford, *The Sutton Hoo Ship Burial*, 3 vols., 1975–83. Most readers of *Arthur's Britain* will be very adequately served by the illustrated handbook by A. C. Evans, *The Sutton Hoo Ship Burial*, 1986. Meanwhile, new excavations have begun, concerned especially with the other barrows in the Sutton Hoo cemetery and with the general background to the major burial; as yet, only brief interim reports have appeared.

Weapons and warfare form an important theme of *Arthur's Britain*. M. J. Swanton deals with *The Spearheads of the Anglo-Saxon Settlements:* Royal Archaeological Institute, 1973, and supports this with *A Corpus of Pagan Anglo-Saxon-types*, *BAR* 7, 1974. H. Härke dismisses the myth of 'Anglo-Saxon laminated shields at Petersfinger', *Med. Arch.* 25, 1981, pp. 141–4. The written evidence for 'Aspects of the warfare of Saxons and Britons' is considered by Alcock in *ESW*, chapter 15.

Major artefact studies have included J. N. L. Myres, *A Corpus of Anglo-Saxon Pottery of the Pagan Period*, 2 vols., 1977; this must be read in the light of critical reviews of Myres's methodology, for instance by D. Kidd, *Med. Arch.* 20, 1976, pp. 202–4; and T. M. Dickinson, *Arch. J.* 135, 1978, pp. 332–44. Papers too numerous to list individually on the typology and technology of metalwork, especially jewellery, are to be found in the volumes of *ASSAH*.

Early Christian (Chapters 5, 8 and 10)

Since the publication of *Arthur's Britain*, both the history and the material remains of the early Church have attracted a burgeoning interest, especially through architectural surveys and excavations – the latter, however, still on nothing like the scale common in Germany. It is only possible here to indicate some major syntheses and discussions.

C. A. R. Radford examines 'Christian origins in Britain', *Med. Arch.* 15, 1971, pp. 1–12. C. Thomas, *Christianity in Roman Britain to AD 500*, 1981 and subsequent revisions, is a major and mature study. The same author's *The Early Christian Archaeology of North Britain*, 1971, which covers a wider area than its title might suggest, is by contrast a pioneering work with all the advantages and dis-advantages which that implies. In addition to structures, it does deal with the inscribed standing stones which are of such importance in Wales and Dumnonia; of these, a new corpus for Wales is promised shortly through the collaboration of the National Museum and the Royal Commission on Ancient Monuments. Despite its misleading title, S. Victory, *The Celtic Church in Wales*, 1977, is a slight but useful survey.

The papers from a major conference have been edited by S. M. Pearce as *The Early Church in Western Britain and Ireland: Studies Presented to C. A. Ralegh Radford*, *BAR* 102, 1982. An outstanding benefit from the setting up of a Churches Committee by the Council for British Archaeology has been R. Morris, *The Church in British*

Archaeology, CBA Research Report 47, 1983; chapters 1–4 of this are especially relevant here.

The churches of the Anglo-Saxons are now covered exhaustively with the completion of the corpus by H. M. Taylor and Joan Taylor, *Anglo-Saxon Architecture*, 3 vols., 1965–78. E. Fernie, *The Architecture of the Anglo-Saxons*, 1983, will provide a sufficient guide for the ordinary reader. W. Rodwell, *The Archaeology of the English Church: The Study of Historic Churches and Graveyards*, 1981, is a fascinating introduction to the methodology of such studies. Finally, the state of the art is well represented in the conference papers in honour of H. M. Taylor, edited by L. A. S. Butler and R. K. Morris, *The Anglo-Saxon Church*, CBA Research Report 60, 1986.

Conclusion

To conclude: *Arthur's Britain* set out – with many cautions and reservations – my position on the Arthur of history as it appeared to me in the late 1960s. How far has that position been modified by all the subsequent research, of which a sample is listed in this supplementary bibliography?

It is axiomatic, for a start, that archaeology cannot prove the historicity of Arthur, except through the highly unlikely discovery of an unambiguously inscribed memorial stone, or some personal object like the signet ring of the Frankish king Childeric or the well-known Alfred jewel. What archaeology can do is to provide an increasingly rich picture of the material possessions and way of life of the Celtic inhabitants of Britain and the Anglo-Saxon settlers; and in particular of the weaponry and ostentation of a heroic society.

To this extent, the original excavation at Cadbury, and especially the reconsideration of the defences and the feasting hall, published in *Proceedings, British Academy 58, 1982*, and subsequently in *ESW*, chapter 13, demonstrate the architectural setting appropriate to a British war leader about the end of the fifth and beginning of the sixth centuries AD. Particularly important here is the abandonment of the interpretation which saw the role of Cadbury as essentially that of a campaign base for the defence of Dumnonia against Saxon aggression from the Thames Valley, and its replacement by the hypothesis that the refortified Cadbury was a permanently occupied political and administrative centre. It seems very likely that this was in some sense a descendant of the nearby Roman *civitas* capital at Ilchester, by then in a decayed state. This is not to say, however, that any romanized authority ordered the move to the Cadbury hilltop and the refortification of the derelict Iron Age ramparts, as appears to have happened in the late fourth and early fifth centuries in northern Gaul. The chronological gap between the end of effective Roman authority in AD 410 and the rebuilding of the Cadbury defences about AD 460–70 is too great to admit such an hypothesis.

The comment made above, that any archaeological demonstration of the historicity of Arthur would depend on the discovery of an inscribed memorial or personal object, makes the point that historical proof must be based on a written source, however brief. My own use of written sources has been mildly criticized by the late Dr Kathleen Hughes, and vigorously – and, as I have indicated above, sometimes less than scrupulously – attacked by Dr David Dumville. Does anything remain of a case?

Following a comment of T. Jones, 'The early evolution of the legend of Arthur', *Nottingham Medieval Studies* 8, 1964, pp. 3–21, especially p. 6, I asked the question, on p. 88 above, 'if the whole weight of reasoning and reasonable scepticism is brought to bear on Arthur, what remains as the irreducible minimum of historical fact?' In 1971 I answered that it was the entry in the Welsh Annals on the battle of Camlann; and I went on to draw certain wider implications about Arthur as a great warrior. I would answer in the same sense today; and I would do so for three reasons.

Firstly, our knowledge of the annals of Britain and Ireland, and of the way in which the earliest annals came to be compiled, is not so advanced or so perfect as to allow us to say with certainty that a particular entry cannot have been entered contemporaneously, whether in a running set of annals or in the margin of an Easter Table. Obviously I am excluding here all those Irish annals which go back to the pre-literate period; but western Britain was certainly not illiterate in the early sixth century.

It follows that, while it can be shown that the Camlann entry – and, for that matter, the Badon entry, stripped if necessary, as

T. Jones would have it, of the Arthur reference – do not derive from an Irish source, this does not tell us anything surprising; they are, after all, about events in Britain. They relate to an area which was Christian and therefore literate, and which had the means of making and preserving just such a record, until it came to be incorporated, by stages obscure to us, in the permanent form of the Welsh Annals.

If this possibility is rejected, then we are entitled to ask when, and under what circumstances, were these two entries originally compiled? Did they represent some possibly sound tradition, not necessarily one to which any firm chronology was attached? Or were they and the person of Arthur simply invented, probably, as the *Historia Brittonum* would suggest, sometime before the early ninth century?

This brings me to my second point. It is sometimes said that if Arthur had not existed, it would have been necessary to invent him. This is at best a facile remark; but more seriously, it surely inverts the logic of the case. This is that if Arthur had never existed as an historical figure, then why was it necessary to invent him in later centuries, and then insert notices of him, retrospectively, into the Annals and the *Historia Brittonum*.

This argument reinforces that deployed on p. 359 above: that given the undoubted historicity of Ambrosius as a great British war leader in the later fifth century, why was it found necessary to invent Arthur at all? To Ambrosius we should also add the name of Riothamus, as a well-documented Briton, capable of taking a large war band to intervene in military events in Gaul in the later fifth century; a person well equipped to fill the heroic role which came to be attributed to Arthur.

My third point concerns the possible chronology of events in that half-century. I accept that Gildas is almost our only source for the events leading up to the battle of Badon, and that therefore any attempt to date them must be hazardous in the extreme. I also accept that Dumville has rashly proposed a Gildasian chronology (in *Gildas: New Approaches*, SCH 5, 1984, p. 83) which is not consistent with the interpretation which I wish to propose; but I find Dumville's chronology incompatible with the archaeological evidence.

In my view, taking the fluctuating fortunes of war from the first God-given victory under Ambrosius up to the siege of Mount Badon and beyond (since Badon was not the last of the battles, as Gildas makes clear), the chronology implied is too long for all these battles to have been fought under the leadership of Ambrosius. Here, then, Arthur may be fitted in as the commander at Badon.

As long ago as 1959 K. H. Jackson, writing on 'The Arthur of History' in R. S. Loomis (ed.), *Arthurian Literature in the Middle Ages*, p. 1, asked 'Did King Arthur ever really exist? The only honest answer is, "We do not know, but he may well have existed." The nature of the evidence is such that proof is impossible.' Even today, it would be impossible to fault that statement; though we might be justified in believing that today we have a better idea of the nature of the evidence, and a sharper concept of the character of the proof that we might require.

Something more should be said, however, about evidence and proof in the currently prevailing climate of reductionism, to which so many references have been made in this supplementary bibliography. The reason given for concentrating on a meticulous analysis of written sources, coupled as it so often is with a refusal to attempt to draw wider inferences from them, is that the subject is in its infancy. What this means is that the study is vigorously alive, with keen and critically minded scholars making exciting contributions to it. A healthy discipline will always remain, in these terms, in its infancy.

But another test of the health of a discipline is that it should also be producing wider syntheses or explanatory models of the processes, historical or other, which are implicit in the evidence, and which indeed created the evidence originally. However vigorous or meticulously critical the study of the details of the evidence may be, the exercise remains sterile unless it does contribute equally to wider interpretations.

Moreover, there is an essential feedback from the syntheses or model-building to the narrower work on the details of the evidence. One test of the validity of the details is the way in which they cohere; and this can be examined only at the wider level. Gaps in the synthesis, weaknesses in the model, may point to weaknesses in our knowledge and understanding of the evidence, and thus to areas which demand special attention from researchers.

Obviously, there must be a balance between the detailed, but inherently sterile, analysis and the broader, but probably flawed, synthesis. I believe that the value of *Arthur's Britain* is that it provides one half of that balance. Many of the scholarly papers listed above provide the other half.

P.S. Inevitably, since this Supplementary Bibliography was compiled, other relevant books and articles have appeared. A selection must be added here. Among principal texts and translations (pp. 366–8), D. Jenkins, *The Law of Hywel Dda: Law Texts from Medieval Wales translated & edited* (1986), and A. O. H. Jarman, *Aneirin: Y Gododdin, Britain's Oldest Heroic Poem* (1988) provide up-to-date translations and commentaries on these basic texts. J. M. Wallace-Hadrill, *Bede's Ecclesiastical History of the English People: A Historical Commentary* (1988) furnishes the long-awaited commentary volume on the Colgrave & Mynors text and translation (1969; p. 367).

Finally, two major papers on fifth-century history are: I. Wood, 'The fall of the Western Empire and the end of Roman Britain', *Britannia* 18 (1987), 251–62, and M. E. Jones & J. Casey, 'The Gallic Chronicle restored: a chronology for the Anglo-Saxon invasions and the end of Roman Britain', *Britannia* 19 (1988), 367–98. The latter article vindicates the Gallic Chronicle of 452 (above, pp. 105–6) as 'a contemporary and reliable framework for the primary phase of the Anglo-Saxon conquest'.

Index

432 | INDEX

FOR THE BEST IN PAPERBACKS, LOOK FOR THE 🐧

In every corner of the world, on every subject under the sun, Penguin represents quality and variety – the very best in publishing today.

For complete information about books available from Penguin – including Puffins, Penguin Classics and Arkana – and how to order them, write to us at the appropriate address below. Please note that for copyright reasons the selection of books varies from country to country.

In the United Kingdom: Please write to *Dept E.P., Penguin Books Ltd, Harmondsworth, Middlesex, UB7 0DA.*

If you have any difficulty in obtaining a title, please send your order with the correct money, plus ten per cent for postage and packaging, to *PO Box No 11, West Drayton, Middlesex*

In the United States: Please write to *Dept BA, Penguin, 299 Murray Hill Parkway, East Rutherford, New Jersey 07073*

In Canada: Please write to *Penguin Books Canada Ltd, 2801 John Street, Markham, Ontario L3R 1B4*

In Australia: Please write to the *Marketing Department, Penguin Books Australia Ltd, P.O. Box 257, Ringwood, Victoria 3134*

In New Zealand: Please write to the *Marketing Department, Penguin Books (NZ) Ltd, Private Bag, Takapuna, Auckland 9*

In India: Please write to *Penguin Overseas Ltd, 706 Eros Apartments, 56 Nehru Place, New Delhi, 110019*

In the Netherlands: Please write to *Penguin Books Nederland B.V., Postbus 195, NL–1380AD Weesp*

In West Germany: Please write to *Penguin Books Ltd, Friedrichstrasse 10–12, D–6000 Frankfurt/Main 1*

In Spain: Please write to *Longman Penguin España, Calle San Nicolas 15, E–28013 Madrid*

In Italy: Please write to *Penguin Italia s.r.l., Via Como 4, I-20096 Pioltello (Milano)*

In France: Please write to *Penguin Books Ltd, 39 Rue de Montmorency, F-75003 Paris*

In Japan: Please write to *Longman Penguin Japan Co Ltd, Yamaguchi Building, 2-12-9 Kanda Jimbocho, Chiyoda-Ku, Tokyo 101*

PENGUIN HISTORY

The Germans   Gordon A. Craig

An intimate study of a complex and fascinating nation by 'one of the ablest and most distinguished American historians of modern Germany' – Hugh Trevor-Roper

Imperial Spain 1469–1716   J. H. Elliot

A brilliant modern study of the sudden rise of a barren and isolated country to the greatest power on earth, and of its equally sudden decline. 'Outstandingly good' – *Daily Telegraph*

British Society 1914–1945   John Stevenson

A major contribution to the *Penguin Social History of Britain*, which 'will undoubtedly be the standard work for students of modern Britain for many years to come' – *The Times Educational Supplement*

A History of Christianity   Paul Johnson

'Masterly ... It is a huge and crowded canvas – a tremendous theme running through twenty centuries of history – a cosmic soap opera involving kings and beggars, philosophers and crackpots, scholars and illiterate *exaltés*, popes and pilgrims and wild anchorites in the wilderness' – Malcolm Muggeridge

The Penguin History of Greece   A. R. Burn

Readable, erudite, enthusiastic and balanced, this one-volume history of Hellas sweeps the reader along from the days of Mycenae and the splendours of Athens to the conquests of Alexander and the final dark decades.

A History of Latin America   George Pendle

'Ought to be compulsory reading in every sixth form ... this book is right on target' – *Sunday Times*. 'A beginner's guide to the continent ... lively, and full of anecdote' – *Financial Times*

FOR THE BEST IN PAPERBACKS, LOOK FOR THE 🐧

PENGUIN HISTORY

The Penguin History of the United States   Hugh Brogan

'An extraordinarily engaging book' – *The Times Literary Supplement*. 'Compelling reading ... Hugh Brogan's book will delight the general reader as much as the student' – *The Times Educational Supplement*. 'He will be welcomed by American readers no less than those in his own country' – J. K. Galbraith

The Making of the English Working Class   E. P. Thompson

Probably the most imaginative – and the most famous – post-war work of English social history.

The Waning of the Middle Ages   Johan Huizinga

A magnificent study of life, thought and art in 14th- and 15th-century France and the Netherlands, long established as a classic.

The City in History   Lewis Mumford

Often prophetic in tone and containing a wealth of photographs, *The City in History* is among the most deeply learned and warmly human studies of man as a social creature.

The Habsburg Monarchy 1809–1918   A. J. P. Taylor

Dissolved in 1918, the Habsburg Empire 'had a unique character, out of time and out of place'. Scholarly and vividly accessible, this 'very good book indeed' (*Spectator*) elucidates the problems always inherent in the attempt to give peace, stability and a common loyalty to a heterogeneous population.

Inside Nazi Germany   Conformity, Opposition and Racism in Everyday Life
Detlev J. K. Peukert

An authoritative study – and a challenging and original analysis – of the realities of daily existence under the Third Reich. 'A fascinating study ... captures the whole range of popular attitudes and the complexity of their relationship with the Nazi state' – Richard Geary

PENGUIN HISTORY

The Victorian Underworld Kellow Chesney

A superbly evocative survey of the vast substratum of vice that lay below the respectable surface of Victorian England – the showmen, religious fakes, pickpockets and prostitutes – and of the penal methods of tl .t 'most enlightened age'. 'Charged with nightmare detail' – *Sunday Times*

A History of Modern France Alfred Cobban

Professor Cobban's renowned three-volume history, skilfully steering the reader through France's political and social problems from 1715 to the Third Republic, remains essential reading for anyone wishing to understand the development of a great European nation.

Stalin Isaac Deutscher

'The Greatest Genius in History' and the 'Life-Giving Force of Socialism'? Or a tyrant more ruthless than Ivan the Terrible whose policies facilitated the rise of Nazism? An outstanding biographical study of a revolutionary despot by a great historian.

Montaillou Cathars and Catholics in a French Village 1294–1324
Emmanuel Le Roy Ladurie

'A classic adventure in eavesdropping across time' – Michael Ratcliffe in ·*The Times*

The Second World War A. J. P. Taylor

A brilliant and detailed illustrated history, enlivened by all Professor Taylor's customary iconaclasm and wit.

Industry and Empire E. J. Hobsbawm

Volume 3 of the *Penguin Economic History of Britain* covers the period of the Industrial Revolution: 'the most fundamental transformation in the history of the world recorded in written documents.' 'A book that attracts and deserves attention ... by far the most gifted historian now writing' – John Vaizey in the *Listener*

PENGUIN ART AND ARCHITECTURE

An Outline of European Architecture   Nikolaus Pevsner

With its readable brevity and its combination of warmth and scholarship, Pevsner's classic history remains an unsurpassed introduction to western architecture, from the basilicas of Rome to the skyscrapers of the twentieth century.

Style and Civilization: Neo-Classicism   Hugh Honour

'Hugh Honour's elegant and enthralling work is the first study by an English author of neo-classical architecture, painting and sculpture … what Mr Honour defines with superb clarity as neo-classicism is a stark process of elimination' – *Observer*

Palladio   James S. Ackerman

In this brilliantly incisive study, Professor Ackerman sets Palladio in the context of his age – the great humanist era of Michelangelo and Raphael, Titian and Veronese – examines each wonderful villa, church and palace in turn, and tries to penetrate to the heart of the Palladian miracle.

Ways of Seeing   John Berger

Seeing comes before words. The child looks before it can speak. Yet there is another sense in which seeing comes before words … These seven provocative essays – some written, some visual – offer a key to exploring the multiplicity of ways of seeing.

Style and Civilization: Mannerism   John Shearman

'He has cut through the detritus of psychological guesswork, shown that the word mannerism has a precise meaning in its own time … Shearman's essay ranges across sixteenth-century music, literature and architecture as well as art: it is a model of breadth and concision' – *Observer*